The Camel's Neighbour

There are many horizons that must be visited, fruit that must be plucked, books read, and white pages in the scrolls of life to be inscribed with vivid sentences in a bold hand.

Tayeb Salih, *Season of Migration to the North*

The Camel's Neighbour

Travels and Travellers in Yemen

Andrew Moscrop

Signal

Signal Books
Oxford

First published in 2020 by
Signal Books Limited
36 Minster Road
Oxford OX4 1LY
www.signalbooks.co.uk

A catalogue record for this book is available from the British Library

ISBN 978-1-909930-89-6 paper

Cover Design: Tora Kelly
Typesetting: Tora Kelly
Cover & Text Photographs by Andrew Moscrop
Printed in India by Imprint Press

Contents

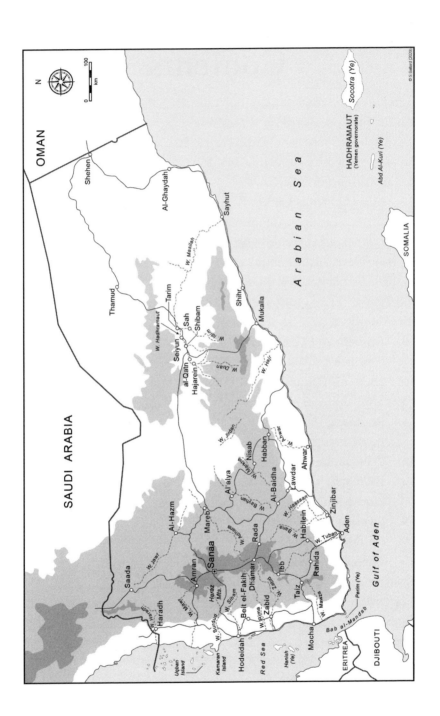

Introduction

SILENTLY THE LAST STARS WERE swept away. The eastern sky became brushed with blue, and the silhouettes of towerhouses were inked against the heavens. From somewhere far off, the echoing voice of dawn rose like vapour in the cool air. *Allaaaaah u akbar.* God is the greatest. More voices followed, distant, closer, becoming entwined, from all directions intermingling and overlapping above the city. Until as many muezzins pierced the silence as minarets pierced the sky and that celestial blue was filled with sound. From loudspeakers on every mosque, the amplified voices resonated in empty streets, rattled shuttered windows, and roused the city's sleeping residents. I was already awake. And I listened as the prayer calls slowly faded, ethereally as they had arrived. The quiet that followed had a different quality, of an emptiness waiting to be filled, a void made stark by its interruptions. A dog's sentinel hacking, the squeal and clang of a metal door on un-oiled hinges, a pink note of cirrus touching the sky. Still it was dark; still early. Too dark and too early to subject my world indoors to electric glare. A match scraped then flared. Slowly, a slender candle flame spooled up and cast its wavering glow over the notebook. The circle of illumination flickered and swayed, moving with my every breath as I scratched inky thoughts across the pages. Then at last the sun crested the eastern hills, lighting the tops of towerhouses, and the candle guttered.

God was gazing down from above. Craning my neck, I gazed back. His face on the chapel ceiling stared at me from a backdrop of brilliant ultramarine. It was a colour that spectacularly usurped his golden halo; it was a remembered skyscape of silence and blue. To reach the Byzantine frescoes of Mystras I had walked the few miles from Sparta. From Mystras a narrow path continued across the Taygetos Mountains. This trail led on toward the very tip of Greece, to the beginning and the end of Europe, where the continent crumbles in rocky islands and bouldering peninsulas into the Mare Mediterraneum; the sea at the middle of the earth. It was October 2014. The days were shortening, the path was long, and by the time I reached the mountain refuge it was after dusk. And it was closed. 'Some refuge,' I thought, and worse, before bedding down beneath the gusting clouds and creaking pines. Once, among these glowering crags, leathery Spartans had abandoned their feebler infants to the Fates. Many centuries later Patrick Leigh Fermor described a twilight ascent by jeep into these same mountains. Fermor was my companion this evening. 'Such is the force of suggestion,' he had written, after hearing of the exotic Taygetos mountain folk, 'that the first shepherd seemed to resemble, in the jeep's headlamps, a light-skinned Yemenite.' Two incidental lines, mere droplets of Fermor's mellifluous narration. Yet in that fitful night, under a racing sky and straining branches, the shepherd whom Fermor fixed in prose became animate again, among a tangle of shadowy trees, touched by the light of my head torch. His wild black curls flared for a moment in the headlamp's beam, such was the force of suggestion.

Parched rocks, bleached white as bones, rolled and cracked underfoot as I descended the next morning from my night upon the Taygetos. A dry, boulder-strewn riverbed ran down from the mountains and I followed the sun-blanched watercourse to Kardamyli, the colourful Greek seaside village where Leigh Fermor had made his home. It was, according to Freya Stark, a home 'loved and lovely, full of cats and books and stone benches under olive trees'. A lifetime ago, or just a few weeks before I was born, Paddy the Hellenophile poet-warrior was visited here by Freya, the grande dame of Arabian travels. On 24 July 1976 she wrote that 'Paddy Leigh Fermor is giving last touches to his book - a journey at eighteen from England on foot to Istanbul.' Fermor was now aged sixty-one. It was a time of last touches to old beginnings. Stark was well into her eighties and in between two trips that she would make that year to Sanaa, the capital of Yemen, in March and November of 1976. She had visited the city once before, thirty-six years earlier, in 1940, when Europe was at war and Yemen remained determinedly peaceable.

I too had wanted to return to Sanaa. It was a yearning to reconnect with something, with people and places that I had known when I lived in Yemen, eight years before. An urge to reflect upon changes, and to revisit what was unchanging. In that autumn of 2014, a gap between work contracts and an absence of other commitments might have been the opportunity that I was looking for, or it might have been the cause of my reflective mood. Either way, the Foreign Office advised against all travel to Yemen. It warned that the country had become unsettled by popular unrest and political uncertainty. In September, a coup d'état installed a new regime in the capital. I contacted a friend in Sanaa who advised me to postpone my visit until things had settled a little. And so I had abandoned thoughts of Yemen and travelled instead to Greece. But thoughts of Yemen had not abandoned me, and memories resurfaced. In the silence of a Byzantine chapel. Amid wakeful shadows and my starstruck reading in the Taygetos Mountains. And, later, among the hard-won terraces, the mountain-top villages, and the broken and abandoned towerhouses of the Mani peninsula. Events in Sanaa moved swiftly, with suicide bombings, ground attacks, and airstrikes. I exchanged emails and Facebook messages. Abdulghani said he was doing fine, but had been bombed out of his home. Najla was well, but she had sought refuge in Lebanon. Adnan wrote that his son was dead. Walid hoped to see me soon. Khaled wrote to tell me that he was planning to flee to Aruba. *Aruba*?! I never heard back from Ibrahim. And in my replies I struggled increasingly to know what to write.

Yemen became the name of another conflict. News outlets called it a 'forgotten war'. Marginalised in the news media, if Yemen was mentioned at all it was usually accompanied by images of bombed out buildings, emaciated children, or angry-looking men brandishing automatic weapons. Uncomprehending of the dearth of news stories, unable to relate to the few I found, and unable now to return to Yemen, I returned instead to my diaries, beginning with my last entry, written on my last morning in Sanaa, before the sun had risen over the eastern hills, when the sky was still a silent untroubled blue. And I returned to the narratives of those travellers from Europe who had visited Sanaa before me, from the sixteenth to the twentieth century, from the men of the East India Company to Freya Stark.

I found contrasts and connections between my own writings and those of past travellers. Our writings said something about Yemen, but they said more about how Yemen has been variously imagined and portrayed, from the Land of Sheba of the Old Testament to the al-Qaeda hotbed of the War on Terror. But what relevance did any of this have now? As I reflected upon what had been a formative period for me in Sanaa I had begun to write, but to what purpose? What point was there in reading or writing anything about our past experiences in Yemen when the present situation there was changing so dramatically and so devastatingly? Was it useful? Was it even appropriate to look at Yemen without focusing on the current conflict? How else does a war get forgotten? The answers were not immediately clear. And then events interceded.

Khaled had not reached Aruba. But in a sequence of pictures posted to his social media account, his face appeared against the silent blue of the Mediterranean, haloed by a sunset orange lifejacket. The image was familiar. Countless news articles that summer had described, with differing degrees of compassion, the movement of refugees toward Europe. Many arrived and many drowned. On television and in the press, families were pictured escaping from conflict in the Middle East by the only route open to them: a dangerous sea crossing, with a flimsy-looking life vest. But the image of Khaled in a dinghy was especially harrowing because we had drunk tea together many times in Sanaa, because we were friends, and because at that moment I was on the other side of the Mediterranean, having returned to Greece to work as a doctor in a camp for refugees. The thought of meeting Khaled under such cruel circumstances was terrible to contemplate. The thought of him not making it to safety was worse.

Most Yemenis had been trapped by the fighting. Millions had been displaced from their homes, but relatively few had been able to leave the country. They were boxed in by the desert, the sea, and the Saudis who were bombing them. Some made it to Oman, others fled to Djibouti or Somalia. Scarcely any Yemeni refugees reached Europe: a fact that Khaled must have known when he boarded a boat on the Mediterranean. In the camps where I worked in Northern Greece most people came from Syria, others were from Iraq and Afghanistan, but none came from Yemen. It might have been the relative absence of Yemenis arriving on European shores that had allowed the war in Yemen to be 'forgotten'. But it was clear that in Europe not only conflicts had been forgotten. With the war in Syria, there was a marked discrepancy between disgust expressed at the widely reported atrocities being perpetrated with barrel-bombs and mass-exterminations, and an apparently dispassionate reaction to the people who escaped. Similarly, while once we had sent our own soldiers to fight in Iraq, now we resisted offering sanctuary to people who fled from the killing there. Even if we remembered the war, it seemed we could forget its victims, or forget our common humanity. In the crisis of Europe's collective failure to adequately respond to the arrival of refugees, the images and narratives of war, or of helpless victims, appeared to elicit little empathy. The borders were closed. In the refugee camps, as I worked among people who had experienced trauma and enforced journeys, and as

I witnessed the continued suffering of families who had lived for months in tents and derelict warehouses with no idea of what the future held for them, I too had found it almost possible to become inured to the pain that surrounded me. But just as the photograph of Khaled boarding a boat on the Mediterranean breached some emotional barrier, so did the photographs that people had carried from Syria on their smartphones. Images of families, friends, pets, cars, and homes: these things had been transformed by war from being mundane to being extraordinary. While once-unimaginable horrors - the destruction of one's home, say, or the annihilation of one's family - were now taken for granted, things once taken for granted had now become unimaginable or seemed lost to some distant and impossible past. The smartphone pictures served an important purpose. Far from being merely nostalgic, they were proof of that past and of how very different it was to the present, and they were symbols of hope for a different future. When anyone invited me to view their saved images, I was moved by the generosity of that invitation and by all that had been taken from them. The evidence of lives interrupted, everyday lives not unlike like my own, with similar concerns, values, and aspirations, forced an acknowledgement of how easily and how terribly our existence can be upturned, and how it is only the accident of circumstances that separates us. Something in all this encouraged me to return to reading and writing about Yemen; to prove that how things are is not how they always were, nor how they need remain; and to remember not a war, but our shared experiences.

- 1 -
Truth

- Ludovico di Varthema, 1504 -

YOU WOULD HAVE COME FROM the west, squinting into the early sunlight as you made your way toward the Old City. Through the street market of Bab as-Sabah; its name, aptly, means 'Morning Gate', I am told. The gate has long since gone, and by the hour of your arrival padlocks would have been jerked from shop fronts and tarpaulin sheets whisked from market stalls. Vendors would already have unfurled their emporiums into the street, or unfolded sun umbrellas over caskets of coolly enticing pears, sweet plums, and luscious pomegranates. Men wearing dazzling white robes with daggers thrust into their ornate waist belts would have caught your eye. You would have caught theirs too, with your foreign clothes and your sunglasses. And they would have offered you greetings.

Salaam Alaykum! Peace be upon you.

Wa alaykum salaam! And upon you, peace.

You know some Arabic? It would surely have been Nabil calling out to you, as he arranged the embroidered pashminas in his tiny boutique. 'Maybe tomorrow,' he would have called if you had chosen not to stop. Seeing the young girls who walked holding hands and chattering on their way to school you might have noted that their mothers and older sisters were hidden by veils and *abayas*, and that might have felt strange. Until you were distracted by the much stranger sight of an old man herding two live goats from the backseat of a battered taxi. Or a pillion passenger gripping half a lamb's carcass as he buzzed away on the back of a motorcycle. The pitiable squabbling and squawking of chickens near the meat market would be followed further on by the plucked up-tempo notes of a Yemeni lute, twanging from a tinny radio somewhere. Perhaps a young boy steering a wheelbarrow loaded with bread rolls would have swerved in front of you, spilling a wonderfully oven-fresh aroma into your path. Or a frying pan of boiling bean stew, bubbling and spitting, might have been wielded through the crowd by a uniformed waiter, trailing steam as he hurried along the street. I can almost smell the fried onions and spices. By now, you see, shops and stalls would have been abandoned for breakfast. Sugary tea, flat bread, and beans, delivered from one of the many restaurants and devoured by the huddled groups of hungry traders. On past a few more stalls selling vegetables or cigarettes, and shops offering the component parts of animals or mobile phones. Then, at its eastern end, where the street terminates abruptly, plunging steeply into the dry riverbed know as *al-Sayilah*, you would have halted. Of course. There you would have stopped, wide-eyed I suggest, to take in your first prospect of the Old City. An extravagantly disordered terrace of biscuit-coloured brick, traced with lines of broad white plaster and rising in towering blocks of irregular height. It all creates an impression of... gingerbread houses? You would not have been the first to say so.

Crossing the narrow stone footbridge over the *Sayilah*, you would have passed above the city's major watercourse. Almost certainly it would have been dry. The embankments have been bricked and the bottom paved so that the *Sayilah* serves mostly as a sunken thoroughfare for traffic. But if you were to have visited in the rains, you would have seen a very different motion; the flow of vehicles replaced by a remarkable torrent of run-off from the surrounding hills. Truly, the road becomes a river for a few weeks every year and it is for this that it is named; *al-Sayilah*: The Flood.

Reaching the opposite bank you would have arrived at a building that soared magnificently from the pavement. Upwards, from the white plaster of the ground-floor facade, lines of stucco scaling the walls, marking ornate borders around shuttered windows, and laying bands of zigzagging chevrons about the building like banners. Up and up, three storeys, until your gaze reached the outline of the flat roof. There, at each corner of the building, set into the plaster, a pair of ibex horns curved into the sky, gracefully or grotesquely depending upon your point of view. Like all the towerhouses of the Old City, the construction was both elegant and imposing. But this particular house was unique. It was my home.

Your hammering of the gong-like door knocker would have echoed inside. My tugging on a string in the third-floor vestibule would, ingeniously, have drawn back the bolt to unlock the portal. And then you would have been able to push open the heavy wooden door. Your eyes would have taken a moment to adjust. It would be dark when you came in from the street. The ground floor used to be a stable for donkeys, a storage area for firewood; little need for windows then. Watching your footing on the stairs at the back of the house, you would have ascended. The spiral was dizzying, the stone block steps were tall, and it would have been easy to stumble in the darkness. But the way became less hazardous as you went up, as holes in the brickwork let a little daylight onto the stairwell. The building was once the home of a wealthy family but had since been divided into three separate flats and on your way up you would have passed the door to the first-floor apartment. Then a few more thigh-testing steps, on past a pair of wooden shutters on the wall; no, not a window, the shutters open into a small stone cage that sticks out from the masonry: in the days before water pipes and roof-top tanks, a bucket on a rope would have been lowered and raised from here to supply water to the second-floor kitchens. Those kitchens had been converted into another stand-alone apartment. Another twisting climb. Another shuttered wall niche: I have no idea what function this one would have served originally, being set into the stairwell's central pillar, but I used it to store the key to my apartment. Admittedly, leaving my door key in a niche outside my door might have seemed a little negligent. But I am sure that you would have understood my security lapse if you had felt the weight of it. The key was cast in iron, bigger than my hand span and too large for even the deepest trouser pocket. It was quaint, but impossibly clumsy. Once, prompted purely by intrigue, I had a duplicate made and watched a metalworker in the *suq* trace the key's knotted geometry onto a huge iron blank then begin methodically to cut away the design with a hacksaw. 'Come back tomorrow,' he told me.

A final turn of the staircase and four more breathless steps would have brought you to the door of my apartment. Welcome. You would have had to excuse my humble and unpractised efforts at hospitality; my perhaps too-eager offerings of pomegranate juice (assuming it was still in season), coffee (I always had the finest from Al-Kabous), or tea (there would have been fresh mint). I never grew familiar with having guests. Few friends would pass through Yemen. And most other expatriates and many of my local colleagues would tend to avoid the Old City, put off by its lack of parking spaces, unreliable electricity, and the amplified noise from its abundant mosques. Or else drawn to the modern suburbs by the lure of restaurants and supermarkets. Even then 'security' would have provided a further, often definitive, deterrent. The high walls and barbed wire surrounding suburban compounds were deemed to offer greater protection than the neighbourhood bonds and community cohesion found in the Old City. Choosing to live here, rather than in accommodation approved by my employer, I had been obliged to sign a document waiving their responsibility for my safety and surrendering any assistance in the event of an emergency. All of which might have explained my awkward hosting and my enquiry, astonished and delighted, as to what on earth brought you here?

For Ludovico di Varthema it had been a 'longing for novelty'. Evidently bored in Italy, he had sought 'to behold the various kingdoms of the world' and 'give a very faithful description'. His ambitions would be fulfilled by his travel and travel writing. In 1504 Varthema became the first European to visit Sanaa. He is better known, though, for being the first non-Muslim to enter Mecca. That most holy of Islamic cities was then and remains today strictly off-limits to non-believers, so Varthema travelled disguised as a Muslim. And from Mecca he journeyed to the Red Sea coast where he found passage on a boat bound for that distant corner of the Arabian Peninsula now known as Yemen. Varthema did not call it that. He used an epithet invented by the Romans over a thousand years earlier and still applied by Europeans until late into the nineteenth century: 'Arabia Felix', Blessed or Happy Arabia. It was not a happy landfall for Varthema. Upon reaching the port at Aden, Varthema's Muslim disguise unravelled. Accused of being a Christian spy, he was promptly arrested and thrown into the prison of the local sultan.

All this, and all that is known of Varthema, is recounted in his own travel narrative, his *Itinerario*, first published in 1510. A woodcut on the frontispiece of early Italian editions portrays Varthema sitting with a vast terrestrial globe between his knees, plotting a course across the huge cartographical sphere. It is a fanciful image. Nothing in Varthema's account of his rambling passage suggests that he ever charted his route, and it is highly improbable that he ever had access to a globe. But cartography and discovery upon a spherical earth were powerful themes in sixteenth-century Europe. And their synergy could be expressed in mutually endorsing printed representations. So Varthema is pictured with a globe. And a 1532 world map features a cartoon of Varthema in one corner. He is seen striding across a distant landscape with knobbly knees and a knobkerrie. On the map, illuminated by Holbein the Younger, another image depicts an incident in Varthema's jailbreak: he is shown with his arm raised, holding a stick, and dragging a sheep, about to brutally club the animal. For in Yemen, Varthema and two fellow-inmates hatched an improbable plan to escape from the sultan's prison. Eschewing what in 1504 might not have been such well-established traditions of overpowering guards, making ropes out of bedclothes, or digging tunnels with teaspoons, Varthema and his companions 'arranged that one of us should pretend to be mad'. 'The lot fell upon me,' he reported. And so, determined to demonstrate his lunacy in the belief that this would secure his release, Varthema promptly accosted a sheep and attempted to engage it in conversation. 'I seized it and demanded of it if it was a Moor, or a Christian, or, in truth, a Jew.' When the sheep made no reply, he says, 'I took a stick and broke all its four legs,' just as Holbein depicted. Three days later Varthema performed the same cruel farce with an ass. And then, still more unpleasantly, with a Jew. 'I cudgelled him to such an extent that I left him for dead,' he wrote. The sultan's wife was apparently greatly amused. If Varthema's version of events is to be believed, he had to fight off her lustful advances. 'She kept me before her for two hours,' he claims, 'contemplating me as though I had been a nymph, and uttering... "O God, thou hast created this man white like the sun... Would to God that this man were my husband..."' From which Varthema drew a general conclusion about 'the partiality of the women of Arabia Felix for white men'. It was after his eventual release from captivity, facilitated by the sultan's lascivious wife, that Varthema made his brief excursion to Sanaa.

For all his vainglory and occasional bigotry, it is hard not to be impressed by Varthema, or at least by his courage, curiosity, and quick thinking. Having left home in his early thirties, his longing for novelty spurred him through Arabia, Persia, India, Sri Lanka, and the Spice Islands. For five years he journeyed alone as far east as Java before returning to Italy. Claiming to have 'procured the pleasure of seeing new manners and customs by very great dangers and insupportable fatigue', he hoped that his readers might 'enjoy the same advantage and pleasure, without discomfort or danger.' The 1532 world map testified to those dangers and to the unknowable mysteries of Varthema's destinations: there were sea monsters in the Indian Ocean and its cartography had changed little since Ptolemy.

Here then was a self-styled writer-explorer for the sixteenth-century European armchair traveller. A Jew-bashing adventurer who could not only outwit the Arabs, but confirm that even their own wives thought them inferior to fair-skinned men. A travel writer when such things were becoming popular. Following the printing of Varthema's original Italian text in 1510, a Latin version was swiftly produced and the work was subsequently translated into German (1515), Spanish (1520), again into German (1530), French (1556), and Dutch (1561). In this age of discovery and incipient empire-building, Varthema's writings were not only valued as a source of entertainment, but also as a source of information about imperial prospects. Tellingly, his English translation was commissioned by the Crown.

That first English version of Varthema's *Itinerario* appeared in 1577. It was translated from Latin by Richard Eden, a Cambridge graduate and failed alchemist. Nearly three hundred years later, John Winter Jones, Deputy Principal Librarian of the British Museum, found Eden's 1577 translation 'extremely imperfect: many passages are totally at variance with the original, and many others are omitted.' Jones committed himself henceforth to 'a faithful representation of the original work'. His new translation was published in 1863 by the Hakluyt Society, a subscription book club founded early in the Victorian era that specialised in accounts of historical voyages. 'It is impossible,' says Jones in the preface, 'to peruse Varthema's narrative and not feel a conviction that the writer is telling the truth, that he is recording events which actually took place, and describing men, countries and scenes which he had examined with his own eyes.' Truth and faithfulness were imperative for Jones. But the belief of even the most trusting Victorian reader would surely have been strained by Varthema's brief report on Sanaa.

> The walls of this city are of earth, of the height of ten braza, and twenty braza wide. Think, that eight horses can go abreast on the top of it. In this place many fruits grow the same as in our country, and there are many fountains. In this Sana there is a Sultan who has twelve sons, one of whom is called Mahometh. He is like a madman: he bites people and kills them, and then eats their flesh until his appetite is satisfied. He is four braza high, well proportioned, and of a dark brown colour. In this city there are found some kinds of small spices which grow in the neighbourhood. This place contains about 4,000 hearths. The houses are very handsome and resemble ours. Within the city

there are many vines and gardens as with us.

The text written by Ludovico di Varthema and translated by John Winter Jones was subsequently edited and extensively footnoted by one George Percy Badger, an Anglican chaplain who had once lived in Aden. To the above passage describing Sanaa, Badger added footnotes of such long-windedness that they threatened to usurp Varthema from the page entirely. First he commented upon the dimensions of the city walls, referencing later visitors who had confirmed Varthema's claim about their breadth of twenty braza (a braza being a unit of measurement equivalent to the English fathom or brace, corresponding to the length of a man's outstretched arms). Then Badger stated solemnly that despite his investigation of the then ruling imam, he had 'not succeeded in discovering any notices corroborative of Varthema's statement regarding the cannibal propensities of one of his sons'. He cited the explorer Richard Burton who had read Varthema some years earlier and appeared to rationalise the cannibalism of the sultan's son by remarking that 'Louis XI of France was supposed to drink the blood of babes'. But Burton had recognised that here and elsewhere Varthema's account was 'disfigured with a little romancing'. Meanwhile Badger seemed to take Varthema's observations at face value. He omitted to acknowledge the possibility of fabrication, or metaphor perhaps, in the anecdote of a flesh-eating ruling elite. Like John Winter Jones who felt a conviction that Varthema was telling the truth, Badger was concerned with confirming the veracity of Varthema's tale, not pointing out elements of implausibility or evidence of invention.

Explaining the motive for his travels, Ludovico di Varthema had described his determination 'personally, and with my own eyes... to investigate some small portion of this our terrestrial globe... remembering well that the testimony of one eye-witness is worth more than ten hear-says.' The valuing of eye-witness testimony over hear-says or rumours is indubitable, but seeing with one's 'own eyes' does not guarantee the incontestable 'truth' that John Winter Jones perceived and that George Percy Badger laboured to prove. Idiosyncrasies of individual experience, perception, and memory created Varthema's uniquely personal set of observed 'truths'. For any witness who puts pen to paper, selective descriptions, omissions, choice of terminology, phraseology, and metaphor all contribute to creating an account that is unavoidably subjective. Not only subjective, but subject to a particular set of cultural values which, for Varthema, permitted Jews to be beaten up without qualm and determined that fair-skinned men were superior to other races: actions and assumptions that went unchallenged and notably unremarked upon by Badger the bountiful footnoter.

Beyond subjectivity, there is a further element in the matter of truth-telling. Embellishment. Varthema did not actually claim to have witnessed cannibalism in the streets of Sanaa, yet he embellished his account with this story. How far then can a story be so elaborated or exaggerated before it becomes untrue? The nature and extent of acceptable embellishment must vary according to the nature and extent of established truths. In his *Itinerario*, Varthema was both founding new truths and upholding old ones. He broke the news to his readers that the body of Mohammed did *not* float suspended in the air above Mecca as had been rumoured. And having traversed the Red Sea on his way to Yemen he could knowingly proclaim 'that this sea is not red, but that the water is like that of any other sea'. New truths. But his account of Sanaa recoursed to old ones. Europe was already well-furnished with tales of cannibalism among the natives of foreign lands. Holbein's illustrations for the 1532 world map included images of cannibals butchering and spit-roasting human corpses. It was a familiar trope. In his narrative, Varthema seems more startled by the scale of the city walls than the sultan's cannibalistic son. And his description of murderous flesh-munching is bounded by prosaic comments about the varieties of fruit trees and the availability of spices. The embellished story of the sultan's son, remarkable and unbelievable today, may have seemed unremarkable then. It may have been as plausible and as consistent with known truths as observations of the local flora.

Varthema's entwining of observation, speculation, and invention or rumour lies firmly within a tradition that stretches all the way from Herodotus to, say, Bruce Chatwin. Theirs is a probing of the borders of what is known and unknown, a traversing of familiar beliefs and an exploration of new ones, a discovery of novel and original truths. And their method may be less diminishing of their worth than defining of their genre; a genre that does not fit neatly into the categories of 'fiction' or 'non-fiction' that might have been recognised by certain Deputy Principal Librarians of the British Museum. Ultimately, for the travel writer, and for the reader of travel writing, the matter of truth may be less relevant than the matter of trust. The contract between writer and reader is implied by Varthema. He has seen with his 'own eyes', but his readers must be satisfied with his testimony as an 'eye-witness'. He promises 'to give a very faithful description', but true to his prejudices and perhaps those of his readers, he perceives no contradiction between the deceptions perpetrated amidst the Arabs (pretending first to be a Muslim, then later a madman, among other deceits) and the assertion that he will report truthfully to his readers. Trust and Varthema's trustworthiness are further assured by his flattering anticipation that readers of his book will be 'other studious men'; men like him, who would have seen things the way he saw them, if only they had been there. Which hints at a final fiction in what has become a consideration of truth in travel writing, for in addition to the inherent subjectivity of storytelling and inclination toward embellishment, there is the invention of the reader. All writers imagine their readers. Varthema may have imagined a papal censor, and he may well have adjusted his account accordingly. I have imagined you, though it will be clear that this is preposterously ambitious. Who, after all, can say what you would have seen, and what you would not, if, one morning in Sanaa, not so many years ago, you had walked through the market of Bab as-Sabah, heading east, into the sun? You may have to trust me.

- 2 -

Myths of
Strangeness

- Pedro Páez, 1590 -

MY NEIGHBOUR WAS A CAMEL. A dromedary. The sort, that is, with a single hump, a lolloping stride, and a pair of astonishingly expressive nostrils. She lived and worked in the barn next door. Blindfolded to prevent her getting dizzy, tethered to a huge wooden pestle that turned in a colossal stone mortar, she trod ceaseless circles on the sawdust floor, grinding sesame seed into oil. Day after day, round and around, an interminable journey. At some point I was corrected: the camel was a male. Sesame mill camels are *always* males, Ali told me. He had pointed. I had stooped and peered. Neutered, apparently. And it was not interminable: the camel was given Fridays off. Ali oversaw the production process, filling the mortar's funnel with seed throughout the day, and flicking a crop at the camel's behind if he dawdled. Ali was my neighbour too. He lived with his wife in a small loft above the mill, distanced only slightly from their domesticated animal, from the stench of rotting cabbage leaves, and from the flies that buzzed insanely about the glistening boulders of camel excrement. Their sesame oil was not cheap: two hundred riyals for a recommissioned carbonated drink bottle containing the turbid yellow liquid. A can of locally mass-produced 'Girl' brand cooking oil four times the size could be purchased at less expense. But camel-milled oil retained a market niche. It was free from impurities and had unique properties, according to Ali. Good for both skin and hair care, and in the event of minor ailments (Ali feigned a sore back) or illnesses (he demonstrated a coughing fit) the oil could be used topically or orally for self-medication.

As though contesting the curative powers of the camel-milled oil, on the opposite side of our building stood a pharmacy. With white walls and glass display cabinets, shelves stacked with bottles and blister packs of medications, it had the generic interior design and decor of dispensaries everywhere. A glass-fronted serving counter was furnished with toothpastes and bars of soap, baby powder and disposable nappies. Behind this sprawled the pharmacist. He had kept a section of the glass clear of toiletries and baby care products, creating a window in his merchandise through which he could inspect any customers while remaining comfortably reclined on a mattress behind the counter. I had heard that Yemen's universities taught pharmacy in English, and I had been assured that the pharmacist was suitably qualified, but on each of my occasional visits to his store, be it for throat lozenges, pain relief, or sticking plasters, he would only ever muster a single word of English, a lackadaisical enquiry: 'Antibiotic?' I had also read in the *Yemen Times* that one-third of antibiotics in the country were counterfeit and, befitting sugar pills, it appeared they might be taken like candy without prescription. Invariably, I would decline the pharmacist's offer, confident that my sore throat, headache, or inconsequential injury would resolve without the need for untrustworthy antimicrobial therapy. Besides, acknowledging the trade in fake drugs, the pharmacist's medicaments seemed unlikely to be any more efficacious than camel-milled sesame oil, which at least made no spurious claims about its content and had a time-honoured heritage.

Camels have been a feature of life in Sanaa for centuries. They have milled oil, drawn water from wells, and transported produce and people. Pedro Páez, the second European to document his visit, had arrived in the city much troubled by the 'very vile gait of camels when hurried'. 'We endured great hardships during those days,' he later recalled of the journey to Sanaa. Páez and his fellow-Portuguese travelling companion, Antonio de Montserrat, were brought to Sanaa as prisoners. The two Jesuit priests had been sailing from India to Ethiopia in February 1590 when pirates seized their vessel off the coast of Arabia. Later Páez described how they were dragged by their captors, stumbling, across the scorched and stony desert, blinded by the sun, blighted by sand storms, and beguiled by desperate mirages. Eventually, the pitiable pair had been put upon the backs of two vile-gaited camels and taken to the Turkish pasha in Sanaa. For, as Páez stated matter-of-factly in his subsequent account, 'all Portuguese prisoners belonged to the Great Turk'.

The Portuguese and Ottoman Turks had been skirmishing for over a century. Their clashing histories were those of two expanding and competing empires. Battles had begun around the Mediterranean, but the voyage of the first Portuguese ship around the African Cape in 1488 opened up a new theatre of conflict and of trade. Nutmeg, mace, cloves, and pepper had long reached privileged European kitchens from the East via overland spice routes, but the Portuguese sea passage around Africa circumvented Ottoman and Venetian middle-men. When Vasco da Gama returned to Lisbon from India in 1499, his ship carried a small fortune in spices. More vessels set out from Portugal and the sailors aggressively established forts at strategic locations around the Indian Ocean. Portuguese became the lingua franca of the region's ports and the de facto currency became the *real de a ocho* or 'pieces of eight', a coin stamped from silver mined in South America. Attention then turned to the Red Sea. In an effort to monopolise the spice trade, the Portuguese sent ships to sever the Red Sea passage between India and Suez. But the Ottomans responded purposefully, capturing Portuguese vessels and occupying Aden in 1538. Pasha Suleiman the Magnificent was determinedly enlarging the Ottoman Empire. Mecca and Medina were already under Turkish control. To secure those holy cities and ensure control of regional trade, Suleiman's forces had moved along the Red Sea coast and headed inland. The Ottomans occupied Sanaa in 1547 and made it their provincial capital. 'The Great Turk' was thus established as the territory's supreme power some forty odd years before the unfortunate arrival of the Portuguese priests Pedro Páez and Antonio de Montserrat, as prisoners on the backs of two camels.

It was on an afternoon in November 2005 that the camel and the pharmacist had become my neighbours. An autumn glow had filled the cooling city, turning it to polished amber and making even the shadows seem luminous. In the walled garden behind the building that was to be my home in Sanaa, a light breeze had puffed the sleeves of Ibrahim's cotton shirt as he shuffled from the shade of a honeysuckle. Seeing me arrive he had dropped the gushing hosepipe, pushed a flat cap back from his brow, and wiped his palms upon the pair of baggy grey corduroys that hung about his waist.

'You must be Andrew.' He shook my hand firmly. 'It's my pleasure. And what a beautiful afternoon...' Behind the little round lenses of his wire-rimmed spectacles Ibrahim's eyes squinted warmly in the sunlight. His drooping ashen moustache twitched to a voice roughened with cigarettes and made sonorous with age. 'And you're here to see the apartment... Come...'

From the garden we had ascended slowly and haltingly, effortfully, until we stood in the stairwell in front of the door to the third-floor apartment. There was a moment of suspended promise, of expectations hanging in balance, as Ibrahim fumbled with a clutch of three enormous keys tied together with a length of twine, trying first one, then another, until the last key turned with a clunk in the lock. The door opened and we stepped onto the flagstones of the apartment's vestibule. In front of us, and on either side, were three sets of ornately carved double wooden doors. Ibrahim swung open the pair facing us and led me through into the *mafraj*, the main living and eating area. Then he paused, remembering, and suggested that I remove my shoes. The floor of the room, and the walls and ceiling, were entirely covered in pure white plaster. Sunbeams fell in gilded slabs through broad windowpanes, before collapsing, splaying in lazy parallelograms, warming our feet. The room spanned the entire front of the apartment, looking out across the *Sayilah*'s traffic flow, over the activity of Bab as-Sabah, toward the late afternoon sun which hung suspended above the city. The house was a half house: a house facing west; one facing south was said to be complete, east-facing was a quarter house, and a north-facing house was no house at all. Light, light, light, might have been the estate agent's patter in Sanaa; location a subordinate concern. The wool-stuffed mattresses furnishing the *mafraj* made the space seem blithely uncluttered and immoderately comfortable. Ibrahim patted the upholstery, rousing a dust plume that swirled and blazed in the sunlight before settling back to its dormancy. At head height, around the walls, heavy plaster lines wriggled and sculpted themselves ingeniously into occasional fitted shelves, calligraphy, and lampshades. Another lampshade, hanging from the ceiling, had been crafted from a huge gourd, dried and hollowed. Also dried and hollowed, and hung upon the wall, was the partially inflated skin of a dead sheep. Intact in its entirety, complete with a withered scrotum, the stiffened ram skin had a texture like desiccated suede or nubuck as I prodded it, perplexed. 'For carrying water in the desert,' Ibrahim explained. It was precisely the sort of container that Pedro Páez had described carrying on his camel journey more than four hundred years earlier. Ibrahim muttered that it would need oiling if I wanted to use it.

Adjoining the apartment's vestibule, beyond the other pairs of carved doors, were two further rooms through which illumination would move like a sedate diurnal resident. A large bedroom with an east-facing fanlight of painted glass fragments became daubed in kaleidoscopic spectacle for a few early hours every morning. Opposite was a much smaller room, white-plastered, south-facing, and so warmed and brightened throughout the day. When light filtered through the single window and a breeze shifted the translucent curtain it was like being submerged in some brilliant undersea cave. The quiet seclusion would soon draw me here to read on late mornings and sunny afternoons. Outside the apartment, just across the stairwell, was a small kitchen. It was equipped with a gas stove, a rust-covered sink, a cracked laminate worktop, and an ant infestation. Beyond the kitchen was the bathroom, furnished with a temperamental wall-mounted water heater, a dribbling shower, a Western-style toilet with an uncertain flush mechanism, and a funny smell that emanated unremittingly from the drain. Previous occupants of the apartment had been two women from Copenhagen. Ibrahim had grumbled about the stiletto holes left in the *mafraj*'s plaster floor. Their prior residence was also evidenced by the glossy Danish magazine left next to the toilet and the tube of anti-cellulite lotion and other sundry toiletries scattered about the bathroom. Later I would discover in a kitchen cupboard the sort of angular stovetop coffee pot that I had always associated with continental Europe and never quite known how to operate. Already I had noted the Danish flag stuck to the refrigerator. It was faintly reassuring in a familiar, homely sort of way. The kitchen of my Suffolk childhood had contained an inexhaustible big blue tin of Royal Dansk Danish butter cookies. I still recall the sense of strangeness in a neighbour's house when I was offered a selection of Bourbons and Garibaldis from a reused Quality Street tub.

On the staircase, Ibrahim directed me to the roof and I scampered up to a vista of satellite television dishes and steel water storage tanks fixed atop the flat roofs of towerhouses. Beyond were domes and minarets and distant mountains; a captivating skyline. Back down the steps, I found Ibrahim sitting in the darkening stairwell. He lifted his cap and swept a hand across the gleaming surface of his head.

'Well,' he sighed, 'if you want to take it, it's yours. But it's not cheap. And the *mafraj* floor needs re-plastering, and that won't be cheap either.' His gaze fell upon my face, questioning. I was only passingly engaged in a conversation about rental payments and water rates. Still adrift amid the defining constants of sunlight and whitewashed walls. Distracted by the intriguing contrasts between ornamented extravagance and a sort of unadorned naturalness: the fanlights' vivid hues against the pure white interiors; the stucco's strict geometry beneath the roof beams' warped curves; the vestibule's ornately carved doors and its rough-hewn flagstones.

'The style is traditional Yemeni,' Ibrahim had told me. But I had been reminded of Friedensreich Hundertwasser, and of the Austrian architect's assertion that an uneven floor is a melody to the feet, and that 'the straight line is a godless line'. My new home in Sanaa had been built with exactly that amalgam of human feeling and divine inspiration. It was uplifting.

'I'll take it.'

A movement behind Ibrahim's moustache might have been a smile. Then he levered himself to his feet.

'Here's the key,' he said, encumbering me. 'You can move in whenever you want.' Descending the stairs, 'Get the first two months' rent to me whenever you can,' he called over his shoulder. 'And you have an open invitation. You are always most welcome to join us in the garden.' Ibrahim's puffing footsteps dropped away, returning him to the watering of his plants.

Sanaa's gardens had been known to foreigners as far back as Páez and Montserrat. Portuguese sailors captured by the Turks were commonly enslaved in the city's green spaces. Pedro Páez himself remarked upon Sanaa's 'numerous gardens and orchards with many of the fruits that there are in Portugal'. That hint of his nostalgia for home is understandable, for the two Jesuits were held captive in the city for over five years. Once ransomed, they returned to Portuguese India in 1596. Montserrat died soon after, but Páez, undeterred, made plans to embark once more upon the journey that had led to their capture: to Ethiopia.

Why Ethiopia? King Philip of Spain and Portugal, prompted by political and mercantile ambitions, had already sought accord with the Orthodox Christian Kingdom of Ethiopia. The African country represented a potential ally against the perceived Muslim threat to European Christendom and, more pressingly, against the Ottoman control of Red Sea shipping. But less worldly concerns inspired the Jesuits. Ethiopia had received Christ's teachings from the apostles Matthew and Bartholomew, long before the Christianisation of Europe. Nonetheless, in the sixteenth century the Jesuits committed themselves to converting Ethiopia's Orthodox Christians to Catholicism. Following his failed attempt to reach Africa in 1590, and not dissuaded by his capture and subsequent imprisonment in Sanaa, Pedro Páez finally arrived in Ethiopia in 1603 and remained there until his death nineteen years later. During those years of evangelising missionary work, he composed a two-volume *História da Etiópia*, in which he quite literally wrote himself and his religious order into the country's history. In this work Páez also recorded his brief account of captivity in Sanaa.

Some four centuries later, on that November afternoon after we had looked around the apartment, while the sunlight still marbled coolly through the trellised vines and the heady scent of honeysuckle enveloped us, Ibrahim added his own minor addendum to that History of Ethiopia. Between 1936 (when Mussolini annexed Ethiopia and proclaimed his Italian East African Empire) and 1941 (when the Italians were ousted and Haile Selassie was reinstated as emperor), Ibrahim's father, along with many other migrant Yemeni workers, had earned good money in Ethiopian construction projects (hydroelectric plants, railways, and so on). Ibrahim recalled his early childhood in Addis Ababa, his family's return to Yemen, and his father purchasing the Old City towerhouse in Sanaa 'with a bag of silver coins'. When his father died, Ibrahim's older brother inherited the building. But when maintenance costs proved unaffordable, Ibrahim bought him out. With his father's eye for profit, he converted the three storeys into three self-contained apartments and set himself up in the real estate market. Though his interests were mostly economic, in the garden I saw a sentimental motive.

The numerous gardens and orchards witnessed by Pedro Páez, irrigated by camel-drawn well-waters and fertilised with camel dung, would once have provided the city's denizens not just with fruits like those in Portugal, but also animal fodder, and medicinal plants. Most of these plots had long been abandoned, left parched and barren, allowed to become no more than refuse dumps or public toilets. A few, like the open allotments of the al-Qasimi quarter, were still productively tilled for vegetables and herbs. But from my subsequent explorations in the city, peering from rooftops, over walls, or through the cracks in their stonework, it was apparent that the verdure of Ibrahim's enclosed garden was uncommon. Hidden behind high walls, Ibrahim's assiduous watering and cultivation had created a rare leafy enclave of fruit trees and flowering plants. On most weekends he would drive in his rattling car from his home in the new town to the garden of the Old City towerhouse. Pottering amid the shrubbery, preparing a leisurely al fresco lunch for friends, or spending the afternoon chewing *qat* in the garden *mafraj*, Ibrahim had created a sanctuary.

The idea of a hidden garden of earthly delights has perennial charm. That very notion had fortified the Portuguese and Jesuits in their early contacts with Ethiopia. The explanation is an irresistible digression... A lush Christian kingdom in the East had been envisaged and mythologised over centuries in medieval Europe. Its existence was widely accepted, but it remained shrouded in mystery, nurturing wild conjecture and elaborate fable. Its ruler, Prester John, was believed to be a descendant of one of the Three Wise Men and to be endowed with preternatural powers, as well as inconceivable wealth. His luxuriant realm was said to contain incredible marvels and extraordinary treasures. There were centaurs and fauns, pygmies and giants, fountains that cured illness, others that ran with wine or honey. There was a looking glass in which any distant corner of the kingdom could be seen. Gold was so abundant that it was used to tile roofs. In imagination and in a presumptive geography, this earthly paradise was close to the Garden of Eden. Yet the precise whereabouts of Prester John's kingdom had long been subject to speculation. India was initially suspected and later Central Asia, but growing familiarity with both those regions confirmed that their inhabitants were unequivocally unchristian. Opinion eventually favoured Africa, specifically Ethiopia, where the population was known to follow Christ's teachings. Portugal's interest in Prester John and his kingdom burgeoned as more of its ships sailed down the African coast. The Portuguese dispatched envoys to Ethiopia, the Ethiopians dispatched envoys to Portugal, and the two countries established a bond of common religion. In Europe, the legendary figure of Prester John was unhesitatingly conflated with the real-life Christian Emperor of Ethiopia. In Ethiopia, the locals were bemused by the foreigners who insisted on referring to their esteemed ruler as 'John'. Ultimately, the relationship of mutual respect was undone. In part this was due to the long-term residence in Ethiopia of a small number of Portuguese Jesuits. Prominent among them was Pedro Páez.

For the Jesuits, the pope was Christ's representative on earth. As the differences between the Ethiopians' religion and the pope's Catholicism became increasingly apparent, and in order to justify converting locals from their Orthodox Christianity to the Church of Rome, the Jesuits set about denigrating the native religion. In their preaching and in the history of

Ethiopia written by Pedro Páez, the 'errors', 'wrongs', and 'heresies' of the Ethiopians were catalogued and denounced. Perspectives on Ethiopia shifted from visions of admiration and religious commonality to an emphasis on strangeness and immorality. The kingdom was no longer rhapsodised, its ruler was no longer revered. At the same moment, the idea of Prester John and his kingdom was becoming increasingly irrelevant. The Age of Discovery was replacing fable with fact and Europeans were growing confident in their capacity to conquer the world without recourse to lost Christian kings. The undermining of the myth and its progressive unimportance are, of course, related phenomena. Once capable of testing the truth of our myths, we no longer have need of them. The Prester John myth died in the seventeenth century. It had been a reassuring fable. The thought of a Christian kingdom hidden somewhere in Africa must have offered comfort to those early Portuguese sailors as they sailed around the coast of the continent, before some of them landed up in the gardens of Sanaa.

Backing onto our garden, just a stone's throw or a shinny-over-the-wall away, was Yusuf's house. With friends and cousins from nearby towerhouses, twelve-year-old Yusuf and his younger brother made their playground in front of the building where I lived. On any given day the cobblestones between the camel and the pharmacy might become a football pitch, a wrestling ring, or a water pistol combat zone. And when the games were interrupted by a vehicle's lumbering passage along the narrow street, the stage was set for something like a fairground or a rodeo as the boys raced to leap upon the tailgate or running boards, clinging to the fairings with fingers and toes while the driver pulled on the steering wheel with one hand and waved the children away with the other.

Soon after I moved into the building, seeking to ingratiate myself with these local youngsters, I arrived home one day bearing a bag of confectionaries for them to share. It was a strategic blunder. My new-found extortionists were eager to exploit the possibility of further gains and for weeks after I had been hounded relentlessly for more candies. In the periods of boredom between their urban adventures, the behaviour of the kids veered from befriending to bullying, and I came to tolerate their capricious conduct with equally fickle indulgence or frustration. Among us all, Yusuf showed a constancy and maturity beyond his years. Following my confectionary misjudgement Yusuf had surprised me at our next encounter. Rather than demanding more sweets, he instead insisted that I accept a gift from him, something like half a chocolate bar, still sticky from pocket warmth and not remotely appealing, but a kindly and appreciated gesture at least. Eldest of eight siblings, Yusuf had developed a precocious self-sufficiency, galvanised by his father's ill health. On weekends he frequently found employment in our garden, performing odd jobs for Ibrahim. Once, aboard a city bus, I caught him truanting from school, working as an impromptu fare collector and extracting his cut from the takings. Another time, after a hawk had crash-landed in the garden with a broken wing and Ibrahim had nursed it back to health, Yusef found the bird and sold it for a tidy sum. But Yusuf retained an underdeveloped sense of vulnerability. His eager risk-taking would impel him to shinny and jump from ever-greater heights. So when his distressed younger brother summoned me urgently one day saying that Yusuf needed a doctor, I hurried around the corner to their house with an uneasy apprehension.

The foetor of sickness hung in the air and an oil lamp struggled to push away the shadows. Yusuf, shivering beneath a blanket and glistening with perspiration, acknowledged me with just a flicker of his usual grin. Stepping closer, I saw the grotesque purple lesions that blotched his face and hands. His mother entered the room, stooped, lifted Yusuf's shirt, and exposed a strange bluish eruption that spread across his torso. Crouching beside him I reached instinctively to check a pulse. When his mother laid a hand upon his chest I noticed that the awful discoloration of his skin did not blanch beneath her fingertips. But then my clinical gaze was distracted. There was an extra finger on his mother's hand. And the unexpected sixth digit was tainted purple at its tip. Lifting my hand from Yusef's wrist I found my own fingers were stained purple too. 'From the pharmacist,' his mother replied to my quizzical expression and handed me a bottle of gentian violet. Dimly I recalled the purple-coloured anti-fungal tincture, not from my work in hospitals, but from its application as a supposed cure-all to the characters of Joseph Heller's *Catch-22*. On further examination, and to my great relief, beneath the strange and terrifying appearance of his literary skin splotches, Yusuf bore nothing more concerning than the familiar vesicular lesions of chickenpox.

Finding the familiar amid the strange has abiding appeal. Whether it is a Christian ruler in an African kingdom, or Danish accoutrements in a Yemeni apartment; walled gardens in Sanaa containing fruit trees like those in Portugal, or honeysuckle like that in Suffolk. It may be human nature, an innate way of making sense of the world, or it may be merely a nervous habit, born of anxiety and apt to sustain it as strangeness is shied away from. For just as lamplight makes the shadows darker, being drawn toward the familiar only makes the strange seem stranger. It is the stuff that myths are made of. And yet it may also be the source of their undoing. When Pedro Páez discredited the Prester John myth, he did so by emphasising the strangeness and denying the familiarity of Ethiopia's Orthodox Church. Yet of the familiar and the strange, it is strangeness that is the more mythic. And it is true to its mythic nature (and it is a liberating truism - the very opposite of a Catch-22's inescapable paradox) that reaching out to touch what is strange makes it strange no longer.

I had intended to enquire about the practice of daubing purple fungicide over children with chickenpox. But after finding the pharmacist reclined as usual behind his glass-fronted showcase of toothpastes and nappies, and after asking him for some medication to treat Yusuf's fevers, my clinical curiosity was again distracted. As the pharmacist pushed a box of paracetamol across the glass counter top toward me, I saw that on his right hand he too had an extra digit.

It had no longer seemed strange that one of my neighbours was a camel and another was a boy painted purple. But then there were those extra digits. They had seemed strange when strangeness was otherwise diminishing. Afterward I wondered if those additional little fingers revealed an unending strangeness. Or undid my sense of familiarity. Or whether they merely reflected my place outside a pool of interrelatedness and quotidian intimacies no more strange than those of my own family. Not really strange at all then, just different. I had become the camel's neighbour. And my neighbours and I were slowly becoming less strange to one another, and more familiar.

- 3 -

Journal Writing

- John Jourdain, 1609 -

'A TEMPERATE AIRE,' WROTE JOHN Jourdain, 'neither too hott nor too cold; but upon the waye in the mornings it is as cold as in England.' Jourdain was the first Englishman to visit Sanaa, and he was right about the weather. Upon my own way in the brisk mornings I soon made it a habit to stop at the local bakery, for a couple of bread rolls shovelled fresh from the brick oven would serve as pocket warmers during my commute. Jourdain meanwhile had warmed to his theme: 'I never felt soe much cold in any place as by the waye in the mornings before sonne rizinge, with a hoare frost on the grownd.' He spent a week in Sanaa during June 1609, when the temperatures would have been relatively clement. But having come from the sultry coast, ascending more than 7,000 feet, the city's mountain cool would have felt decidedly chilly.

Some four hundred years later, in the winter following my own arrival, I walked along Bab as-Sabah each morning on my way to work. Mansour would be standing behind his fruit stall, blowing on a steaming glass of tea held clamped between the palms of his fingerless gloves. At the pashmina shop Nabil would be whistling and wrapping one or more of his scarves about him. I had paused once to hear his recollections of snow falling upon Sanaa's Great Mosque, not knowing if he was exaggerating, but not thinking it too far-fetched. Reaching the end of the street and leaving the Old City behind me, I would pass too briefly through the warm air of the underpass and emerge on Tahreer Square. The prickly pear vendor outside the telecommunications building would see me coming. Selecting a thumb-sized cactus fruit from the pile in his wheelbarrow, grasping it in his protective rubber gauntlet, he would knife through its spine-covered skin and expose a succulent ball of orange flesh for me to pluck. I had become a regular customer. This, despite an excruciating first encounter in which, too eager, I had grasped at the barrowed fruit and spent the rest of the day tweezing cactus bristles from my fingers. Nearby squatted the *miswak* seller, with his twigs aligned in rows on a cloth spread over the pavement. They had looked talismanic, or like the component parts of some conundrum I could not fathom. But staring at the mysterious array of twigs one morning, I had been informed that in fact they were natural fluoride-containing toothbrushes from the native Arak tree. Still I could not comprehend their appeal. Chewing the bitter tip of one of these twigs and scrubbing it about my mouth as instructed had resulted in a single, sore experience of bloodied gums, sufficient to ensure that I never adopted the practice.

Continuing on my journey, a toothless mouth would open up in front of me. 'TAXI! TAXI!' the empty oral cavity would bawl in my face. My path across Tahreer Square was frequently blocked by this old gentleman with no dentures and finger-thick spectacle lenses. Either his salesmanship was undeterred or my recurrent rejection was unremembered. 'TAXI! TAXI!' He would point to a decrepit vehicle parked nearby, but I always smiled without stopping, disinclined to place my life into his tremulous hands.

At the bus terminus there were no signs, no stands, no ticket counter, and no information office. Only the fleet of veteran minivans, revving angrily, battle-scarred, or resting silently, awaiting repair. Each beaten-up Toyota HiAce had been rendered to its role with a re-fit of the seating (four rows of benches), a re-sprayed colour scheme (white with yellow speed stripe), and a driver-specific refurbishment (tastes varied, but fake-fur dashboard covers were popular). The first gear manoeuvrings of the worn vehicles and the travel plans of commuters were all directed by a squat, ricket-bowed man. He issued commands with his walking stick and a voice like rusted iron being dragged over rubble.

'Jumhuri, Jumhuri, Jumhuri!'

His rallying cry for a bus passing by the Jumhuri hospital made signage and information offices superfluous. Finding passengers and filling seats earned the old man ten riyals from the driver; twenty if the day was slow and more shouting was required than usual. Twenty riyals was my bus fare to get across the city, equivalent to about six pence. It seemed a meagre wage for the old man's single-handed administration of the city's public transport system. He knew my route and on this particular occasion the bow-legged old man had waved me towards the single space remaining on the back seat of a bus. Not a particular occasion really; just one on which I had decided to document events during my journey to work. John Jourdain was a far more conscientious diarist. Keeping a journal was, after all, a contractual obligation of his employment as a 'factor' or trader for the East India Company. At the age of thirty-five he had joined the Company and the crew of the *Ascension* as they set sail for India in the spring of 1608. He arrived in Sanaa the following year.

I ducked inside the Jumhuri bus. A near-crawl brought me to the back seat where I had squeezed alongside an unshaven soldier, a thin-faced elder, and a spectacled student in jacket and jeans. We were squashed shoulder-to-shoulder on the least comfortable and most resented row of seating. We knew our buttocks would shortly be subjected to an uncushioned battering as the bus lurched along potholed roads. We expected our kneecaps to be forcibly crushed into the back of the seats in front at each pick-up, drop-off, and engine stall. But none of us had thought for a moment about moving forward from the back row to the more adequately upholstered seats toward the front of the bus where two women sat with ample elbowroom. It was unthinkable for a man to sit beside any woman other than his wife. This proprietary custom could be the cause of considerable disruption. A woman wishing to board a bus might pose a puzzle only solved by vociferous debate and cumbersome relocation of the male passengers. I had learnt to be mindful of my feelings at such moments. My first reaction had been to resent the woman who appeared to cause the disturbance. There was a shameful delay before I acknowledged that the gendered societal restrictions must be far more exasperating for her than for me.

The engine snorted and we rumbled away. West down al-Bawnia Street beneath cedar branches and over rutted tarmac, bounding alongside the mud wall of the British Council's compound, I peered through the window at the fleeting city. A fanfare from the radio heralded the eight o'clock news and told me I was already late for work. Beyond the broken traffic lights at Suq al-Qa, somebody on board yelled and we swerved to a stop. An arthritic shadow creaked from the second row, prised itself into the sunlight, and stood, stooped and fumbling for the fare of twenty riyals. Through the cracked and crudded glass I watched a young girl herd a flock of sheep across the road, mewing and pooing. Day labourers waited on the pavement nearby, squatting next to picks and shovels. Others sat with paintbrushes and rollers, plasterers holding trowels, and plumbers carrying carpetbags stuffed with wrenches and hacksaws, or clutching orange plastic cistern floats. I hoped, but never knew, if these glimpsed figures would find work. I guessed that they didn't know either, and again my own discomforts and inconveniences seemed of little account. We had moved on, until the sharp rap of a coin against a window signalled one of the women wanting to disembark. A chorus of male voices yelled at the driver and we pulled up at al-Jumhuri. A large billboard promoted the latest private ultrasound technologies while a rusting hand-painted sign encouraged uptake of government-funded immunisations and maternity care. The woman clambered out and swayed towards the hospital gate, her pregnant abdomen barely visible under the figure-obscuring black *abaya*.

Speeding onto Zubeiry Street, we joined the city's East-West highway A podium-mounted policeman at the intersection waved his baton ineffectively while cars dodged and swerved, honking contemptuously. Engines fumed, traffic lanes melted into one another, and stoplights on an overhead gantry blinked in bewilderment, but everything was in order. The motion accorded with principles that were only apparent when they were defied, like the time I had attempted to get to work on a bicycle. A small crowd had watched me set off from the bike shop on Zubeiry Street, and witnessed me pedalling no more than a couple of hundred yards before a motorbike careered toward me on the wrong side of the road, ploughed over my rear wheel without stopping, and left me with a mangled wreck and a lesson learned.

The bus continued accelerating, slowing down, dropping off and picking up, while our heads whipped back and forth, and our hands gripped the seats in front. We passed banks, travel agents, baklava shops, and office blocks, then further on were government buildings and austere high-walled compounds. Another intersection and another policeman, this one wielding his baton like a weapon and managing to hold back the tide of traffic. Hawkers manoeuvred among the stationary cars, pushing an unpredictable assortment of merchandise against windows. The boxes of tissues and bottles of water seemed like marketable commodities, potentially too the bags of lemons, but I had struggled to imagine the demand among rush hour commuters for brightly coloured beach towels, or inflatable plastic dinosaurs. It was an implausible commercial intermission before we set off again. Eventually my turn had come to holler for the driver to halt. Scrabbling to emerge from the back seat onto the roadside, screwing up my eyes in the sunlight, I pushed a coin into his palm before he trundled off.

April 4 The winde at E.S.E., a fresh gale; and wee steered awaye N.

West, and N.W. & by West. In the evening wee had sight of land, on our starboard side, beinge the coaste of Arabia Felix.

John Jourdain documented how the ship 'perfectlie made the land of Aden' and how he stepped ashore with Captain Sharpeigh on the morning of 8 April 1609. It was the first British footfall upon what would one day become a cornerstone of empire. But for now, Aden was firmly in the hands of the Ottomans and the nascent British Empire consisted of only a few tentative colonies in North America and the Caribbean. Yet early trading missions undertaken by the likes of Jourdain gradually extended British influence to new territories in the East, and the commercial pursuits of the East India Company over the ensuing decades would ultimately create the basis of British rule in India.

Queen Elizabeth had granted the East India Company a Royal Charter in 1600. This Charter assured the Company exclusive rights to all English trade from the Cape of Good Hope to the Straits of Magellan. English sea captain Francis Drake had sailed between those distant points two decades earlier when he followed the Spanish in circumnavigating the globe, crossing the Indian and Pacific Oceans. When the Spaniards complained about Drake's incursions into their oceanic 'territories' Queen Elizabeth countered that 'the use of the sea and air is common to all' and Drake had routed the Spanish Armada soon after. Alongside this increasing maritime confidence of the English was a growing consciousness of the spice trade profits that they were missing out on. In 1592, during a period of undeclared war with Spain and Portugal, the English Royal Navy captured the *Madre de Deus* on its return voyage to Lisbon from the Far East. Laden with ambergris, ebony, jewels, precious metals, and a huge quantity of spices, the ship's cargo was worth an estimated half-million pounds: almost half the size of the English treasury at the time. Yet despite the obvious yields, Portugal's sea empire was already beginning to decline. Piracy and shipwrecks had taken their toll, and so too had the rising costs of goods being bought in Europe to trade overseas. Expenses began to outweigh returns and eventually there was neither sufficient money nor manpower to sustain Portugal's outpost forts and ocean fleets. Dutch traders moved into the spice trade and began setting prices for the

British markets. The turn of the century and the Royal Charter marked an opportunity and an imperative for the English East India Company.

Twelve months had passed since Jourdain, Captain Sharpeigh, and the rest of the crew of the *Ascension* had departed from Woolwich dock in March 1608. Hopes were high that this fourth voyage of the East India Company would be a lucrative expedition. The Company's three previous voyages had more than doubled their money on imports of pepper, cloves, mace, nutmeg, indigo, and silk. In London the *Ascension* had been loaded with 'yron, tynne, steele, and cloth'. The plan was to sell the metals and material, buy spices in India, and, if possible, establish a permanent trading post or 'factory' at Aden or the Red Sea before returning home. But negotiations at Aden did not go smoothly. After Jourdain and Captain Sharpeigh had come ashore, the Ottomans refused to allow them to return to their ship. The *Ascension*'s crew responded by capturing a couple of Turks. And the first trade between England and the inhabitants of southern Arabia was a hostage exchange.

The double-dealings continued with a dispute about custom fees that left the Ottoman authorities insulted and the English merchants feeling swindled. If they were unsatisfied, the Turkish governor thundered, they could explain their quarrel to the pasha in Sanaa. Jourdain responded feistily: 'I awnswered him that for my owne parte I was very willing to see the Bashaa.' And so, toward the end of May, John Jourdain and his fellow merchant Phillip Glascocke embarked upon the journey from Aden to Sanaa, accompanied by the Turkish governor's secretary who was charged to deliver them to the pasha. They took with them the contested sum of money for the Ottoman ruler to allocate as he determined. But Jourdain admitted in his journal that he had set out fearing that the Governor of Aden 'would secreetlie have putt us to death and so keep the money to himselfe'. Here then was the uneasy context for John Jourdain's visit to Sanaa, and for his maundering commentary upon the weather.

Fireballs seemed to be falling from the sky, hurtling toward me, one after another. The light ricocheting from windscreens flared briefly but violently as each vehicle blasted by while I stood at my drop-off point on Zubeiry Street, dazzled by the blazing cars, waiting for a break in the traffic. After crossing the road I had entered a suburb of stray dogs and semi-constructed buildings, detouring around broken cars and hopping over piles of rubble. On the street leading to the office where I worked a group of men were crouched around a bowl of steaming bean stew. Each had a Russian-made automatic weapon hung over his shoulder or lying close to hand. These were the blood relatives and bodyguards of a tribal sheikh who lived nearby.

'Yaaa!' I had been sighted. One of them shouted, pointed at me, and reached for his Kalashnikov.

'Welcome!' He had moved his machine gun to make space for me, then gestured toward the communal dish. It was an invitation for breakfast.

The Turkish ruler was still in bed. Having reached Sanaa and been summoned to the Ottoman court, Jourdain 'stayed three howers before wee could have admittance to the Basha, hee being asleepe'. It was after noon when the Englishman was finally ushered past courtiers and hushed ranks of noblemen into a 'faire gallerie' where the pasha sat 'upon a high stoole laid with crimson velvett'. After kissing the pasha's gown he was asked to explain his presence. At which point in Jourdain's narrative it becomes apparent that the dispute with the Governor of Aden had served usefully as a means of gaining audience with Yemen's Ottoman ruler. Jourdain delivered a letter, written in Portuguese, requesting permission for the English East India Company to establish a trading post upon Yemen's coast. The pasha refused. Such a request, he announced, 'could not bee permitted without expresse order from the Great Turke', that is, from the sultan in Constantinople. On the subject of the disputed money from Aden, Jourdain was discreetly advised by one of the Turkish administrators not to mention it, for 'if he did he should surelie paye for itt'.

Later, Jourdain noted that upon being gifted several lengths of English cloth, two barrels of gunpowder, and two pistols, the pasha 'seemed not satisfied with the present'. In a 'discription of the cittie' he alluded to the many hostages held by the pasha in his castle 'as pledges of peace of the citties and townes which are under the subjection of the Turke'. And he wrote that although Sanaa was 'yealdinge little comodities for marchandize', it was 'a very firtill cittie for all provision of victual and fruite, and reasonable cheape'. He recounted too the assurance from local merchants that his own 'tynne' and 'yron' 'would sell at a good rate'. Jourdain did not describe his motives for writing and for detailing his findings. But it is clear that his journal entries were no mere jotting of observations and incident, of those things that he happened to see or that happened to happen. Rather, they were a deliberate documentation of diplomatic encounters and local politics, of trade prospects and likely profit margins. And when not analysing markets he was noting navigational details: wind directions, harbour depths, latitudes, and so on. His journal was purposeful and pragmatic. The information it contained could determine the success of future voyages.

The purpose of my own journal writing was less immediately apparent. Like Jourdain, I had never made my motives explicit at the time, but in documenting such mundanities as my bus journey to work, I suppose that I had thought vaguely (and correctly as it turned out) that some future self would be grateful for my record of events. A similar sentiment stimulated Jourdain, though the self in question was not his own and his incentive had a rather more robust basis, for upon his return to London he would be expected to deliver his journal to his employer. So even as he feared for his life on the road out of Aden he was duly noting the distances travelled and details of local towns. And after his encounter with the pasha in Sanaa he had diligently set about making his commercial enquiries on the subjects of local merchandise and the potential market for English goods. Just as Jourdain's journal spurred on his questions, my own diary encouraged a sort of contemplative inquisitiveness as I endeavoured to establish some comprehension of what went on around me. Diary-writing is an inherently reflective undertaking. But reflecting now upon my reflections then, I wonder whether there wasn't also something defensive about my journal writing; about approaching events hidden behind a notebook, or defining their meanings at a safe distance, unchallenged.

Eventually, Jourdain's journal arrived at the Fenchurch Street offices of the East India Company in London. Curiously, it was lost soon after, but not before a copy had been made. Somehow, and some decades later, the handwritten facsimile of the journal fell into the possession of Sir Hans Sloane, the inveterate Irish collector. Upon Sloane's death in 1753, his amassed cabinet of curiosities and his gargantuan library (including Jourdain's journal) were bequeathed to the nation, forming the basis of the British Museum. The journal was forgotten about for over a century, but after being rediscovered the text was published in 1905, accompanied by a biographical sketch of the author. Jourdain was portrayed as a tragic character. Having grown up in Lyme Regis he was said to have joined the East India Company because 'his business was a failing one' and 'his relations with his wife were not satisfactory... he chose exile in the Indies as a means of escaping domestic unhappiness.'

My own self-imposed exile had been imbued with significantly less pathos. In the summer of 2005 I had been attempting to fix an air conditioning unit in the Boston apartment where I was then living when the telephone rang. I put down a screwdriver, knowing nothing about air conditioning units, and picked up the phone, knowing little about Yemen.

'But you know about the polio outbreak there?' The question came from my research supervisor.

'Yes, of course.' I had recently completed a degree in public health and was now researching global polio eradication efforts.

'There's a job come up. I thought you might want to apply.'

'Golly.'

'Are you interested?'

'In going to Yemen?'

I had worked hard to go to medical school, failed, tried again, and eventually succeeded in becoming the first in my family to go to university. But my clinical studies were dispiriting and my first hospital job would divest me of confidence. Much of my time at university had been spent longing for the vacations and looking back, they feel more formative than my formal education. Long summer breaks were spent reading novels and working in a variety of factory jobs, earning the money that would allow me to abscond on solo excursions to the newly independent countries of Eastern Europe and parts of Asia. Oddly, though, I don't recall any interest in visiting the Middle East. Otherwise, the most enjoyable period of my undergraduate career had been a year spent in London studying the History of Medicine. My final dissertation had focused on the social experience of Britain's 1947 epidemic of polio, which struck me as fascinating at the time. Subsequently, international public health, the study of population health issues including polio epidemics in the so-called developing world, had seemed to offer a means of pursuing my interest in foreign cultures while distancing myself from the disillusions of my clinical career.

In truth I had known precisely nothing about Yemen. I would not even have been able to locate it on a map. Whether despite, or because of my ignorance, after discussing the job proposal with my supervisor I had politely expressed my lack of interest. Once the conversation ended and I had hung up, I looked up Yemen on the internet. The BBC News website gave an impression of a nation clinging to peace and stability about as tenuously as it seemed to cling to its distant corner of the Arabian Peninsula. When a friend called a few minutes later to make plans for the evening I had mentioned the Yemen job as a sort of comical aside.

'Yemen?!!' he exclaimed. 'Awesome! That'll be amazing.' I had listened to his impressively well-informed outline of the country's politics and history. Then he told me I was sure to get the job if I applied, that I'd be great at it, and that I'd find Yemen fascinating.

'It is a generall rule with the English that if they have but a parcell of faire words given, that there neede noe more feare.' Having taken his leave of the pasha in Sanaa, John Jourdain journeyed to the Red Sea port of Mocha where the *Ascension* lay at anchor. He was appalled to find the ship's company wandering about ashore, unprotected. 'If the Turks had pretended any villanie against us,' he fumed, 'they might at one clapp have taken Generall, marchants and maister.' Next they could have 'taken the shipp'. Jourdain thought the English sailors a guileless lot and it was all 'very careleslie done'. Still riled, he noted that 'the Turks themselves say: If thou wilt have anie thinge of an Englishman, give him good words and thou shalt bee sure to wynne him.' In my relevant experience though, susceptibility to flattery may be a symptom of insecurity, or uncertainty, rather than simply a national affliction. I had been back on the telephone to my research supervisor within the hour, enquiring about the job in Yemen, while the air conditioner hummed reassuringly in the background.

The *Ascension* departed the Red Sea and reached the Indian coast at

Gujarat by the end of August 1609. Eschewing the need for a local pilot to guide them onwards to the port at Surat, the crew set sail across the Gulf of Cambay: waters notorious for their shoals, sandbanks, and strong tides. Jourdain's diary records how the *Ascension* soon ran aground. The grounding tore off the ship's rudder and broke the skiff that had ferried the sailors between ship and shore. 'Nowe troubles begin to enter into mens harts, seeinge our ruther gone, our skiffe split... and our long boate not sufficient to save our men, which made us all doubt our lives.' The men laboured through the night to repair the skiff and enlarge the longboat. But by the afternoon of the next day there was two foot of water in the hold and the two inadequate rowing boats were hastily lowered overboard.

On Captain Sharpeigh's orders the Company's money chests were broken open so the crew might help themselves to as many pieces of eight as they could carry. A scramble ensued for the silver coins. Jourdain feared a mutiny, 'as comonly there is att such times'. Another scramble followed for the longboat. Clambering down a ladder over the ship's side, clinging to the rungs, Jourdain was pressed upon by the crush of heavily silver-laden sailors that tumbled after him. 'It was everyone for himself. Life beeing sweete, with greate paines I hunge by the hands.' Shoved or slipping, he ended up in the water and was dragged unconscious aboard the longboat by his collar. The crew had thought him drowned, but he spluttered back to life. And with the entire company eventually squeezed into the two small vessels, hoping to reach the Indian coast, it was after midnight when, as John Jourdain recounted, they 'putt of from the ship, singing of psalms to the praise of God...'

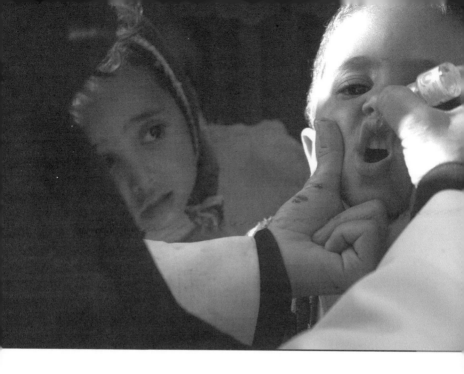

- 4 -

Global Health &
Global Wealth

- Sir Henry Middleton, 1610 -

ON CHRISTMAS DAY IN THE year 1610 Mr Pemberton's Boy was abandoned by his comrades. The English crew of the *Trades Increase* had been captured by Turks on Yemen's coast. They were put in irons and forced to march to Sanaa where the Ottoman pasha would decide their fate. Mr Pemberton's Boy fell ill during the journey. He was left behind in the town of Taiz while his erstwhile companions continued on their long slog to Sanaa. Later he heard that his shipmates had been put to death in the capital. And he was told that his own life would be spared only if he converted to Islam. When Mr Pemberton's Boy refused, he was overpowered, dragged to a hammam, stripped naked, and forcibly circumcised. Such were the facts as recorded subsequently by Sir Henry Middleton, commander of the *Trades Increase*.

Meanwhile, grimy and bedraggled, angry and manacled, Middleton and the rest of the sailors had pushed on toward Sanaa, where in fact they were imprisoned, but not executed. Middleton later recalled how 'two great men came and tooke me by the wristes', dragging him before the pasha.

> He, with a frowning and angry countenance, demanded of what Country I was, and what I made in those parts? I answered, I was an Englishman, and a Merchant, and friend to the Grand Senior, and came to seek trade.

Eighteen months had passed since Jourdain had stood upon the 'Turkie Carpets' amid the rows of Ottoman officials in front of Yemen's Turkish ruler. Eighteen months during which time nothing had been heard from Jourdain, Captain Sharpeigh and the crew of the *Ascension*. Now, restrained at the wrists, it was Sir Henry Middleton, another employee of the East India Company, who confronted the Ottoman pasha in Sanaa. 'He said, it was not lawfull for any Christian to come into that Countrey, and that he had given warning to Captaine Sharpeigh, that no more of our Nation should come thither. I told him, Captaine Sharpeigh was cast away upon the Coast of India, and came not to England to tell us so much, which had we knowne, wee would never have put our selves into that trouble we were in.'

The 'trouble' was not only the incarceration of Middleton and his men in Sanaa, but how 'treacherously and vilely' they had been treated on the coast at Mocha. An embittered Middleton opined that 'the covetous Turkes would leave no Villanie nor Treason unattempted.'

Christmas Day 2005 had marked the beginning of another national vaccination campaign. Over the next three days, tens of thousands of vaccination teams would visit every household in Yemen in order to vaccinate the country's children against polio. Nasser worked for the government's vaccine programme. He was responsible for monitoring and managing local immunisation activities and resolving any problems. We had met several times through work and I had arranged to accompany him on this first morning of the polio campaign, but when our progress was halted at the city's perimeter checkpoint it became quickly apparent that I was not going to make his job easier.

'He won't let us through,' Nasser said, nodding toward the soldier on duty. 'He's concerned about you being kidnapped.' Sighing, Nasser had reversed the four-by-four off the road. Kidnappings of foreigners were not unheard of in Yemen, but they never occurred anywhere near the capital. And the risk of abduction had never before prevented my passage beyond the city limits. I voiced my indignation. There was no chance of me being kidnapped, I said. The suggestion was absurd.

'No.' Nasser calmly interrupted my outburst. 'He's not worried about the risk of you *being* kidnapped. He's concerned that you've *been* kidnapped. He thinks *I* might have kidnapped you.'

The uniformed figure stooped to peer through the driver's window, inspected me with an expressionless gaze, then conferred briefly with Nasser.

'He wants to see your passport.'

I pointed out rather petulantly that we were only leaving the capital, not the country. Nasser smiled patiently and waited for me to produce my passport. I admitted that I had not brought it with me. Dimly I acknowledged that I was making Nasser's day more difficult. A longer discussion ensued, until the soldier seemed to grow weary of the conversation and walked back towards the barricaded checkpoint.

'He can't let us through until he gets permission from his commander,'

Nasser informed me, then pre-empted my next question. 'His commander doesn't arrive until nine o'clock. At the earliest.'

My watch said seven thirty. I asked Nasser what he thought we should do.

'Wait.'

I suggested trying to bluff our way past with some of the official-looking documents that we carried from the Health Ministry, but Nasser was unconvinced. He sat for a moment, then climbed out of the vehicle and wandered over to where the soldier stood. Returning after a few minutes and hoisting himself back into the driving seat, Nasser manoeuvred the four-by-four out in front of the checkpoint once more. The soldier waved us through dismissively and we drove away. I had no idea what had happened. 'I told him you were Russian,' said Nasser. I still had no idea. 'He doesn't care anymore if you are kidnapped,' Nasser explained. I still wasn't certain whether this was a joke or an ingenious subterfuge. Sanaa's troops had fought against Soviet-backed soldiers from the south during the civil war a decade earlier. Nasser was well attuned to the local resentment that persisted toward Southerners and Russians. He was not only from the south of Yemen, but had studied in Moscow during the 1980s. Now, evidently cheered by his evasion of the military, he regaled me with recollections of his glasnost-era exploits: shaving off his moustache, starting smoking, discovering pop music and women. As Sanaa slipped away behind us, Nasser pushed cigarettes to his clean-shaven lips and hinted at sexual adventures back in the USSR.

We stopped at a turn-off about an hour outside the city. The landscape had flattened, the wind picked up, and grubby clouds fled over dusty plains. Nasser and I waited for the district's health director to join us. He arrived, a little flustered, keen to demonstrate that local immunisation activities were proceeding as planned. His suit flapped officiously as he fought to flatten a map across the bonnet of his car. With his finger, the director traced the house-to-house routes of his vaccination teams across the cartography while the map's wind-blown sheets bucked rebelliously. Then he pointed to two women walking towards us. Squalls tugged at their veils and clipboards. One of them carried a cumbersome grey cool box. The pair were instantly recognisable as vaccinators. University students, they said when they had reached us, currently on holiday and keen to earn a little extra income by helping with the immunisation days. A little theatrically, the director removed one of the vaccine vials from their cool box and inspected the heat-sensitive strip on its label that showed it had been stored at the correct temperature.

'Things didn't go smoothly here during the last campaign,' Nasser told me when we were back in our vehicle and following the director's car. 'The director struggled with the organisation. Understandable. It's a difficult job. But that's why I'm here. And that's why he's nervous.'

A short drive brought us to a settlement where the dirt had been carved-up and walled-off into a mosaic of compounds, each compound containing a single-storey home. It was the territory of another vaccination team. Dhekra and her male companion both wore white, knee-length clinical coats. Hers was buttoned-up swelteringly, his was open and stained at the breast pocket with a splodge of purple ink from a leaking fibre-tip. In our brief introductory exchange, Dhekra gave an immediate impression of intelligence and no-nonsense. When she knocked loudly at an iron door and we heard a female voice reply to say that the man of the house was not at home, Dhekra had turned towards us and rolled her eyes.

'Well, is his father in?' she shouted.

We waited. Slowly and with creaking joints, the door opened and an aged man invited us into a tiny courtyard. Drying clothes hung from a washing line and drying dung cakes leant against the breeze-block walls. A canvas screen, frayed and patched, was draped across a doorway. The canvas twitched and unseen hands impelled a child to toddle forward into the courtyard. Dhekra instructed her male colleague as he coaxed the child into looking upward then squeezed a couple of drops from a vaccine vial into the toddler's open mouth. A brief pause to ensure that the vaccine was swallowed and not spat out, then the child's finger was coloured with the purple fibre-tip pen, marking him as having been vaccinated. For every home in the country this would be the seventh polio vaccination visit in nine months. For vaccinators, children, and parents in Yemen, the routine was now familiar and perfunctory.

For my own parents, polio had been the summer plague. Swimming pools and cinemas had been closed for months as local authorities sought to halt the seasonal epidemics that swept through post-war Britain, leaving children crippled or caged in iron lungs. For me, a child growing up in the

1980s, polio was simply the one vaccination that I did not fear: three sugar lumps wetted with polio vaccine had offered sweet reprieve in the schedule of tetanus injections and TB jabs. But for many children at the start of the twenty-first century, polio still represented a real threat of paralysis and death, despite determined international efforts to eradicate the disease.

A few days earlier, in a darkened conference room in Yemen's Ministry of Health, an aged slide projector had thrown a map of the country against the wall. Red dots had spotted the chart, speckling the Red Sea coast and clustering around Sanaa. 'Each dot represents a confirmed case of polio,' a government epidemiologist had informed the small gathering. The first cases had occurred during February 2005 in the coastal city of Hodeidah. The number of cases grew. Slowly at first. Two cases initially. Another the following week. Two more the week after, three the next, then nine, and then the virus had spread beyond Hodeidah. Seven weeks after the first cases were diagnosed, the city had recorded twenty-three polio-affected children and the disease had disseminated to five other regions. By the end of April, over fifty new cases of polio were being diagnosed in Yemen every week and the disease had appeared in almost all of the nation's twenty-two governorates.

'We're staring at the whites of the eyes of this thing', the Director of the Global Polio Eradication Initiative had declared. The Initiative had been launched at the World Health Assembly in Geneva in 1988. Its aim was to wipe out polio altogether, just as smallpox had been wiped out a decade earlier. Fifteen years of intensive vaccination efforts had dramatically reduced the number of countries in which poliovirus circulated from 125 when the initiative began, to just six in 2003. During the same period, the annual incidence of polio had plummeted from 350,000 cases to fewer than 700. But then in August 2003 communities in northern Nigeria refused to allow their children to be vaccinated. The reduction in population immunity to polio led to a local resurgence of the disease and the virus then began to spread.

Early in 2005, a five-year-old boy from Nigeria was diagnosed with polio in Saudi Arabia, on the outskirts of Mecca. It was the first recorded case of polio in Saudi for ten years and it occurred just weeks before the start of the annual Hajj pilgrimage. The Director of the Global Polio Eradication Initiative, staring at the whites of the eyes of polio eradication, feared a catastrophe. Two million pilgrims were expected to arrive in

Mecca for Hajj. If the poliovirus was circulating in the city, it could spread among this congregation. The virus would be transported along a multitude of routes as the Hajjis returned to homes all over the world. Disease outbreaks could then occur in countries that had previously been polio-free. Suddenly, polio eradication was in jeopardy.

The Saudi government swiftly instituted emergency immunisation measures and the feared outbreak of polio in Saudi Arabia never occurred. But neighbouring Yemen was less well prepared. Hodeidah, Yemen's major port city, was a common point of disembarkation for people journeying by boat from Africa and local immunisation rates had been low when the polio virus arrived. The ensuing outbreak of childhood paralysis was represented by the red dots that mottled the map in the Ministry of Health. More projected maps of the polio epidemic flicked across the wall of the conference room, followed by charts of escalating case counts and tables of immunisation coverage. Then came Yemen's president. 'This picture,' announced the epidemiologist, 'shows His Excellency launching the first of our National Immunisation Days.' The right hand of the president appeared alabaster white in the camera flash, pinching a tiny vaccine vial between forefinger and thumb above the head of a swaddled infant. His face bore an expression of stern, but benevolent, concentration as he let the droplets of oral polio vaccine fall into the child's mouth. A crowd of background figures watched as the President of the Republic cut a hybrid icon of baby-kissing politician and child-anointing holy man.

Six national polio immunisation campaigns had been carried out in the year so far. During the three days of each campaign, thirty-five thousand people volunteered to ensure that every home in Yemen was visited, and that all four million children in the country aged under five years received three drops of polio vaccine. It was an extraordinary endeavour. To support the vaccination efforts, posters, pamphlets, and promotional banners appeared in the streets. Public announcements, interviews, and live phone-ins with polio experts were featured on local radio and national television. Imams endorsed immunisations in mosques, teachers informed pupils about vaccines in schools, and vehicles with loudspeakers attached to their roofs drove through city streets and remote villages blaring promotional messages that had been pre-recorded onto audiocassettes. In the days leading up to the vaccination campaign that commenced on

Christmas Day, the poster image appeared in Sanaa of a man with a snow-white beard and a distinctive hat. I recognised his face. He was Imam Yusuf Al-Qaradawi, Muslim cleric and Al-Jazeera celebrity. His portrait on publicity material accompanied the text of a lengthy fatwa proclaiming his support for polio vaccinations. It was an important and hugely positive intervention. So it was with some sadness that I remembered how I recognised him. Eighteen months earlier Al-Qaradawi had visited Britain. His brief time in London had been entirely overshadowed by media furore surrounding his view that Palestinian suicide bombings were a legitimate weapon of the weak.

Just off the coast of Yemen, an Arab fisherman warned Sir Henry Middleton: 'The Pasha that last was, was very bad, this a little better; but all the Turkes in general starke naught.' Nonetheless, when the *Trades Increase* dropped anchor at Mocha the English mariners were welcomed ashore with courtesy and ceremony by the occupying forces of the Ottoman Turks. Soon though began the 'trouble' that Middleton later spoke of in Sanaa. He recalled a 'bloudie Massacre'. The unsuspecting English sailors were violently and murderously assaulted in a surprise attack. Eight men were killed and several wounded by the Turks. The fisherman's caution had gone unheeded and John Jourdain's presentiment of the Turks' 'pretended villanie' had been unheard. Middleton was knocked unconscious, shackled, and brought before Mocha's resident Turkish aga. 'With a frowning countenance, he asked mee how I durst be so bold as to come into this their Port of Moha, so neere their holy Citie of Mecca?'

Middleton was in command of the East India Company's Sixth Voyage. Aboard the *Trades Increase*, he had sailed from England on 1 April 1610, rounded the Cape of Good Hope in July, reached Aden in November, and from there had sailed on to Mocha where he ignored the fisherman's warning that the Turks 'starke naught'. After he and his men had been assailed by the Turkish soldiers, and following his reproach by the frowning Turkish aga, Middleton recorded in his journal how that night he was confined 'in a dirty Dogges Kennell under a paire of staires'. He continued with unfettered self-pity: 'my lodging was upon the hard ground, and my pillow a stone, my companions to keepe me waking were griefe of heart and multitude of rats.' His grief turned to anger and Middleton was soon fuming about Treachery and Vileness, Villanie and Treason. When he was subsequently chained to his captured comrades, his grievances found prosaic focus in the fact 'that one could not goe aside to ease himselfe, but the rest in a row must goe with him, to their great annoyance.' Bruised and begrudging of the toileting arrangements, the sailors then endured a forced march from the coast up to Yemen's capital.

Like John Jourdain before him, Middleton had been obliged to keep a journal for the East India Company. And like Jourdain, he noted the dramatic change in climate during the journey to Sanaa. And he recorded the abandonment of Mr Pemberton's Boy.

> We arrived at the Citie of Ties [Taiz] on Christmas day... A youth of Mr Pemberton fell sicke in this towne, and was left with the Governor thereof, for that he was unable to travell. I kept no Journal from this time forward; but this I remember, we found it very cold all the way from Tyes [Taiz] to Zenan [Sanaa], our lodging being the cold ground... every morning the ground was covered with horie frost: and in Zenan wee had Ice a finger thicke in one night, which I could hardly have believed, had I not seene it.

On reaching Sanaa, Middleton, restrained at the wrists, was taken before the pasha to give an account of himself and his crew. It was then that he declared himself 'an Englishman, and a Merchant', and rather less convincingly, a friend of the Grand Sultan in Constantinople. And he claimed that if he had known of the Pasha's dislike of foreign visitors he would never have come to Yemen and landed himself in so much trouble. If only he had been forewarned by Captain Sharpeigh, John Jourdain, or any of the crew of the *Ascension*, but they were all 'cast away upon the Coast of India'. The Turkish ruler was evidently unimpressed. He promptly threw Middleton and his men in jail. Middleton later wrote of the prison conditions that 'many of our people fell sicke and weake through griefe, cold, naughtie aire, bad diet, evill lodging, and waightie irons.' He recorded few other details of Sanaa, though in analogies fitting for an English merchant seaman he compared the pasha's palace to London's Royal Exchange and noted that the city was 'somewhat bigger than Bristoll'.

Despite all the griefe, naughtie aire and waightie irons suffered by the sailors in Sanaa, and despite Sir Henry Middleton's imprisonment in Mocha with a multitude of rats in a dirty dog's kennel under the stairs, the most pitiable figure in Sir Henry's narrative remains Mr Pemberton's Boy. Abandoned on Christmas Day, he was left alone and unwell among strangers, then heard that his comrades had been put to death and had his own life threatened. By the time Middleton and his men were released from their incarceration and returned to Taiz two months later, Mr Pemberton's Boy had been 'forced to turne Turke'. Evincing a fascinated horror of that fate, Middleton described in some detail the means by which the Turkish governor had 'circumcised him perforce'. Evidently, the minor surgical procedure undergone by all male Muslim children was a source of terror and tarnish for the English sailors. To 'turn Turk' meant to convert to Islam. The phrase was also used metaphorically to denote an act of betrayal. Either way it was deprecatory. And even when the turning had been involuntary, as in the case of Mr Pemberton's Boy, both body and soul were irredeemably smirched with sexual violence and religious apostasy. In his journal, Middleton never deigned to note the Boy's name. And when Middleton passed through Taiz with his crew on their way back to the coast from Sanaa, the Turkish governor of the town refused to release the youth. Once more Mr Pemberton's Boy was left behind by his comrades.

'My husband will kill me.'

The district health director hammered with his fist, but the woman refused to open the door. 'He doesn't want our son to be given the polio vaccine,' she shouted from within the house. Nasser and I stood nearby. One of the vaccination teams had telephoned the director about a mother who did not want her child to be vaccinated.

'They must be new to the area,' the director muttered. 'I've never had this problem here before.'

The house stood alone on a dirt road, a rutted track that cleaved through a landscape of winter wheat and stretched away toward the ragged silhouettes of dark distant mountains. The wind had died and nothing moved. Except far off, just below the horizon, where a moving car tore a dust cloud between the earth and sky.

'But why will your husband kill you?' the director cried through a broken windowpane in the building's crumbling stone wall.

'He won't.' The voice sounded alarmed by the suggestion.

'But you said...'

'My husband said he will kill me if I let our child be vaccinated. I won't let that happen.'

'Why not?'

'I told you. Because of my husband.'

Dhekra, if she was still with us, might have rolled her eyes.

'Why does your husband say that your child must not be vaccinated?' the director yelled.

'I don't know. But you can't vaccinate my son.'

The director looked to Nasser and asked if he should call the police.

'To do what?' Nasser asked.

'To make her... vaccinate the child?' The director suggested weakly.

Nasser called to the walls of the house. 'Where is your husband?'

'He's away,' the woman shouted. 'Back at sunset.'

'OK.' Nasser turned to the director. 'Come back after sunset and talk to her husband. And don't call the police,' he added. 'Unless of course he kills her. In which case you should, obviously...' Nasser stopped talking and pointed to someone approaching from the fields. Amiably he greeted the man who set down his farm tools to shake hands. They stood talking for some time and later I heard from Nasser the story that the woman's husband had told him. The family were from the coast. They had scraped a meagre existence from the littoral until the husband was offered a house and employment here as a sharecropper by his brother-in-law. They had arrived only a few weeks earlier. Before leaving their last home, during an earlier round of immunisation days, a vaccination team had visited them and their two children had been given the polio vaccine. Their two-month-old daughter became ill the very next day. She died soon after. The man blamed the vaccine. Nasser sought to rationalise the situation. Could they be sure that the vaccine had caused the death of their child? There had been many immunisation campaigns this year and children often became unwell, so could it be coincidence that their child's death followed one of the campaigns? Many thousands of children had been given the vaccine and had they heard of any other children dying afterwards? Yet perhaps they knew of children who had been paralysed by polio because they were not vaccinated? To which the farmer replied that he had only seen a small number of polio victims in his life, but he had witnessed many deaths from TB and malaria on the Red Sea coast. If we were so worried about his children, he wanted to know, why were we not doing anything about *those* diseases? Nasser admitted afterwards that, uncharacteristally, he had been unable to provide a good answer.

Over eighty thousand children aged under five died that year in Yemen. Around one in every fifteen of those born would die before their fifth birthday (in Britain the figure was less than one in a hundred). Most of these deaths would be due to readily treatable causes like malnutrition, pneumonia, and diarrhoeal diseases. Had the five hundred cases of polio that occurred during Yemen's outbreak elicited disproportionate concern? That suggestion, implied by the farmer, was difficult to refute with conviction. There was a marked discrepancy between the concerns of the government health authorities, alarmed by the sudden spread of polio among the population, and the concerns of those individuals whose children too often contributed to the statistics. The authorities, and observers like myself, had simply become inured to the annual death tolls. I was neither surprised, nor unsympathetic, when parents expressed suspicion or refused to allow their children to be vaccinated during the immunisation days in Yemen.

'Less than a third of homes have a piped water supply,' Nasser reminded me as we drove back towards the city at the end of the day. 'And far fewer are connected to a sewerage system.' Healthcare access outside of a few urban centres was extremely limited. Widespread poverty meant that child malnutrition was rife and more than half of children in Yemen would grow up stunted. The assumption that parents would simply be thankful when they were offered vaccines to protect their children against polio no longer seemed tenable; not while so many of their other basic needs remained unmet and while there were so many undeserved and unjust dangers to their children's health.

Arriving back at Mocha and back aboard the *Trades Increase*, Sir Henry Middleton was incensed by the harms and humiliation that he had experienced. Angrily he demanded recompense from the Turkish aga. Blockading the port with his heavily armed ship, he held the town and its trade to ransom. Menacing the Aga of Mocha with his ship's cannons, he threatened to 'batter the Towne about his eares'. Indian merchants endeavoured to intercede, eager to reinstitute trade. One even paid for the release and return of Mr Pemberton's Boy from Taiz, 'decently apparelled in new clothes after the Christian fashion'. The investment in unTurkish attire suggested an especially earnest attempt at redress. But Middleton was only concerned with his own 'losses and disgraces' and he remained determined to exact revenge.

The threatened battering might have been exactly what Mocha's Turkish aga had originally feared. When it first arrived at the port, Middleton's ship, the *Trades Increase*, would have been an intimidating prospect. It was the largest merchant ship ever built in England and far larger than any other boat in the Red Sea at the time. And it was armed with dozens of cannons, a fact unprecedented among local trading vessels and seemingly inexplicable for a ship claiming to be concerned only with commerce. Mocha meanwhile had no defensive wall and its few guns would have been no match in number or in range for those carried aboard the English ship. The aga would have been understandably anxious. From the outset, the *Trades Increase* seemed to threaten the aga's own immediate safety and that of his town, as well as the maritime trade upon which they depended. Furthermore, as the aga pointed out after his soldiers' surprise attack on the English sailors, Mocha lay 'so neere their holy Citie of Mecca' that he would be held accountable if the Christians attempted any assault on that city of Mohammed's birth. Finally, the aga in Mocha was under instruction from the pasha in Sanaa, who himself was under orders from the Great Turk in Constantinople, to kill or capture any Christian sailors who ventured into the Red Sea. The fearsome hierarchical authority of the Ottoman Empire and the vulnerability of the aga in the chain of command were made apparent when Sir Henry Middleton stood before the pasha in Sanaa. Middleton requested a letter guaranteeing that upon their release he and his men would suffer no further harm from Mocha's aga. 'Is not my onely word sufficient to turne a Citie upside down?' the pasha replied testily. 'If [he] wrong you, I will pull his skin over his eares, and give you his head: is he not my slave?' All of which, though hardly a justification for the aga's 'bloudie Massacre' of the English sailors in Mocha, may at least provide some explanation for it.

I may have misjudged the concerns of the aga in Mocha. And I may have misunderstood the sentiments of those parents who refused to allow their children to be vaccinated against polio in Yemen. But without some effort to empathise and reflect upon the perspectives of others the world will remain a dangerous and incomprehensible place, and we will remain fearful of unwarranted hostilities toward English sailors and irrational resistance to vaccinations. I may also be mistaken in positioning in parallel the stories of global economic exploitation pursued by the East India Company and the global humanitarian endeavour undertaken by the Polio Eradication Initiative. But these stories are connected. It was, after all, overseas expansion of the sort administered by the East India Company that stimulated European interest in 'tropical medicine'. Initially, this interest was purely for the sake of protecting empires and European colonials. Only much later did efforts to improve 'global' or 'international' health purport to address the wellbeing of colonised and once-colonised peoples, for example, through the eradication of smallpox and, later, polio. A continuum of evolving medical science and institutions, directed by evolving economic and political concerns, connects seventeenth-century English overseas traders to my involvement in twenty-first-century polio eradication efforts. And it is the inheritance of power relations established in the colonial era that permits wealthy countries to determine the health priorities of poorer ones. If the health agenda and allocation of funds had been decided upon by people in those once-colonised countries where polio persists, or by those people in populations among whom outbreaks have occurred, they may have prioritised other diseases to address, or even other issues entirely, such as education, food, or water supplies. Which is not to contest the fact that polio eradication, if or when it happens, will be a good thing, but that it will have been achieved at great cost. And the achievement, I suspect, will be more celebrated in Geneva than in Sanaa. For now though, as I write, the global Polio Eradication Initiative continues to stare at the whites of the eyes of the thing.

When I arrived home shortly before dusk on Christmas Day, the neighbourhood kids had a new game. A cross in a circle had been chalked onto the front door of my house in Sanaa, indicating that a vaccination team had visited, but that nobody had been at home. Now the chalk mark had been reimagined, becoming a target for Yusuf and the boys who hurled darts made from chicken feathers and old syringes. I was tired, but I recall at that moment being overwhelmed by the thought of the four million children who would be vaccinated against polio during the three days of the campaign. And it was impossible not to be moved by the determined efforts of those thousands of vaccinators who would visit every home in the country during the polio immunisation days. Whatever doubts or scepticism I may have harboured, I have never witnessed a more powerful, nor more positive, human endeavour.

- 5 -

On the Origins
of Coffee

*- Representatives of the Dutch and English East India
Companies, 1616 & 1618 -*

BY NOW WE WOULD BOTH have needed a restorative libation, a mid-morning pick-me-up. And you would recall that I had offered you coffee, promising you the finest from Al-Kabous. You would have been sitting on the low mattress in the *mafraj*, that domestic space between city and sky. Cross-legged perhaps, your knees level with your hips, spine erect, calmly ergonomic. Or, if you were not used to sitting so close to the floor, you might have positioned yourself a little awkwardly, with both feet in front of you, arms folded around your knees, your back arched forward, rather strained. In which case I would have suggested the posture commonly adopted on this shallow seating: one knee up, the other curled under, with an elbow resting upon a cushion; a sort of semi-reclining sideways slouch, a lolling. It is a position of both physical ease and social utility, comfortable and convivial; for during large communal gatherings it would allow you either to recline, open to the discussion of the group, or lean in close toward your neighbour for some more intimate conversation. For now, though, it would be just you and I here in the *mafraj* on the third floor of our towerhouse in Sanaa. And before settling myself opposite you I would have pottered off to the kitchen at the back of the building.

While I am filling up the inherited Danish coffee pot and firing up the gas stove, you might have taken the opportunity to look around. The windows of the room were set low in the wall, offering perspectives intended to be viewed from where you would have sat, so that even without getting up you might have gazed out over rooftops, minarets and mountaintops, but mostly sky, an uninterrupted blue. It would have been bright outside, a hot sun-drenched glare, but inside it would be cool, and the sunlight would not yet have slipped in to join us. You would have been aware of the background thrum of traffic on the *Sayilah* and the air would have carried the faintest memory of incense. Before you, on a low wooden table, there would have lain a couple of A5 notepads, faint-lined, their edges a little battered, the tattered fringes of torn out pages still caged in their buckled spiral bindings. And if, without wishing to be nosy, you had flipped through one of these notebooks you would have found paragraphs of scribbly handwriting in blue and black ballpoint pen with pencilled annotations. The same handwriting, a little neater, a little smaller, would have filled another notebook, hard backed with heavier pages, dense dated entries in fine-tipped brown ink: my diary. A scattering of stationery upon the table: the brown fibre tip pen, some HB pencils and a sharpener. A candle or two, wax-welded to a couple of unmatched saucers. A mobile telephone with a black and white screen. A laptop computer that could be connected to the World Wide Web via an Ethernet cable if I took it to the internet café on the other side of town. All this would have been covered by a layer of dust. Not the powdery dust of ages. Not the floury dust of forsaken surfaces and furrows swiped by supercilious fingertips on shelves and mantelpieces. It was a dust like fine sand. A dust that gritted the teeth and matted the hair when the winter winds picked up. It was a dust that could blow in on an afternoon breeze, through an open window or a careless crack in the glazing. A dust that entered stealthily and swiftly deposited a tide of sediment over furniture and floors. This was a dust that did not so much conceal the presence of things as reveal their absences. An oblong where yesterday a book had been placed. A circle marking a coffee cup removed. A dust that did not seem to describe time, but loss.

Having set the coffee to boil I would have returned, to ask whether you would want milk, and to apologise for being able to offer only the evaporated variety from a can. Al-Momtaz ('The Excellent') evaporated milk was the only sort produced by Yemen's National Dairy and Food Company. Perhaps you might have preferred your coffee black? Still, there could be no more fitting beverage to accompany our reflections on early European visitors to Yemen. When Pedro Páez, the Portuguese Jesuit, was served 'cahua' during his journey to Sanaa in 1590 it was one of the first recorded European experiences of coffee. Not coffee as we know it; Páez described 'water boiled with the rind of a fruit that they call *bun*, which they drink very hot instead of wine.' This was *qishr*. It remained the more usual form in which coffee was prepared in Yemen: not with the roasted beans, but using the dried husks or 'rind'. Anywhere else the husks are a waste outcome of the coffee production process, but in Yemen they are brewed in the so-called Greek or Turkish style, with heaps of sugar and flavoured with cinnamon, cardamom, ginger. Not what you were expecting? Perhaps you might have preferred tea? But you need not have worried, for as well as selling coffee husks, Mr Al-Kabous was an unfailingly reliable purveyor of Yemeni beans and it was these that I would have purchased and used to prepare our coffee this morning. Yet it is the huge hessian sacks of husks that I recall from his stall in the *suq*, and Mr Al-Kabous' hand, sun-blotched and wrinkled like dried tobacco leaf, rising and falling; the same repetitive motion that you might use to stroke a much-loved cat; fingers curling about a handful of desiccated husks, lifting them then letting them drop, over and over, with the sound of waves receding over shingle.

Once upon a time, Yemen had been the world's exclusive source of coffee and Mocha, the Red Sea coastal town, had been its principal entrepôt. In June 1609, while the *Ascencion* lay at anchor in Mocha's harbour awaiting the return of John Jourdain from Sanaa, one of the ship's crew had recorded that the founder of Mocha was also 'the fyrst inventour for drynking of coffe'. There is still a consensus that the Arabs of Yemen were the first to adopt coffee drinking in the fifteenth century. Inland meanwhile, Jourdain had learnt that 'the seeds of this cohoo is a greate marchandize, for it is carried to Grand Cairo and all other places of Turkey, and to the Indias.' Just as he observed, by the early years of the seventeenth century Yemen's coffee, or 'cohoo', was being transported for sale across the Islamic world. 'And as it is reported,' Jourdain wrote somewhere in Yemen's highlands, 'this seede will grow at noe other place but neere this mountaine.' Not only the earliest brewers of coffee, Yemenis were its first cultivators, roasters, and distributers.

Yet although Yemen is where the coffee bean was reared, its origin was in Ethiopia. The coffee plant, *Coffea arabica*, is believed to have arisen in the Ethiopian highlands and various apocryphal accounts describe its properties being recognised after unusually vivacious goats were witnessed in the plant's vicinity, having eaten its berries. And while Yemenis were the first to habitualise coffee drinking, the Ethiopians ritualised it, and the coffee ceremony still holds an important place in Ethiopian culture. At an Ethiopian restaurant in Sanaa, I had once experienced the formal rite of coffee making and drinking. A slender woman in a white dress had slipped through a curtain of wooden beads, lit a charcoal brazier, and filled the room with swirls of fragrant smoke as she roasted a handful of coffee beans. It had been briefly intoxicating, before a stocky young man wearing jeans and a Manchester City football shirt swept through the bead curtain.

'Hey! You English?' he beamed at me. 'Which city you from my man?

Liverpool? Chelsea? Arsenal?'

My small Suffolk village must have been disappointing. 'Ipswich Town,' I tried.

'Near London?' he asked. 'London man?' We settled on London.

His accent was an enigma. It was effortless, though not quite fluent, English, intoned with a lilt that might have come from the West Indies, but a drawl that sounded as though it could be from the States.

'And where are *you* from?' I asked in my ignorance, keen to source his intriguing pronunciation.

'I'm from Ethiopia,' he exclaimed, as though it should have been obvious. 'It's an Ethiopian restaurant man!' He looked at me with a bemused expression. 'We're all from Ethiopia.' And really, I suppose it should have been obvious.

The woman lifted the pan from the coals and poured the still-smoking coffee beans into a stone mortar. Then she began to grind them, slowly and methodically.

'How long have you been in Yemen?' I asked the Ethiopian in the Man City shirt.

'Been here near two years now.'

'And before that?'

'Back home! In Ethiopia man! I came over with the contraband. Smuggled in on a boat like the whisky and gin. Whoooa that boat was terrible. Not so far to travel, but everyone is sea-sicking all over the place and I'm praying we don't get taken by pirates or sharks.' His voice rose and fell, racing then slowing to draw out a vowel. His name was Soloman and he needed little prompting to narrate the recent events of his life: the death of his parents, the rumour of a distant relative in Yemen, the journey from his village to the coast, a tough job in a port to earn the money for his passage, and a hope-filled but terrifying journey across the Red Sea.

'All the time in the boat I'm thinking of pirates and sharks, pirates and sharks. 'Cos that's all anyone says about the sea in Ethiopia.'

Behind him the woman had decanted the roasted coffee grounds into a clay flask, poured in some hot water, and planted the vessel carefully among the hot coals of the brazier.

'And true man, the day before I left, news comes back to port about a boat crossing the sea and the boat got attacked by pirates. They fed the men to the sharks and the women got all taken and done with. So when we're coming over - near fifty of us in this little boat - I'm all the time looking out for pirates. And they're hard to tell 'cos they're in little boats too. Just like the fishermen. And only if you look hard you can tell them far off. See if them's fishermen, there'll be fish and so there'll be birds following the boat. And if there ain't no birds, then there ain't no fish, and them ain't no fishermen and you'd do best to get away real quick. But they can move fast and when they move real fast that's when you know for sure they ain't fishermen. And by the time you see they ain't got no fishing gear, only guns, it's too late man. But we see no pirates. And no sharks. And I made it here, safe, to Yemen. Man that was almost two years ago.' Soloman ceased talking.

Silently, the woman stood, approached carrying the flask, and tipped the flagon to pour a long, slow, slender stream of black syrupy coffee that pooled and rose in a tiny cup, foaming and steaming.

'And did you find your long-lost relative?'

'No man. But someone else here from Ethiopia said he had a friend with a restaurant in Sanaa and he asked me if I was looking for work and I said I was and he said maybe he could get me a job and he did and that's how I ended up here.'

'So, where *did* you learn your English?' I asked, sipping the delicious oily brew.

'Ethiopia man! I picked it up on the coast, from the sailors and the American movies. You're the first real English-speaker I've met.'

My own preparation and serving of coffee would have been neither as elegant nor as enthralling. Still, by now, surely, our coffee would have been ready and I would have returned from the kitchen bearing two unmatched cups, accompanied by an unmistakable aroma and perhaps a packet of Abu Walad Sandwich Biscuits. The brew would have been thick and dark, with a slight foam crema and a rich bouquet. The flavour would have been earthy, heavy, raisiny. This was the 'something hot and black' tasted by Dutchman Pieter van den Broecke when he travelled to Sanaa in 1616, seven years after Jourdain, seeking permission to establish a Dutch trading presence on the coast. Two years later, the Englishman Joseph

Salbank undertook the same journey with the same request. And before long both the Dutch and English East India Companies were trading from their competing 'factories' in Mocha. Savouring the lingering chocolatey aftertaste, I would have joined you, soothed and settling myself agreeably on the low upholstery.

Once established in factories on Yemen's coast, European merchants were able to profit from the regional coffee trade that John Jourdain had reported. Soon it was English ships transporting beans from Mocha to Grand Cairo and supplying coffee to the Shahs of Persia and the Mughals of India. Still, for the time being coffee drinking remained an oriental custom and the coffee trade remained largely confined to Indian Ocean ports. The East India Company only began sending regular shipments of coffee beans back to England once a viable domestic market was established. The opening of the first coffee houses in Oxford and London during the 1650s initially relied upon coffee procured in the Levant that had been brought from Yemen overland. As the drink turned from exotic curiosity to commercial viability, and then into a profitable commodity, the East India Company began shipping coffee to England. Soon more coffee was being brought back to London than was being sold in the East. And from London, Mocha coffee was distributed to the rest of Europe so that by the end of the seventeenth century, the English East India Company had turned the import and export of Mocha coffee into a lucrative business. Yet neither the Company's market dominance nor Yemen's production monopoly was to last.

A decade after the English established their factory on the Red Sea coast, tribesmen from Yemen's highlands forced the Turks out of Sanaa. The Ottomans were soon ousted from Mocha too. Commerce was disrupted for a while, but then, for a brief moment in history, Yemenis were able to exert control over their coffee trade. Export of coffee seedlings was prohibited and coffee growers were rumoured to part-roast the beans in order to prevent their germination. Yemenis also deliberately propagated the myth, reported by John Jourdain, that coffee could grow only in their mountains. But despite these efforts to ensure exclusive control of the market, the cultivated plant was soon appropriated. Pieter van den Broecke has been rumoured to have made off with several coffee bushes during his visit to Yemen in 1618. It is said that he took the plants back to Amsterdam's Botanical Gardens where, apparently, they thrived and were later used to establish coffee in the Dutch dominions. Certainly it is true that shortly after European traders began visiting the market town of Beit el-Fakih ('Beetlefucky' as it was commonly rendered in English), close to Yemen's coffee hills, the coffee plant began appearing in European colonies. The Dutch planted in Java, the British in Jamaica, and the French carried the bean to other Caribbean territories. As slaves and plantations made the product cheaper elsewhere, Yemen's importance to the global supply of coffee gradually diminished. The port at Mocha silted up and the town that Sir Henry Middleton had once threatened to batter about the ears of its Turkish ruler slowly crumbled into the sands.

As for the fate of those early English visitors to Sanaa: his ear-battering threats behind him, Henry Middleton and the crew of the *Trades Increase* departed from Mocha and reached India in October 1611. They were surprised one morning off the coast near Surat to see someone signalling to them from the shore; a pale figure waving a turban from behind a sand dune. Middleton sent some men in a rowing boat to investigate. Then, darting from his hiding place, racing across the beach, there came a white man in Indian dress, running into the water, wading out toward the English sailors. He carried few possessions, perhaps only his journal. It was John Jourdain, last seen two years before, scrambling over the side of the sinking *Ascension* and rowing toward the Indian coast singing psalms to the praise of God. Jourdain and the rest of the ship's crew had survived their shipwreck on the nearby shoals and made it safe to shore. Most of the men had then sought to return from India to England overland and most were killed in Baghdad during the attempt, but Jourdain had put his faith in the Company and awaited an English ship. Fortuitously rescued, Jourdain sailed on with Sir Henry Middleton aboard the *Trades Increase* to the English trading post at Bantam, Java. There, while the ship was careened for repairs, she toppled onto her side, was battered by waves, burned by the Javanese, and became a wreck. Middleton more or less went down with his ship in an equally inglorious fashion, dying at Bantam, from illness or injury, in 1613. Jourdain returned from Java to England and his family in the summer of 1617, but he departed again before the year was out and not long after, during an altercation with Dutch ships off the east coast of Malaysia, he was shot and killed. Mr Pemberton's Boy, whose actual name seems to have been Richard Phillips, was not mentioned again in the journals of either Middleton or Jourdain, nor in any of the East India Company correspondence that I have found.

Tink, tink, tink. The ringing peels of metal upon metal. Tink, tink, tink. Louder, closer, the sound coming from outside. Tink, tink, tink. It would have been the gas seller at this hour of the morning, on his circuit of the Old City, pushing his wheelbarrow loaded with propane canisters, chiming out his passage with the incessant tapping of a spanner on an empty cylinder. Until a summons yelled from a window halted his passage. The sound would have returned us to the present, or to the near past of my time in Yemen. It was around that time, when coffee aficionados in Europe and America had begun obsessing over speciality single origin coffees, that rumours of coffee being sundried on rooftops in old stone villages and hulled in camel-driven mills began to stir a renewed interest in Yemen's coffee beans. But there were no boutique growers or distributers to capitalise on the potential, only Mr Al-Kabous and a few farmers west of Sanaa who struggled to maintain the quality of their crop and to ensure that there were no stones among their roasted beans. The prospective resurgence of Yemen's coffee trade has not yet occurred. Mocha, once synonymous with the very origin of coffee, is today only obscurely acknowledged in the English term for an espresso-based chocolate-and-hot-milk beverage, and in the name of the Bialetti Moka Express, the stove-top coffee-pot that I had inherited from the Danish residents of the apartment and that I had eventually learnt how to operate.

Such quiet coffee-drinking in Sanaa had become impossible by the time of my writing. In September 2014, troops from north Yemen's armed Houthi movement overthrew the national government and took control of the capital. Neighbouring Saudi Arabia led a coalition that responded in March 2015 with airstrikes intended to crush the Houthis. That much I knew from the limited news coverage of events. From friends in the country I learnt that the conflict swiftly disrupted supplies of food, fuel, water, and electricity. Petrol was blockaded or requisitioned for the Houthi army, and public transport costs soared exorbitantly. No fuel remained for water pumps and electricity generators, so drinking water was rationed and the city lived in darkness. As people swapped petrol generators for gas-powered ones, the price of gas cylinders doubled, then tripled, before their supply also failed. Coffee-drinking became an occasional indulgence.

At first, as the Saudi air strikes destroyed homes, hospitals, and schools, journalists in Yemen reported the mounting civilian death toll and the growing numbers of injured and internally displaced people. But journalism declined as press freedoms were curtailed then egregiously violated by the Houthi army on the ground. Individuals who did not display overt support for the Houthi war efforts began to be targeted. Foreign reporters were threatened and intimidated, prompting most to leave the country. Local journalists were killed or kidnapped. For well over a year the website of the *Yemen Times*, Yemen's English language newspaper, was not updated. The last headline, dated 12 June 2015, remained fixed, like an epitaph: 'At Least 6 killed in the Old City of Sana'a on Friday'. The story described a devastating airstrike and a denial from the Saudi coalition that they had anything to do with it. An accompanying photograph revealed the damage to a familiar row of towerhouses. The bomb had landed just a few hundred metres from the house where I once lived. I returned to the website periodically, hoping for some better news. But it was always the same headline, the same story, the same tumulus of rubble and dust marking the bombed-out rupture in an urban terrace. Until the story was taken offline.

By now my old friend Khaled had left Sanaa. The last I heard from him was in January 2015 when he wrote that he was planning on leaving Yemen and heading to Aruba. And I had wondered whether that was a mistake, whether he had some other place in mind. I looked up Aruba on the internet. A Dutch-administered island, just off the coast of Venezuela; it seemed an idyllic location, but an unlikely destination: I couldn't think how Khaled would get there, or what he would do when he arrived, unless he had connections in the Caribbean. But Khaled's family were from Eritrea. I recalled him telling me so years before as we had sat together drinking tea.

We were friends of a friend initially, until that mutual friend left Sanaa and Khaled and I continued to meet up. We were the same age and we were each attempting to learn one another's language. We struggled, but there was a shared sense of humour that surmounted any language barriers, and we were both pretty idle on the weekends. We would convene at Tahreer Square on occasional Friday afternoons, sitting in the ebbing sunlight, sipping sweet milky tea brewed in vast metal teapots above roaring gas flames in a side street behind the post office. The tea was served in the take-away cup of an emptied Al-Momtaz evaporated milk can.

Then late in 2015 Khaled uploaded a photograph of himself to Facebook. He stood amid trees and grass. It was a backdrop that looked like nowhere in Yemen. Comments in Arabic were either wishing him well, or wishing they were with him. Khaled had boarded a boat in Mocha, crossing the Red Sea and the Gulf of Aden, a two-day journey, risking pirates and sharks. In August 2015 he had reached Berbera, in Somalia. Then he too went offline.

- 6 -

Freedom of Expression

- Carsten Niebuhr, 1763 -

A FLY, TRAPPED, BUZZED AND beat itself against the inside of the dust-covered windscreen. A man lay dozing on the rear seat. The heat was stultifying. February's still, dry air and the sun directly overhead had made the midday torrid, and the stretched-out 1970s-era Peugeot 404 estate seemed to bask languidly in the car park. Next to it was a second, identical vehicle. Its open trunk yawned widely, creating a shady refuge for two figures sat hunched beneath the lid. They smoked lazy cigarettes, murmured in hushed discussion, and slowly stirred the torpid air with legs hung over the tailgate. A thin man in a tattered *futah* approached and slapped a damp rag onto the chassis, sliding it down the length of the automobile, wiping a silty line along white paintwork that dazzled hotly beneath its layer of grime. The itinerant valet then mopped his brow. And apparently re-evaluating his task, he plopped the cloth back into his rusty bucket and wandered away. Nearby, the drivers of the two vehicles argued about which of them would take me to Manakha.

'Mine is half the price.'

'Ya, but mine is almost full.'

'But I'm going straight there!'

'Ya, but I'm going to leave sooner. Look, my car is almost full!'

The ubiquitous white Peugeot 404 estates provided transport beyond the city on much the same basis as minibuses within Sanaa, waiting at well-established departure points for a full load of passengers. The French vehicle manufacturer had become so synonymous with long distance travel in Yemen that to journey 'by Peugeot' meant taking any shared intercity transport, even if, as in a few rare instances, the car undertaking the road trip was actually a Toyota. Seven hundred riyals was the price of a seat in the car heading to Manakha. But the second driver had intervened, offering to sell me a seat in his vehicle. He was going to the coastal city of Hodeidah, but would drop me mid-way, at the turn-off from the main highway, from where I could find transport for the short onward journey to Manakha. This second option would cost more, but I might depart sooner if the Hodeidah-bound car filled up first.

'Look, if he goes with you he'll still have to wait again to get from Al-Maghrabah to Manakha.'

'It'll be better than waiting here all afternoon with you.'

'But I will charge him half as much, I tell you!'

Devoid of any spirit to engage in squabbling and having both time and money enough for either outcome, I had retreated beneath the spattered shadow of a fig tree and waited for events to unfold. The sun crawled a little further toward the west. A scrawny dog came, sniffing at the hot earth, and then left. The trunk of the Manakha vehicle opened and closed as a youth wearing a shiny black tracksuit slung a holdall into the back, before clambering onto the rear seat next to the sleeping man. Occupants now numbered six. Ten was a full load. In the Hodeidah-bound Peugeot, seven paid-up passengers had been joined by an eighth who strapped a suitcase to the roof and claimed a seat. After this activity, a stifled atmosphere of unvented vexation gradually reasserted itself. The two drivers scowled, tapped things impatiently, and the afternoon looked set to curdle. The dog returned periodically, aimlessly parading the welts upon its flank, unthreatened by my sluggish shooing. Time felt as though it had slowed, as if it were melting, or just weary.

But time, of course, was constant. Even on the most swelteringly listless days it progressed with unerring reliability. And for that reason Carsten Niebuhr had begun by counting his footsteps.

'When it was hot I walked 1,580 double paces,' Niebuhr observed after tallying his steps for half an hour. 'And when it was cool, 1,620 double paces.'

By timing the duration of each stage of his journey through Yemen, and factoring in the effects of ambient temperature, Niebuhr could now calculate the distances that he covered. Coupling this technique with regular magnetic compass bearings, he was able to plot his progress across the landscape with reasonable accuracy. Variations on this method used the strides of horses, mules, donkeys, or dromedaries, all of which, Niebuhr noted, had a less temperature-dependent gait than himself.

Carsten Niebuhr was the map-maker for the Royal Danish Expedition to Arabia Felix. Departing from Copenhagen in January 1761, the Expedition had set out to achieve nothing less than the scientific illumination of the Old Testament through the application of modern instruments and methods. Arabia Felix, being relatively untouched by Europe and, it was assumed, relatively unchanged since the time of Moses, was thought to offer the ideal laboratory for research that would elucidate the Holy Scripture. The lives and language, clothing and customs of the

Arab people would be examined to reveal unimagined contextual truths. Flora and fauna referred to in the canons, but unknown in Europe, would be catalogued. Study of the Red Sea tides would explain the miracle of the Israelites' flight from Egypt. And, thanks to Niebuhr, biblical locations would at last be accurately charted upon European maps. It was to be an epoch-making venture. Scholars from across Europe submitted questions for the expedition team that ranged from the prescient (are the Arabian deserts the beginning of a drying-out process that will affect the whole earth?) to the profane (does a circumcised man experience more pleasure during sexual intercourse?).

Six expedition members were judiciously recruited to capitalise on their various areas of expertise. Friedrich Christian von Haven, the eminent Danish philologist, was to study and record contemporary Arab customs and colloquialisms. Peter Forsskål, the esteemed Swedish botanist and student of Carl Linnaeus, was to collect and describe botanical and zoological specimens. Other members of the team included the German artist and engineer Georg Wilhelm Baurenfeind, Danish physician Christian Carl Kramer, and Swedish ex-soldier Lars Berggren who would act as porter. Finally, there was Carsten Niebuhr, the mathematician and cartographer. While Forsskål and von Haven competed for the position of seniority and predominant authority within the expedition, twenty-seven-year-old Niebuhr charted a more humble path. Youngest of the group, the son of peasant farmers from the flat marshlands of Friesland, he had received almost no formal education until his early twenties. Yet it was he who would secure the expedition's outcomes and conscientiously narrate the journey through his diary. And at each day's end, after his double paces had ceased and the heat had dissipated, but before settling himself to document the day's events, Niebuhr would unpack his saddlebag and carefully unwrap his astrolabe, quadrant, and telescope. Then, lifting his attention from his footsteps to the stars, with practiced astronomical observations and the new Lunar Distance Method for determining longitude, he confirmed the coordinates of where on earth the Royal Danish Expedition had come to.

'Khalas!' Enough! The Manakha driver had hurried to pull me to my feet.

It was settled: I would ride with him. A gentleman had arrived along with his portly wife, their infant, and two older children, all of them wishing to travel to Manakha. The passenger quorum had been achieved. I was pushed headfirst into a cramped position next to the youth in the tracksuit. The family of five piled in beside two men on the seat in front of me, which shoved back sharply into my shins. I winced, and my head banged against the roof. 'Yalla!' The trunk was secured, the doors had slammed, the driver climbed in alongside two other front seat passengers, and the engine fired. We set off. I counted thirteen of us. Romping onto Zubeiry Street, our overloaded charabanc was soon embraced by the familiar guff of engine noise and exhaust fumes. In front of me a bundle of headscarf bounded by the backs of two huge hairy ears had rotated to reveal an old man's wrinkled face. He observed me steadily with eyes that welled up like springs. I offered a self-conscious greeting. Rivulets formed as the old man's face crumpled into a smile.

'*Hollandi*? *Franci*?' he enquired.

'*Engilterra*', I replied.

'Engiiilteraaaa...' He muttered, stretching his vowels and rotating his head back round.

'Married?' asked the husband, lingering a little longer in his attention before my negative response returned him to the task of placating his children.

'Not married...' Mumbled the headscarf and the hairy ears. The shiny youth beside me positioned a pair of earphones on his head, clicked on a portable cassette player, and closed his eyes.

It was not by chance that I was leaving Sanaa on the second weekend of February, 2006. In what had become known as the Danish Cartoon Crisis, twelve images of the Prophet Mohammed had been published in a Danish newspaper, causing offence to huge numbers of people across the globe. There were public protests in Turkey, Pakistan, Iran, and Iraq. When thousands of Muslims took to the streets in Kuala Lumpur, the Malaysian Prime Minister stated that a huge chasm had opened between the West and Islam. As more European newspapers re-printed the Danish cartoons, more protests occurred and more violence ensued, with hundreds of demonstrators teargassed, wounded, or killed. Tempers were no less inflamed in Yemen. Boycotts of Danish consumer goods had been organised across the Muslim world and posters appeared in Sanaa extorting people not to purchase Bang & Olufsen stereo systems, Ecco shoes, Grundfos water pumps, Jarlsburg cheese, Lego bricks, Lindberg spectacles, Lurpak butter, and Hempel antifouling marine paints. If any of these products had been available in the country, they would have been utterly unaffordable to the average Yemeni. But the positioning of the posters themselves - on buses, shopfronts, cars, and street corners - became an expression of defiance.

Likewise, drinking tea without milk became a symbolic gesture: shunning dairy products that might have had European origins. Still, most of the people I had spoken to in Yemen thought the cartoons offensive, but not worthy of being too much offended by, and certainly not warranting violence. But when I repeated this sentiment to a Moroccan acquaintance in Sanaa, he had angrily accused me of arrogance and I was forced to confront the meaning of the cartoons for someone who saw his religion being persecuted. Oppression in Palestine, atrocities of the War on Terror, humiliation in Guantanamo and Abu Ghraib, all these were cited. 'And now you draw pictures of the Prophet as a terrorist?' His enraged rhetoric drew on a familiar logic. It was the same reasoning that had conflated Sadam Hussein with Osama bin Laden and constructed the Axis of Evil. It was the lamentable opposition of 'us' and 'them'; the corollary of being 'with us or with the terrorists'.

Early in February, it had become known that mass demonstrations against the West were planned for the forthcoming weekend in Sanaa. Security announcements advised foreigners to stay in their homes. My habitual weekend wanderings through the city would be curtailed, but I had no intention of confining myself to my apartment. Instead, I had decided to head to the Haraz Mountains, a two-hour journey from Sanaa. So I was squashed in the rear seat of a Peugeot 404, next to the youth with the shiny tracksuit, behind the man with the watery eyes, stuck in a traffic jam on Zubeiry Street when, above the horns and the engine noise, I heard shouting. And above the vehicle roofs I saw placards and banners moving slowly towards me.

For weeks an uneasy apprehension had intensified among Sanaa's non-Muslims. Foreigners, for the first time, had begun to take an interest in the imams' Friday speeches. Had the Danish cartoons been mentioned? Had

Western nations been condemned? Had there been calls for any actions targeted at foreigners? The answers, invariably, were no. But with exemplary cooperation, the Danish consul and the Yemeni police coordinated a cautious evacuation operation, gathering Sanaa's small community of Danish expatriates at the Sheraton hotel, then escorting them under armed protection to the airport where a plane was waiting to fly them back to Copenhagen. Many other foreigners decided, or were instructed, to leave the country, including the staff of the British Embassy. But I had opted to remain, and now I was trapped in a stationary Peugeot, watching the crowd pushing closer through the gridlocked traffic. Fists punched the air and pounded on car bonnets. A Danish flag burned. 'No God but Allah!' The shouting grew louder. 'Danish Devils!' The slogans were familiar from international news reports. Then the crowd was upon us, hands raining down upon the vehicle, thundering. And I wondered what symbolic significance I might hold for the mob, and whether this was how it ended, in the wrong place at the wrong time. Heads turned toward me, with watery eyes and headphones. I was aware of people peering in from outside as they marched past. The face of a young man pressed up against the rear window, stared at me, then smiled. The demonstrators moved on, the crowd thinned, and the traffic began shunting slowly forward.

The relief that I felt at passing unscathed through the protest might have been shared by my companions. Or they might simply have been happy at not having had their travel plans too much disrupted by events. Either way, the car was filled with ebullient chatter as we crossed the city bypass and started switchbacking up the Hodeidah Road toward the mountains. At the perimeter checkpoint a soldier poked his head through the open rear window and pointed at me.

'Where's he from?'

'Engilterra.' Announced the old man with the watery eyes, before I could think of claiming Russian citizenship. 'He's not married.'

The soldier waved us on. Slouched low in my seat, I was not spotted at a second military checkpoint and my fellow travellers flicked conspiratorial glances in my direction as we motored on unhindered, my nationality and marriage status deftly smuggled past the unwitting authorities. Continuing, climbing, between low scree slopes and distant rock faces, we passed through villages glimpsed in fleeting snatches of concrete homes, plastic bags, and rusting broken-down vehicles. Journeys along this route were often hair-raising rides of hairsbreadth overtaking on hairpin bends. Six weeks earlier I had travelled to Manakha on the first day of *Eid al-Adha*, the Festival of Sacrifice, and seen instalments of ritual slaughter being enacted in every village we passed through. Cows were being dragged in bellowing panic, carcasses cleaved into pieces, sides of flesh carried over shoulders, and a carnage of discarded bones and hooves littered the road in bloody puddles. All of which provided scenic distraction from the stomach-churning driving of the Peugeot racers. Behind the wheels of their 404 estates, these intercity drivers seemed invariably intent on chasing near misses with a blare of horns and a blaze of glory.

Suddenly, the husband of the corpulent woman convulsed, his son leapt from his lap, the daughter shrieked, and the driver delved into the glove compartment and tossed a polythene bag over his shoulder. But it was too late. The old man cast a teary eye over the yellowy stains of baby sick that now covered his *thobe* while the infant coughed and spluttered unapologetically. All the car doors opened simultaneously when we stopped at the next settlement and everyone, except the woman and her three children, jumped out. Her husband went in search of tissues with which to wipe the drying scraps of vomit from his sleeve, the driver with his two front seat passengers wandered off to buy *qat*, and the old man with the sick-stained *thobe* hobbled discreetly behind a wall for a moment. I was happy to stand and extend my limbs. 'Ya! Whoa!' The cry from behind me came as a surprise. I had not been aware of the young man squashed into the trunk of our vehicle, but now he too shouted out an order for *qat*.

When we set off again I counted fourteen of us. With my head pressed into the vehicle's roof and only a small triangle of glass through which to view the world, mine was an awkward vantage point. But while the mountains had been obscured as they rose up before us, now that we began to descend I was able to look down into a valley of terraced *qat* plantations dotted with concrete watchtowers. In the distance, a concertinaed succession of jagged ridges fell away into unfathomed crevasses, before the precipitous drop down to the coastal plains.

'Suq al-Hami. Tell him, "Suq al-Hami".' The old man directed the husband.

'Suq al-Hami,' the man in front said, turning toward me.

Following his comfort stop in the last village, the old man had watched me scrawl a few lines in a notebook. Having deduced, quite correctly, that I was documenting our journey, he thereafter announced the name of each village as we passed through it. The effect was surreal and salutary. Surreal because my journey narrative was now being narrated in real time by one of its protagonists. Salutary because as we had watched each other, the old man's idea of me as an interested foreign traveller and his consequent assistance was both more astute and more generous than my trivial caricature of him as an aged fellow with leaky eyes and a weak bladder.

'Mofhak,' the old man announced. We stopped in Mofhak. One of the *qat* chewers from the front seat got out to approach a concrete home, knocked loudly upon its metal door, yelled at the windows, and then slumped back into the car. A burly figure appeared from the back of the house with a hessian sack thrown over his shoulder. He seemed to struggle beneath the weight of his burden, groaned, and hollered at the driver for assistance. Then the bag began thrashing and with a gasp he dropped it to the ground. The head of a live goat burst from the sack's drawstring neck. 'Allah!' cried the driver. The goat mewed loudly. Neither the driver nor the goat appeared happy with the proposed transportation arrangements and a vociferous argument about appropriate payment occurred before the two men attached the goat in the sack to the roof rack.

Off again. I now counted fifteen of us. The bagged animal banged intermittently upon the roof and goat piss dribbled in wind-blasted streaks across the triangle of glass beside me.

'Beni Mansor.' The backdrop to the old man's commentary had changed. We no longer shuttled around steep mountain slopes, but roller-coastered along a gorge of layered black rock mottled with patches of yellowish grass, short spiky trees, and cacti.

'Beni Mhura.'

The stout woman pushed a plastic bag behind her veil, coughed, shuddered, and transferred the contents of her stomach into the bag then hurled it from the open window, all without waking the infant that slept on her lap.

'What does "Beni" mean?' I asked her husband.

'Land of. Or Sons of,' he explained. People and place. Leaving behind the ancestry and territory of Mhura, hurtling around a rock outcrop and narrowly avoiding a collision with an oncoming car, we swerved off the tarmac for a moment in a noisy cloud of dust. The woman reached for another plastic bag, the infant screamed, the youth in the tracksuit woke, and the old man issued an invocation to Allah as the goat exploded in a wild flailing panic, sprinkling piss though the open window into my face.

'Manakha.' We had arrived at our destination.

Two years and three thousand miles from their embarkation in Copenhagen, having travelled via Constantinople and Cairo, the six men of the Royal Danish Expedition arrived upon the Yemeni coast. In February 1763, they decided to base themselves for a few months in the waning coffee town of Beit el-Fakih. From here, Carsten Niebuhr, the German cartographer, and Peter Forsskål, the Swedish naturalist, conducted radial sorties. Together they mapped and botanised, gathering the Arabic names of places and plants, unconcerned that their respective interests in astronomy and flora gained them a local reputation as alchemists or magicians. Niebuhr noted happily that in Yemen's mountains they felt as safe as 'even in the best regulated states of Europe'. And they were not 'subjected to any of those difficulties which, even in Europe, are generally troublesome to travellers'. But this easy tranquillity would not last.

Returning to Beit el-Fakih at the beginning of April 1763 and re-joining the expedition team, Niebuhr found the Danish philologist von Haven wracked by 'a violent fever'. Niebuhr himself soon suffered similarly and attributed their symptoms variously to food (he thought they ate too much meat), weather (they spent too long in the cool night air), and the inherent difficulty of being a European in Arabia (their constitution being not 'in accordance with the land'). The physician Kramer was in no position to correct him, for medical science had not yet discovered the cause of malaria. Von Haven's fever worsened. He became delirious and died in Mocha the following month. None of the Expedition team seemed much upset by his demise: he had been a conceited and petulant colleague. But his death confirmed the perils of their situation. Before long all five of the remaining expedition members had fallen sick. They headed inland, considering the 'refreshing rains' of the highlands 'to agree with our constitutions' more than the 'oppressive heats' of the coast. Still,

Niebuhr ached and vomited. Forsskål the botanist could not continue and soon was buried by his comrades. Berggren, the hardy trooper, became too ill to travel, but proved too ill to remain, for after it was agreed that his comrades would continue without him, he caught them up a few days later, complaining that in their absence he had been refused lodgings, his condition apparently being so grim that landlords feared they would have to bear the cost of his funeral. Meanwhile, Niebuhr had pressed on to Sanaa, the Expedition's intended destination.

Cautiously we unfolded ourselves into the damp chill of evening. I pushed the rear seat forward, extricated myself from the vehicle, and stretched. The boy from the trunk helped me with my backpack while our driver manhandled the goat from the roof and our travelling companions dispersed into the darkening town of Manakha. The sun had long since fallen behind some towering peak, violet clouds bruised the sky, and dusk bore the scent of fresh rain. After the noise, motion, and containment of the car journey, the quietude was disconcerting, the loss of companionship a little disheartening. I followed a muddy track out of town, toward al-Hajarah, where I would spend the night. A cluster of tungsten constellations flickered far off, then disappeared abruptly as electricity failed that distant village. The starless night closed in, dense and disorientating. An unamplified prayer call, echoing and faint, only emphasised the immensity of the void. But I knew the road and knew the *funduk* in al-Hajarah where I could get a meal and a bed: certainties sufficient for me to slowly embrace the stillness, the silence, and solitude.

Suddenly the sky flared in front of me. A sweeping beacon became a halo of glowing cumulus. Then the aurora descended to earth, slapping molten upon the wet road as the glaring headlamp hurtled over a rise in the track and sped toward me, briefly becoming a clamorous Toyota with a single functioning front light. Noiseless black swiftly engulfed the vehicle's slipstream. Stray dogs at the roadside ignored my passing. Two figures in white *thobes* drifted by without word. A cricket trilled then fell silent and the waxing moon slipped glancing between vagrant clouds. A puttering growl reverberated and, turning, I discerned a motorcycle pushing its beam up the mountain road like a solid slab of luminescence, before sound and light both vanished behind an outcrop. Moments later my shadow was projected monstrously onto the cloud ahead as the motorbike grumbled up behind me and halted.

'Al-Hajarah?' asked the rider.

Of course. The road led nowhere else.

I mounted the rear of his idling machine and we veered away, carelessly spilling light across the unilluminated landscape. Our journey lasted only a minute or two, for with power cuts and cloud cover depriving me of waymarkers I had unknowingly walked most of the distance to the village.

In a fountain-splashed stateroom richly furnished with Persian rugs and fine silks, Imam al-Mahdi Abbas sat cross-legged, resplendent in a white turban and green robe with gold filigree. The reception of the Danish Expedition in Sanaa's palace was elaborately prepared for and enthusiastically attended by the imam's retinue. Not since the early encounters between trading companies and occupying Turks had European interest in Yemen extended much beyond the coastal ports and the pursuit of profit. The Turks had been expelled from Yemen a century before and so it was a Yemeni imam who welcomed Niebuhr and his colleagues to Sanaa and requested that they display to the assembled audience their intriguing array of magnifying glasses, microscopes, and thermometers.

The imam had already put a house at their disposal and sent them gifts of sheep and sweatmeats; now he offered the Danish Expedition leave to remain in the city for a year. But Niebuhr was not even well enough to stay through this initial meeting: he had to excuse himself, overcome by waves of nausea. Twelve months' rest in Sanaa might have benefited their health. And they might have found much in the city and its environs to fulfil the Expedition's scientific purpose. But the recent deaths of Forsskål and von Haven, and the sickness of the survivors, had bled the Expedition of its impetus. Niebuhr calculated an accurate latitude for the city, paced the walls, and produced a map of Sanaa, but it was a modest and distracted output. News that the last English trading ship of the season would shortly be departing Mocha for Bombay prompted the men to hurry back toward the coast after only ten days in Sanaa.

'Along a bad road among bare hills', on 26 July 1763, the four fever-wracked survivors of the Royal Danish Expedition to Arabia Felix departed from Sanaa, the apotheosis of their journey now behind them. In his excursions with Forsskål four months earlier, Niebuhr had found an 'agreeable aspect' in Yemen's hills, but now they were only 'bleak and wild'. The valleys once 'beautiful and rich' had become home to 'a few wretched hamlets'. The reservoirs 'of excellent fresh-water' had turned 'putrid' and unhealthy. The 'legions of locusts' that attacked the men were driven away only by 'a violent storm'. Their trials seemed unrelenting. 'Next day the road was still worse... the most rugged road I saw in all Yemen,' Niebuhr recorded. And yet, 'our next day's journey was upon a still more disagreeable road. Nothing can be worse,' he thought, 'than the roads between Mofhak and Sehan.' But things did get worse. A narrow path skirting a sheer cliff face 'had broken a gap eight feet deep'. Niebuhr judged it 'absolutely impassable'. Seeing the gaping cleft in the path, the party's Yemeni guides 'were of the opinion that we should return straight to Sanaa'. But for the Europeans, febrile and aching, there would be no going back. Theirs was a race against time. In desperate haste to reach the coast and the ship that might rescue them, they 'resolved to fill up the gap with stones' and set about repairing the narrow causeway. By evening they were able to cross safely.

Dimpled by cloudburst and indented by sheep hooves, the sandy path traced steeply upward, gaining height swiftly away from the *funduk* where I had spent the night. Curving away either side of me, agricultural terraces extended in sweeping meanders in and out of gullies and around outcrops, towards distant profiles that climbed stepwise up and down the precipitous terrain. From below, the shadowed stone walls of the terraces looked like ladders as they scaled the mountainside; from above they looked like contour lines, as though the morning light had sought to survey the landscape, then thought better of it as wave upon wave of terraced plots fell away, folding over one another, tumbling into deep crevasses and twilight shadows, places where the sun never entered and sound never left. Far below, perhaps a couple of kilometres down, was the Wadi Sehan. And down there somewhere, among the cacti and acacia, between the crags and boulders, carving around rock faces and dropping over escarpments, would be the trail taken by Niebuhr,

Kramer, Baurenfeind, and Berggren as they had scrambled from Sanaa to the coast. Somewhere down there too, perhaps, their unceremonious memorial remained in the repair work to that broken path.

As I walked, following one of those contours, shadows began to overtake me, slipping all too easily over the corrugations of topography. The weather was drawing in, dark palls descending to touch distant peaks, nearby ridges becoming rugged grey opacities. These were Niebuhr's 'bleak and wild' hills, made intimidating and forbidding by fevers and the fear of death. Even without those perils, still the landscape was imposing. The villages that scaled seemingly inaccessible slopes and the houses perched valorously upon cloud-swept mountaintops were an audacious riposte to the geography.

Wheat sheaves, tight-bound, lay with their heads flopped over the edge of a terraced plot. As I rounded a corner the crop was swaying and falling before an old farmer's swinging scythe. Behind him was a swath of stubble and three girls who dropped the sheaves that they were bundling and fled at the sight of me. The ageing farmer waved away my apologies. 'They run from work at every opportunity,' he said, smiling thick furrows into a kindly face. The girls disappeared into a stone house nearby. Its façade had been recently re-painted with white chevrons and zigzags and in front three hammocks had been hung between apricot trees. The rustle of leaves in a grove of eucalypts caused us both to glance up towards the branches and to the glowering sky. Aloud I wondered whether it would rain. '*Inshallah*,' the man replied, then stooped with surprising suppleness to pick an ear of wheat from the soil. He rolled the wheat spike between his praying fingers, blew the chaff from his cupped hands, then lay them open, presenting a few kernels on palms cracked and calloused with labour. If God willed it, and if his three filial helpers returned, he would have time to reap his ripened crop before the rain set in. A stentorian rumble overhead summoned us back to our respective tasks. The farmer, readjusting his grip on the scythe, asked where I was going.

'To Kahil.' It was a three- or four-hour walk. I had planned a longer hike, but the *funduq* owner in al-Hajarah had curbed my ambitions with dire forecasts of torrential afternoon downpours. Touchingly too, he had biro-ed a sketch map of a route round to Kahil, from where I could drop back down to Manakha and then get a Peugeot ride back to

Sanaa. But the simplified representation in blue ink bore little relation to the unfolding scenery. Niebuhr would have been unimpressed. Latterly a German publisher was rumoured to be producing a trekking guide to these mountains, but I never came across a copy.

'Is this the way to Kahil?' I asked.

'It's one way to Kahil,' the old farmer replied, laughing, and pointed me onward.

Crouched in a rock cleft and shadowed by overhanging cliffs, the village of al-Ayn had a grey forlorn aspect. Terraces abandoned to whatever vagrant seeds blew in had sprouted weedy straggles while mosses scuffed their dilapidated stone walls. Eucalypts encroaching and shedding ragged shreds of bark exaggerated an appearance of neglect. Yet the satellite dishes that scanned the churning sky and a moraine of plastic waste falling away from the hamlet confirmed its continuing population. Behind a parapet of rusting tin cans that contained a rooftop potager of mint and parsley, a woman paused while drawing in her laundry to observe my approach. Seeing the barometer of her clothesline and reckoning moisture in the air, I waved, but passed quickly, pulling my collar up against the misty breeze that wisped across the path.

A straw hat's wide brim hid the face of a young girl who skittered by without raising her head, herding her flock of sheep back toward the village. The mist thickened as it swept in, concealing the gloomy roil of higher cloud and reducing visibility to no more than a few feet. Dark spots began dotting rocks and an irregular, hastening rhythm tapped upon my backpack. Then came a rupturing blast of thunder and the sky emptied. Rain streamed down my spectacle lenses and hissed into a plot of shrivelled maize stalks. I stopped beneath the dripping branches of a solitary tree and waited, soaked trousers clinging miserably to my thighs. The deluge ceased only a little less suddenly than it had begun, the sky brightened, and the cloud lifted to reveal a line of electricity pylons and a scampering flock of fugitive sheep that led the way onward from here.

Kahil balanced on a wedge. Geologic accident and almost Pythagorean geometry had created the triangular rock pedestal on which the village perched. Towerhouses scaled the vertiginous slope with ever-increasing temerity, climbing toward the apex and a sheer cliff face at the edge of which stood a house so boldly located as to demonstrate its bravado to the far horizon. When a stray shaft of sunlight illuminated the village, storm-washed and cross-hatched by a still slanting drizzle, the scene was of quite breath-taking improbability. A donkey raced past, clattering and slipping over stone and mud, chased by another girl with a soaked straw bonnet clutched to her brow. Slower, I had followed the runaway and its pursuant up the incline, into the village. Here the improbability lost its picturesque charm. For every house in Kahil whose walls had been lately repainted there stood another not repaired for a generation, its stonework collapsing, alabaster smashed, and wooden window shutters hanging half-off rusted hinges. From the lofty escarpment, the view under lifting cloud and breaking sunshine reflected the same story: for every inhabited village and cultivated terrace was another emptied and forsaken. Tethered tenuously by the overhanging electricity cables, the rural hamlets still required drinking water to be drawn up by hand and the propane canisters used for cooking were carried much further than the three flights of stairs up to my apartment in Sanaa. The sky had brightened, but the hardship remained apparent. A dying wind whipped away the last black clouds and dried the stones of the old staircase that carried me down from Kahil to the taxi stand at Manakha.

The journey was over for the members of the Royal Danish Expedition. Having raced from Sanaa to the coast, the four men arrived back in Mocha, feverish and exhausted. They were bed-ridden, back in the house where von Haven had died barely three months before. Boarding the English merchant ship that they hoped would assure their salvation, Carsten Niebuhr was the only one of them still able to walk. The others needed to be carried aboard. The vessel sailed from Yemen on 23 August 1763. The artist Georg Baurenfeind deteriorated and died six days later. Lars Berggren was dead the next day and both bodies were buried at sea. Carl Kramer, the physician, endured his passage to India, but died on reaching Bombay. Niebuhr would be the Expedition's sole survivor and he was to be responsible for ensuring its outcomes.

With its empirical and reductionist approach to religious orthodoxy, at its outset the Danish Expedition had represented a quintessential Enlightenment project. But Carsten Niebhur resisted the trends and tropes of Enlightenment-era travel writing. While Benjamin Franklin's Native Americans and Captain Cook's Pacific Islanders would uphold the utopian ideal of an alternative society, demonstrating mankind's innate goodness and the decay that had set into European civilisation, Niebuhr's experiences of the Arabs and Muslim lands were more balanced. 'I found the Arabs to be just as humane as other cultured people,' he wrote with equanimity, 'and I experienced pleasant and unpleasant days in the countries I visited.' Niebuhr's voice intones respect, not romanticism. He was open-minded by habit. With unfamiliar foods, for example, 'to Europeans, it is just as inconceivable that Arabs eat locusts with pleasure, as it is unbelievable to Arabs, who have never had contacts with Christians, that Christians consider eating oysters, crabs, shrimp and the like to be an enjoyable meal. In this way the one is as valid as the other.' Neither better nor worse, but both equally valid. Similarly while in Sanaa, invited to kiss the imam's palm, Niebuhr had knelt, reached out, touched the potentate's hand, and was startled by the shattered silence as a herald cried, 'Allah preserve the Imam', a shout loudly repeated by all the courtiers present. But then, 'it occurred to me that what was happening at this ceremony was rather like what happens at home when we call for three cheers.' Again, both were equally valid. As for the hardships endured in Arabia Felix, he reflected with admirable magnanimity that 'one doesn't always travel with pleasure in Europe either.'

Though he appeared receptive and unassuming at the outset of the journey, Niebuhr's capacity to move beyond superficial differences and embrace fundamental commonalities seems to have been a product of the expedition. Arriving in Constantinople in 1761 he had found the Turks daunting, perceiving 'their language, their dress, and their entire demeanour so strange that I did not hold out any great hope of finding much further pleasure in these Eastern Lands.' Yet by the time he returned to that city in 1767, having journeyed from Sanaa by way of Bombay, Muscat, Shiraz, Persepolis, Babylon, Baghdad, and Palestine, Niebuhr had acquired a fluency in local dialects, adopted Arab dress, grown a beard, and come to live in every way according to the routines and customs of the region, even taking on the name 'Abdullah'. The Danish Expedition, transformative for Niebuhr, was also transformed by him. What began as a Eurocentric scientific exploration of Arabia for the purpose of better understanding Western Christian tradition, became something closer to an ethnographic appreciation of the region and its people in their own right.

Niebuhr's respectful approach toward Arabs and Arabia, and to other people and cultures more generally, holds a remarkable relevance for our own times. Arguably too, the contemporary pertinence of his colleague Peter Forsskål may be less obvious, but at least equally important. The year before the Arabia Felix expedition, Forsskål had published a pamphlet entitled *Thoughts on Civil Liberty*. The text included a radical demand for the freedom of the printing press. It was precisely arguments about press freedoms and freedom of expression that had been used to justify publication of the Danish cartoons of the Prophet Mohammed. In the minds of proponents, these freedoms were supposedly being threatened by Islam and supposedly defended by the Danish newspaper. The protests and violence that followed apparently only confirmed the danger of being intimidated into silence or self-censorship. At the time I had been deeply suspicious of the anti-Islamic content of the cartoons, as well as their destructive consequences, but the rhetoric about freedom of expression being both a human right and an essential feature of democracy appeared persuasive. It was only when considering a contemporaneous but seemingly unconnected news story that the duplicity of claims about freedoms had become apparent to me. In February, 2006, just days before the protests in Sanaa and my departure to Manakha, the Islamic preacher Abu Hamza had been on trial at the Old Bailey in London. Hamza, known for having only one eye and two hooks for hands, as well as for his incitement to violence, was accused, among other things, of 'using threatening, abusive or insulting words or behaviour with intent to stir up racial hatred'. Quite rightly, Hamza was found guilty of this and other crimes and sentenced to seven years in prison. The point that his conviction demonstrated was that freedom of expression did not bestow freedom to insult or cause hatred. Not, at least, without retribution. And yet that point appeared to me to apply to the Danish cartoons as much as to Hamza. Retribution, or even an acknowledgement of wrong-doing, had in fact been exactly what the protesters in Sanaa and elsewhere in the Islamic world had been calling for. And this is exactly what Peter Forsskål had argued in his pamphlet of 1759. He had stated explicitly that freedom of expression should not be exploited to cause harm to others, and that any such harms should be punished.

In the wake of the Danish cartoon crisis, the Expedition to Arabia Felix was revisited. Following the cartoon controversy, Denmark was keen to rehabilitate itself in the Islamic world and the 250th anniversary of the Expedition's commencement appeared to offer an opportunity. The members of the Danish Expedition could deliver a conciliatory message of respect and commonality. In addition to Carsten Niebuhr-themed exhibitions at Copenhagen's National Library and National Museum, the Danish Ministry of Foreign Affairs began planning a calendar of educational activities and cultural events that would take place during 2011 in Ankara, Cairo, Damascus, Beirut, Tehran, and Yemen. But contemporary events would prove more powerful than historical ones. In 2011, the planned new Danish Exhibition to Arabia was prevented by the upheaval of the Arab Spring.

- 7 -

Intolerance

- Nineteenth-Century British Soldiers & Physicians -

DOCTOR FINLAY'S PATIENT SUFFERED FROM that most difficult to treat malady: contempt for his physician. His condition deteriorated rapidly and after just three days Finlay diagnosed 'evident symptoms of being tired of my medicines'. Robert Finlay was Assistant Surgeon to the British Residence in Mocha. The sick man was Imam Al-Mahdi Abdullah, ruler of Yemen. Disobeying the doctor's orders, Imam Al-Mahdi 'confined himself to his Haram', purportedly 'for fear of catching cold'. But, according to Doctor Finlay, 'by this trifling conduct his fever continued six weeks'. The imam's prolonged period of convalescence in the women's quarters seems to have aroused Finlay's suspicions. 'I am told he has more than 100 women in his Haram,' he noted.

In July 1823 the imam had requested the urgent attendance of a medical man in Sanaa. Doctor Robert Finlay was duly dispatched from the British Residence to Yemen's capital. It was an unprecedented invitation and a rare opportunity. Yemen remained 'a country little known' to Europeans. Few since Niebuhr had visited the interior. Finlay was briefed by his superiors 'to avoid all political discussions and also the appearance of being on a political mission, but to collect every information relative to the country and its politics.' So, having accepted his assignment, the doctor became a spy. His subsequent report to the Bombay government made the little-known country sound uncivilised and unappealing. 'The natives,' he recorded on his first day out from Mocha, were 'very insolent and troublesome and the country much infested with thugs and robbers.' The local sheikhs were 'constantly plundering', the highlanders were continually 'committing robbery', and even the 'Imam's rapacity' was said to be renowned. Nothing could dispel Finlay's conviction of the incessant threat of brigandage: neither the fact that he had nothing stolen, nor the fact that, on the contrary, he was gifted camels for his travels and a sheep for his dinner on at least one occasion.

Finlay and I had both studied medicine in Edinburgh, and we would both turn thirty in Sanaa, but there the commonalities end. I felt little affinity with this bigoted physician. In Sanaa, Finlay was impressed by the Persian carpets, crimson velvet, and 'rich gold cloth' of the imam's throne room. Briefly impressed too by the imam's diamond ring, his green silk gown, and the gold lace that trimmed his turban. But he was perplexed by the jumbled miscellany of horse trappings, silks and swords, empty bottles and matchlock pistols that so cluttered the imam's private rooms that 'there was scarcely room left for him to move. On his pillow were fixed 6 gold and silver watches, all going...' Finlay was also perturbed by the imam's fondness for 'spirituous liquors', by his ten wives, and by the hundred women in his harem. He found nothing admirable in the imam's intellect, for 'all his conversation was on trifles'. And he saw 'nothing dignified or commanding in the Imam's countenance'. Doctor Finlay decided that Imam Al-Mahdi Abdullah, ruler of Yemen, was 'exactly resembling the Abyssinian slave'.

Finlay's analogy is poignant. It reveals both an unpleasant colonial racism, as well as an unsettling familiarity with slavery. British subjects and ships had been prohibited from participating in the buying and selling of slaves by the Slave Trade Act of 1807. Yet six years later, when William Milburn's *Oriental Commerce* was published in London, it still included the cost of an Abyssinian slave on the Red Sea coast. 'A good female slave' could be had for 60 dollars, Milburn told his readers: the price of a dozen cows, or a herd of goats. A male slave was valued at 40 to 80 dollars, 'according to age'. As late as 1843, the Anti-Slavery Society reported slave-trading occurring openly under a British flag in Mocha. Though the British authorities seem to have turned a blind eye, Doctor Finlay's remark suggests that Abyssinian slaves were in fact a familiar sight.

Mocha remained 'the principle port in the Red Sea frequented by Europeans', according to William Milburn. Seeking to contribute to 'the commercial interests of the empire' and drawing on his own experiences, in his *Oriental Commerce* Milburn enumerated local exchange rates for the various foreign coins circulating in Mocha: Spanish and Mexican dollars, French and German Crowns, gold Venetians, Gingerlees, Gubbers, Stamboles, and Xeraphims. And he itemised a 'list of Articles procurable at Mocha, with Directions how to chuse them':

> *Acacia, Acorus, Asphaltum, Balm of Gilead, Carpo Balsamum, Xylo Balsamum, Civet, Coffee, Dates, Hermodactyl, Junctus Odoratus, Myrrh, Natron...*

Milburn's *Oriental Commerce* depicts Mocha as a cosmopolitan entrepôt of exotic currencies and alluring commodities. It hints, too, at the especially avaricious pursuit of Eastern trade by British merchants who sought profit in any currency, from any product, according to a moral code that was controversial even by the standards of the time. In 1820, British traders at Mocha had demanded additional trading rights, reduced customs duties, and the waiver of anchorage fees. When their terms were refused, they simply bombarded the town until it yielded.

... Rhinoceros' horns, Rhinoceros hides, Sagapenum, Salep, Senna, and Sharks' fins...

An eyeball gazed back at me, lustreless and lifeless. My finger prodded cold flesh. I flipped the gill flap and a gash of pink filaments had opened up. The scales gleamed like burnished steel.

'Ok?' asked the restaurateur. While I had examined the fish, he had been studying my face.

'Ok,' I replied. The fish looked remarkably well after its long journey over the mountains from the coast. A carving knife was sunk deep behind its head, the blade drawn swiftly down its spine, glistening purple innards were tugged out and the body was splayed open. The two opposing sides of flesh were licked by a paintbrush primed with fiery red marinade and the preparation was complete. Tossed through a hatch and snatched into the kitchen, our dinner was lowered at the end of a metal rod into a wood-burning tanoor.

'Can we have some shrimps too?' I asked.

The restaurateur nodded and yelled toward the hatch. 'Ya, Aliii!... *Jimburi!*'

We had rolled through a glittering conurbation of airline offices, supermarkets, and shopping malls to arrive at the restaurant in Sanaa's up-market Hadda district. Richard's composure behind the wheel of his four-by-four inspired confidence and my toes had long since stopped twitching for an imagined brake pedal when taxis pulled out in front of us, or motorcycles raced toward us. Richard merely bounced the heel of his hand upon the horn without lifting his foot from the accelerator. Middle-aged, or late middle-aged, I suppose, he lived in the same building as me in the Old City, in the first-floor apartment, and he worked at Yemen's Ministry of Agriculture on a project funded by the European Union. Richard was responsible for managing something called a 'market information system'. If pressed he would say it was 'something to do with the price of mangoes'. It was a Wednesday evening, the end of the working week in Yemen, where the two-day weekend took place on Thursday and Friday. Inevitability, we had talked about work as we drove through the suburbs.

'Ali's still pestering about this conference in Dubai. He's drawn up a budget with a daily allowance of two hundred dollars for a ten-day trip. And the conference only lasts four days!' Ali was the project accountant. According to Richard, when he had arrived in Yemen at the start of his assignment, Ali had been carrying all of the project funds - amounting to several hundred thousand dollars - in the boot of his car. It was not the first time I had heard Richard bemoan the accountant's generosity with his own expenses. A few weeks earlier Ali had invited Richard to his home for dinner and requested five thousand riyals to purchase a large goat for the occasion. Richard told me how he had dispensed the cash, watched Ali leave the office early to buy the goat, and then been surprised later that evening at Ali's house when he was served chicken.

'Drunkenness,' according to Charles Cruttenden of the Indian Navy, was the 'prevailing vice amongst the higher classes in Sanaa'. Cruttenden and his companion Jessop Hulton enjoyed double measures of moral outrage during their visit to the Yemeni capital in 1836. 'Twice we were at the private apartment of the Imaum, and each time we left perfectly disgusted,' Cruttenden recounted. 'The Imaum with five or six dancing and singing girls, got shockingly drunk, and he seemed surprised at our refusing to join him in drinking raw spirits.' This was Imam Al-Mansur Ali, son of the Imam Al-Mahdi whose fevered fondness for the hundred women of his harem Doctor Finlay had been unable to cure thirteen years earlier. Cruttenden, scandalised, wrote that Imam Al-Mansur Ali was 'rarely sober after midday'. Despite his self-righteous tone, Cruttenden was generally less disdainful than Finlay. Still, he too was convinced that parts of the countryside were 'infested with robbers'. He reviled certain 'unfavorable specimens of the Arab' and repudiated 'the bigotry of the Arab'. Which sounds bigoted. And causes me to wonder whether an accusation of bigotry, or intolerance, inevitably expresses the bigotry or intolerance of the accuser toward the accused? So, if I suggest Doctor Finlay and perhaps Charles Cruttenden were bigoted and intolerant toward the people in Yemen, does that demonstrate my bigotry and intolerance toward Finlay and Cruttenden? And is my attitude toward these nineteenth-century Englishmen any better than theirs toward the Yemenis? There is, I would argue, a significant difference between making judgements about groups of people ('the Arabs') and judgements about the specific behaviour of individuals (Finlay and Cruttenden). But still, the questions remain. Are my judgements of characters in another historical epoch any more valid than theirs of the 'natives' in a foreign country? Should I tolerate their intolerance?

It was just the sort of question that Richard and I might have discussed or disputed over dinner at Al-Shaibani's. A popular establishment, even at this late hour it was crowded with men whose hands moved busily, sweeping up rice or gesturing at serving boys. Stark Formica and flourescent tube lighting accentuated the animation. Multiple Shaibani restaurants had sprung up along Hadda Street. There was Shaibani Modern, Shaibani Super Deluxe, Shaibani al-Beek, and Shaibani Royal. One of them was the original, the others had cashed in on the branding. I never figured which was which and it didn't much matter: we had our favourite. The restaurateur spread sheets of old newsprint like a tablecloth between us, his palms shuffling and patting the paper while his head snapped about distractedly, acknowledging his customers and instructing his staff. When our fish arrived, charred and curled, it was dropped onto yesterday's headlines. Richard looked approving. The blackened scales embraced flesh cooked to deliciously tender perfection. Curried shrimps came still simmering in their stoneware bowl. Then the bread, *rashoosh*, a thin unleavened whorl of tossed and layered dough, wide as a car tyre, the topmost stratum scorched crisp and flaking from the softer, chewier, underside. A waiter asked if we needed spoons: we were foreigners after all, anomalies among the Yemenis. We would have been anomalous even in England. It was an unlikely friendship. Richard, a self-confessed Conservative; me, a decade or two younger, with a broadly opposing worldview and political perspective. Which might have made the question of tolerance more acutely relevant, and more vexed.

In response to the waiter's enquiry though, we were both of like mind: neither of us wished to sacrifice our tactile experience for the conceit of cutlery. Richard tore into the fish while I began to shred a layer of *rashoosh*. We talked and ate as other dinners arrived and departed. 'Eat first, talk later,' a Yemeni friend would admonish me whenever I attempted to interrupt a meal with conversation. For most of the Yemenis I knew, the main meal, consumed at midday, was a quick and functional affair, unhindered by discussion. But Richard and I would eat slowly, arguing or agreeing to disagree, and any lingering quarrel would sooner or later be assuaged by a comic anecdote from Richard's varied career. He had been an Army cadet at Sandhurst, trained as a builder and as a barrister, worked as a meat trader in the East End of London and as a development consultant in Bulgaria and Kazakhstan before he arrived in Yemen. All of which had endowed him with an incomparable collection of yarns. One of the best was The Tale of Carlos the Gangster. Carlos was a cockney criminal imprisoned for carrying out no fewer than seventeen armed robberies. Richard had met him shortly after his release from jail. I relished the retelling of how Carlos described his eventual capture by the police and I had the impression that Richard relished it too. He would put on an East End accent.

Carlos: So there I was, run to ground, the game was up and I was all in, surrounded by fuckin' coppers all armed to the fuckin' eyeballs, and I looked at me shooter lying near me, and I knew I could reach it, and I knew I'd be quicker than them coppers, and I thought 'fuck it!'

Richard: Carlos, what did you do?

Carlos: Ten years.

The rewards had diminished. Oriental commerce had dwindled in Mocha. Coffee revenues had declined and Britain's interest in the Red Sea shifted from trade to transport. Hitherto, almost all contact between London and British India had occurred via the Cape route: a sea journey around Africa lasting at least four months. The alternative, much shorter, Red Sea passage via Suez remained an arduous and dangerous undertaking. Sandstorms and the shimmering refractive effects of the desert heat frequently conspired to scupper navigation in the Red Sea, while scattered reefs and submerged rocks threatened wreck. Sailing ships were often beleaguered or becalmed by unpredictable winds, and the waters between Africa and Arabia were notorious for their irregular currents. A solution to the problem of propulsion in unreliable sailing conditions was promised in the early decades of the nineteenth century by the development of the marine steam engine. And in the 1830s, a thorough hydrographic and geographic survey of the Red Sea was undertaken to make steam pilotage safer in what chief surveyor Robert Moresby described as a 'heated funnel of reef-bound sea'.

Ultimately it was Aden, not Mocha, that the British judged to be the best coaling station for steam ships undertaking the Red Sea passage. The decision was informed by Moresby's survey findings and by administrative concerns: Aden had a deep harbour and a good water supply for the refilling of boilers; it was also part of an independent sultanate that the Ottomans could lay no claim to and it was equidistant from Bombay, Suez, and British interests on the East African coast. A pretext for appropriation of the port was provided in January 1837 by the shipwreck of the *Deria Dowlat*. The Indian-owned vessel had been sailing under English colours when it ran aground near Aden. Surviving passengers and crew were purportedly 'grievously maltreated' and the wreck was looted by pirates. The British accused the local sultan of complicity, branding him a 'barbarous robber', and coercing him into conceding control of Aden. Royal Marines commandeered the port in 1839 and 'Aden became a British possession,' according to the *History of Arabia Felix or Yemen* written by Captain Robert Lambert Playfair and published two decades later. In Playfair's view, the past justified the imperial present and the story of Arabia Felix or Yemen was a story of successive occupations, chronicled in chapters devoted to each occupying power: Abyssinian, Persian, Portuguese, and Turkish, until the 'First Appearance of the British in the Red Sea' and culminating in a final chapter on 'Aden since the British conquest'. One person's conquest is another's unwarranted invasion. One person's bribe is another's gratuity. One person's theft is another's restitution. Or so my tolerance and relativism might seem to suggest. Even so, the British seizure of Aden would appear to have had more in common with, say, the culpable armed robbery of Carlos the Gangster than the merely questionable opportunism of Ali the Accountant.

Of all Richard's anecdotes, perhaps my favourite was The Tale of Joe Cursley, or Richard's Earliest Encounter with Yemen. 'Joe was from up North. Not one of the toffs at all. And before officer training at Sandhurst he'd enlisted as a private soldier. Prince of Wales regiment.' In Al-Shaibani's restaurant a flaky strip was ripped from the circle of bread. 'Shortly after he joined them they were all sent off to Aden. An emergency deployment, back in 1967.' Bread was dabbed into the bowl of shrimps. 'And after that he came to Sandhurst. So Joe was the only cadet with a service medal.' Oily shrimp broth dripped onto the newsprint. 'And whenever we were all brought out for inspection by some general or whatever, it was always the same routine: Joe would be put at the front row, with his medal all polished and proud, and I would be put at the back somewhere.' Dribbly shrimpy bread was chewed methodically and I waited for Richard to continue his account between mouthfuls. 'I couldn't see a bloody thing from the back, of course. And there'd be some general parading somewhere along the front of the ranks in Number One dress with his spurs and sword.' Then the fish tail was lifted and white flesh fell from its spine. 'When they came to Joe, him being the only one of us with a medal, the generals would always stop to ask him where he got it.' A morsel of fish was pinched between fingertips. 'And Joe would always bark out his answer at the top of his voice.' Then swallowed. 'So, stood at the back, all I knew of those parades was the "clink, clink, clink" of the general's spurs, then a pause, and then Joe, right on cue, shouting: "Aden, Sir!" And I suppose that was really all I knew of Yemen for a long time too.'

Britain's annexation of Aden in 1839 riled the Ottomans. Though they had been absent from Yemen for well over a century and a half since their forced departure in the 1630s, the Turks now laid claim to the country. They asserted that the imam in Sanaa had merely been entrusted with the administration of their dominion. Turkish soldiers returned to Yemen in 1849 and re-entered Sanaa in 1872. The intervening decades witnessed the Ottoman army fighting against considerable resistance, and at great loss. Charles Millingen, another British military physician, visited in 1874. At a citadel occupied by Turkish troops close to Sanaa, he had counted the cost of their possession: '700 Turks who perished during the siege lie in an adjoining field.'

Fourteen years after the Ottoman forces returned to Yemen's capital, Major-General Felix Thackeray Haig saw there 'the marks of Turkish rule - decay, poverty, and squalor'. Visiting Sanaa in 1886, he witnessed the effects of 'heavy and capricious' Ottoman taxation - the citizens were miserably impoverished and brutally oppressed. The guns of the city's Turkish fort, he noted, were aimed 'not to the outside, but upon the town.' Yemen was no longer infested with thieves and the natives were no longer bigoted Arab specimens. The perspectives of British visitors had shifted from disdain when the Yemenis had their independence, to sympathy when they suffered under a rival empire. These perspectives, of course, said less about the people of Yemen than about the British visitors themselves, and about how, if it came down to it, the Yemenis could be treated by the British. If the capture of Aden in 1837 had been belligerence, supposedly justified by the wrongs done to the British, the colonisation of Sanaa would be munificence, justified by the wrongs done to the Yemenis by the Turks. 'There can be no doubt English rule would be welcomed,' thought General Haig. The Yemenis were 'quite capable of appreciating the benefits of a wise and enlightened government.' After all, in Aden, 'the spectacle of a wise, firm, and just rule there presented has made a deep impression upon the whole population.' When Haig delivered his report to the Royal Geographical Society, he emphasised that Yemen 'possesses a climate quite suitable for European colonisation.' Moreover, it was rich in iron ore, coffee, and coal, which would make it a valuable possession if the Turks were ever 'obliged to evacuate Yemen'. All of these political considerations were a striking expansion of Haig's purported purpose, which he had said was to have a look at the country and its inhabitants 'with a view to ascertaining whether it might be possible to do anything for their Christianisation.' For having retired from the Madras Engineers, General Haig had dedicated himself to evangelical strategies. He thought all Arabia 'open to the Gospel' and that Sanaa would be an apt location for a Christian mission (though he duly acknowledged that any converts would 'probably be exposed to violence and death'). Much like Doctor Finlay, who had avoided the appearance of being on a political mission while gathering political information in Yemen, General Haig had observed the oppression of the Yemeni people, noted the direction of the Turkish cannon, and considered the possibility of British colonisation, while travelling with the Bible Society's agent from Aden. Approaching Sanaa, he had written to his young daughter in England, assuring her that he had been assiduously saying his prayers, every morning and every evening.

It was to spite a military father that Richard had abandoned his career in the armed forces. He decamped from Sandhurst just two weeks before Passing Out. On leaving he took with him a battery of anecdotes, an impressive knowledge of British military history, and a certain particularity about shining his shoes. In the right mood, he would sometimes introduce himself as 'Senior Cadet, retired'. At our first meeting he had not been wearing any trousers. Some days after moving into the Old City apartment I had heard a footfall in the stairwell, listened to a key clunk in a lock, waited for a while, then forced myself downstairs to knock on the door of my unknown neighbour and say hello.

'Hello.' The door was opened by a slightly greying, slightly balding man wearing black socks and a pair of blue and white striped underpants. 'I thought you were the cleaner.' He chuckled. Somewhat disconcerted, I managed to convey my name, the fact that I had moved into the apartment upstairs, and that I hadn't meant to disturb, before we shook hands and I departed.

Richard's relationship with his cleaner in fact turned out to be much less racy than that initial encounter suggested. They had met in the Ministry of Agriculture where, despite his degree in geography and near-perfect English, Mohammed had been employed to sweep floors and scrub toilets. He became an affable but unpredictable presence in Richard's apartment, disappearing for weeks, then turning up unannounced to commence a marathon effort of dusting and washing up. Humble, kind-natured, and slightly camp, Mohammed had a habit of making the world both more complicated and more entertaining. Like the time he had been looking under the stairs for a broom and discovered an object that looked rather like a large cake tin. He had shown it to me and as I tried to take the lid off, wondering at the unusual matt black finish of this piece of bakeware, Mohammed had intervened. 'Oh no, please don't Mister Andrew,' he said, sounding agitated, 'I think it might be a bomb.' Richard had a look, supposed that it might be a landmine or something, made a pot of tea, and telephoned our landlord to ask if he would arrange for the disposal of some unexploded ordnance.

'This isn't a bomb!' Ibrahim exclaimed when he arrived. 'And we never used land mines.' He looked aghast at the suggestion. Then, with something like nostalgia, he declared, 'This is the magazine from our old Chinese machine gun.' Which still amounted to live munitions and Mohammed, Richard, and I were all happy to see the thing leave the building slung under Ibrahim's arm. The incident did not reflect well on Richard's diligence during cadet training, but I wondered nonetheless whether it had the makings of a future anecdote; Mohammed the Cleaner and the Cake Tin Bomb. Mohammed meanwhile seemed to have been unnerved by the discovery of weaponry among his cleaning equipment and had not been seen since. The consequent state of Richard's kitchen might have explained why we were eating out at Al-Shaibani's this evening.

'Good scoff.' Richard tapped appreciatively at the earthenware dish, empty but for the heat-crusted dregs of shrimp sauce clinging to its edge. Across the newspaper was strewn the debris of our meal: scraps of bread, an empty bowl, and the skull, spine, and blackened skin of our fish.

- 8 -

The Gift of Reading

- Joseph Wolff, 1836 & Henry Stern, 1856 -

YOUR SHADOW IN THE NOONDAY city would have splashed hard across the cobbles, pooling as you stood, then flowing easily beneath you as we walked. Towerhouses would have risen up around us, reaching heights of eight, nine, as many as ten storeys, stories upon stories, revealing then concealing themselves, the skyline leaping then plunging among houses with no numbers, along streets with no names. The whole effect could be dizzying and disorientating. We might have navigated by the skybound minarets of mosques and the city quarters to which they lent their names: Nahrayn, Talha, Dawd, Fulayhi, and onward. Or we might have lowered our gaze and followed the trails of steel water pipes that lay gleaming, half-embedded in the pavement, as they strained in strict linearity and right-angled severity to negotiate the convolutions of the Old City. Eventually we would have found our way to the heart of the Muadh quarter and a narrow alley leading to the library of Architectural Studies. It would almost certainly have been closed.

'Hmmm... We are open... Any day... From nine until, hmmm... one thirty.' The librarian's hesitant English had given the impression of a contemplative soul, or of someone who was only partially present even during the rather limited library opening hours. On my first visit, he delivered such a detailed description of the workings of the photocopier in such an impossibly distracted manner that I half wondered whether one or other of us had fallen asleep: either I was dreaming, or I was listening to the monologue of an obsessive somniloquist. When he heard that I was looking for a book in English about Sanaa, the librarian pulled a couple of dusty PhD theses from a nearby shelf. I must have looked unimpressed. I had come with a very specific objective, hoping to find a very particular book. *San'a: An Arabian Islamic City*, edited by Robert Serjeant and Ronald Lewcock, is a monumental study of Yemen's capital. An ambitious attempt to view the city from a multitude of academic angles, it contains geographical, historical, and anthropological chapters, as well as detailed architectural descriptions. The tome was published in 1983 in a limited edition of 2,000 copies. Once, in a London bookshop, I saw a copy for sale, but was put off by the £450 price tag and the 'no browsing' sign.

'And, hmmm... We have this very important book...' The librarian unlocked a glass cabinet behind his desk, withdrew a weighty volume and carried it carefully to one of the nearby reading desks. 'Very important,' he re-emphasised, setting the volume down with veneration, all four-hundred-and-fifty-pounds-worth and six-hundred-and-thirty-two pages, complete with colour inserts and an inscription in blue biro from Serjeant and Lewcock to Yemen's president. I sat, scanned the contents pages, glanced at the index, looked at the photographs, then began to read. The first chapter on the city's geography included a description of how hand-dug wells and donkey-drawn water had been gradually replaced by drilled boreholes and diesel-powered hydraulic pumps, and how these were steadily depleting the local water table. I read that the city's diminishing underground water reserves were threatening a water crisis that could make Sanaa the first capital in the world to run out of water. Chapter Two described the ancient aqueducts or *ghayls* that had once brought water from far distant hills, but which had run dry since the early 1970s. I read that around that time a network of underground plastic water channels had been installed to ensure the urban water supply. But as an influx of motorcars replaced donkeys, vibrations from the vehicles damaged the plastic water pipes, causing them to crack and leak, dampening the foundations of many vulnerable structures, weakening them, and threatening the collapse of Sanaa's unique architectural heritage. The emergency response included the laying down of those superficial metal water channels that still remained, tracing their silvery trails through the streets underfoot. Water, exhausted or mismanaged, seemed the greatest threat to this Arabian Islamic city.

'I am sorry.' Indeed, the librarian appeared genuinely crestfallen. The library would be closing in ten minutes, he informed me.

'But, I thought you closed at one thirty?' It was just a little after eleven.

'Hmmm. Yes. We are open any day from nine in the morning until one thirty in the afternoon. Except Wednesday. Today is Wednesday. On Wednesday we close at eleven thirty.'

I asked if it would be possible to photocopy a few pages of Serjeant and Lewcock's book before leaving.

'Ah. Yes, we have the photocopier. But,' again he looked apologetic, 'I'm sorry, it is broken. The, um, hmmm, engineer came yesterday to fix it. He almost fixed it. But, tomorrow he will fix it, *inshallah*.'

'Is the library open tomorrow?'

'No. I am sorry. We are open, hmmm, any day, from nine until one thirty. Except Thursday and Friday. We do not open on Thursday and Friday.'

'And I don't suppose I am able to borrow any of the books?' Mercilessly vengeful, I must have been determined to squeeze every ounce of penitence from the librarian.

'I am sorry,' he said again, then disappeared as I resignedly stuffed my notebooks and stationery back into my bag.

Not long after the publication of *San'a: An Arabian Islamic City*, one of the authors, Australian architect and conservator Ronald Lewcock, produced a much slimmer book on the subject of the city. When I saw it being sold by an online retailer for a sum of just thirteen pounds I had unhesitatingly placed an order. The response was decidedly less immediate. I received first an email confirming an estimated delivery date some six weeks hence. A second email later informed me of a two-month delay and amended the delivery date accordingly. A third email postponed this date further and a fourth email further still. After twelve months I had given up all hope of ever seeing the book and my order remained outstanding a decade later.

The librarian returned. 'You can keep it. It's a gift,' he said and handed me a pristine copy of Ronald Lewcock's *The Old Walled City of San'a*. I was astounded. Ever since the failure of my internet book-buying efforts I had given up hope of ever seeing the title, let alone acquiring it.

'But please, if you find any other book about Sanaa, could you give it to us?' he asked. 'We are trying to build up the library.' I should have told him that where a global online retail company had failed, he had succeeded. And I might have advised him that if he also wished to succeed in building up a library, he might reconsider giving away his books quite so readily. But instead I just looked a little dumbstruck and said how enormously grateful I was for the gift of the book.

For Joseph Wolff it appeared to be a matter of faith. In a small town on the road to Sanaa he had given an Arabic translation of *The Pilgrim's Progress* to the town's governor. The governor responded by inviting him to spend the night. Next morning Wolff busied himself handing out more classics of religious-themed English literature to the locals, noting that 'Robinson Crusoe was admired, also, as a great prophet'. Arriving in Yemen's university town of Zabid, Wolff introduced himself to an Islamic scholar who promptly took two books from his shelf and, 'to Wolff's greatest surprise, they were a Bible and a New Testament in Arabic, with his own name written in them'. Wolff reported having inscribed the books before giving them to a man in Baghdad who, it transpired, had forwarded them to Yemen. The scholar then gave Wolff a manuscript in Arabic, which bore the name of the German explorer Ulrich Seetzen. The gift might have been a warning. Seetzen had passed this way some twenty-five years earlier and then been found dead nearby. Poisoned, it was rumoured, on the orders of the imam in Sanaa. But Joseph Wolff was undeterred. He was, by his own account, a missionary of indomitable zeal. By the time he reached Yemen in 1836, he had already survived being shipwrecked on Cephalonia, bastinadoed in Bokhara, enslaved at Khorasan, and forced to walk naked for 600 miles across Afghanistan, or so he claimed. At the Indian hill station of Shimla, the English colonials had believed him to be mad. At the slave market of Khorasan he had been valued at just twenty-five shillings.

Wolff had been born into a Jewish household in Germany, the son of a Bavarian rabbi. But after converting to Christianity he left home at the age of seventeen. Then, in Vienna, Rome, and Cambridge he dedicated himself to the study of theology and Eastern languages, including Arabic, Aramaic, Hebrew, Persian, and Syriac. Brimming with linguistic learning and a proselytising fervour, Wolff embarked upon his first missionary journey in 1821, aged twenty-six. Five years spent preaching and distributing bibles in Persia, Egypt, and the Levant won few converts, but the publication of his journals earned a small reputation for Wolff in London. Returning to England, he expeditiously married the sixth daughter of the Earl of Orford, before setting off upon his next mission.

Wolff in fact considered himself 'a great friend of the ladies'. The few ladies mentioned in his travelogues tend to have a hereditary title and to retire early after dinner, but Fanny Parkes was an exception. She met Joseph Wolff in Allahabad in February 1833 while her husband was in the employ of the East India Company. In her memoirs she described Wolff as 'a strange and most curious-looking man... his complexion that of dough, and his hair flaxen. His grey eyes roll and start, and fix themselves, at times most fearfully; they have a cast in them, which renders their expression still wilder.' Doughy-faced and squint-eyed, according to Mrs Parkes, Wolff 'roams about the world in search of the lost tribes of Israel'. Those Ten Lost Tribes were said to have descended from the Children of Israel and to have been 'lost' since the time of the Old Testament. At different moments in the history of European expansion overseas, Afghans, Native Americans, indigenous people of the Andes, and the Japanese had all been ascribed descent from one or other of the Tribes. Wolff repeatedly found remnants or rumours of the Lost Tribes during his travels. In Malta he heard they were in Bokhara. In Samarkand he was told they were in China. He thought he met their descendants in the Hindu Kush. And in Washington, 'one of the Indians' confidently asserted their Israelite heritage, having being informed of it a few years earlier by a 'Mrs Simons, from Scotland'. Undaunted by such dubious leads, Wolff had 'not the slightest doubt' that 'the Indians in America are the descendants of the Khivites'. They had left the land of Canaan and journeyed via Kamchatka, thought Wolff. Near to Sanaa, he 'spent six days with the children of Rechab', a community said to have travelled with the Tribes of Israel to the Promised Land. Using the third-person narrative and scripted dialogue that is a feature of his account, Wolff recalled his encounter with the Rechabites in Yemen.

> He told them that he had seen twelve years back, one of their nation in Mesopotamia, Moosa by name.
> Rechabites. 'Is your name Joseph Wolff?'
> Wolff. 'Yes.'
> They embraced him, and said they were still in possession of the Bible which he had given to Moosa.

Wolff was always pleased by the thought that his reputation had preceded him. To that end, the liberal gifting of books was both a means of spreading the word of God, and spreading the name of Joseph Wolff. Not just a matter of faith then, but self-promotion. When it came to his own book, Wolff would dedicate his *Travels and Adventures* to Benjamin Disraeli, then Chancellor of the Exchequer, later Conservative Prime Minister, and, like Wolff, a convert to Christianity from Judaism. The gesture might have looked a little toadying.

'They drink no wine,' Wolff noted of the Rechabites he met in Yemen, 'and plant no vineyards, and sow no seed, and live in tents, and remember good old Jonadab, the son of Rechab.' His observations certainly appeared to accord with the biblical description of the 'Children of Rechab' who had been commanded to remain nomadic and prohibited from drinking alcohol (and whose name was hence appropriated by a friendly society of the English Temperance Movement). No such abstemiousness was found in Sanaa. The imam 'was drunk from morning to night, and the Jews furnished him with brandy and wine,' said Wolff, corroborating the account of Charles Cruttenden who had visited that same year and found the imam 'rarely sober after midday'. In an almost equally immoderate gesture, while he was in Sanaa Joseph Wolff arranged for the Rechabites to be sent eighty volumes of Hebrew bibles and testaments. Presumably he enjoyed inscribing his name in each book.

'Sanaa, called in Genesis, chapter x. verse 27, "Uzal",' offered 'magnificent' views and 'beautiful gardens'. But 'the climate is most wretched,' Wolff decided during his 1836 visit. He developed a fever, blamed the weather, and departed, but apparently not before baptising a handful of the city's Jewish residents. Upon his leaving, the Rabbi of Sanaa gave Wolff a copy of the 'History of the Jews of Yemen'. That history was one of mercurial oppression. Jews had been expelled from Sanaa in 1678, then permitted to return the following year. In 1762 the city's synagogues were destroyed by order of the imam, though his successor allowed their rebuilding. For centuries Jews had been forbidden to build houses higher than two storeys, or to remain outside the Jewish quarter after dark. And sometime in the early nineteenth century Sanaa's Jews were tasked with the duty of removing dead animals and excrement from the city. Whether or not Wolff read the book that he had received from Sanaa's rabbi, he soon gained first-hand experience of local religious intolerances. On his way back toward Yemen's coast, Wolff was accosted by a band of 'Wahabites... with fury stamped upon their faces'. They were appalled by the unIslamic content of Wolff's earlier book donations.

'The books you gave us, on your way to Sanaa, do not contain the name of Muhammad, the Prophet of God.'
Wolff replied, 'This circumstance ought to bring you to some

decision.'
'We have come to a decision;' and, saying this, they horse-whipped
Wolff tremendously.

Wolff eventually returned to England and in 1845 became the vicar of Isle
Brewers in Somerset. He was said to occasionally interrupt his sermons
to the West Country folk with a burst of Hebrew song. There too, 'well
knowing that his temperament would not allow him to write a calm
history', Wolff began dictating his *Travels and Adventures* to obliging
friends. This method of having his stories transcribed might explain
why they are retold in the third person. Or, the constant self-reference to
'Wolff' might reflect the narcissism that characterised his narrative in the
eyes of some contemporary critics. The *Spectator* thought his *Travels and
Adventures* 'artless, outspoken, gossiping'. Another reviewer dismissed it
as 'anecdote and egotism'. Wolff admitted that 'vanity and ambition' had
been 'his great enemies all though life', but the urge seemed irresistible. At
one moment he snorted that he would be 'mad to compare himself with
Plato, Pythagoras, and Aristotle', but he then proceeded to do just that,
before then boasting that the Afghans considered him a prophet.

Still, for the reader, and for the listener, there was something peculiarly
enthralling about the prattling of this puffed-up preacher. The missionary's
voice had thundered in 'a phrenzy of zealous fervour, until he shouted
out as if bellowing to a camel-driver in the desert,' wrote an anonymous
contributor to *The Bristol Times* after Wolff delivered a late Sunday
morning sermon. 'I never was more interested, or rather *entertained*, by
any man from the pulpit before,' he continued, 'though I knew my roast
duck was being carbonated at the time,'

In 1861 Wolff oversaw completion of the new village church in Isle
Brewers. It was consecrated by the Bishop of Bath and Wells, and celebrated
one August afternoon on the vicarage lawn. That same year, following the
death of his first wife some months earlier, Wolff remarried. And 1861
also witnessed publication of the complete edition of Wolff's *Travels and
Adventures*. The author portrait on the frontispiece reveals how fifteen
years of pastoral life had turned the doughy-faced missionary into a
double-chinned and gouty-looking old man. Nonetheless, circumstances

had awoken in Joseph Wolff 'a most burning desire of going forth again'. 'Armenia, and Yarkand, with other places in Chinese Tartary' were his professed destinations, 'with a Bible in my hand, and the Cross figured on my gown'. Of the fact that he was by then aged sixty-five, Wolff reasoned with typical grandiosity that 'Moses undertook his mission to call the children of Israel out of Egypt, when eighty years of age.' He died at home in Isle Brewers the following year.

My introduction to Joseph Wolff had come by courtesy of the librarian and as a consequence of the repair of the photocopier. Serjeant and Lewcock's monumental *San'a* contained a chapter on 'Western Accounts of San'a, 1510-1962' and included a complete bibliography of writerly European visitors. The librarian helped me to locate their stories. Their descriptions of Sanaa rarely bore much resemblance to the modern city around me, and the characters, their context, and their reasons for coming were not always admirable. But they revealed a history of intriguing encounters. Besides, I sensed that these were, in some awkward way, my forebears. And so I read. On sunny afternoons I immersed myself in the small south room of my apartment, bathed in the warm radiance that filtered through the curtain stirred by a breeze, the sunlight undulating calmly as though reflected from water. Then after dark I was drawn toward the convivial glow of the teashop by the *Sayilah*, accompanied by photocopies of Ludovico di Varthema, John Jourdain, and Joseph Wolff.

'Whaaa, ya, Whoaa!!!' In the fiery pit of his teashop Ali had turned up the heat. He shouted at nobody in particular and nobody took any notice. Ali would continue the business of tearing lids off condensed milk tins, sloshing and stirring water on the boil, and spooning out heaps of tea and sugar. Grey stubble scuffed his jowls and two or three jutting canines splintered from his jaw. A scraggy turban slouched upon his head, a stained *futah* hung about his waist, and epaulettes flapped at the shoulders of his torn military sweater. Orders were taken with a toss of the head, payments were cast into a rusty can, empty milk tins were hurled aside, and Ali breathed fire. He was notoriously ill-tempered. His tea was notoriously overpriced. But his teashop was celebrated. In part this was due to Ali being generous with the milk, not excessive with the sugar, and never allowing the tea to over-boil. But mostly it was because of his unrivalled location on the west side of the *Sayilah*. From the fold-up iron chairs outside Ali's establishment the prospect of tower houses on the opposite bank was superlative. The teashop was furthermore located next door to the al-Mahdy mosque, enabling the pious to intersperse their prayers with tea-drinking and the less devout to interrupt their tea-drinking with prayer. All of which conspired to make Ali's diabolical temperament tolerable. It was here in the evenings that I often drew up a chair, set down my glass upon the pavement, and read contentedly while tealeaves swirled then settled in their milky currents. Until, at some point, I would be joined by someone who wished to talk to a rare foreigner in Sanaa. Or until, at some point, the electricity failed. The sweeping illumination from vehicles passing along the *Sayilah* was of little use to read by, so on one occasion when the streetlamps cut out I had moved closer to the blue flame of Ali's gas stove with my book or whatever photocopied pages I was absorbed in. Seeing my struggle and showing a solicitude that surprised me, Ali had placed his only candle upon the table in front of me. The electricity returned, I finished reading, finished my tea, and left. When I returned shortly with a newly purchased pack of two-dozen candles it was the only time I ever saw Ali smile and following this reciprocated exchange he favoured me with an extra half cup of milky tea upon my every visit and never once screamed at me.

At a coffee shop on the road to Sanaa, the Arabs had made room for Reverend Stern to sit down. Stern seemed surprised: this was 'contrary to the selfish character of their nature,' he thought. 'Patiently,' he then 'endured all the torments which a thermometer at 98°, and twenty unwashed and unclothed Ishmaelites, could inflict.' Two decades after Joseph Wolff's visit, Reverend Henry Aaron Stern had sailed to Yemen in August 1856 from Jeddah. There, he wrote, 'amidst fever and cholera, the shrieks of the living and the groans of the dying, I was enjoying excellent health.' But then the cholera that had swept through Jeddah struck Stern too, inflicting 'the most excruciating agonies'. 'The hand that now writes this might long since have mouldered on the barren shores of the Red Sea,' he would claim later, 'had not the certainty that Arabia Felix was waiting for the message of salvation supported me in my sufferings.'

Like Wolff, Henry Stern had grown up in a Jewish home in Germany, converted to Christianity, and then moved to England. Unlike Wolff, who had relied on the patronage of sympathetic benefactors to fund his missions, Stern was capable of abiding by societal conventions and institutional expectations and was appointed by the London Society for Promoting Christianity Amongst the Jews. In nineteenth-century Europe and the Islamic world, Jews commonly experienced discrimination and persecution. Proselytising efforts to convert them to Christianity appear no less pernicious. They also seem out of touch with contemporaneous movements toward European Jewish emancipation and proto-Zionism, and even out of touch with new forms of anti-Semitism based on race rather than religion, against which Christianisation would offer little defence. Incredibly though, the Society for Promoting Christianity Amongst the Jews continues to exist today as The Church's Ministry Among Jewish People. One of the Society's founders was the abolitionist hero William Wilberforce; suggesting that, from an evangelical perspective, there was nothing contradictory in holding that all men were equal under God, but that not all men's Gods were equal. Adhering to that precept, Reverend Stern in Yemen distributed New Testaments among a community of Jews near Manakha and 'cheerfully... explained to them, how Christianity was only mature Judaism'.

Neither Wolff nor Stern was especially interested in attempting to convert Muslims, but neither were they especially successful in converting Jews. Rather, their missionary accomplishment lay mostly in the travails that they endured. From Manakha, Stern continued toward Sanaa. The Jews had warned him to walk barefoot, for his shoes, they said, would raise suspicions that he was a Turk 'and a Turk is lawful prey'. Stern's bare Christian soles soon became 'pierced and lacerated'. There was further hardship on paths that 'threaded up and down dizzy heights, where a false step, or the shifting of a stone, would have hurled the unfortunate wayfarer into ravines of immeasurable depth.' And yet more 'toil and fatigue' was suffered beneath the 'fervid rays of the cloud-defying sun', among 'barren and naked rocks, reflecting from their rugged and flinty sides a fire that made the blood boil and the perspiration stream.' In the threat of the abyss and the heat of hellfire, the landscape had become persecutory.

'Alone, in an unknown country, and among a savage fanatic people': Stern's description of his journey's perils not only added drama, but symbolic, spiritual significance. He followed an archetype of triumphalist travel writing, which of course required something to triumph over. Yemen, an 'unknown country', could be made threatening and the Yemenis could be portrayed as 'savage': making an ideal setting for an allegorical Christian drama. Joseph Wolff, for all his rambunctious bumptiousness, had been as much inclined toward morality tales as Stern. But while Wolff had delivered *The Pilgrim's Progress* to the Arabs, Henry Stern retold it to his readers - casting himself as the Christian character in John Bunyan's allegory who leaves his home and journeys via the Slough of Despond and the Valley of the Shadow of Death to the Celestial City. After all his suffering along the road, Stern's first vision of Sanaa was suitably ecstatic: 'as if by enchantment, we beheld before us one of the most ancient and famous cities, with its quaint palaces and gardens, tapering minarets and glittering cupolas, rising like an oasis, out of the midst of desolation and death.' Truly, a Celestial City.

In the Jewish Quarter, Stern's preaching to a small crowd on the subject of Christ's 'sublime teachings, superhuman miracles, and infinite holiness' provided a climactic denouement.

> There was a breathless silence among the eager listeners, not a sound was heard, nor a word uttered; they all appeared amazed and confounded at the sublime truths I set before them.

The eventual mismatch between the alleged awe of his audience and the actual number of converts was accounted for by Stern: 'if the dread of their Mahomedan taskmasters had not, like a menacing spectre, floated before their minds, not one among my audience would have left the room without avowing his faith in the crucified Redeemer.'

Stern's distrust of the Mahomedans elicited an attitude of equal suspicion among them. Guards were sent to his home, his movements were confined, and his donkey-load of bibles was embargoed. When he sought justice from the Governor of Sanaa he was welcomed cordially as 'Sheikh-el-Nazarane' and given permission to distribute his bibles freely. In return, the governor's only request was for 'a description of the fire-carriages and wire words'. The missionary once more endeavoured to enlighten, but once more he failed. Later he claimed sorely that 'had Watt and Franklin themselves occupied my place, and explained their immortal discoveries, the telegraph and railway would still have been ascribed to the skill of magic.'

Patronising toward the Jews and churlishly unpleasant to the Muslims, it took less than a fortnight for Reverend Stern's unpopularity in the city to reach its zenith. 'The public clamour against me began to be too loud and vehement to resist it much longer.' At least one of those who befriended him was beaten up on account of it. Stern himself remained unscathed in Sanaa, but with what might have been divine retribution he was punched in the face soon after leaving. 'Once more,' he wrote of his departure, 'I grasp my pilgrim's staff, and set out on my dreary and perilous journey.' He really did seem to perceive himself enacting Bunyan's allegory.

Some years later, Stern's ordeals garnered a greater audience following his role in Britain's preposterous military expedition to Abyssinia. A diplomatic spat between the two countries had prompted Abyssinian Emperor Tewodros II to imprison a visiting British missionary: none other than Henry Stern. Calls for his release came from other missionaries and the British Consul in Abyssinia, but Tewodros had them locked up too. Negotiations led nowhere and after four years Queen Victoria announced that an expeditionary force would free the captives. Some 13,000 troops, 16,000 mules, 8,000 camels, 3,000 horses, and 44 trained elephants were sent from Bombay. Aided by the construction of a small coastal port and a purpose-built light railway, the British expedition spent three months traversing four hundred miles of mountainous terrain to reach the emperor's fortress in 1868. Tewodros released his handful of hostages, but the British troops anyway bombarded and plundered his fortress. Tewodros was found dead, having killed himself with a pistol once gifted to him by Queen Victoria. Reverend Stern returned to England and found in his experiences material for another book and a career as a public speaker.

The stillicide came hesitantly. An erratic tapping, as though tentatively awakening something dormant. A cool breeze in March had become a chilling bluster, whipping dust up from the streets. It was the harbinger of coming storms. For after the rising dust came falling rain. At first the city had darkened each afternoon; the air thickening, cloud curtains dropping, and a pattering of precipitation blotching the dirt. Then the saturated monsoon winds of the Indian Ocean crashed against the mountains around Sanaa, unleashing their torrential cloudbursts. Timid splashes swelled to become downpours. Sheets of gravelly rain turned the *Sayilah* from a road into a river and turned the streets of the Old City into tributaries.

By the time I walked home after work the afternoon rainfall had usually ceased. Stepping cautiously among murky rivulets, I quickly learnt a new and transient geography of submergent potholes, flotsamed vegetables, and slicks of sheep shit in the market on Bab as-Sabah. The footbridge over the *Sayilah* would be crowded with spectators. They gathered to watch daredevils jump into the fast-moving currents; to goad youths who tried crossing the channel, wading deeper and deeper until the push of water threatened to topple them; to laugh at the cars abandoned by drivers who had attempted some ill-advised short-cut, only to find their vehicles afloat; but mostly the crowds came to stare at the sheer volume and force of rushing water. The energy released from the heavens was a marvel to behold. The city slowed, the traffic stopped, we stood and stared. The unfamiliar weather and uncharted waterways were a revelation. Despite all I had read about Sanaa's water and its conduits, I had never been able to conceive the annual flood surge. It had seemed implausible, if not impossible. And when it came, it upended my assumptions. I had unthinkingly supposed that if the *Sayilah* were to flood then its water would flow south, toward the sea; down, toward the bottom of my city map. It was disconcerting to watch the water running north, never reaching the ocean, spilling into the desert, struggling to replenish the underground aquifers that were the city's depleting water source.

At dusk the cobbles remained damp and dark, as though the shadows had soaked into them and night would soon seep up from the ground. At Ali's teashop the folding chairs were a tangle of steel tubing, collapsed and hurriedly brought in from the rain. Awkwardly one wet evening I attempted to unfold one of them while holding a steaming glass of tea. My struggle did not go unnoticed or unassisted. The stranger who intervened drew my seat up next to his own on the paved embankment overlooking the deluged *Sayilah*. The water boiled beneath us, glittering with tungsten sparks caught up in the eddies. No need for candles this evening; the electricity remained on and every puddle contained a streetlamp. The man who had carried my seat offered me a cigarette and began asking questions in rusty English. I was a Nazarene? A Christian? Not really, but sort of I supposed. So I knew about the flood? The Ark? In the Bible? He delivered his enquiries with vigorous gestures and emphatic eyebrows. And Noah, I knew about Noah? Yes, I did. But did I know about the son of Noah? No. I did not. Wide-eyed, hands thrown up in an exaggerated expression of surprise, his response was a set-up for the enthused account that followed. The son of Noah, after the flood, was helped by a bird. He was nearly one hundred years old. The son of Noah, not the bird. The bird dropped something... I waited. Something... The translation was obviously difficult and I didn't understand the term when it was spoken in Arabic. His brow furrowed, he reached down, picked up a pebble, held it aloft between finger and thumb, and held his eyebrows up too in an expression of astonished triumph. A stone! Yes, a stone! He tossed the pebble into the *Sayilah*'s torrents. After the flood, a bird had carried a stone and dropped it here. *Here*! And that was how the son of Noah knew where to build his city, the city that would become Sanaa. It was the story of the city's genesis. The story of Shem, son of Noah. The story of how Shem had been guided by a bird to found a city here after the flood had subsided. A story from before the Ten Tribes, told and retold for centuries, well before stories were written down. It was a gift. That evening I remained until late, long after the storyteller had departed. Until only a cold sludge of tealeaves remained at the bottom of my glass and the conversations of tea drinkers had been replaced by the quiet rushing of water. Until Ali extinguished the hiss of his gas flame, then hissed and shooed the cats from his doorway, while the cats hissed back indignantly.

- 9 -

Pictures Taken

- Joseph Halévy, 1870 & Renzo Manzoni, 1877-80 -

I HAD BEEN DRAGGED BEFORE the man who carried a musket over his shoulder. He wore a turban of shiny indigo and a beard of silver-grey, a leather bandolier across his chest and a sprig of basil in his headdress. The effect was impressive, but a little intimidating, since the gun barrel that he gripped at the muzzle was pointing at my guts. 'This is a tribesman,' proclaimed the man who had brought me and still held me by the arm. 'You must take his photograph.' A small crowd watched, amused, as I levelled my camera. I was about to release the shutter when the man stopped me. He rearranged the striped cotton shawl draped over the tribesman's shoulder, stepped back, tipped the old tribesman's jaw up just a little, then flicked me a nod. I took four photographs before I was allowed to disappear back into the crowd. It was a good-humoured encounter, poking fun at me, at the tribesman too I suspect, and at our respective roles. I didn't stop to ask the old tribesman how he felt about it. Looking at it his expression in the photograph now, I find it hard to know. Despite the weapon and the gruff masculinity, there seems a plaintive tilt to his brow.

The square inside Bab al-Yaman was all spectacle that morning. It was Thursday, the start of the weekend. The al-Rudwan mosque was half-hidden behind boiled egg sellers and spiced potato stalls. Business was lively at the newspaper stand; a brisk trade in periodicals and portraits of the president. Two boys with sports jackets hoisted over their forearms jibed back and forth, keenly hawking their garments. Pink clouds of candyfloss drifted lazily, following a sweet seller who meandered through the crowd. Women in black *abayas* passed by, tugging their husbands by the sleeve of their white *thobes*. I had been observing these scenes from behind my camera when the enforced meeting with the tribesman neatly upended my spectator position. A group of tourists arrived, also brandishing cameras, wearing wide sunhats, and clutching guidebooks. The 4th edition of the Lonely Planet guide to Yemen had advised new arrivals in 1999 that 'a good starting point is Bab al-Yaman'. It is a sign of changing times. A 5th edition seems unlikely to be published anytime soon. And Bab al-Yaman, the South Gate, was once the *only* starting point: the gate through which all foreign visitors were obliged to enter the city. Evil persons and venomous snakes were said to be unable to cross its threshold. Its parapets were periodically adorned with severed heads. At dusk, the gate's colossal wooden doors would have been shut and bolted. High up on one of those doors, it had once been pointed out to me, there remained a shallow crater; the indentation left by a Turkish cannonball. Yet the Bab seemed too ornate to be truly imposing, with its red and black dressed stone, Romanesque pillars and decorative flourishes. The flanking turrets seemed stout and almost jovial, their white crenellations like paper crowns. And since the gates were now always left wide open, it was impossible to approach that gaping arch without glimpsing too the jumble of extraordinary domestic architecture and vibrant communal life beyond. Through the Bab, a ceaseless tide of people surged. Most headed straight on, across the square and into the *suq*. A few veered left, toward Sanaa's Great Mosque. It is said that the mosque was constructed upon the order of the Prophet Mohammed himself in AD 630. And it is said to incorporate materials salvaged from a cathedral that had been constructed one hundred years earlier by Christian Abyssinians in Sanaa. The cathedral, once the largest Christian building outside Europe, is believed to have contained marble and mosaics sent by the Byzantine Emperor Justinian. It has long since fallen to ruin. But the mosque is still standing and still in regular use. According to Ronald Lewcock and the copy of his book that I had been gifted by the librarian, the upcycled wooden lintel of the Great Mosque's southern entrance incorporated carvings of vine tendrils, leaves, and crosses. Several of its stone columns and capitals allegedly featured early Christian and Byzantine designs. I never saw them myself. I had never been permitted to enter. The mosque was open to worshippers, but closed to visitors. The custodians had apparently become exasperated by inconsiderate tourists. Among their forebears, it seems, was the Frenchman Joseph Halévy.

Halévy had been warned about the dead cat. It was one of numerous occasions upon which he was warned, and then rescued by his Yemeni companion, Hayyim Habshush, when the warning was ignored. Habshush later wrote admiringly of Halévy: 'illuminator of my mind'; 'master of all my knowledge'. But the French Orientalist never acknowledged the coppersmith from Sanaa who had accompanied him on his journey through Yemen in 1870. In his writings, Halévy not only omitted to mention his Yemeni guide and colleague, but contrived to erase him by claiming actions that Habshush had in fact undertaken as his own. Habshush had been indispensable to Halévy. He had found archaeological remains that Halévy would later take credit for discovering; he had navigated and negotiated accommodation and safe passage; and not infrequently Habshush had intervened in order to keep Halévy alive. And so, the story of the Great Mosque and the dead cat.

Halévy had been sent to Yemen by the Académie des Inscriptions et Belles-Lettres. He was tasked with finding and copying inscriptions from the ancient kingdom of Saba, the biblical land of Sheba, home of the queen famed for her encounter with King Solomon. For the purpose of his academic expedition, Halévy adopted the guise of a rabbi from Jerusalem and sought assistance in Sanaa's Jewish quarter. It was there that he met the Jewish metalworker Hayyim Habshush. With Habshush, Halévy collected the fragments of Sabean script that he took back to Paris, where he then deciphered and described them in his 1872 *Mission archéologique dans le Yemen*. He would be rewarded with a professorship of Oriental languages. While in Sanaa, Halévy had been determined to see the Great Mosque. But being dressed as a rabbi made a visit to the Islamic holy site a delicate and potentially dangerous undertaking. Habshush recounted the story of a European Jew who had visited the city and wanted to witness the procession of the imam and his entourage to the mosque for Friday prayers. The visitor's request was only accepted after he agreed in writing that he would endure all those abuses to which a Yemeni Jew might be exposed. Accordingly, he was obliged to suffer the insults and stones that were hurled at him from the crowd as he watched the imam's retinue pass by. But when a dead cat flung in his direction struck the visitor's beard, he angrily hurled the carcass back into the throng. Seized and dragged before the imam, the visiting Jew accounted for his actions by claiming that the written conditions to which he had agreed included no reference to dead cats. Apparently only the imam's amusement at this indignant pedantry saved the visitor from punishment. Despite these forewarnings, Halévy remained insistent. He made his way to the Great Mosque. And when the crowd turned hostile toward him it was Habshush who intervened to smuggle Halévy back to the safety of the Jewish quarter.

Accepting the guidance of the Lonely Planet authors, we might have begun our mid-day city tour at Bab al-Yaman. 'Make sure you carry twice as much film as you think you will need,' those authors had advised, in an age before cameras became digital. Instead of turning left toward the mosque, you and I would have headed north, straight on then bearing right, moving slowly toward the *suq*. Slowly because the narrow street would have been crowded with people, acknowledging you with curious glances or friendly grins, greeting you with 'hellooo' or 'sura', which, if you didn't know, means 'picture'. Heaven forbid your Arabic was worse than mine: the words around you would have been baffling, a tangle of rolled rrr's and glottal stops, knotted sounds being choked or gargled. Thanks to some patient language tutors and conversational taxi drivers, my spoken Arabic had improved substantially in Yemen, but it remained only middling, and I never learnt to read or write. Meanwhile, my grasp of French, German, and Italian has always been poor to non-existent. And so the travel accounts of those non-Anglophone authors who visited Sanaa soon after Halévy remain mysterious: Albert Deflers' 1889 *Journal d'une excursion botanique*; Eduard Glaser's *Von Hodeida nach Sanaa vom 24. April bis 1. Mai 1885*; Renzo Manzoni's *El Yèmen: Tre anni nell'Arabia Felice. Escursioni fatte dal settembre 1877 al marzo 1880*. All are unfathomable. In reading as in travel, language defines the limits to our encounters. Joseph Halévy's visit, documented by him in French, is only revealed to me by his guide, Hayyim Habshush. Habshush wrote an account of their travels together two decades later. He wrote using Hebrew script in a phonetic transliteration of his vernacular Sanaani Arabic: a method similar to the way I tried to write down Arabic words and phrases using the Latin alphabet. Fifty years later, the German-Jewish scholar Shlomo Dov Goitein helpfully collated and translated Habshush's text into English. Such decodings are marvellous to me. And it is regrettable that while I might have acted as a passable guide in Sanaa, I would have been of only limited use as a translator.

So, carrying twice as much film as you thought you might need, you might have recoursed to the visual; swinging your camera up to your eye and peering through the viewfinder, as in the age before photographs were taken with tablets and telephones held at arm's length. You might have composed close-ups of passing faces, or swopped the zoom lens for a wide-angle to frame the sacks of coffee beans or stalls selling scarves. On the busy lane to the *suq* you might have stepped back from the path of a swarthy figure carrying a sack of grain on his shoulders, or to make way for a woman herding her children, or to dodge a cyclist pedalling past in a streak of gelled-back hair and pop music blaring from a portable stereo attached to his handlebars. Or you might have been stepping back in order to rewind your roll of exposed film, in the way that people once did. Or you might have been retreating into the technicalities of aperture settings and shutter speeds, f-stops and hundredths of seconds. But if you had stepped back from the human traffic in the hope of getting some natural-looking shots, candid or spontaneous, you would quickly have become bored or irritated in the attempt. Because people would not have become so quickly bored with you and your rolls of film would have been filled with images of inquisitive onlookers. Had you pointed your lens toward the date seller, curled and flicking an indolent flywhisk over his stall, he would have paused, taken a handful of dates and offered them to you. And so, odd as it may seem, in all your photographs, it would have been you who was the centre of attention.

The same irony and the same concern for imagery are apparent in Renzo Manzoni's *El Yemen*. The 1884 travelogue, written by the grandson of the Italian novelist Alessandro Manzoni, has never been translated into English. But it uses a visual language to describe the experience of being in Sanaa. Manzoni belonged to a small group of travellers who had begun collecting foreign light upon collodion plates and bringing these back to Europe. Following the innovation of the Daguerreotype, but before the ubiquity of Kodak, he was the first person to photograph Yemen's capital. Manzoni's published account contains engravings made from his prints.

There are pictures of people and buildings, and fold-out panoramas of the city. Portraits are formal, subjects are passive. People in Sanaa are seen standing stiffly, staring straight at the camera, framed against blank backgrounds, their bodies captured whole and in their entirety to provide a complete document. The same starched formality evinced in Manzoni's image of an Arabian horse is apparent in his picture of 'alti dignitary di Sanaa', which shows six figures wearing sandals, draped shawls, and turbans. Their facial expressions are obscured amid dense beard growth and cross-hatched ink, but their eloquent hands are clasped together, clutching *jambiyahs* and prayer beads, or placed protectively upon the shoulder of a young nephew while the youth has turned his face away warily. Next to him, another beardless boy scowls at the camera, at Manzoni stooped beneath his camera hood, and at us.

The relaxed profile headshot of Manzoni on the book's frontispiece offers a sharp contrast. The Italian photographer is portrayed very differently, and far more empathetically, than the way in which he captured his subjects in Yemen. The first camera in Sanaa established what would become a familiar inequality between photographer and the photographed. Even the double-page spread of Sanaa's twenty-four-man Turkish garrison, despite all the epaulettes and medals, Fez hats, moustaches, and crescent moon belt buckles of the men who stand squinting in the light, still manages to look like a strained school photograph.

By now, with the sun directly overhead, the light would have been too harsh for photography. For that reason, and for another that I would explain later, I would have suggested that you put away your camera as we approached the *salta* shop and the bread sellers who stood outside. We would have bought two rounds of bread from one of the women at the entrance, then ducked in through a low doorway. If you had withdrawn into a visual world, the *salta* shop would have dragged you out. There is a damp heat and an aroma rich with oil and spices. There are discordant clashes and shouted conversations. It would all be a little overwhelming at first. Dark wet noise, loud hot smells. You might have taken a moment to adjust to our new surroundings before we squeezed our way onto rickety benches either side of a long table that has seen better days, bashed and repaired, excoriated and re-painted. Our fellow diners, sitting elbow to elbow or at a forearm's distance opposite, might have included a policeman in uniform, two men in single-breasted suits, a man in rags, and a group dressed with jackets and *jambiyahs* over their *thobes*. You would have had to yell your order. No matter if your knowledge of Arabic was rudimentary. You could not go wrong. There was only one dish on the menu. *Salta* is a Yemeni specialty. A beef stew topped with foamy whipped-up fenugreek flour. Beyond that, the contents seemed to vary. Leeks, egg, okra, rice, carrots, potatoes, a teaspoon, and what appeared to be the wooden handle of a paintbrush had all made appearances in *saltas* that I had enjoyed; attesting to the truth of the assertion that the most important ingredients of a good *salta* are the heat and clamour of the *salta* shop. You would have needed to shout louder if you wanted the waiter to hear you. Louder than the infernal roar of the gas burners, and louder than the other customers.

Salta!

You *could*, I suppose, have gone wrong. Perhaps with the pronunciation. Richard, whose Arabic was even worse than mine, once gave five hundred riyals to twelve-year-old Yusuf and instructed him to fetch some take-away *salta*. Yusuf soon returned, to Richard's consternation, laden with lettuces; five hundred riyals-worth of *salata*.

Ya, whoa! SALTA!

A young waiter would have nodded in acknowledgement before being lost amid the silhouettes and the vapours. He would have been last seen heading toward the *salta* chef who stood among oversized cooking pots, aloft, a wavering apparition melting like ghee in the heat above the stove. The chef too would then disappear completely behind a belch of steam as the lid was lifted from a vast metal cauldron big enough to contain a couple of whole sheep. Only his hands would be visible, ladling soup into bowls held up by serving boys. Then the waiter would have reappeared. Uniformed in a knee-length burgundy-coloured coat and looking like a 1950s hotel concierge, he would have deposited two bowls of thin soup on the table in front of us. Then he would be gone again. The soup, *shurba*, would have been meaty, oily, and delicious. A dribble might have made for your chin as you drained the last of it. Then the waiter again materializes, with a dish of fire-blacked stoneware balancing precariously on an empty tin can, steadying it with a piece of cardboard that protects his fingers from the heat. Cautiously he would have pushed the dish onto the table. It would have spluttered and fumed, spat and steamed, then slowly exuded a pale green froth of fenugreek onto the furniture. Together we would have attacked it with the flat bread, whipping the foam into the boiling stew.

Which would have brought me back to the subject of the bread sellers and your camera while we waited for the *salta* to cool. I had been warned, but like Halévy I had chosen to ignore the warning. On a prior occasion, as I approached the four figures draped in printed Indian fabrics, their faces entirely covered, bread piled high upon their heads, perhaps I imagined that because I could not see them, they could not see me. Perhaps I thought that I could hide behind my camera. Perhaps I hoped they wouldn't mind if I took their picture. Or perhaps I didn't care. But the bread sellers were justly furious. To photograph a woman was *ayb*; a shame or disgrace. Not a religious prohibition, but a societal one; not *haram* then, but anything *ayb* was nonetheless powerfully proscribed. Pressing the shutter release button on my camera had been an affront. The bread sellers launched a vehement tirade. A dead cat flung in my direction might not have been unwarranted.

I imagine the camera in Manzoni's hands to have been a more benign tool than the technology that I held in mine, or that you might have had in yours. While he fiddled with his cumbersome tripod and fragile glass plates, his subjects would presumably have had plenty of time to consider their consent to the protracted method of his image making. Moreover, the certain knowledge of being the first photographer in Sanaa would surely have prompted Manzoni to recognise that he himself was as novel and unusual as the people who stood or sat opposite him on the other side of the camera's glass eye. That sense of novelty has worn off. In many contexts photography has become so pervasive and prosaic as to be assumed an unremarkable reflex. That unthinking automaticity allows us to assume that the novelty and the noteworthy are the things we photograph and not us photographing them or the act of photography itself. Only this explains why you might have felt a little irked when people behaved 'unnaturally' in front of your camera: as if your frustrated attempts at candid or spontaneous photographs were themselves in any sense 'natural'.

On the other side of the Old City, at Tahreer Square, there were career photographers with aged Chinese cameras who carried props for people to pose with while their picture was taken. Flower garlands, ceremonial swords, and one of the photographers even had a bird of prey which perched upon his shoulder, dribbling a line of white excrement down the back of his jacket. There were no automated photo booths. When I needed a passport-sized photograph for my visa renewal, I was directed to a studio where the photographer snapped a few pictures of my face and then, unprompted, photoshopped away my acne and the broken veins on my nose. The results were contrived images, with swords and falcons or artificially smoothed skin, but like Manzoni's deliberately constructed photographs, their unnaturalness was made plain.

Perhaps Manzoni's ponderous method made him conscious of

the potentially distancing and dehumanising effect of putting a lens between himself and someone else. And perhaps it was this that made him conscientious about asking the names of those people whom he photographed. Or perhaps it was simply fastidiousness. Regardless, all twenty-four members of the Turkish garrison are identified beneath their fold-out image. Too often I have been more like Halévy in his dealings with Habshush, rather than Manzoni in his interactions with his photographic subjects: I have taken without proper acknowledgement, not bothering to record names. There have been times, as with the bread sellers, when to my shame I have not even asked permission. And other times when I have not asked what impact making a photograph might have upon someone's dignity; or asked whether the image will be an empathetic portrayal; or whether I would feel comfortable taking a photograph in an equivalent setting, or of a similar subject at home; or whether I would mind if the roles were reversed, if I was the one being photographed; or how I would react if a stranger were to photograph my children, or my ageing parents.

After the old tribesman at Bab al-Yaman and the bread sellers outside the *salta* shop, another encounter in Sanaa caused me to reflect with some disquiet upon the action of my photography. Close to the al-Nahrayn mosque, an old man sitting outside had struck me as photogenic. I had asked and he had assented, and so I had taken his photograph. It was a nice image. I gave the picture of the old man to Adnan, a local artist friend, who used the photograph to create a pen and ink drawing, rather like the engravings made from Manzoni's prints. Adnan's drawing hung in Yemen's National Gallery for a while, until he gave it to me, and then I gave it to my Old Man, who still has it on his wall at home. Sometime after I had taken the photograph, I saw the old man in Sanaa again, once more sitting on the steps outside the mosque. While I watched, he was gently helped to his feet by someone I took to be a relative, a son perhaps. The old man looked frail and as he stood upright the handsome face that I had photographed became clouded with uncertainty and confusion. Thinking back to the moment when I had asked whether I could take his picture, I wondered whether he had really understood, or whether he had merely nodded genially, and whether I had simply exploited his senescence. I never asked his name.

What was the purpose of these pictures? Once, I had truly believed that they captured a moment in time. But the young nephews photographed by Manzoni have died long ago. Manzoni, pictured in his handsome twenties, grew old and died in his sixties. The old man I photographed was young once, the youths I photographed will become old; it is we who are captured by time and not it by us. We can no more capture time in a photograph than we can grasp sunlight in our palm. Here then lay the real purpose of my photographs; a mere trick of the light, markers of lost moments, of unalterable actions and inactions, revealing nothing more or less than our ephemeral nature.

'At Least 6 killed in the Old City of Sana'a on Friday'. I continued to return to the website of the *Yemen Times*, hoping that the headline had changed, that the news was better, that the online newspaper was operating again. But everything remained unaltered. At 2am on the morning of Friday 12 June 2015, a bomb had been dropped on the al-Qasimi quarter of Sanaa's Old City, killing half a dozen people, injuring many more, and destroying several homes. In Britain, the *Guardian* and *Daily Telegraph* both ran the story, accompanied by photographs of the obliterated houses.

'I am shocked by the images of these magnificent multi-storied tower-houses and serene gardens reduced to rubble,' UNESCO's Director-General was quoted as saying, after she had seen the pictures. 'I am profoundly distressed by the loss of human lives as well as by the damage inflicted on one of the world's oldest jewels of Islamic urban landscape.' Leaders of the Saudi-led war coalition denied responsibility, but bomb fragments from the site matched those from their other air attacks. Amnesty International denounced the airstrike and did not hesitate to name the perpetrators. They also named the victims. Hassan Yahya Abdelqader, his brother Rashad, his son Abdullah, his cousin Shawqi, and his wife Amat al-Malik. Amat had been six months pregnant.

There was much to be abhorred here. The civilian deaths. The killing of a pregnant woman. The fact, made apparent in the *Yemen Times* headline, that the attack was carried out on a Friday, the Islamic holy day. Perhaps too the violation of Sanaa's traditionally 'protected' status; a status that had been generally, though not entirely, honoured by warring tribes for centuries. But arguably most significant of all, the airstrike on Old Sanaa was a contravention of international humanitarian law. Sometimes referred to as 'the law of war', international humanitarian law, or IHL, is a set of internationally recognised principles intended to limit the effect of armed conflict; for even wars have rules. Under those rules, all warring forces are obliged to take precautions to prevent or minimise civilian casualties. Attacks in which there is no evident military target, that do not discriminate between civilians and military objectives, or that cause disproportionate civilian harm, are unlawful. Following the airstrike on the Old City of Sanaa, the website yemenwarcrimes.blogspot.co.uk reported an interview with Mohamed al-Mansour, brother to Hassan and Rashad, uncle to Abdullah, cousin to Shawqi, brother-in-law to Amat al-Malik, and unmet uncle to Amat's unborn child. 'There are no Houthis nor armed men in our neighborhood. And my family doesn't belong to any political party or any armed movements,' Mohamed said, conveying the stark facts of a war crime. 'Everyone knows that we are peaceful and everyone knows the value of old Sanaa with its ancient history, especially al-Qasimi neighbourhood.' I remembered the al-Qasimi neighbourhood well. Its expansive gardens and many palm trees had made it an especially attractive part of the Old City. Photographs of the now-obliterated terrace had once featured prominently in promotional tourist material.

UNESCO responded to the continuing threat of Sanaa's further destruction by promptly placing the Old City on its World Heritage in Danger list. But soon after, the United Nations Human Rights Council resolved not to establish an investigation into violations of international humanitarian law in Yemen. The two decisions by the two UN organisations - an action and an inaction - appeared conspicuously contradictory. The Human Rights Council's decision not to investigate potential war crimes was strikingly at odds with UNESCO's recognition of the damage and continuing endangerment of an urban residential area populated by civilians. But the proposed war crimes investigation had been blocked by those members of the Human Rights Council that supported the Saudi-led war coalition. Those members included both the UK and US.

War crimes, like other crimes, when they are not investigated and when the perpetrators are not punished, become permissive. They set precedents. And serious violations of international humanitarian law continued to be committed by all parties to the conflict in Yemen. On one side, the Saudi coalition continued to drop bombs on civilian targets. Laser-targeted airstrikes were carried out on homes, hospitals, markets, mosques, weddings, funerals, and schools. The Saudi coalition also illegally obstructed the delivery of humanitarian aid to Yemen. On the other side, Houthi rebels carried out forced detentions and evacuations, recruited child soldiers, and siphoned off any humanitarian supplies that made it through the Saudi blockade.

Before he left Sanaa, before he boarded a boat in Mocha to cross the Red Sea and the Gulf of Aden, my old friend Khaled had been under pressure from Houthi commanders to enlist in their cause. It was the threat of having to participate in an unjust war as much as the hardships and the dangers that he faced in Sanaa that had prompted him to flee. We kept in contact through occasional Facebook messages, and I kept abreast of his progress through the updates that he posted. Having crossed the sea from Yemen to Somalia, he found work in a photographer's studio in Mogadishu. It was a nice city, he wrote. The people were friendly, the climate was comfortable, the Italian architecture was interesting, and the food was, well, not bad, but not what he was used to (the locals enjoyed eating pasta mixed with banana). Then, after Khaled had been living in the Somalian capital for seven months, a colleague of his was shot dead in the street. Khaled suspected the involvement of al-Shabaab, the militant jihadist group. He no longer felt safe. By then he had earned enough money to move on, and he boarded a plane to Sudan.

Sudan was hot, too hot. People could only sleep, rouse themselves to eat, and then sleep again. Khaled rarely saw any chairs: he concluded that if you were not moving then you were lying flat out. Images and updates on social media continued to document his journey. In March 2016 he posted some photographs of the central market in Khartoum. In April there was a picture of his boots and backpack, then some goats and trees. At the end of May someone wrote on his Facebook page asking if anyone had seen or heard from him lately. He hadn't been responding to messages. The last time he had been in contact was a couple of weeks earlier, to say that he was leaving Sudan and intending to journey overland to Libya. Nobody had heard anything since. There were only rumours of people smugglers.

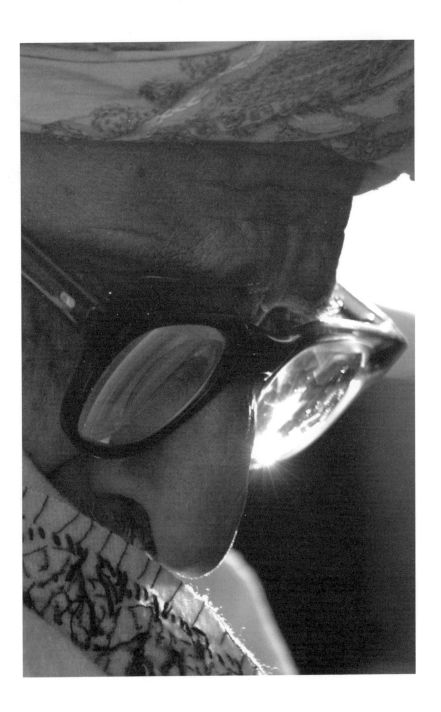

- 10 -

Passports and
Their Uses

- Walter Harris, 1892 -

THE INVITATION HAD COME FROM the British Ambassador. The lion, unicorn, and crown embossed in gold on the stationery had elicited my resentment. To honour the eightieth birthday of Queen Elizabeth a celebration would be held at the ambassador's official residence in Sanaa. Richard's company had been courteously requested. Mine had not.

'I imagine it'll be quite an event,' he said, pouring tea into two mugs, 'and quite a crowd. Government people, company directors, heads of organisations; they all turn out for this sort of thing.' Richard set down the teapot and sat opposite me at his kitchen table. 'They've invited all the British nationals in the city.'

'So why didn't I get one of these?' I waved his invitation card with its royal coat of arms.

'I can't think.' He took a sip of tea. 'Brigitte's got one.'

'She's not even British.'

'Yes, it does seem strange.'

Ordinarily, invitation-only celebrations of the reigning British monarch would have held little interest or appeal for me. But under the circumstances I felt a little left out.

'You did register with the embassy?' Richard asked.

I must have looked a bit blank.

'Well, that might explain things.'

Soon after my arrival in Yemen I had telephoned the British Embassy in order to register my presence in the country. Someone had advised me that I should and, though it seemed a rather unnecessary formality, I was prepared to conform to the convention. The woman who answered the telephone at the embassy informed me that if I wanted to register I would have to appear in person, with my passport, on the other side of town, during the embassy's rather inconvenient opening hours. Was it really necessary, I wondered?

'It's probably a good idea', said the English telephone voice, sounding indifferent.

I pushed for some more tangible reason.

'In case anything should happen.'

The conversation ended and I tried hard to imagine how, in the event of 'anything' happening, any value could derive from my having registered at the British Embassy. In the end I never bothered.

'Well, you can hardly expect the ambassador to invite you to his party if he doesn't know you're in town', Richard pointed out.

British nationals had not always been welcomed with party invitations. And when something of the 'anything' sort occurred to Walter Harris in Sanaa, he found the British government's response to his predicament decidedly unhelpful. Born into a wealthy English family in London, educated at Harrow, and supported by a generous inheritance, Walter Burton Harris had grown up to become a man of independent means and scant responsibilities. Following the fashion of European exoticism, he settled in Tangier. While there he became fluent in Arabic, filed a few stories for *The Times*, and wrote a book recounting his travels in *The Land of an African Sultan*. Harris had been living in Morocco for four years when, at the age of twenty-five, he set off on his journey to Sanaa, intending 'to throw light upon the present condition of the Yemen'. Arriving in the latter part of the nineteenth century, Harris saw Yemen's Ottoman occupiers struggling to control opposition to their 'exorbitant taxation and oppression'. The harder they pressed down, the more resistance arose, and the harder they pressed. 'There is no nation in the world that can put down a rebellion as the Turks can,' wrote Harris, 'but they have a great objection to anyone seeing the process.' Harris planned to bear witness to that process; stealing into Ottoman Yemen and reporting what he found.

So Harris, the affluent young Englishman, arrived in Aden aboard a P&O steamer, but when he crossed from British-occupied Aden into Turkish-occupied Yemen it was upon a camel, in the semblance of an impoverished Greek merchant. 'No Englishman crossed the frontier into Turkish Yemen in January of 1892. No; the only stranger was a penurious Greek shopkeeper of Port Said.' Harris was delighted with his disguise. His personal fortune meant that he really had no need to earn a living from journalism, but he was eager to make a name for himself and he relished an adventure and the retelling of his exploits. A later author would remark that 'Harris loved to tell stories, especially about himself'; observing a tendency to make 'his own part in any yarn he was telling into a hymn to his own cleverness, cunning, bravery, popularity and importance.' After his return from Sanaa, Harris wrote that 'all he can boast to have brought back with him is a story of travel and adventure.' The self-deprecation is rather affected, but his published *A Journey Through the Yemen* sets an undeniably thrilling pace through a dramatic succession of anxious moments and narrow escapes.

Reaching Sanaa in 1892, Harris evidently assumed that he would cast off his Greek storekeeper's outfit and be congratulated on the ingenuity of his deceit. After enjoying a brief 'saunter through the bazaars', he entered 'the residence of his Excellency Ahmad Feizi Pasha, Governor-General of the Yemen'. In 'a handsome room, surrounded by quite a number of his staff', the Turkish pasha reclined upon a divan, drawing on a water pipe. Unfortunately, the Turks understood neither Harris' English, nor his Moroccan Arabic. But undeterred, and having been 'pleasantly received', Harris proudly flourished his passport: a single sheet of paper, valid for a single journey, printed with elaborate script in both English and French, signed by the British Foreign Secretary and emblazoned with the royal coat of arms. Harris himself had been 'dazzled by its splendour'.

His passport was a novelty. The ease of cross-border train travel within Europe and the growth of intercontinental tourism had ushered in an era of generally unrestricted travel for those who could afford it. France abandoned the use of passports altogether in 1861 and several other European countries followed the example. Not until the First World War were authorised travel documents widely reintroduced to control the movements of refugees and spies: a temporary measure, it was presumed at the time. The small number of individuals to whom British passports were issued during the 1890s were usually already known to the Secretary of State for Foreign Affairs. As though conscious that his passport denoted personal connection and class privilege, Harris seems to have believed that it would serve as an irrefutable letter of recommendation and an inviolable assurance of protection. Or perhaps he simply assumed that the splendour of its 'seals and titles and stamps' would dazzle the Ottomans too. The pasha in Sanaa summoned a French-speaking Armenian who would translate the document's content into Turkish.

'Pint of Guinness please, Abdullah.' We had met once before. Born in Saigon, Abdullah embodied a demographic of diminishing probability:

from the tiny Muslim community in Vietnam to the miniscule Vietnamese population in Yemen, and one of only a handful of bar jobs in Sanaa. After the communist takeover of South Vietnam in 1975, a few hundred Vietnamese had been airlifted to Yemen. They were Muslims, possibly descendants of ocean-going Yemeni traders from many centuries before, but more crucially many had compromising connections to the fallen South Vietnamese government or to the American military.

The beer came from a can, but Abdullah served it in a dimpled tankard that he took from the refrigerator. I raised my glass. He smiled and tossed me a packet of salted peanuts. A young Queen Elizabeth watched us from a framed photograph above the bar. This was the Lion and Jambiyah Club, operated by the British Embassy. Abdullah pushed a plastic laminated menu towards me. Lasagnes for carnivores and vegetarians, chickens Kieved and Cordon Bleued, an all-day breakfast and the speciality Club Curry. Guinness was a meal in itself. I passed the menu back to Abdullah. Upon my first visit I had been told that there were three establishments in Sanaa where it was possible to obtain a pint of beer: the Russian Club (with its sticky floors and prostitutes), the newly-opened Movenpick Hotel (spotless, but eye-wateringly over-priced), and the British Club (the acquaintance who had invited me flung out an arm in a sweeping gesture intended to look magnanimous and welcoming, but I thought it a little pompous). Peach-coloured walls were adorned with regimental badges and British Military crests. A corkboard was papered with drawing-pinned notices advertising second-hand vehicles and gym equipment for sale. Muscular men defended a pool table, swigging from beer bottles and swaggering with boozy insouciance (the ambassador's close protection team, a voice had whispered in my ear).

I had vowed never to return. But another acquaintance implored me to make up the numbers in a pub quiz team. Long ago I had also vowed never to attend another a pub quiz. So it was with a twofold sense of failed resolve that I quietly exhibited my ignorance of Popular Entertainers, Sport, and General Knowledge. During a break in the quiz proceedings somebody introduced me to an embassy employee who asked if I was planning to attend the Queen's Birthday celebrations. On hearing that I hadn't been invited she backpedalled swiftly, aloof and suddenly uninterested. The guestlist had been finalised months before. Names could not be added now. Invitations were 'rare as hen's teeth', she informed me, and if I turned up without one I would simply be turned away. Security would be tight. Nearby the men of brawn were still watching over their patch of green felt, pool cues held like bayonets. Childishly, I felt snubbed by the withheld party invitation. Neither the Geography round nor a second pint of Guinness did much to lift my spirits.

The taxi ride had been the most engaging part of the evening. The cab driver dozing behind his wheel at Tahreer Square had rubbed his eyes, fumbled beneath the dashboard for the ignition wires, revved the engine hard into life, and yawned a 'bismillah' before we set off. Shattered windscreens, missing body panels, bumpers tied on with string; there was not a taxi in Sanaa without an affliction. Windows that would not open or would not close, seats that could not be tilted forward from a semi-recumbent angle or shifted backward from thrusting one's knees into the glove compartment; these were mere discomforts. Headlights that did not come on, wing mirrors that had come off, doors that opened unexpectedly, dashboard instruments that never moved, seatbelts that never existed; these were life-threatening conditions. This evening's vehicle suffered from a potentially fatal imbalance of the steering that inclined it to drift toward the oncoming traffic. Fortunately, I was distracted by the driver. Like so many other taxi drivers in the city, he doubled as an impromptu language tutor: a service for which I would happily double his fare. By the time we passed the Taj Sheba Hotel he had woken up and introduced himself as Zayd. At the bottom of Ali Abdul Mogni Street he was bemoaning the traffic and pollution in the city. As the policeman waved us across Zubeiry Street he was telling me about his wife and children who lived sixty miles away while he lived in his cab and sent home his earnings from the capital. 'This used to be the city's airport,' he said as we rumbled along a broad strip of tarmac, veering left then being wrenched right. Petrol prices had gone up, the government had removed fuel subsidies; the conversation seemed to follow the steering, wandering and lurching in trajectories determined by Zayd's desperate sleep-deprivation. He was vehemently denouncing US President George Bush when we turned off the main road onto an unpaved, unlit street, lined by high-walled villas and vacant sentry boxes. We struck a dog with the glare of our headlights then stopped at a roadblock. I gave Zayd a few hundred-riyal notes and he gave me his mobile telephone number, with an invitation to call him whenever I needed a ride. I continued on foot past a group of body-armoured soldiers and a dead cat lying in a pothole. In response to my knocking, a head peered out from a hatch in a metal door. The door would be opened in response to a password that I did not know or the presentation of a passport that I had not brought. So it remained closed. And I remained outside. And I waited in the dark while a member of the quiz team that I did not want to join was found to vouch for me. By which point I had been not having a good time already.

The Armenian translator arrived, the pasha put down his water pipe, and the assembly of Sanaa's Ottoman officials fell silent. Cautiously, the translator conveyed in Turkish the content of the passport that Walter Harris had presented, with all its seals and titles and stamps, its lion, unicorn, and crown. 'Suddenly his Excellency's manner quite changed,' Harris noted with some surprise. After being welcoming and cordial, the pasha 'became very red and irascible'. Awed apparently by his own lustre and the dazzling splendour of his paperwork, Harris had failed to anticipate the embarrassment that he and his document would cause to the Turks in Yemen. With the Englishman's unexpected arrival in Sanaa, the pasha's failure to control the country and secure its borders was being blithely demonstrated in his own salon. Harris was accused of espionage. The pasha, 'scarlet as a tomato', ordered his immediate imprisonment. The reaction was 'explicable', Harris later conceded. 'Nor do I complain very much of it', he wrote. 'Not so, however, with the action of H.M. late Secretary of Foreign Affairs...' An exchange of telegraphic communications ensued between London and the prison cell in Sanaa. 'I was informed, in one of those elegant despatches of the Foreign Office, that I had entered the Yemen on entirely my own responsibility, and must bear the results of my actions myself!' Harris was furious. The Foreign Secretary, according to Harris, 'entirely ignored the fact that my passport, - demanding that I should be allowed to pass without let or hindrance and that I should be afforded every assistance and protection of which I might stand in need in the Ottoman Empire... - bore his own signature!' Harris later wrote to the Foreign Secretary asking 'whether the wording of my passport was of any value... and to this day I have been unable to obtain a reply.' And to this day the wording at the front of a British passport has changed little.

> Her Britannic Majesty's Secretary of State requests and requires in the name of her majesty all those whom it may concern to allow the bearer to pass freely without let or hindrance, and to afford the bearer such assistance and protection as may be necessary.

Harris had mistaken that wording. It is not a demand; it is a request. The *request* for passage 'without let or hindrance' and for 'assistance and protection' is made precisely *because* the secretary of state can neither demand nor guarantee those things when British citizens are abroad in foreign countries; not because the secretary of state will intervene to ensure them. Which might uphold my doubts about the value of registering at the embassy.

Perhaps the Foreign Office would not have objected to Harris' escapade if it had gone undetected. The British government may even have been grateful for whatever intelligence he acquired during his travels in Yemen. But as things stood, Walter Harris was just as embarrassing to the Foreign Secretary in London as he had been to the pasha in Sanaa. The Turks might misconstrue his actions as having been approved by the Foreign Office, and any intervention on his behalf could only substantiate suspicions of state-orchestrated espionage. Besides, he had misused his passport. Here Harris illustrated a further point about passports: they are not an assurance of good character or behaviour (just as a passport does not guarantee the safety and security of the traveller, it does not guarantee the safety and security of the State in which he or she travels). But for bad behaviour they can be revoked or withdrawn. Then as now, a passport remains Crown property; issued to, but not owned by, the bearer.

Though a passport confers no rights, not even the right of ownership, it may permit privileges. So I had carried mine with me one evening in June as Richard drove us toward the residence of the British Ambassador in Sanaa.

'Well, you look the part,' Richard assured me. I had shaved and put on a shirt.

A pair of metal gates rolled back. Security guards crouched to inspect the underside of our vehicle. An attendant waved us toward a parking spot and we stopped alongside a black sedan with two little Pakistani flags flying on its bonnet.

'So far so good.' Richard pulled on the handbrake and flashed me a smile. I was nervous and said nothing. Other people were arriving. They looked smarter and more sophisticated than me, and they all had invitations. These were being checked by a man in a tuxedo. When he extended his palm to receive my gold-embossed card I seized his hand, shook it heartily, and slipped past in what I hoped was a moment of brief confusion: a quick glimpse of my burgundy-coloured passport with its gilded coat of arms and a blur of my Caucasian skin. Along with the other guests, I was then welcomed personally to the Queen's Birthday celebrations by the ambassador, grey-haired and black-tied, with that familiar sweeping arm gesture.

Crowding the ambassador's lawn, wine glasses in hand, crisply attired foreigners chattered while waiters enlisted from the Indian-run Taj Sheba in town slid among them proffering canapés and aperitifs. 'Christ! Real EM Forster stuff isn't it?' Richard remarked before he plodded off toward the buffet of butter chicken, hariyali lamb, and curried vegetables. There was also a seafront-style cabin serving battered fish goujons and chips in paper cones, and a piano quintet playing what I guessed was probably Elgar. There was a twelve-foot-high inflatable clock tower that might have been modelled on Big Ben, or on the Aden clock tower that had been built by the British in 1890 to look like Big Ben. There were clusters of what I took to be representatives of international organisations and development agencies, foreign ambassadors and their spouses, and dour-looking men who probably worked for oil companies. 'So how did you end up here?' They meant in Yemen, not the party, for nobody else knew that I had not been invited. I answered the question a few times, apathetically, before detaching myself. Orbiting, out of place, I began moving with the uniformed waiters, and became acutely aware of the men who glanced about moodily, wires extending from earpieces to their lapels, handguns bulging beneath their dark suits. I didn't really recognise anyone, or anything. This wasn't Yemen, it wasn't Britain, or not the Britain I knew. The clergyman who stood alone on the lawn looked like a throwback to another time and place, with his cream cotton

jacket, dog collar, and slightly lost expression, but, lost and alone, he also
looked like the only authentic presence. Perhaps my discomfort reflected
nothing more than my own social awkwardness, but my brooding was
interrupted by the sombre notes of 'God Save the Queen', followed by the
piano quintet's dystonic performance of Yemen's national anthem. The
ambassador's speech was then ungraciously cut short by a malfunction
of the microphone and soon the party dispersed at a seemly hour amid a
flurry of exchanged business cards. I declined an invitation to continue
on to the Club House. Richard had a more enjoyable evening. It had
reminded him of his Sandhurst days, he told me on the drive home.
And he had heard from an embassy source that the women from the
piano quintet were being taken to a firing range next morning to shoot
Kalashnikovs at rocks.

Walter Harris had enjoyed a good night too. 'What a night it was! One of
those nights in a lifetime which can never be forgotten.' During his journey
to Sanaa, Harris had stopped in Dhamar, four days south of the capital,
and there he had been invited to a celebration. 'The first to come were
half-a-dozen Arab tribesmen, with long wavy black hair and a scarcity of
clothing... strange lithe beautiful creatures.' The tribesmen were followed
by some fat merchants and Hadhrami musicians. Harris found the men-
only event exquisitely gratifying and described the occasion in sensual
terms.

> The cool dim light of the swinging alabaster lamps, the flashing
> spears heaped together in the corners, the wonderful dark crowd
> of swarthy men, the steam of the brewing coffee issuing from
> strange jars, the rich dark carpets and gaudy cushions, the murmur
> and the blue curling smoke of the pipes - ay, a dinner-party in
> Dhamar is worth seeing! And then the soft music and singing of
> the musicians, whose tall beautiful figures moved slowly here and
> there as they played strange melodies!

The night ended with Harris making an unexpected and climactic
contribution to proceedings. 'I brought out my electric machine,' he
wrote, 'and, the guests joining hands, felt, for the first time in their lives, a

shock.' For reasons not otherwise apparent, Harris had brought with him a small, hand-powered electrical generator that he now cranked up, and pleasurably discharged upon his unsuspecting company. 'They smiled, and asked for more.'

Through a haze of Cuban cigar smoke and Havana Club rum, a few weeks later I understood better that it wasn't simply my own awkwardness that had made the Queen's Birthday such a strained experience. Despite having been omitted from the British Ambassador's guestlist, I was inexplicably invited to a party at the Cuban Envoy's residence. 'Have you ever been to Cuba?' Richard asked suspiciously. 'Or met a Cuban recently?' I had not even read *The Motorcycle Diaries*. A DJ mixing mambo and meringue, a dance floor in a basement crowded with Cuban medical staff from Yemen's hospitals, and a few other assorted foreigners like me. I had no idea how I had found myself on this alternative list. The Cuban Ambassador delivered a short welcoming speech, his wife distributed cigars, and their daughter whirled as if electric under the strobe lights. Beneath sober portraits of Presidents Saleh and Castro, an American drank Mexican beer and talked earnestly to me about the importance of resuming normal diplomatic relations between Washington and Havana. Later, a Cuban woman encouraged me to feel the rhythm and use my hips more. I left around midnight, thanking the ambassador and thinking how much more fun the Cubans had.

'As I lay down my pen I conjure up in my mind the desert rides under a myriad of stars; I feel upon my cheek the soft balmy southern breeze... once more, but this time with a smile, I spend five days a prisoner.' An unfettered nostalgia permeates Harris' account of his time in Yemen; from his arrival in Aden (on 'one of those terrible still tropical days, motionless, silent, oppressive', two years after the construction of the Aden clock tower that was later inflated in facsimile on the ambassador's lawn) right up to and including his incarceration in Sanaa. The Turkish governor-general released him from prison after five days on condition that he depart the country immediately. He took a moment to explore, but after visiting a few sites in the city Harris soon opined that 'there is, in fact, but little to tell of the former grandeur of Sanaa.' The romance was almost over. He had longed for fountains to 'splash their crystal waters into the clean air', for the pavements to echo with 'the bells and anklets of dancers', but he found only the 'rough voice and rougher tread of the Turkish Troops'. Turning his aesthetic sensibilities toward the pasha's residence, Harris was disappointed that 'the simple old Arab taste has been changed for decoration of Louis Quatorze'. 'By no means bad of its kind,' he wrote of the pasha's décor, 'but still sadly out of place.' Not out of place in Sanaa, but out of place in Harris' idea of how Sanaa ought to be. Even the 'purely and essentially Yemenite' architecture failed to enthuse him; he found it merely 'impossible to describe... for it is a style that exists nowhere else.' For a style lacking precedent, Harris lacked romanticised preconceptions, and without them his descriptive powers seemed to fail him.

'Of all the sights offered by the city,' he decided, 'the population presents the most interesting.' There were Turkish soldiers, 'ill-fed, ill-clothed... with only one boot perhaps', and portly pashas whose luxurious attire had been 'bought with the money that ought to feed the soldiers'. There were Hejaz merchants, 'slow and stately, with strange glassy eyes that speak of hashish', and there were the Tribesmen 'with bronzed skin and raven-black locks'. It was characteristic of Harris to save his most florid prose for the men whom he encountered or observed upon his travels. 'While the men are often almost divinely handsome, the women are just the contrary, being generally thickly built,' he wrote. His descriptions reveal an obsession. Early in the Yemen Journey his eye had settled upon 'my Arab Apollo'. 'Tall, lithe, and exquisitely built, his skin of dull copper hue showed off the perfect moulding of his limbs... Except for a small loin-cloth of native indigo workmanship, and a small blue turban, almost lost in the spreading masses of raven hair that burst from beneath its folds, he was naked.' For Harris, the desert sands, stars, and warm southern breezes had been the exotic backdrop to an erotic fantasy.

It came as a surprise to some when, five years after the publication of his *Journey Through the Yemen*, Walter Burton Harris married Lady Mary Savile, daughter of the Earl of Mexborough. It came as a surprise to her when, after the ceremony, Harris revealed his predisposition toward the intimate companionship of young boys. And it seemed to come as a surprise to Harris when the bride promptly abandoned the honeymoon and eventually had the marriage annulled on grounds of non-consummation.

Lady Mary never remarried. Harris returned to Morocco, becoming *The Times'* correspondent there and residing in a sumptuous villa on the edge of Tangier along with his Arab houseboys. An ambitious social climber who courted Moroccan royalty and notable colonials alike, while still occasionally infuriating the Foreign Office with his outspokenness, Harris enjoyed the sense of being a man of some importance, or at least reputation, within Tangier's expatriate community. In accounts of his excursions 'in the Near, Middle and Far East', until his death in 1933, he continued to seduce readers with the fantasies of an Englishman abroad.

I had been generally less enamoured than Harris with my status as an expatriate: too conscious that it invoked unearned privileges of colour and country of origin. But it was hard not to collude with those privileges at times, and privileges quickly beget a sense of entitlement. Moreover, escaping the constraints of home and not always needing to conform to local conventions could compound delusions of grandeur. How else but as a privileged expatriate could one receive a gold-embossed invitation to an official celebration of the Queen's Birthday? And how else could one have the boldness to gatecrash the event?

- 11 -

Costume & Class

- Leland Buxton & Aubrey Herbert, 1905 -

ON 2 MARCH 1905, JUST a little after lunch, the Mayor of Cambridge received a telegram. This unexpected communication announced the imminent arrival of the Sultan of Zanzibar. The mayor checked and rechecked his calendar, then flicked through his diary in case he had missed something, but there were no visitors scheduled for that afternoon. Nevertheless, four tall, dark, bearded figures wearing flowing robes and flamboyant turbans soon alighted from the London train. They were accompanied by an interpreter who translated their unintelligible speech. The mayor dispatched his carriage to the railway station, donned his chain of office, and welcomed the sultan and his entourage. Crowds of spectators stopped to applaud the Zanzibar delegation as the mayor accompanied them on a tour of Cambridge. But he regretted not having had time to arrange a more impressive reception for his distinguished guests. Before long the sultan and his retinue made their excuses and departed for the ten-to-eight train back to Liverpool Street, while the Mayor of Cambridge returned to whatever other mayoral duties awaited him. The deception was only revealed afterwards, once the grease paint had been washed off and the exotic outfits had been returned to a London theatrical costumier. The story was widely reported; from the *Taunton Courier* to the *Whitby Gazette*. A group of Cambridge University students, dressed up and blacked-up, had carried off what became known as the Sultan of Zanzibar Hoax. Leland Buxton was one of those spurious African dignitaries in Cambridge. Equal audacity had imbued Buxton's first encounter with Aubrey Herbert a few weeks earlier. In the opening sentence of his account of their journey together through Yemen, Aubrey Herbert recalled the meeting: 'One day, early in 1905, I met Leland Buxton in the Lobby of the House of Commons, and, in ten minutes conversation, we decided that we would try to reach Sanaa.'

Leland Buxton also produced an account of his travels with Aubrey Herbert. It began rather less compellingly: 'The chief disadvantage of a journey to Sanaa lies in the preliminary stay at Hodeidah which it involves.' Even for 'Englishmen equipped with passports,' wrote Buxton, 'at Hodeidah many formalities are necessary, - the candidate's pedigree, social position, and object in the country have all to be investigated.' If the Ottoman administration in Hodeidah *had* investigated, they would have found Leland William Wilberforce Buxton and Aubrey Nigel

Henry Molyneux Herbert to be of exemplary pedigree and enviable social position. The content of their ten-minute introductory exchange in the Lobby of the House of Commons is not recorded, but it must surely have included the preening and fluttering of those markers of breeding and upbringing that, under any other circumstances, would have rendered all travelling papers unnecessary: Eton, Harrow; Balliol, Trinity; the Carnarvon Earldom, the Buxton Baronetcy. And to explain their 'object in the country' to the Mutasarrif of Hodeidah, the pair had devised a strategy of diaphanous camouflage. Herbert, speaking in French, claimed that they were 'rich and noble Englishmen' who wished to visit Sanaa en route to India, where they intended to shoot tigers. 'Et lions,' added Buxton. 'The Mutesarrif, awaking from a dream, said that there were no lions in India.' It was a slight deceit. Much slighter than the Sultan of Zanzibar prank. Lions and tigers aside, the pretence of Herbert and Buxton to be 'rich and noble Englishmen' was not really a masquerade at all. It was a self-evident truth. Wealth and aristocratic underemployment were prerequisites for their venture. No disguise was necessary now for them to play upon the novelty of foreign race and the privilege of social position.

Buxton had just turned twenty-one and Herbert was four years older when the pair reached Yemen via Suez in August 1905. At Hodeidah, after an 'indescribable scrimmage' with the acquisitive customs officials over Herbert's typewriter, they set about soliciting the services of mules, muleteers, a troop escort and 'native servant' for their journey. But they struggled to organise everyone for the hour of their departure. On successive mornings they rose at dawn only to find one or other of the members of their entourage absent. And those who were present were unsatisfactory. The troop escort was 'insufficient and insubordinate'. An Arab servant swiftly garnered their disdain: 'He tasted all Leland's medicines and he wore my underclothes,' Herbert whined.

In all there were seven pairs of underpants. Three shirts. Thirteen socks. Item by item, my clothes had been sorted and counted by the man at the launderette. In the background, another man in a sleeveless vest with glistening biceps and a big moustache was swinging a steam press up and down. Up, and he rearranged the position of a crumpled jacket or a creased trouser leg; down, and with a hissing stamp he disappeared in a gushing vapour cloud. My fourteenth sock was found. Laundry fees were not determined by the volume or weight of washing, but by the category and quantity of clothing items. So each load was itemised before being washed; every garment tallied on a pre-printed carbon-paper inventory. An American acquaintance had once described her embarrassment at a local laundry upon having her most intimate undergarments held aloft and subjected to scrutiny, apparently defying classification. Richard preferred to take his laundry to the upmarket Taj Sheba Hotel where it would be dealt with by a Filipino maid. The laundry man disentangled a pair of my winter long johns. He paused thoughtfully before biroing a tick in the box marked 'trowssers'. Steam mushroomed up to the ceiling and the figure in the vest reappeared, muscles working like oiled pistons, moisture droplets glimmering on his whiskers before he disappeared again. When all my clothing had been counted, the laundry owner scrawled a phonetic Arabic spelling of my name at the top of the completed checklist, tore off the top copy and handed it to me, suggesting that I return in a day or two. The list intrigued me. The forty clothing items named in both Arabic and Latin script included four different types of headscarf. There were also Mokeets, F Blades, Walsteoats, Ksshwans, and Beloweets, none of which were ever ticked on my inventory, their mysteries remaining undisclosed, their names revealing only the lingering fascination of a foreign wardrobe.

Arab costume had long enthralled visitors and dressing à *l'arabe* was once an essential part of the Arabian travel experience. Herbert and Buxton might have been a little disappointed. Travelling as rich and noble Englishmen meant that they wore relatively unexciting tropical khakis and pith helmets. The only enthralling parts of their outfits were the underclothes that had captured the attention of their Arab attendant. Disguise was occasionally necessary, as when Walter Harris crossed the frontier dressed as a penurious Greek shopkeeper, but more often Arab garb was adopted for the sheer frisson of dressing up and living out an alter ego. And despite the apparent subversion of status, these altered guises only served to uphold established assumptions about race and social superiority. After all, an upper class Englishman might pass as an Arab, a Greek shopkeeper, or a Zanzibari sultan, but the reverse was presumed to be impossible. Implicit were ideas about who had the power to deceive and who was susceptible to deception.

Within Sanaa, society had its own engrained stratifications too, with social classes determined by descent, defined by occupations, and distinguished by their attire. Turban style and the tilt of a *jambiyah* could reveal a man's station. The Sayyids were a literate elite who claimed descent from the Prophet; they wore white muslin over their pill box hats, bore their ornate curved daggers at a slight angle on the hip, and, rather like the aristocracy to which Herbert and Buxton belonged, they were entitled to exclusive positions in administration and the judiciary that ensured their privileges were maintained. Below them were the blacksmiths and blade-polishers, tinsmiths and silversmiths, stonemasons and bricklayers; all these asserted tribal ancestry and were attired with indigo turbans and blades in sheaths shaped like fish hooks. At the bottom of this caste hierarchy were the Akhdam; forbidden to carry arms, to own property, or to enter most professions, they lived in slums, undertook menial tasks, and were systematically marginalised. Above the 'untouchable' Akhdam, but beneath the blacksmiths, was another social group. Without ancestry of note, they carried only small knives and performed tasks of dependent service. They were cobblers, tanners, butchers, barbers, and, latterly, laundry operators.

For a while I thought myself outside any such social layering, but there were different classes of foreigner in Sanaa too. The Indians and Filipinos who worked in the city's service sector were referred to as 'migrant workers' and often held in low regard. Those of us given the more prestigious appellation of 'expatriates' were simply wealthier, mostly white, and we usually held passports from Europe or North America. Though my skin colour already marked me out as a privileged foreigner, my status was affirmed by my clothes, specifically by the fact that it was not me who was washing them. In my expeditions to the launderette, to ATMs and moneychangers, and in my purchases at the shops, I not only defined my status, but I came to define my self. These, after all, were the routines and rituals by which my existence in Sanaa was paced out.

Every couple of days I would visit Abdul's hole-in-the-wall store. Bold red capital letters paint-brushed onto the metal shutters proclaimed that this was a 'SOBERMARKET'. Abdul stood behind a door-width countertop, in front of shelves stacked with all manner of household provisions. When Walter Harris visited Sanaa thirteen years before Herbert and Buxton he had found shops stocked with 'every imaginable article', 'from tins of sardines and inferior Turkish cigarettes to photograph frames and musty chocolate creams.' Abdul's Sobermarket continued in that tradition. Mostly Abdul and I met to exchange two small jerry cans: my empties swopped for his that had been refilled at one of the city's water purification plants; a more environmentally sound practice than buying and selling drinking water in endless plastic bottles. But had I needed any other item I could have named it and Abdul would have rummaged in a dark recess before presenting it to me. There were two exceptions. The first was obviously alcohol; obvious even without Abdul's punning shop title (which may have been unintentional). The second was toilet paper, for which I had to visit the Al-Huda upmarket supermarket on Zubeiry Street. But sugar-filled soft drinks, single-use shampoo sachets, individual cigarettes or whole packets, powdered milk, paper tissues, tins of tuna, toilet cleaner: all these were available at Abdul's, along with cans of Al-Momtaz condensed milk, boxes of Abu Walad Sandwich Biscuits, and bottles of Abaya shampoo that promised to 'keep your abaya black'. Despite being unfamiliar, these Yemeni processed foods and domestic goods managed to elicit a remarkable nostalgia thanks to the historical authenticity of their decades-old packaging designs. The grinning Abu Walad biscuit boy had a mullet haircut. The Al-Momtaz lady, clutching a steel milk churn to her bosom, was wearing a dress with shoulder pads. Most remarkable was the woman on the cans of fenugreek-flavoured Green Girl Ghee, produced by the Yemen Company for Ghee & Soap Industry. She was depicted with her hair uncovered, wearing a black and white striped pinafore over a gingham blouse, stirring the contents of a frying pan over a stovetop that was all silver knobs and coiled black heating elements. Even the lime green background perfectly recalled the chipboard veneer kitchen units from my childhood years ago and miles away.

'I went to the East by accident,' recalled Aubrey Herbert, 'as a young man may go to a party, and find his fate there.' It is hard to believe. If there was a party, Aubrey Herbert was sure to have gone by invitation, certainly not by gatecrashing and probably not by accident. Nor did he find his fate by accident either; it had been bestowed upon him at birth. Herbert was born into the English nobility, but blighted by congenital eye disease. The former benefit went a long way toward enabling him to overcome the latter disadvantage. By the time of his trip to Yemen, the family connections of 25-year-old Herbert had already got him a job as an honorary attaché; first in Japan, then Constantinople. His going East was not by accident. Before that Herbert had been at Oxford, where his near-blindness might have impeded his studies had his wealth not permitted him to employ a personal secretary and dictate his exam papers to a newspaper reporter. Accidents of fate would not be permitted to determine his future. Abysmal eyesight did not prevent him gaining a first class degree in Modern History, as well as a reputation for scaling Oxford's dreaming spires (though it may have contributed to him falling through a roof on the High Street and then being apprehended at gunpoint by the startled manager of the bank into which he had tumbled). Nor did being partially sighted impede the trajectory of his later political career: Herbert became a Conservative MP in November 1911. And it did not hinder his travels: he visited the Balkans on several occasions and was twice approached to take the throne of Albania. And his visual impairment did not prevent Herbert from serving in the First World War. He circumvented the regulation fitness tests by paying a military tailor to cut an officer's uniform for him and when the Irish Guards marched out of Wellington Barracks to board a troop ship bound for Belgium, Herbert was waiting on the pavement and simply fell in alongside them. But he took a bullet in the guts only a fortnight later during the retreat from Mons, where even the entrenched class distinctions of the British military afforded inadequate protection. After the war, when a retinal detachment necessitated the removal of his better eye, Herbert was rendered blind. His friend TE Lawrence (of Arabia) wrote a letter to him suggesting he 'retire to a solitary place', then write and rewrite his memoirs. Aubrey went to Portofino, where his family owned a house, and there, 'tranquilly and nostalgically', he 'listened to his diaries as they were read to him' and he dictated his book of travels, including the account of his Yemen journey.

'A letter?' I thought I had misheard.

'Yes,' said the bank teller, curtly. She slid a sheet of blank notepaper toward me.

'Can I borrow a pen?' A pen followed.

Seeking to open an account at the International Bank of Yemen I was asked to provide evidence of my identity and my employment, and then told to write a letter to the manager of the bank. I had wandered away, pondering this, only to return to the bank teller.

'What should I say in the letter?'

'Ask him if you can open an account.' Of course.

In the lofty banking hall scrums had jostled in front of the cashiers and a Kalashnikov-equipped security guard watched a man stuffing piles of Yemeni notes into a sports bag. On the opposite side of the bulletproof glass was a dreary-looking world of grey filing cabinets, beige computer terminals, and matching shirts.

'Does the manager have a name?'

'Yes.'

'So, um, what is it?'

'Just call him the Bank Manager.'

Elbowing some space at a desk among the men filling out cash withdrawal slips, I began my correspondence.

'Dear Mr Bank Manager...' I wrote, feeling rather facetious.

The bank manager's spindly limbs splayed from a fat leather armchair. He glanced up to murmur a greeting. Brought through to a back room, I introduced myself and handed over the letter that I had hastily written. Sweeping a pile of *qat* stalks from his desk, the bank manager placed the missive in front of him and sat contemplating it. In the long, discomforting silence that followed I became convinced that my application would be declined. Nervously I began to babble, describing my employment in Yemen, how long I would be remaining in the country, and offering assurances as to my credit rating.

'He doesn't speak any English.' I was interrupted by the bank teller whose pen I had borrowed.

'Does he read English?'

'No.'

A signature swept across the bottom of my incomprehensible supplication, a purple-inked stamp banged down on the sheets of accompanying paperwork, and I was waved away. My application had been approved. And after depositing a lump sum and collecting my debit card the next day, I was able to withdraw US hundred-dollar bills from either of the capital's two ATMs.

In the summer of 1923 Aubrey Herbert was back in Oxford. Returned from the family home in Italy, his autobiography was almost complete, but his loss of vision was tormenting him. At a Balliol College dinner an old tutor advised that having his teeth taken out would restore his sight. Herbert's assent to this implausible suggestion seems startling, but more orthodox medical practices had little to offer. His doctor had thought him in rude health ('said I had the complexion and the morals of a debutante'), cautioning only and bizarrely that he 'must not eat curry before breakfast'. The extraction of several molars was a last resort. And a last act. Following the procedure Aubrey Herbert developed septicaemia and died at the age of forty-three.

'I am greatly saddened this week by Aubrey Herbert's death,' wrote John Buchan in September 1923. The author of *The Thirty-Nine Steps* thought Herbert 'the most delightful and brilliant survivor from the days of chivalry'. According to Buchan, Herbert had 'the most insane gallantry that I have ever known - a sort of survivor from crusading times. I drew Sandy from Greenmantle from him.' Sandy Arbuthnot, fictional polyglot and master of disguise, had been introduced to readers in chapter two of Buchan's *Greenmantle*:

> He rode through Yemen, which no white man ever did before. The Arabs let him pass, for they thought him stark mad and argued that the hand of Allah was heavy enough on him without their efforts.

Herbert's premature death became the stuff of legend, for he was half-brother to the 5th Earl of Carnarvon, famed for financing the excavation of Tutankhamen's tomb. When Herbert died six months after Carnarvon, and within a year of the Pharaoh's tomb being opened, it appeared to substantiate rumours of Tutankhamen's curse. Commemorated in Buchan's fiction and in Pharaoh myth, Herbert was also remembered in the posthumous homages of his grandchildren; offspring from the marriage of his daughter to the author Evelyn Waugh. Auberon Waugh penned Herbert's entry in the *Dictionary of National Biography* and Margaret Fitzherbert (*née* Waugh) wrote a 250-page biography of her maternal grandfather. Today, his stone effigy lies in a small Devon church, reposed, like a medieval knight, to paraphrase John Buchan.

After withdrawing money from the ATM, my necessary next step would be to Tahreer Square and 'Al-Dooby for exchange'. The moneychanger's walls were papered with used notes from distant times and places; Estonian Kroon, Chinese Renminbi, Greek Drachma, Peruvian Sol, a Rhodesian dollar, and Metical from Mozambique. A Sanaani tune would be jangling from a transistor radio, a puff of cigarette smoke would rise, and a smirk would creep across Mr Al-Dooby's face as I placed my hundred-dollar bill upon the Formica counter-top. He would reach behind him for a brick of thousand-riyal notes, then scuffle about in a drawer for a tuft of fifties and hundreds. Tatty and torn, the lower denominations looked even older than his wallpaper. But the Riyal only became Yemen's legal currency in 1962. It had replaced the Maria Theresa Thaler. For more than two centuries the silver Thalers, named after the Habsburg empress, had been the preferred coinage of Arabia and North Africa. Carsten Niebuhr reported seeing hoards in Sanaa in 1763, accrued from the coffee trade at Mocha. Following Maria Theresa's death in 1780 the coins continued to be produced using the original dies, with the date stamp unchanged in order to ensure their acceptance abroad. The 1867 expedition to rescue Henry Stern in Ethiopia had taken 5 million newly minted Thalers. The Maria Theresa Thaler was a trusted, standardised unit of bullion. Minted in Austria, the coin's silver content was strictly defined and stringently controlled. Its inscribed edge discouraged clipping and forgery was prevented by the intricacy of its design, which on one side featured a generously busted profile of the empress - said to have added to the coin's appeal. In 1905, Aubrey Herbert's companion Leland Buxton observed the charm of children in Sanaa wearing headdresses adorned with 'Maria Theresa dollars'. But he resented having to use the Thalers. 'Carrying a quantity of huge silver coins,' he wrote, was 'one of the chief inconveniences of travelling in the

Yemen.'

Buxton had already noted 'the chief disadvantage' of a 'preliminary stay at Hodeidah'. Eventually though, with the assent of Hodeidah's mutasarrif and an escort of one hundred and fifty Turkish troops, Herbert and Buxton had departed from the coast and headed for Sanaa. In 1922, distanced from events by a decade and a half, by the First World War and the loss of his eyesight, Herbert, infused with tranquil nostalgia on the Italian coast, recalled the appeal of Yemen's capital. Ancient 'mystery' and 'glory' were the city's allure, along with the fact that 'at that date hardly any Englishmen had been to Sanaa.' His travelling companion Buxton had written a more prosaic account immediately after their return from Yemen. His rather plodding 'A Journey to Sanaa' imparted 'advice to those who wish to visit' and was published in *Blackwood's Magazine* in 1906. 'Go to the Yemen,' Buxton had told his readers. 'But,' he conceded, 'this advice applies to those alone who wish to travel in moderate comfort only.' At his lavishly appointed family home in Portofino, Herbert was less restrained in his recounting of the moderate comforts that awaited travellers in Yemen: he and Buxton had spent the first night of their journey in a 'reeking hole' and the next in 'a foetid room that smelt like leprosy'. On the coast their sleep had been prevented by 'the heat and the flies', in the highlands by the 'piercing cold' and fleas.

Dictating his account, just as he had dictated his Oxford essays and exam papers, Herbert apparently had no compunction about plagiarising images or metaphors from his travelling companion's earlier account, or even repeating whole sections of Buxton's 'Journey' more or less verbatim. Presumably, when Herbert listened to his diaries being read to him in Italy, Buxton's published work was read to him too, and he lifted from it freely. So both narratives describe, in almost identical phrases, how travelling by night, 'sleep came so close' that passing Arabs seemed but shadows, or figments of a dream. And how the 'almost insufferably brilliant' moonlight brought to mind the Israelites 'being led by a column of fire'. By the time of their arrival in Sanaa, the two accounts are virtually indistinguishable.

Or if not plagiarism, perhaps it was simply a shared perspective. The two young aristocrats after all shared similar upbringings and educations, at exclusive boarding schools and then at Oxbridge. That uniformity of background reflected the norms of England's upper classes. And the uniform social class of visitors to Sanaa around this time reflected norms of travel and of travel writing. Less privileged visitors might have told a different story, might have seen and represented Yemen differently, but among these elite English visitors there is a constancy and partiality of outlook as they tell us what Yemen was like and what should be done about it. Both Buxton and Herbert thought that Yemen would be much improved by a railway to the capital. Aubrey Herbert, by now a Tory MP, specified that the railway should be British and was 'looking forward to the day' when the country was controlled by Britain. There is a certain sort of traveller for whom the chief function of travel is to demonstrate how much better things are at home: a dangerous trait when combined with imperial ambitions.

In Yemen, in 1905, the new Imam Yahya had been incensed by foreign empire building. He was infuriated by the Anglo-Ottoman Boundary Commission and the demarcation of a frontier between British- and Turkish-controlled parts of the country: as if the land was theirs to divide! A prolonged drought that year, coupled with the widespread belief that corrupt Turkish officials were responsible for the ensuing food shortages, prompted the imam to rally Yemen's tribes and conquer the capital. The Turks landed thousands of fresh troops, laid siege to Sanaa, and before long the starving citizens had once more surrendered to Ottoman rule. Buxton and Herbert arrived in Sanaa soon after these events and were appalled by what they found. The pair saw 'a grey and tragic town, with the savage memories of famine written upon it'.

No matter how much they wished to admire Sanaa's scenic charms, the suffering that surrounded them frustrated any such naïve pleasures. 'It is a town of quaint streets and very picturesque corners,' wrote Buxton, but those streets were 'too often guarded by the corpse of some dead mule.' The vultures were 'full-fed and lazy and the dogs have all been eaten during the siege.' Herbert recalled 'a silent city', except for the calling of the muezzins and the cawing of the carrion crows. Sanaa's population had fallen from 70,000 'to a meagre twenty thousand all told'. In the city's Jewish quarter, 'like the dream of some haunted painter,' Buxton thought, 'the men are still skin and bone'; there were 'cavernous cheeks', 'begging eyes and clutching hands'. 'When we appeared and inconsiderately gave some small charity,' Buxton went on, 'a crowd followed us greater than ever the Pied Piper drew after him, keening and protesting their need for our money, and truly, for upon almost all there are still the signs of starvation.' Sixteen years later, the words and memories were echoed with precision by Herbert: 'a crowd followed us greater than ever the Pied Piper drew after him, asking piteously for alms... Their need could not be exaggerated; famine stared at us.'

Herbert and Buxton arrived in Sanaa just months after the siege of the city had ended, and mere months too since the Sultan of Zanzibar Hoax and the pair's snappy meeting in the House of Commons. For the two rich and noble Englishmen, both of whom had been born with silver spoons and had thoughtlessly bemoaned the inconvenience of carrying silver coins in Yemen, their arrival in the impoverished and famine-stricken city has the mood of an elaborate jape turned sour.

One hundred years later, such widespread starvation seemed a thing of the past, yet poverty persisted. Each afternoon an aged man sat on a step near my home, cradling in his lap a forearm scarred by old injuries. The other arm was poised not quite upright, the hand not quite clenched, not quite extended, as though grasping at something not yet there, or still clasping something that had been taken from him. He held this absence up to eyes that could not see it. The desperate life of the blind beggar in Sanaa contrasted starkly and sadly with that of the visually impaired Aubrey Herbert a century earlier. A thin warbling tone would escape his lips and he would continue singing, sightless eyes continuing to roll in his fleshless face, as the bony fingers closed tightly around the few of Mr Al-Dooby's notes pressed into his palm.

Before the war broke out in March 2015, Yemen was importing around ninety per cent of its food. Most of those imports came through the port at Hodeidah. After the Saudi-led coalition bombed the docks and instituted a naval blockade, the imports diminished suddenly. Some humanitarian supplies still arrived, but these were mostly seized by the Houthi army. For the people, food prices rose sharply. And when the exiled government seized control of the Central Bank, salary payments were terminated and a crisis of liquid currency ensued. People could no longer afford to buy what little food was available.

When the head of the UN's Office for Humanitarian Affairs visited Sanaa in 2016, what he saw was nothing like what I remembered. It felt more akin to what Buxton and Herbert had witnessed one hundred years before. 'I saw the desperation, fear, and resignation in the deep-sunken eyes of people I met who have lost all hope,' the official reported to the UN Security Council. He said that Yemen was facing a 'man-made brutal humanitarian disaster'. The country was 'one step away from famine'.

These days, famine is defined according to specific criteria. For a famine to be called a famine, a minimum mortality rate must be reached, along with a minimum prevalence of childhood malnutrition. By definition then, once a famine is called a famine, it is in many ways too late. Too late to undo that mortality. And too late to avoid the lifelong consequences of malnutrition for the children who survive it. They will suffer impaired cognitive development, an increased incidence of disease, and for those stunted girls who reach adulthood there will be a greater risk of complications during childbirth. All of which will cause the effects of a famine to be felt long after the food shortages have been resolved. To call Yemen 'one step away from famine', or, in the words of Oxfam and the World Food Programme, 'on the brink' of famine, was to highlight the seriousness of the situation before those morbid criteria were met. But really, in the twenty-first century, criteria for famines should be redundant. There should be no famines to define. Food shortages are preventable. Famines could be a thing of the past. If they occur it is as a consequence of human decisions and human actions or inactions. In the case of Yemen, the humanitarian disaster was indeed brutally man-made by the bombing of the port and the shipping blockade. As one commentator remarked, people were not starving, they were being starved.

By this time, in the autumn of 2016, several months had passed since there had been any news from Khaled. His social media posts had dried up. The last I heard he was in Sudan, having journeyed from Yemen and Somalia. He had been planning on entering Libya and crossing the Sahara. It was only much later that I learnt what had happened. How he had paid two hundred dollars to a people smuggler to take him across the Libyan Desert. How there had been no food on the journey, save for a few handfuls of rice. How there had been no drinking water, save for the few grimy wells and pools that they passed in the desert. And how, as he crossed the border into Libya, he was told that there would be no going back. And as he climbed aboard a truck for the two-week journey across the inhospitable landscape, he was also told that if he fell out, the truck would not stop. He held on tight, knees up to his chest, crammed in among the dozens of other refugees, the cramps in his legs worsened by dehydration. Even after the truck ride was over Khaled remained uncomfortable in Libya. Other Yemenis there were mostly associated with al-Qaeda, so people suspected that he was a member of the terror group too. Such suspicions were difficult to allay, al-Qaeda connections were almost impossible to disprove, and a presumption of guilt was a threat to life and freedom. A Yemeni friend wrongly accused of terrorist links had spent five months in a Libyan jail. And American drones were said to be hunting down al-Qaeda suspects in the region. As a Yemeni in Libya, Khaled was not safe.

In Yemen it was his African heritage that had often been a burden. Khaled had been born to a Yemeni father and an Eritrean mother. His skin was just a fraction darker, his curls a fraction tighter than other natives of Sanaa. It mattered. For in addition to the rigid and seemingly inviolable class distinctions that benefited some and brought suffering to others, there were racial discriminations in Sanaa. 'Muwalad' was the label applied to a child who had a non-Arab parent. The term implied a lack of purity and it was used disparagingly. Moreover, Muwaladeen were commonly discriminated against by officials and in law. Even within this racial prejudice there were degrees of disfavour. A Muwalad with a parent from Europe or Asia was treated better that one with a parent from Africa. In Yemen Khaled had been the African, in Africa he would be the Yemeni. Neither status was tolerable, but in North Africa he was in real danger. And he was still on the move. Determined to get out of Libya as quickly as he was able, Khaled made his way to the coast, intending to reach another continent, one unknown to him and still out of sight, across the sea.

- 12 -

Heroism

- Arthur Wavell, 1911 -

'IT IS NOT BY ANY** means impossible to poison a boiled egg,' thought Arthur Wavell. 'But,' he reasoned, 'to do it properly requires more ingenuity than the ordinary Turkish policeman possesses.' January 1911. Sanaa was again under siege. This time it was the Turks who remained trapped within the city walls. Arab tribesmen, led once again by Imam Yahya, had attacked from the north and the Ottoman-occupied city was entirely encircled. Arthur Wavell was on the inside. The Arabs in Sanaa were suspicious of Wavell's presence. The Turks were certain he was a spy. Wavell did not trust the Turkish policeman who had been assigned to stand guard in his kitchen, and so he took the precaution of eating only hard-boiled eggs.

You and I would have fared much better. And after lunch we would have emerged, satiated, from the dark cavern of the *salta* shop into the white heat of the afternoon. The rest of the city would have retreated inside. Window shutters, flung open to the breeze, would have dripped their shadows down sun-bleached walls. A woman stepping quickly into the street would have become briefly incandescent, before extinguishing herself in the black lacuna of an open doorway. A couple of boys would have ambled past, defying the sun, wearing wide brims made from cardboard sheets with head-sized holes cut out. And we would have walked on swiftly, hurrying toward the *suq*, and the merciful patchwork of shade sewn by its overhanging awnings.

On just such a roasting afternoon in 1910, shortly after lunch on Christmas Eve, Arthur Wavell had been witnessed strolling through Hodeidah toward the town's baked clay tennis court. Conspicuously, he was 'wearing canvas shoes and carrying a racket', and he stopped to tell everyone he met how unwell he had been. Yet still, despite the heat, and despite his reported ill health, Wavell played tennis all afternoon.

In Hodeidah Wavell had been warned not to visit Sanaa. He was told the Turks would turn him back if he tried. So he was simply assumed to have over-exerted himself on the tennis court when he was confined to bed on Christmas Day. And Boxing Day. And the day after that. Until he turned up in Sanaa.

'Expeditions, like wars, depend for their success on careful preparation beforehand,' Wavell observed, 'on taking the right things and on employing the right persons.' He employed a servant named Ahmad and, intending his travels to be 'of great scientific value', he took an impressive array of empirical instruments and navigational equipment with him to Yemen. A sextant, barometer, and prismatic compass; two types of thermometer, two pairs of binoculars, two lanterns (electric and paraffin), two volumes of the Royal Geographical Society's *Hints to Travellers*, and three watches. Also, 'a Kodak camera with ten dozen films', 'a small case of drawing instruments' and a military sketching board designed to be used on horseback, as well as relevant sections of *The Nautical Almanac*, and a 'complete medical and surgical outfit'. All this was stuffed into 'a fair-sized tin box', along with a chain mail shirt, which, Wavell admitted, 'next time will be left at home'. In the event it was all left behind when, under cover of darkness, and with the cover story of being bedbound after his illness and over-exertion on the tennis court, Wavell and his servant slipped away from Hodeidah in the early hours of Christmas morning. They were headed for Sanaa, and they took with them 'no luggage except a few clothes and a revolver apiece'.

Weaponry and military references weigh heavily in Wavell's account. Far heavier than his purported scientific intent and the weight of surveying equipment stowed in his tin box might lead us to expect, but no heavier than his background would dictate. Arthur John Byng Wavell was the son of Colonel Arthur Wavell. He was nephew to Major-General Archibald Wavell. And, passing through Winchester and then Sandhurst, he was closely followed by his younger cousin Archie (later Field Marshal) Wavell. After officer training, the young Arthur Wavell fought the Boers with the British Army, then mapped Tongaland, Zululand, Bechuanaland, and other British annexations for the War Office, before resigning his commission to buy a sisal plantation and go big game hunting in the East African Protectorate. In Mombasa he developed an interest in Islam, learnt a little Arabic, and planned the journeys in disguise that would take him first to Mecca and later, at the age of twenty-eight, to Yemen.

Like Aubrey Herbert and Leland Buxton, and Walter Harris before them, Arthur Wavell's travels and travel writing were made possible by the luxury of his affluent underemployment. Unlike Herbert and Buxton and Harris, for whom Sanaa had been a final destination, for Wavell it would be just the beginning. His intention had been to 'live for some time in Sanaa before attempting to go farther'. In his travel account, published in 1912 as *A Modern Pilgrim in Mecca and a Siege in Sanaa*, he described how he had envisaged a 'highly perilous' and 'adventurous feat'. From Sanaa, he would 'penetrate if possible' into Arabia's Empty Quarter - a region 'assumed to be an impenetrable wilderness'. He would penetrate the impenetrable.

Wavell's journey to Mecca and the title chosen for his book were surely inspired by Richard Francis Burton's famed *Pilgrimage to Mecca and Medina*, published in three volumes between 1855 and 1856. Yet his travel plans for Yemen and his choice of terminology reveal the influence of David Hogarth's 1904 *The Penetration of Arabia*. Wavell acknowledged his indebtedness to Hogarth in his book's preface. Hogarth, an archaeologist and later keeper of Oxford's Ashmolean Museum, had written of Yemen that there were 'gaps' in Western knowledge 'for future adventurers to fill'. Here was Wavell's calling.

Years later, with the outbreak of the First World War, Hogarth was recruited to Naval Intelligence. And when he was called upon to compile the Arab Bureau's *Handbook of Yemen*, his influence upon Wavell was reciprocated: in the 1917 British military handbook to Yemen Hogarth duplicated whole sections of Wavell's account of his journey to Sanaa. Among the knowledge gaps that Wavell had apparently filled, and that David Hogarth evidently thought would be valuable to British servicemen in Arabia, was Wavell's description of the Yemeni *jambiyah*:

> a short dagger with a broad curved blade which fits into a U-shaped sheath worn at the waist under the sash. The handle is generally of horn ornamented with silver, and the whole, including the blade, is made locally. No person of the male sex, over three years of age, likes to be seen abroad without his jambeia: it is considered most effeminate. It is amusing to see quite small children, half naked, wearing these formidable knives. The Arabs are very expert in their use. They hold them point downwards and curve inwards, not in the Italian manner, and in attacking aim for the supra-sternal knotch - a blow which, rightly placed, splits open the whole chest-wall, and is instantly fatal.

Somewhere close to the centre of the *suq*, in a cool, dark, cigarette-smoky antique shop, Waleed would have affirmed to us the truth that the *jambiyah* had a symbolic role far greater than the lethal one ascribed to it by Arthur Wavell and then repeated by David Hogarth in his military handbook.

'You used to be able to read a man from his *jambiyah*: where he was from, his tribe, and his profession.'

These ornamental daggers, worn in ostentatious sheaths tucked into ornate waist belts, were once part of Yemen's class-based dress code. 'Now it's different, all sorts of people wear all sorts of blades. They just wear whatever they fancy. Whatever they can afford. Now a man's *jambiyah* only tells you how rich he is.'

That still made them a symbol of status of a sort though. And drawing the blade was a symbol too; one powerful and quite sufficient to avoid anyone having to have their chest wall fatally split open with a single blow. A handful of times I saw a *jambiyah* drawn in anger, once in fear, and none of these occasions resulted in bloodshed.

'Ten thousand dollars.' Only an exceptionally rich man could afford the dagger that would have lain heavily in your palm. Calmly, Waleed would have justified the exorbitant sum. 'There's a lot of silver on that scabbard.' He would have drawn deeply on his cigarette while your gaze returned to the curved leather sheath and its grey metal adornment. 'And it's pure... Very pure...' Exhaling. 'And, of course, the workmanship...' Waleed's voice would have drifted, languid as the ribbons of smoke, while your fingertips explored the fine veins of filigree that tangled and entwined before unravelling and bursting in effortless flourishes.

Around us, relics salvaged from the desert sands would slowly have been burying themselves again beneath layers of Sanaa's dust. A German Luger pistol, a Swiss watch with Indian numerals, a few tarnished Turkish medals, and a cache of Maria Theresa Thalers all lay just about discernible in plate glass display cases. Necklaces of black pearl, lapis, and agate would have overflowed in dribbling lengths from brimming wooden drawers, while chains hung up on the wall dripped heavily with great globes of amber. Offering respite from the mid-day temperatures, the dim interior of Waleed's antique shop was an air-conditioned oasis, and the shop was a genuine trove. To visit was to become lost among beautiful objects and fascinating artefacts while Waleed, chain-smoking, exhibited his polished salesmanship or took the opportunity to complain about the unavailability of gemstones and the poor quality of pink coral from China.

'That scabbard,' Waleed would have pointed with his smouldering cigarette tip, 'was worked by one of the most famous silversmiths in Sanaa,' before tapping at an ashtray. 'Perhaps eighty or ninety years ago... But it's not the age.' He would have purred again emphatically. 'It's the workmanship... Work like that hasn't been done for decades. It will never be done again. Not in Sanaa.' He had the salesman's talent for coaxing your next question and containing within his answer the kernel of your next enquiry. 'There's just not the silver available. And the craft has died. When the Jews left Sanaa they took their skills with them. There were no Arab apprentices. Nobody in the *suq* today can work anywhere close to that standard. And of course it's illegal to use rhino horn these days.' You would have scrutinised the cornaceous hilt. 'Now the handles are made out of cow horn or bone. But before, it was rhinoceros horn from Africa. Kenya mostly.' The East African Protectorate. Big game hunting. 'A rhino horn dagger handle dipped in milk and placed upon a snake bite will heal the wound and cure the victim, so they used to say...' Waleed's voice would have trailed once more. Not just a lethal weapon, nor even simply a symbol of status, the *jambiyah* was an object of enchantment.

Wavell gave little credence to 'knavery of this sort'. Despite his distrust of the Turks and his cautious diet of boiled eggs, he was dismissive of a rumoured plot to assassinate him. He rented a house in Sanaa and engaged the services of an Abyssinian cook and a Yemeni housekeeper, noting that 'both these men had been in the service of Burchardt'. 'A careful and scientific traveller', according to Wavell, Hermann Burchardt had been well known for his photography and ethnography. Less well known at the time was his habit of sending detailed political reports from his travels back to Berlin. Burchardt was on his way to Sanaa, just one year before Wavell's own arrival, when he fell 'victim to an ambuscade of brigands'; murdered in a wadi as he approached the capital. Wavell seemed unperturbed by whispered hints that his housekeeper 'had a hand in the business.' Instead he busied himself with buying carpets and cushions for his new home, along with curtains and a comfortable mattress. 'Furnishing in Arab style is not a very formidable business,' he thought. 'A few small tables for ash-trays, coffee cups, and so on.' Arab décor, like Arab dress, was not difficult for a European. Wavell 'made no special arrangements' with regard to outfit. 'The traveller will perforce adopt the local costume,' he stated nonchalantly, and his book contained a photograph of the author having done just that.

'I have never been so bored in my life as I was during February and March 1911.' A fortnight after Wavell arrived in Sanaa at the end of December, road access to the city was blocked and the telegraph wire was severed by the rebellious tribesmen. The only things now moving in or out of the capital were a few stuttering messages flashed by heliograph. As the siege continued into a third month the effect was stultifying. The tin box containing Wavell's thermometers, barometers, and binoculars, as well as his Kodak camera and his copy of the Royal Geographical Society's *Hints to Travellers*, had not arrived from the coast. An Italian merchant provided a few back issues of a French news weekly, but there was little else to read. 'No chessmen were procurable', but Wavell found some cards and taught his servant to play poker. Shots were intermittently exchanged in a 'desultory manner' between the besieged Turks and the Yemeni tribesmen loyal to Imam Yahya. Meanwhile, behind the city walls, Wavell was confined to his rented apartment with its sundry Arab furnishings, its resident Turkish policeman, and its apparently uninterrupted supply of boiled eggs.

When Waleed locked and shuttered his antique shop for the afternoon, the gold dealers and silversmiths nearby would already have abandoned their workshops. Spice traders would have thrown tarps over their sacks of cinnamon bark and cardamom seeds, metalworkers would have ceased their hammering, and the *suq* would have had an empty feel, as lunchtime marked a lull in manufacturing and shopping. Craft and commerce had long been intermingled in Sanaa and the *suq* was a warren of single-storey shops and workshops. Occasionally there arose a magnificent soaring caravanserai, one of the old warehouses for goods and a way station for those who had delivered them to the city. Now the caravanserai were mostly derelict. Goods were more likely to have been shipped from China than carried by camel train across the desert, and the *suq al-jamal,* the old camel *suq,* now sold only imported hardware and household goods. Sanaa's *suq* had evolved as new products arose and old ones waned. The sale of lamp oil had dried up years ago. The introduction of glass made alabaster almost redundant. The butchers' market no longer offered bloodletting and cupping. In the late 1800s a small group of Greek and Russian traders briefly upheld the *suq al-nazarah,* the Christian market. The twentieth century brought trade in guns and bananas. Almost all the clothing now for sale came from countries further east. Still, local produce maintained its place, in the *suqs* of tinsmiths, coppersmiths, and blacksmiths. And in *suq al-Inab,* the grape *suq,* and *suq al-zabib,* the raisin *suq.* Also, of course, *suq al-qat,* the *qat suq.* From Waleed's antique shop it was just a short walk.

The *qat suq* would have dozed through the morning, only yawning open sometime around noon as *qat* sellers stretched out their wares into the alleyways and haggling crowds arrived from lunchtime eateries.

'Ya, whoa! How much for this?' Men would be shouting in order to be heard, stooping over vendors who sat cross-legged along the narrow lanes, surrounded by their bags of *qat.*

'Four hundred.' The *qat* seller's teeth would be already stained with chlorophyll, his cheek bulging with chewed leaves of the plant. *Qat* for sale in Sanaa's *suq* would have been harvested at dawn on farms outside the city, then delivered by an efficient network of pick-up trucks to the market. There it could be bought as whole branches of foliage or as handfuls of leaves stripped from their stems. You could have selected the leaves of different regions, different growers, and different parts of the shrub, choosing from the stiffer, cheaper leaves of the lower branches, or the juicy, tender, topmost tips. It was an unfamiliar trade and one that had not much appeal to earlier visitors. Peter Forsskål of the Danish Expedition produced the first botanical description of the *qat* plant, *Catha edulis,* but his colleague Carsten Niebhur dismissed its 'disagreeable' flavour. In the *suq,* the prospective buyer would work quickly with discerning eyes and discriminating nose, examining a bag of thumb-sized leaves and breathing their muted scent before testing their turgid blades with judicious fingers. Then he would turn to the seller with an expression of experienced circumspection and the assertion of a fastidious palate.

'Four hundred? Ha! It's not even fit for my donkey.'

The vendor's slow viridescent smile would acknowledge the opening salvo of a transaction.

'Three hundred and fifty.'

'Chew on this. You will see England!' With another green grin you might have been gifted a sprig of *qat* to try. But England, Holland, or America were promises I often heard but never had fulfilled. The effect of *qat* is not hallucinogenic, nor even euphoric. Richard Burton, Wavell's predecessor and exemplar on the pilgrimage to Mecca, encountered *qat* during his journey between Aden and Harar. He had likened its effects to 'those produced by strong green tea'.

'Yaaah!' Another vendor may have yelled and beckoned you toward the cloth sack in which his bundled bags of *qat* were protected from the sunlight. Grabbing one of the plastic bags, he would have untied its knotted top then held it out for your inspection.

'Three hundred riyals.'

Appraising the proffered leaves, but realising that you were being subjected to a far shrewder assessment, you might have strained to adopt a facial expression that conveyed indifference to what was on offer, rather than just ignorance. If the charade succeeded, the *qat* seller might have taken the cue for his own performance; waving dismissively at the leaves that had met with your disapproval, then rummaging in the depths of his sack, withdrawing a second little plastic bag, untying it, and offering it to you with one hand while tapping the side of his nose with a finger. 'From here.' For in Yemen, anything said to be 'from the nose' is a thing of value. Would the leaves have been a little softer? A little greener? A little sweeter?

'How much?'

Another greenish smile. Acknowledging your lack of fluency and pinching the five digits of one hand together, he would have wordlessly indicated the price of five hundred riyals. A bargain, perhaps.

Meanwhile, after shopping for home furnishings and Arab clothing, Arthur Wavell began visiting Sanaa's marketplace to find alternatives or accompaniments to his diet of boiled eggs. He surreptitiously purchased a 'passable claret' from one of the city's Jews and from the same source he obtained four-piasters-worth of hashish that allowed for a lively experiment one afternoon. Wavell's excursions into the *suq* also afforded the opportunity to formulate strong opinions about Sanaa's inhabitants. The Jews 'seem to be the only people to do any real work,' he thought. The small number of Christian traders he found were only occupied with selling Huntley & Palmers' biscuits and tinned sardines to the Turks, or 'discovering Saints Days and other excuses for shutting up shop'. Yet 'the Arab community in Sanaa,' he decided, 'are the laziest people I have ever come across... They lunch about midday, and spend the rest of the day eating kat the national vice.' Quite so. And we would have joined them. For prior to deciding whether the communal chewing of *qat* leaves was so very wicked as to warrant the label of 'national vice', we might have wanted to witness and better understand the practice.

Lunch would have been over by the time we arrived in the garden behind our house. Though Ibrahim repeatedly extended his open invitation, I felt wary of imposing unduly upon his generosity. He remarked once, chidingly, on my 'English foible', but still I felt awkward, and lunching at Ibrahim's expense remained only an occasional pleasure. Still, I always felt at ease bringing my own bundle of leaves to the post-prandial *qat* chew. Beneath a wooden trellis, sunlight would have dappled empty plastic chairs and bougainvillea vines would have reached down toward a trestle table. The table would be cluttered with dirty plates, greasy serving dishes, crumb-strewn bread baskets, and bowls of discarded olive stones. There would have been a couple of brimming ashtrays and a still-warm coffee pot. A cat or three would be licking at a plate of leftover hummus or pawing gingerly at lamb bones. Twelve-year-old Yusuf would have found employment for the afternoon and, perhaps excited by his prospective earnings, he would have grinned as he busied himself with collecting the used cups and cutlery before washing them at the outdoor sink.

The day would have still carried fire, but here, in a shaded and secluded corner of the city, the heat would have felt less intense. And at the edge of the garden the glass door of the summer *mafraj* would have been pushed open and Ibrahim's voice would have invited us inside. Kicking off your shoes at the threshold and entering, you would have found the air heavy with the smell of sweet tobacco and the noise of conversation. And you would have found the assembled chewers lounging comfortably upon mattresses and cushions, coffee cups and ashtrays resting upon a few small tables. It was all the stuff of Arthur Wavell's home furnishing formula. Ibrahim would have gestured toward a space on the length of seating and, cautiously, we would have stepped across a floor already littered with discarded *qat* stalks, between tins of cola, bottles of water, and bags of leaves that acted as place markers. There would have been nods of welcome and shuffling movements to make room for us while the talking continued uninterrupted and the water pipe murmured approvingly. As you coiled yourself onto the mattress, Ibrahim, an experienced and elegant host, would have leant forward to pass you a bottle of water and quietly introduce the assembled faces. Alessandro, an Italian working for a development agency in Sanaa; Abdul-Karim from the Ministry of Water and Environment; Fuad, a political analyst; and an American professor of anthropology whose name you might fail to catch. 'You've just missed Richard,' Ibrahim would have told us. No surprise. Richard and I had different attitudes and attended different parts of these afternoon gatherings. Richard enjoyed Abdu's lunches, but he found little pleasure in 'spending hours munching bloody hedge trimmings'. Untying the polythene bag of *qat* that you had bought in the *suq* and inspecting the leafy contents, it might have been hard not to admit that they did, indeed, appear rather like hedge trimmings. But around you those assembled faces would all be chewing contentedly.

Wanting to join this collective activity perhaps, but still sceptical, you might have hesitated, watching the hands that pushed leaves one at a time into mouths, and watching the mouths that chewed ceaselessly. Then, with impulsive abandon or wary resignation, you might have pulled a stalk from your bag, a leaf from the stalk, and pushed it between your teeth. Crushing the greenery gently with your molars you would have discovered an unfamiliar flavour, bitter but not unpleasant. 'A rather acrid taste of nothing in particular,' suggested Arthur Wavell contemptuously. Like his hero Richard Burton, Wavell likened *qat*'s stimulant effect to that of strong tea, but he admitted to having 'never succeeded in eating enough kat to produce any effect at all'. Registering your apparent displeasure, Ibrahim would have passed you a can of cola and suggested that you sip it to sweeten the sharpness; rather like adding sugar to the analogous tea. And like tea, or like coffee, or like alcohol, the first taste of *qat* holds little of the appeal that later develops.

Displaying a host's largesse, Ibrahim might have tossed you a choice-looking sprig from his own pile. And you, anxious not to offend, would have begun methodically to separate the waxy blades from the fibrous stem, popping each leaf into your mouth and chewing it slowly, concentrating on accumulating the pulverised vegetation in your cheek. An unfamiliar activity, an absorbing task. Munching, but not swallowing. Ruminating. Only belatedly becoming aware of a conversation that might have occurred in English and roused the engagement of all those present.

'...spending their time chewing instead of working, and spending their money on *qat* instead of on food for their family.' The Italian, indignant, might have made an argument not unlike Wavell, who thought the Arabs lazy and whose 'principal objection' to *qat* was 'the enormous amount of time it requires from its devotees'.

'But people do not *choose* to chew instead of work. And *qat* doesn't *cause* unemployment in Yemen. Quite the opposite,' the anthropologist might have taken another leaf before continuing. '*Qat* is a *consequence* of unemployment. If you're unemployed in Sanaa, you fill your time by chewing *qat*. Or you go back to your village to grow it.'

'True,' Fuad would have added. '*Qat* cultivation has made it profitable in live to the countryside. It has limited urbanisation.'

'One of its benefits,' the anthropologist might have observed.

'Its only benefit,' the Italian would have retorted.

'We're sitting here talking and enjoying one another's company: that's another benefit.'

The Italian would have paused; contradicted, but conciliated.

If we had found ourselves sitting, chewing *qat*, while discussing the 'issue' of *qat*, I would not have been at all surprised. Everyone present would have had professional and personal interests at stake. *Qat* was a development issue, an environmental issue, a social and political issue, and a subject of anthropological study. It was also a popular pastime. And, no matter how much I tried to pretend that the afternoon ritual of chewing foliage was the most natural thing in the world, it remained a curiosity, a self-conscious undertaking, fully warranting simultaneous commentary. Besides, discussions such as this seemed to be exactly what *qat* chews were for. But then, in fact, if you and I had been able to shift our attention from the leaf, we might have recognised that this social gathering with its sharing of views and news, accompanied by some communal consumption, really *was* one of the most natural things in the world.

'The government should intervene. Encourage farmers to grow other crops. Coffee or sorghum.' The Italian would have amassed a bulge of *qat* in the right side of his face and be contorting to talk with the left, chomping words and disgorging bite-sized sentences. 'If farmers grew less *qat* they could grow more coffee. They could start exporting again. Increase exports, reduce poverty.'

'Perhaps the government could just encourage the export of *qat*?' the anthropologist would have suggested wryly.

For a moment you would have been amused by the thought of pre-packed *qat* for sale on supermarket shelves, or *qat* being chewed in a chain of high street outlets. Perhaps you would have shared this humorous vision out loud, your voice rendered just a little less distinct by the quid beginning to bulge in your cheek. Could the coolness of *qat* have entered your blood? Or would it simply have been the conviviality of the occasion infusing you with a quickened wit and a garrulous sociability?

'There's no export market for *qat*. It degrades within hours. And it's illegal almost everywhere.' Abdul-Karim would have cast another denuded stalk in front of him. 'And the local market for *qat* is far more profitable than the international market for coffee and the government doesn't have the capability to change that.'

'Then maybe *qat* should be imported,' the Italian would propose excitedly. 'Flood Yemen with *qat*. Import it from Somalia or Ethiopia. The price of *qat* would go down. It'd be less profitable for Yemeni farmers. They'd grow other crops for export instead.'

'Or they would just abandon their farms,' Fuad might have suggested, 'and migrate to the city to try and find work.'

'The problem isn't just money or poverty; it's water. Water poverty.' Abdul-Karim's hands would have paused, interrupting the movement of leaves to his bulging cheek. 'The water's running out. Irrigating *qat* requires huge amounts of water and the water table is dropping faster than it can be replaced. When the country runs out of water, then we'll really have problems.'

The hush that descended would be a moment of shared contemplation, a necessary interlude. By now the *mafraj* would be carpeted with defoliated stalks, our faces swollen with mulch. Only the sibilant opening of a carbonated drink, a throaty expectoration into a spittoon, and the burbling puff of the water pipe would have signalled our continued presence as we each observed our own silent mediations.

Only daydreams disturbed the siege in Sanaa. 'If I were raising a regiment from Turkey,' mused Arthur Wavell, 'it would be from the rough-bearded, unkempt-looking ruffians with dirty uniforms, down-at-heel slippers, and heavy, curved swords of a pattern long obsolete.' Heroes fit for this rough and ready imaginary regiment could be found 'in any garrison town sitting in the dingy cafes sucking water pipes and playing back-gammon'. The fantasy of fighting men, ruggedly masculine, coiled and waiting to spring from their board games into daring acts of courage was a vision both adoring and aspiring. Wavell was longing for action, yearning for the glory of battle. When the besieged Turks eventually repulsed the encircling Arab tribesmen, his vision was ecstatically operatic: 'The band struck up a patriotic air, the bugles summoned the troops to advance, the guns fired salvoes, and the musketry fire swelled to a continuous roar.'

When the siege was over and the band and the bugles and the guns and the musketry fell silent, the Turks made it clear to Wavell that he was to be escorted back to Hodeidah. But he was having none of it. Three months after his tennis court diversion and his getaway in the early hours of Christmas morning, he remained determined to pursue the 'highly perilous' and 'adventurous feat' that had drawn him to Yemen. And he sought help from 'the biggest scoundrel in Sanaa'. This was a man who made his living buying munitions from the Turks and selling them to the Arabs; a man who would 'steal kohl from the eye of his own mother'; who 'feared not god, neither regarded man'. Yet Wavell approached this character and guilelessly asked him 'to play fair' in assisting his escape from the Turks. With his servant, Wavell discussed various strategies for absconding. They could descend the city wall with a rope ladder. Or leave their house disguised as women. Or overpower the Turkish policeman in their kitchen and anaesthetise him using ethyl chloride, now that Wavell's 'complete medical and surgical outfit' had at last arrived from Hodeidah. Or they could entice their Turkish guard to accompany them on a walk outside the city and then just run away. They agreed on this last option.

But the unscrupulous arms trader, kohl stealer, and ungodly scoundrel who had been supposed to meet them outside the city and assist their onward journey never appeared. Double-crossed, Wavell recalled 'we had our weapons and plenty of money, and all Arabia lay before us.' But they had no food, no idea which way to go, and Wavell's servant had managed to lose his shoes. Wavell wavered. He was uncertain how to proceed. And when the Turks discovered his hiding place and Wavell found himself 'looking down a rifle barrel' the adventure was over.

'The expedition which ended here had been an absolute failure,' Wavell wrote. It 'had accomplished nothing whatever, cost a great deal, and entailed a fearful waste of time.' Still, he was able to reconcile himself to having 'had a run for our money'. But if the expedition had been 'an absolute failure', what would success have looked like for Arthur Wavell? Relishing the prospect of peril and adventure, believing that expeditions were like wars, and having fantasies that fixated on old Turkish soldiers with rough beards, his journey to Yemen seems to have been a striving for the heroic, and for some means of proving himself. From David Hogarth's *The Penetration of Arabia* - that chronicle of exploration beyond the edge of empire - Wavell seems to have taken his ideas of where and how to prove his manhood, even if he got no further than the book's Freudian title. But the rite of passage he had hoped for during his warrior expedition into Yemen never occurred.

Five years after the 'absolute failure' of his journey to Sanaa, and two years into the First World War, in 1916 Arthur Wavell found himself once again looking down the wrong end of a rifle-barrel. Near Mombasa, during the conflict between colonial powers in East Africa, Wavell was shot and killed. He was thirty-three years old. And just days earlier he had been awarded the military cross for gallantry.

- 13 -

Impermanence

- George Wyman Bury, 1912-13 -

MOTIONLESS, AN ELECTRIC BLUE LIZARD lay basking in the warm light. Its stillness was unreal, its colour incredible. Face to face with the rock, I had breathed in the hot air. There was no smell to speak of on the stone surface, but my palms as they moved across it were redolent of something like wild sage or thyme. Having sought any vegetation that might serve as a handhold, and having found my footing on the slightest protrusion, I had climbed slowly, and the wadi floor had gradually fallen away. Looking at my roughened fingers and reviewing my precarious position half way up the escarpment, I felt a surge of child-like exhilaration. Gripping a crag, my fingertips dislodged a pebble, sending it rolling then dropping like a lost marble, ricocheting and knocking, clacking down the sandstone. The lizard flicked, startled, bouncing away boulder to boulder as though it were a rubber toy, and the rock came away in my grasp, crumbling into a gritty shower. 'It is very embarrassing to say "Look at that bright blue lizard," and be asked "What bright blue lizard?"' wrote George Wyman Bury. 'You have never taken your eyes off the creature, and yet it has vanished. Such incidents require explaining.' So then, an explanation...

Far below, the Arabian castle had towered above me, resplendent in the morning sunshine, spectacularly capping its isolated rock pillar as if displaced from a dream. Or as if, by some fairy-tale contrivance, the cinnamon bricks and plaster frosting of a Sanaa towerhouse had been swept up and deposited improbably upon an eroded sandstone pedestal in a lush wadi a dozen miles north-east of the capital. Which is more or less what had happened a century or so earlier when Imam Yahya had ordered the construction of his summer residence at Wadi Dahr. Since then the Rock Palace had become a national symbol. Bank notes, postage stamps, bottles of local spring water, and an abundance of souvenirs were all adorned with the building's unmistakable image. Fabulous, disorderly, the palace's multiple storeys and myriad facades clambered on top of one another, driving upward from its sandstone pile. With its labyrinth of chambers and staircases now opened to the public, the Rock Palace had become Yemen's most visited tourist site. Less frequented, though arguably more impressive, were the steep paths that led away from the Palace and up the wadi. Visitors here were rewarded with views of the extraordinary fissure carved into the landscape. The wadi cut a verdant swath of shady orchards into the plains, with fruit trees irrigated by water pumped up from beneath the dry riverbed. The imam's choice of location was exceptional, and it was to Wadi Dahr that I came on occasional day trips when I wanted a break from the city during summer.

Despite the short distance from Sanaa, the journey was not always uncomplicated. The bowlegged bus conductor did not work on weekends and the hesitancy with which his young replacement gestured towards an idling vehicle did not inspire confidence. Being Friday, the bus had taken a while to fill, and when we set off it was along streets lined by empty pavements and shuttered shopfronts. Deposited on a deserted street corner in a suburb I did not recognise, I had been directed toward another minibus that would take me onward to Matbah. I didn't want to go to Matbah, I wanted to go to Wadi Dahr. But from Matbah, the driver assured me, I would find onward transport to Wadi Dahr. And so I hopped aboard.

When I arrived in Matbah it felt like a frontier, a boundary between urban and rural. Farmers' stalls selling fruit and vegetables were pressed amid the breezeblocks and iron support rods of semi-constructed buildings. The boundary was shifting, the city was expanding. A dozen Peugeot share taxis sat by the roadside, all pointing gamely in the direction of Wadi Dahr. But none of the vehicles contained any passengers, or even drivers, and my hopes for an imminent departure evaporated on the tarmac. Outside a nearby café a group of men sat drinking and talking. One of them stood and ambled toward me, sipping at his tea. With a questioning expression he waggled a finger at the sky.

'Wadi Dahr,' I answered to his signalled enquiry.

'One thousand five hundred. Complete.'

Ten passengers might each pay 150 riyals for a seat in a Peugeot to Wadi Dahr, I supposed, but if I wanted to hire the 'complete' vehicle I would have to cover the whole cost myself. Fair, but pricey. And it felt somehow out of keeping with the spirit of my endeavour. So I declined the man's offer. He stared at me, sipped his tea without taking his eyes from my face, then stepped into the road and brought a speeding taxi to a sudden stop.

'Drop the foreigner at Wadi Dahr,' he said, stooping at the driver's open window to instruct the startled face behind the steering wheel. 'And charge him three hundred riyals.' Still holding his teacup with one hand, he opened the rear door of the taxi with the other and shoved me onto the backseat, or, as it turned out, onto the lap of a young man who was already sitting on the back seat. The door slammed behind me, the taxi lurched forward, and the driver yelled above the noise of his engine.

'My name is Ali!' He flashed me a wide grin in his rear-view mirror, then turned and roared at me, still grinning, 'I'm not going to Wadi Dahr!'

'Where are you going?' I cried.

He shouted the name of a place I had never heard of.

'Where's that?'

He yelled again. It was near somewhere else I had never heard of.

'We will pass through Shamlan.' Beneath me was a voice speaking perfect English. 'From Shamlan you may take a motorbike or taxi to Wadi Dahr.' I wriggled, thanked the Yemeni youth, and attempted to lever myself from his lap.

'My name is Mohammed,' he said affably. I introduced myself and shifted a buttock, releasing his arm so that we could shake hands.

'You know, it's easier to visit Wadi Dahr with one of the tourist companies from Sanaa,' he suggested helpfully.

'I prefer to be independent.'

He nodded prudently while I quietly acknowledged the reality that my 'independent travel' usually connoted utter dependence upon the kindness and assistance of folk such as him. Exactly as Mohammed had predicted, our driver dropped me at the motorbike stand in Shamlan, taking just fifty riyals for the trouble.

'Welcome to Yemen,' said the motorcycle rider in English once I was perched behind him, astride the sheepskin saddle cover. Then he opened the throttle. As his camouflage jacket filled with air and lifted from his shoulders, I peered over the straining seams and threadbare fabric to watch the needle of the broken speedometer sit unwaveringly at zero while we gathered pace. Blasted by wind, my watering eyes spattered saline across my spectacle lenses and my vision soon became no more than a blur. The motorcyclist's jacket continued to inflate, pushing against my chest while his headscarf whipped at my face and the engine rattled my limbs. Wind screamed in my ears, tore at my hair, and ballooned my cheeks. I broke into a broad smile. There was an oncoming car, some ineffectual tooting, a last moment, swerving, dust-clouded, off-road deviation in our trajectory before the wadi opened up and swallowed our descent.

Stacks of wooden beehives stood in grassy clearings and old men sat beneath huge sun umbrellas with baskets of peaches, plums, and pears for sale. At the wadi bottom the road surface changed from asphalt to gravel and we decelerated sharply, dropping gears with a lurch that almost threw me. After another mile or so I stood, wiping dust and tears from my spectacles, spitting insects, and still feeling the vibration of the motorcycle in my bones. As I paid for the final instalment of my piecemeal journey, veiled women and their smartly dressed children stepped from pristine off-road vehicles bearing registration plates from Saudi and Dubai, Europeans scrambled from Landcruisers labelled with the logos of Sanaa-based touring companies, and Yemeni men assisted their wives from dented Toyota Cressidas. They would become the black and white shapes who stood upon the terraces and rooftops of the Rock Palace, and the brightly clad foreigners who peered from its windows or pointed cameras at its walls; all diminishing as I ascended the cliff.

As the gradient of the climb decreased I was able to walk upright, and as the sandstone gave way to overlapping layers of crumbling mudrock my cautious steps became crunching footfalls on earth pigments of ochre, umber, sienna, and charcoal. This sedimentary stratum formed a natural terrace, tracing a narrow path between the gravel slopes and vertical sandstone. The rock on one side rose up to a ragged edge of sky and on the other it plunged to the depths of the wadi's panorama. A few wind-scattered seeds, finding rare hospitality in the rockscape, celebrated their good fortune; daisies bunched yellow-white among rubble, there was a spray of golden wheat, and a clump of herbs soft in my palm. Hardier plants made their homes here too. A down-covered shrub brushed against my arm and the skin became aflame with toxins. Occasional stunted trees survived; the long thorns hidden among their feathery leaves drawing blood as I raked past. Stout spine-covered cacti pushed out from boulder clefts, and pin-striped tubules, slender and turgid, branched endlessly like shattered glass before exploding into tiny flowers at their tips. Swallows or swifts swept by with a rush of air, twisting and tumbling. Birds I could not name flapped aloft with broad, black, orange-patched wings. A chestnut-coloured finch or something darted out of sight. George Wyman Bury had been much better at this than me.

Pseudacanthis yemenensis; the Yemen Linnet. 'The bird looks like a sparrow and sings like skylark,' thought Bury. He had spotted it 'among the orchard terraces of Menakha, pouring out its soul in song.' *P. yemenensis* had been previously unknown to European ornithologists, despite being 'much in demand at Sanaa as a cage bird'.

From the mud-flat flamingos and 'stately squadrons of pelicans' around Hodeidah, Bury journeyed inland from Yemen's coast in November 1912. Among the green pigeons, 'common in the foot-hills when the wild figs are ripe', and the sunbirds 'in shot-silk and epaulets of flame', he passed with the piebald larks that 'bustle along the caravan tracks'. Bury followed the ranks of long-tailed rollers that perched upon the telegraph wire as it stretched and sagged between the coast and the capital. That fragile line of Ottoman communication connecting Stamboul and Sanaa ran alongside the 'one road in Yemen worthy of the name'. The hundred and fifty miles of stony track extending east from Hodeidah was protected by numerous Turkish fortifications but remained only passable by mule. 'A mere thread of sovereignty' Bury termed it, unravelling slowly among the mountains and hill tribes. After living for seventeen years in Arabia and having seen 'a good deal of Ottoman rule', Bury felt qualified to offer his opinions. He thought the Turks had made a mess of it. That thread of sovereignty controlled 'an expensive and fragile puppet... an impoverished country which is a constant drain on Ottoman resources'. Unprofitable for the Turks and deadening for the Arabs, he saw a warning for British colonial interests. Bury's book, *Arabia Infelix: or The Turks in Yamen*, was published in 1915. It told of the unhappy relationship between the occupying forces and the subjugated population. It also expressed his pleasure and proficiency in birdwatching. So endearingly enthusiastic are his avian descriptions that I found myself regretting my own lack of birding interest while in Yemen; recognising my likeness in the Turkish Governor of Manakha who admitted to Bury that he had 'been here for years and only seen crows.'

'What are you doing here?' Rounding an outcrop of bare rock and confronted with the visual impact of a shimmering green I had been momentarily stunned. Slowly the tremulous light and bosky expanse took form. Familiar elliptical, thumb-sized leaves quivered and coruscated on branches that bent from pale trunks. Each tree was a uniform twelve-foot high and neatly arranged in well-tended soil. This living organism at least I could recognise and name: I had stumbled upon a *qat* plantation.

'What are you doing?' The figure stomping from the foliage repeated his challenge. No older than myself, with a blast of untamed hair and a pugilist's nose, he squared up to me, muscles twitching. Charged, I guessed, with the task of protecting the *qat* from thieves, he quickly recognised me as a foreigner, one obviously confused, and his bellicosity was promptly defused. He introduced himself as Abdu and thereafter our enquiries of each other became cordial. What was my name? Where was I from? Was I married? Yes, these were his family's *qat* trees. Yes, he lived in a house down there in the wadi. My laboured questions and answers can only have confirmed that I was an unthreatening presence, perhaps a little dim, and that I had blundered upon the plantation by accident.

Moving easily across the terrain, Abdu in his billowing *thobe* appeared as though borne upon the breeze, rather than carried by his pair of weary-looking leather sandals. I followed his sailing footsteps through the *qat* grove and in a further ascent of the canyon wall. A scramble brought us to the edge of the plateau and the ruins of a fortification that overlooked the wadi. The cliff-top ramparts, long-abandoned, still appeared impregnable, but for a single opening in the wall. Abdu and I peered into the enclosed compound. A lonely, desultory goat wandered among pottery shards and broken buildings. Turkish? I wondered. Abdu was unsure. But from the edge of the plateau he pointed out the structures of a recent, personal history. Below, among the rooftops fringing the wadi's sweep of peach trees and palms, was the school that he had once attended. There was the mosque. And directly beneath the *qat* terrace where we had met was his home.

A gunshot cracked. Abdu twitched again.

'Could be *qat* thieves,' he said before the echo had died. 'They get one warning shot.' He returned, running, to his trees.

Cryptolopha umbrovirens yemenensis was a 'modest little chap no bigger than a wren, with a tree-green coat and a light brown waistcoat.' The label of the bird's Latin Taxon includes the name of the Turkish-occupied nation where Wyman Bury found it. *Serinus menachensis*, the Yemen Serin, 'dingy little birds resembling finch-larks', were named after Manakha, the mountain town between Hodeidah and Sanaa. *Sylvia buryi*, the Yemen Warbler, 'a furtive little fellow in sober greyish brown', was named after Bury himself.

Born in Warwickshire, Bury arrived in Aden as an adventurous twenty-two-year-old in 1896. He spent a year living with a local tribe, dressing as an Arab tribesman, learning colloquial Arabic, and using the adopted name of Abdullah Mansur. A photograph shows him bearded, barefoot, wearing a shawl, turban, and carrying a spear. Later he gained employment with the government in Aden, gathering intelligence, but he was accused of taking bribes and forced to leave under a cloud in 1904. In November 1912 he returned to Yemen with the approval of the Turkish authorities and for almost a year he worked as a naturalist on behalf of the Natural History Museum. It was his experiences during this period that he described with an uncommon combination of political and ornithological acuity in *Arabia Infelix*.

'I did most of my work with a double hammerless .410,' Bury remarked, for his birding was not limited to observing and note-taking. He found no contradiction or moral qualm in admiring birds in flight and song, then shooting them out of the sky to be skinned and stuffed. A clean kill could not be guaranteed and some of his targets, like the lammergeier whose wing he shattered with a borrowed twelve-bore, were finished off with a thick blanket and a wad of chloroform-soaked cotton wool. 'The house of an old coffee-broker' just outside Hodeidah provided an ideal setting for his industry. Especially useful was the 'flight of ruinous steps that give onto a coffee-drying platform, where taxidermical specimens may be aired if guarded closely from hovering kites.' 'The guest-chamber is quite stylish,' Bury noted, 'a gap or two in the mud and wattle flooring enable you to keep an eye on your stores below.' He sounded cheerfully oblivious to his unusual choice of marital accommodation.

'*Only picture of my wedding. Hodeidah. Yemen. June 19, 1913. 122°F in the shade*'. The label was scrawled on the back of a photograph that would be treasured for years after. Florence Ann Marshall had travelled from England. From Hodeidah she travelled as Ann Wyman Bury. Ann and

George had met at the Westminster Hospital in 1911. She was working as a nurse when he was admitted with tuberculosis. Following Bury's remission and his departure to Yemen, they arranged to be reunited and formally united on the Red Sea coast. After getting married in a sweltering heat that the bride found quite remarkable, the newlyweds set off the next day for their honeymoon in Yemen and the house of the old coffee-broker. The Wyman Burys seem to have been a spirited match. Yet though they spent five months together in Yemen during the summer and autumn of 1913, George's account of this period barely features his newly betrothed. Her most prominent appearance is in substantiating an allusion to a millipede 'as thick as a stout lead-pencil and half a foot long': 'Strictly speaking he is not a beast, but my wife called him that when she found one in the tent after a rainy evening.' Astonishing that she was not more outspoken. Yet Ann was evidently undeterred. And the happy couple continued to Sanaa, that 'half-forgotten city that the world has overlooked.' The city's towerhouses were 'great, rambling structures, with bewildering passages and unexpected rooms, opening off dark, corkscrew stairs'. To bathe 'you can stand on a stumpy-legged table and drench yourself with a tin dipper from a huge fat-bellied jar of red earthenware.' Presumably Ann Wyman Bury was by now entirely unperturbed by the idiosyncrasies of their honeymoon lodgings. In Sanaa, George continued his specimen collecting. By the time he and his wife departed from Yemen in October 1913, he had sent more than four hundred bird skins to Mr Ogilvie-Grant of the Natural History Museum for description and classification. Glass-eyed, silent, with wings that had once beat Yemen's hot air now stilled, among these lifeless trophies were eight entirely new species and many not previously known to inhabit southern Arabia.

Soaring on the breeze, a distorted warble echoed along the wadi. The prayer call's amplified voice roused me gently. I had been dozing, reclining on the cliff face beneath the meagre shade of a small tree's wispy fronds and thorny barbs. Survival is earned with such vegetative adaptations, protecting the plant from the appetites of feral goats and preventing evaporative water loss, but the skimpy leaves and spiny branches offered scant protection from the sun and I felt my forearms a little scorched.

Across the ravine, steel water pipes glinted, their thin filaments reaching up toward little isolated patches of greenery. Dust followed a shepherd and his sheep as they moved along the dry watercourse below. The mosque fell silent. Other noises returned. Birdsong and the hum of petrol-driven water pumps, the call of the shepherd and the vibrato yawning of his flock. From close by came the stridulate voice of a grasshopper, a sound like the shaking of a saltcellar. I drained the last of my lukewarm water, stood, then skidded, stumbling, down a slope of scree and boulders to the tyre-marked, hoof-tracked, and sandal-printed wadi bottom. The sheep had gone. Prayers were over. Handsomely dressed men, with proud *jambiyahs* in their belts and fresh boutonnieres in their headscarves, stood or ambled together, conversing, inviting me to join *qat* chews. I might have accepted, since Wadi Dahr was renowned for the quality of its *qat*, but I was thirsty and hungry. Besides, there remained the question of how to get home and my chances of finding transport back to Sanaa would diminish as the afternoon rolled by. Scaling the bank of the arid water channel, I left behind its pebble-strewn sands and entered the leafy expanse that I had viewed from above. It was all grassy glades and cypresses, apricot trees that sighed and dipped their lazy branches, empty bottles and littered plastic bags, butterflies like apple blossoms that flitted and teased one another through the orchards.

Halcyon leucocephala, 'that quaint anomaly, the land kingfisher', was spotted by Wyman Bury 'in coy seclusion' among the foothills as the newlyweds approached Manakha. The bird is named after the same woman of Greek myth as Halcyon Days. Soon after the Wyman Burys ended their honeymoon in Yemen, the First World War erupted. Ann and George settled in Cairo where Ann took up work in the Arab Bureau (befriending Gertrude Bell but disliking TE Lawrence) and George finished writing his book. He too made himself useful in the Arab Bureau, contributing to the work of David '*The Penetration of Arabia*' Hogarth and to the Bureau's *Handbook of Yemen*. The 1917 Yemen *Handbook* drew upon Bury's knowledge of the region's tribes and personalities and incorporated excerpts from his *Arabia Infelix*, just as it had included Arthur Wavell's description of the Yemeni *jambiyah*. The fact that the

Arab Bureau considered it expedient to produce a handbook to Yemen might suggest an actual or anticipated battlefront, but the conflict never extended further into Arabia than Allied efforts to destroy the Ottomans' Hejaz railway between Damascus and Medina. And while control of Yemen had been crucial for the Turks to maintain their grip on the Holy cities of Mecca and Medina, after the end of the war and the collapse of the Ottoman Empire, Yemen held little appeal for the British. Their interests in the region were orientated toward maintaining the British Raj through control of Suez, the Red Sea, and the way station of Aden.

George Wyman Bury had joined the British Red Sea Maritime Patrol during the war, precluded from any more active role by his quiescent tuberculosis. Mostly his maritime patrols were routine, guarding against gun-running along the seaboard. But in May 1916 there was news of a German gunboat wrecked on the southern coast of Arabia. Six of the crew survived, ventured inland to Sanaa, then returned to the Red Sea, hoping to reach Germany via Stamboul. Their hopes came to nothing. 'A Turkish rescue party which hurried to the spot found their headless and practically disembowelled corpses with their hands tied behind them,' Bury reported. 'Among their kit was a tattered and blood-stained copy of my book.'

The German sailors had been murdered by tribesmen, their mutilated corpses left drying under the Arabian sun, picked at, quite probably, by the same hovering kites that had once threatened to defile Bury's taxidermal specimens. The blood-stained copy of his book fell eventually into Bury's possession. He does not record his feelings on receiving it. Perhaps it confirmed in his mind a belief that his work could endure beyond death, like his bird skins. Or he might have seen only a token of impermanence, like the wedding photo labelled with faded calligraphy. Or perhaps in that brutal memorial Bury recognised an omen. He was back in hospital a few weeks later, suffering a reactivation of tuberculosis. As his health failed him, he sat out the rest of the war in Cairo, cared for by his wife just as she had cared for him when they first met, until his death in 1920. Ann would outlive George by more than half a century. In her seventies she once again boarded a boat from England to Yemen. But at Hodeidah she was refused permission to step ashore. So, on 19 June 1950, with the temperature again reaching 122°F in the shade, Ann Wyman Bury gazed at that remembered but unreachable shore, on the 37th anniversary of her wedding.

Walking back along the wadi, mindful of how diminutive the Rock Palace had appeared from above, I was almost surprised to find that it still towered over me when I passed it on my return. Piled upon its sandstone column, a pompous appendage to the process of erosion and the passage of time, it looked a little absurd. The sun meanwhile was about to be eclipsed by the rim of the plateau, casting this cleft in the earth's crust into shadow. Already, the rock pedestal on which the Palace sat had fallen into shade, darkening into tones of dried blood, burnt wood, and rusting iron, silently declaring that it had consumed all of these and would outlast them all.

- 14 -

Returning

- Norman Lewis, 1937; Hugh Scott, 1937; & Freya Stark, 1940

-

IN JULY 2006 I TELEPHONED one of the travel agents on Zubeiry Street. We discussed flight schedules between Sanaa and London. Back then, Yemenia, the national airline, was flying the route twice weekly and I reserved a seat on a UK-bound plane departing in a fortnight. We agreed that I would drop by in person after work the next day to collect and pay for my ticket. But on the following afternoon the travel agent had looked at my bank card and apologised.

'Ohhh, so sorry, we don't take cards,' he said. 'Do you have cash?' I did, but not enough. The ATM was at the other end of Zubeiry Street, a fifteen-minute walk away, and the travel agent was keen to close for the day. So I asked if it were possible to hold the reservation for a further twenty-four hours and I would return again tomorrow with the money.

'Take your tickets in the meantime?' he suggested, to my surprise. And I departed with a return ticket to Heathrow in exchange for only my word that I would return with several hundred dollars in cash. Which of course I did, for nothing begets honesty like trust.

News of my travel plans elicited two sorts of request. Yemeni friends asked if I could take items to mail to family members in Europe on their behalf. European friends in Sanaa asked if I could bring things back for them on my return. The country's postal system being notoriously unreliable, I was to provide a surrogate delivery service. Outbound then went a parcel addressed to a Yemeni in Paris, another to Sheffield. Inbound, I was to import Bournville chocolate and Battenburg cake, a rechargeable camera battery and condoms with a recognisable safety mark. Also, underwear from Marks & Spencer and two kilograms of Odlums Brown Bread flour mix. And there were three separate orders for Parmesan cheese. Nobody mentioned alcohol and I supposed that my two-litre allowance was deemed inviolable.

I found the obsession with Parmesan cheese incomprehensible, yet there were those who truly resented its absence in Yemen. Dining once with a Canadian in a hotel far from the capital I had ordered camel stew while he opted for spaghetti bolognaise. 'Where's the parmesan?' he demanded crossly when his dish arrived. The waiter understood little English and his vocabulary did not encompass varieties of Italian cheese. 'Cheese, CHEEEESE!' the Canadian bellowed. The waiter hurried away with the spaghetti. He returned shortly with the bolognaise, accompanied by a small side plate upon which were placed two foil-wrapped triangles of spreadable cheese. My Canadian companion was decidedly unimpressed.

'Airport please.' The taxi driver nodded and we drove off in the wrong direction. It was the morning of my flight to London. 'The airport,' I repeated, anticipating a U-turn, or a little known short cut that never came. 'Yes!' said the driver, pointing dead ahead, in the opposite direction to the airport.

'Where are you from?' I asked. It would not have been the first time that I had been picked up by a provincial driver lacking any knowledge of the city's layout.

'From Sanaa.' Reassuring. Roads around the city were often obstructed by resurfacing or construction projects, so I supposed that this driver, aware of the latest hold-ups on the airport road, was using a circuitous alternative route, until he pulled up and stopped outside the National Museum.

'The *airport!*'

He pointed to the museum.

I shook my head, spread my arms, and made angry aeroplane noises to indicate my intended destination and signal my loss of confidence in our verbal communication.

'Ahhh!' he exclaimed, with a look of recognition.

'Yes!' I cried. 'The airport!' I tapped my watch, he put his foot down, and we accelerated into the traffic. Then we stopped in front of the Military Museum. The driver grinned and pointed toward the Russian fighter jet that sat rusting on the museum forecourt. I ejected myself and my baggage from the taxi, cursing furiously, and strode away without paying. Only after finding a taxi driver who spoke a little English and finding myself only a little late for check-in did my annoyance subside. At which point I realised my error. With all the arrogance and testiness of a Canadian staring down a plate of spaghetti and two processed cheese triangles in Yemen's hinterlands, I had muddled the similar-sounding Arabic words for airport, *mathar*, and for museum, *mathaf*. With shame and self-reproach, I was to leave Sanaa on bad terms. It was a difficult departure.

'Tomorrow it is my intention to set sail,' the skipper announced. 'And if not tomorrow, the day after that.' The departure of the dhow was undecided. The sea journey from Aden to Hodeidah might take three days or three weeks. And if the ageing vessel was becalmed or beset by pirates its passengers might never arrive at all. 'Every aspect of the voyage was attended by uncertainty,' Norman Lewis recalled afterward. 'Only god could be sure of anything,' the dhow's skipper had opined.

On the day after tomorrow, in the spring of 1937, the dhow's single lateen sail was hoisted. Lewis planned to travel by boat to Hodeidah, then continue overland to Sanaa. The journey that followed would give rise to his first book, but it was not all plain sailing. The dhow was pervaded by a fetor of 'dried fish and bilge'. The diet of *qishr* and unleavened bread provoked 'unappeasable indigestion'. And the 'place of ease' was merely a chair hitched to the vessel's side, 'suspended precariously over the sea', 'lashed by wind and spray'. Lewis noted drily of this risky privy that 'in bad weather an enforced visit became an adventure': toileting in rough seas he had found himself hoisted 'high over the cargo' as the ship reeled upon the ocean swell, then 'a moment later... lowered into the cavernous belly of a wave.'

Wry humour did not blunt the moral keenness of Lewis' writing. While his own adverse circumstances were made comic, Lewis was incensed by the conditions in which others suffered. He watched the dhow-builders near Aden hauling wooden beams from ships offshore, shouldering their crushing weight in a 'quick, painful stagger' up the beach, singing chants that became 'a long drawn gasp, a groan'. Human labour was so cheap, Lewis observed, that no jetty had been built to land the materials. Later he saw pearl divers being exploited by a swindling speculator, 'a cruel parasite, lacking any sense of responsibility for the welfare of those he employs'. This harsh taskmaster was predisposed to punish any diver caught trying to keep a pearl for his own profit by setting him 'adrift in a canoe without oars'. 'There is something about pearls,' Lewis concluded, 'that seems to exclude mercy'. An ex-grammar-school boy who had variously struggled to earn a living as an umbrella salesman and a wedding photographer, twenty-eight-year-old Lewis had an acutely sensitive social perspective.

During the sea voyage from Aden to Hodeidah, Lewis' eye ranged keenly over the dhow's thirty-two passengers and crew; 'Arabs of every condition plus a trio of Yemeni Jews'. Ardently recording their stories and experiences in his notebooks and on film, he bore witness to tough lives and created an ethnographic photo-essay. Ever so slightly out-of-focus, the downcast face of the eleven-year-old granddaughter adds gravity to the account of the Jewish family displaced and 'bound for Palestine'. The picture of the young Bedouin shepherd, eyelids touched with antimony and lips drawn to a grin, elaborates his dream of enlisting in 'some foreign country where soldiers wore imposing uniforms and did not have to buy their own rifles'. Captured obliquely, hauling a rope, is the skipper, 'tall, lean, and grave', who called the travellers to prayer in a faltering voice that creaked with the timbers, and who could spin a yarn when the breeze dropped. And when at night the wind died, and Lewis lay awake, the dhow resting motionless 'in a sea glittering with a great hoar-frost of phosphorescence', he believed he was witnessing a passing era. And his prose seemed to conjure those past English seafarers John Jourdain and Henry Middleton, each of whom had also remarked upon the 'hoare frost' traversed upon their own Sanaa-bound journeys more than three centuries earlier.

But Lewis' plan to reach Sanaa came undone when the skipper dropped anchor in Hodeidah. Before Lewis could disembark and continue his journey, the port authorities boarded the vessel. 'Turbans curled like elaborate caracols', the harbour master and his retinue moved 'in a slow, almost dreamy fashion', sitting down with Lewis in silence, watching him 'sleepily, with thin measured smiles'. They sat on the deck, sipped *qishr*, caressed the jewelled hilts of their *jambiyahs*, then politely refused permission for the Englishman to come ashore. From the dhow, Hodeidah, out of reach, seemed to evaporate in the heat, and with it Sanaa, insubstantial as a distant dream. 'We knew that we should never enter the Yemen.' The realisation was stark. Over the years Lewis would revisit his forbidden journey to Sanaa over and over again.

When, some six decades later, Norman Lewis died at the age of ninety-five, he left behind a generous collection of novels and accounts of travel from Indochina to Indonesia, by way of India, Burma, Latin America, Spain, and Sicily. His obituary in the *Guardian* newspaper repeated Lewis' intriguing assertion that he was able to enter a room full of people, then leave, without anybody noticing that he had been there. His biography was titled *Semi-Invisible Man*, after Lewis' own self-description. He believed that he could pass without note, invisibly. The noting, and refusing, of his intended entry into Yemen must have challenged something at his core.

'An acquired knack', Lewis said of what he believed were his unnoticed comings and goings. It was a knack that seemed to speak of a humble nature. For me, though, it was always mere timidity. I find myself able to settle quickly into being or not being somewhere, but my arrivals, and more particularly my departures, are always awkward. My preference is to slink away quietly. That habit, combined with my propensity for forgetfulness, once prompted Ibrahim to remark at a *qat* chew that he only ever knew I had departed when I returned having remembered what I had left behind.

And by now, in the *qat* chew, and in the gloaming, conversation would have dwindled. In the *mafraj* you and I would have still been sitting, while the evening shadows enveloped the garden. With darkness descending outside, the windows looking out would have turned to mirrors, reflecting back at us our dim-lit faces, glinting spectacles, and glowing cigarettes. At this hour, the so-called Hour of Solomon, the atmosphere of the *qat* chew would have changed, from banter and animated discussion to quiet contemplation. The thoughts of chewers would have turned inwards. Surely, with the mass of bitter leaves in our mouths and the pulse of alkaloids in our blood, if we were ever to see England as the *qat* vendors had promised, it would have been now, in this period of collective introspection.

Late into Heathrow I telephoned a Bayswater hotel, then crossed the night-time city by underground and black cab. 'Been scorchin' the past few days,' the cab driver remarked. Elsewhere, Beirut was burning and Sanaa had been ablaze with the news. Lebanon was being bombarded by Israel: retaliation, it was claimed, for the abduction of two Israeli soldiers by Hezbollah militia, which was itself retaliation for the abduction of two Palestinian civilians. In Sanaa, the face of Hezbollah's leader had appeared suddenly on posters across the city and his speeches, replayed from cassette tapes, had rallied crowds. But in London the British government insisted on Israel's right to defend itself and the taxi driver's chatter referred only to the August heat wave.

London felt distant. The language was familiar but the conversations were not. The city was strangely ordered. The traffic was too shiny. Dogs that would have rummaged in Sanaa's rubbish piles had been put on leads and walked ahead of their owners through Kensington. One moment my head was spinning, the next it was being hammered by the forgotten sound of pneumatic drills. And I discovered an unfamiliar feeling of shame in not being invited to join people who were eating; the offer would always have been made in Yemen. Wandering through West London I thought of Sanaa, of my friends, and the conviviality of *qat* chews. As Ibrahim had once said, albeit with a different meaning, my departure was confirmed by remembering what I had left behind.

'To introduce some order into confusion', Norman Lewis studied Arabic for a while upon his return to England. 'I came back with a great collection of words,' he wrote, referring to the fragments of language he had picked up in Aden. Ultimately though, he would not find order in language studies and his great collection of words would not find expression in Arabic. Over the course of his life Norman Lewis published three different accounts of his voyage by dhow from Aden to Hodeidah. For the young man who had intended to reach Sanaa, the journey marked the beginning of a life of travel and of writing. Amid his dozens of other fictions and travelogues, Lewis returned to the dhow voyage periodically, meditating upon its significance, re-introducing order and finding new meaning.

The story evolved. Hodeidah, 'desolate as a cluster of whitened bones' in 1937, became 'a crystalline sparkle of dwellings' in Lewis' 1985 retelling. The port authorities had originally ridden in a rowing boat oared by African slaves, but when Lewis recounted the story in 2001 they chugged about in a motorboat. Yet the most intriguing inconsistency relates to Lewis' thwarted attempt to reach Sanaa. He had hoped to enter and depart from Yemen as easily and inconspicuously as he would later claim to be able to enter and leave a room full of people. And although the fact of his being refused permission to step ashore at Hodeidah remains unchanging, Lewis subsequently imbued the incident with very different meanings. In 1937 the harbour master apparently announced his decision 'suddenly, and for no apparent reason'. In 1985 Lewis alluded to 'a terrible confusion' in which the port authorities thought he was attempting to deliver a shipment of arms. In 2001 he claimed to be the unwitting victim of an 'ingenious subterfuge' perpetrated by a travelling companion whom he suspected of having been in league with the Italians. Lewis' early assertion that 'every aspect of the voyage was attended by uncertainty' appeared as accurate at its end as at its beginning, and was as astute in 2001 as in 1937. And yet, in his final retelling, the last of his published essays, Lewis hinted at a definitive explanation. Tellingly perhaps, he suggested for the first time that the dhow upon which he had travelled 'bore the name *El Haq*': The Truth. This revelation may have been the prelude to other truths. The voyage by dhow had not been the 'journalistic trip' that Lewis described in 1937: in 2001 he revealed that he had been a 'secret agent' equipped with a 'spy camera'.

It is eminently plausible. In 1937 Yemen was a source of some concern for the British government. Italy's occupation of Abyssinia in 1936 had already threatened Britain's control of Red Sea shipping and interests in emergent Arabian oil. Moreover, Mussolini was said to be on good terms with Yemen's Imam Yahya. Yahya's interests, though, were far more insular. The imam had ruled Yemen from Sanaa ever since the end of the First World War had sealed the fate of the Ottoman Empire and the Turks departed from the Arabian Peninsula. Subsequently, Yahya kept his country closed off to a great degree from the outside world and from the trappings of 'modernity'. Purportedly this was to prevent corruption of the pure Islamic faith; presumably it also served to prevent challenge to Yahya's rule. In London, the Foreign Office was eager to understand the imam's political allegiances and the state of his isolationist theocracy. Norman Lewis had been recruited to visit Yemen as a 'civilian observer', taking photographs and making notes as he travelled. In the end, of course, Lewis was unable to glean any knowledge of Sanaa. Yet never 'was a journey richer in experience, and the fact that the avowed object of the expedition remained unfulfilled was of little importance,' Lewis wrote after the aborted assignment gave rise to his career as an author, not an agent.

Mine was a familial mission. My parents were moving house. From my childhood home in Suffolk they were relocating back to Ireland and they had asked me to return from Yemen to sort out my possessions. It was for this reason that in the summer of 2006 I had visited a Zubeiry Street travel agent, collected orders for Parmesan cheese, taken a taxi to Sanaa's airport via two of the city's museums, and arrived at a West London hotel in the early hours after a late flight into Heathrow, before journeying on to Suffolk. The next few days were spent up and down a loft ladder, and opening and emptying boxes, then sorting, discarding, and repacking plywood shipping crates. School exercise books and Star Wars toys. Bicycle bits and model aircraft. Heavily thumbed anatomy textbooks and a rarely used dinner jacket. I discovered lost treasures of the past thirty years, with all their attendant stories. Yet with many of my memories I am aware of only really remembering their last retelling. Which is why, rather than fostering my distrust, Norman Lewis' shifting narratives suggest to me an unusual authenticity and honesty. With each recounting he seems to be struggling to return to the source, to recall actual events, rather than just his last recollection of them. When this appears to expose inconsistencies, it only confirms the challenge of his objective and the changeable nature of memories and their meanings. In Suffolk I threw a lot away, though not enough according to parental wisdom. I kept my old camera, a second-hand Olympus OM10, well-travelled and much-loved. I repacked the shoeboxes full of 35mm Kodak negatives; tiny hundredths of a second in almost-sepia orange. And I recollected other summer homecomings, with mown grass, creosote, honeysuckle, and the backdoor key hidden in the shed. Memories to be returned to someday.

The evening prayer call would have marked the passage of time. One by one we would have excused ourselves. Outside, we would have emptied the green paste of our masticated *qat* leaves into the shrubbery. It is a messy task, no matter how well practiced; sliding a finger along the gums and spitting, then rinsing out your mouth after. The inevitable end to a *qat* chew, an experience that you may or may not have found pleasurable. It is hard not to think that some of my own attachment to these habits and to this temporary home in Sanaa arose predictably and necessarily from my having said goodbye to another home in Suffolk. Our fellow chewers would not have departed, but merely retired, to sit in the warm air, beneath the creeping vines and the evening sky. There would have been a sniff of whisky, the scent of honeysuckle, a thrum of traffic, and the summer nocturne of crickets or cicadas.

Six months after Norman Lewis, two entomologists from the British Museum arrived in Aden. They too were hoping to visit Sanaa. And their preparations had been impressively thorough. Hugh Scott and Everard Britton had sent a written request to Imam Yahya, asking permission to enter Yemen. And they had brought all the necessary equipment for catching and sorting insect specimens: butterfly nets and pooters, meshes and funnels, chisels for lifting bark, and a crowbar for boulders. While awaiting the imam's response, they set about collecting the grasshoppers, locusts, beetles, bees, wasps, butterflies, and moths of the British Aden protectorate. Again their packing was exemplary: insect bodies were fixed with steel pins, enfolded in cellulose wool, or preserved in tubes of spirit. And to protect the specimens from ants, they were placed upon tabletops with the table legs stood in tins full of water. Otherwise though, Scott and Britton had no intention of their expedition becoming waterborne. They planned to reach Sana from Aden overland, avoiding Lewis' thwarted sea route.

Hugh Scott's account of their journey *In the High Yemen* is adorned with the observations of an enthusiastic naturalist; 'buttercups and tall yellow potentilla', 'tufts of golden-yellow primula', and 'mauve flower-heads of homely field scallions'. Scott was especially fascinated by the differences between the flora of Southern Arabia and that of the Horn of Africa; perceiving that the Red Sea had acted as a barrier between evolutionary forms. 'For instance, the giant lobelias of the Tropical African mountains reach as far north as the Eritrean highlands, but are not found across the Red Sea in Yemen,' he wrote. Conversely, some 'European and Asiatic' species such as the Iris had reached Yemen, but not Africa. Meanwhile, the two English entomologists made their own adaptations to the Arabian environment. 'Applying neat brandy from a pocket flask immediately,' they learnt, was the most effective analgesic for wasp stings. Britton discovered the dangers of wading through wadis in search of aquatic insects after suffering 'rather badly from sunburn about the knees'. And when clouds obscured the lunar surveying of their assistants, Scott devised a novel technique for confirming the dates of Ramadan by 'consulting the date of the New Moon in my Cambridge Pocket Diary'.

Still they awaited a decision from the imam as to whether or not they could enter Yemen. 'Could he be convinced of the innocence of our purpose?' asked Hugh Scott. Can we? While the butterfly collecting and floral effusing of the pair appear benign enough, the timing of their visit so soon after Norman Lewis arouses suspicions. As does the use to which their findings were ultimately put. For when the Second World War broke out two years later, Scott became formally attached to the Admiralty. He wrote a lengthy treatise for British Naval Intelligence on *Western Arabia and the Red Sea, 'for use of persons in H.M. Service only'*. At which point his allegiance shifted from the British Museum to the British government is not clear, but the 'innocence' of his journey to Yemen appears questionable in retrospect. Having already found travel writing by Arthur Wavell and George Wyman Bury appearing in the Arab Bureau's *Handbook of Yemen* during the First World War, it may come as no surprise to find that photographs and text from Scott's Yemen journey were reproduced in a strictly restricted document printed 'for official purposes' during the Second World War.

In the event, Imam Yahya not only permitted Scott and Britton a two-month stay in Sanaa, but also granted them a private audience. 'He looked at first glance a very ordinary man,' thought Scott, short, stout, 'and his face, though showing intelligence, would not be taken to show aristocratic breeding.' It is impossible to confirm or refute these rather snobbish-sounding remarks about Yahya's appearance, for the imam imposed a complete ban on images of himself. Partly this was due to religious stricture, but mostly it reflected a strongly held superstition that any reproductions of his image would lead to his untimely demise. Scott admitted to 'some disillusionment' upon meeting the seventy-year-old ruler of Yemen. Yet he acknowledged that, despite appearances, 'the Imam Yahya is far from ordinary.' It was almost an understatement. Imam Yahya - or, to give him his full title, Amir al-Mumenin Al-Mutawakkil 'Ala Allah Rab ul-Alamin Imam Yahya bin Al-Mansur Bi'llah Ahmad ud-din Muhammad Hamid ud-in, Imam and Commander of the Faithful, and

King of the Mutawakkilite Kingdom of the Yemen - was nothing if not extraordinary. He had grown up in in the fortress of Sheharah in Yemen's far north, resenting the Ottoman control of the country, and succeeding his father as imam of the Zaydis in 1904. It was Imam Yahya who led Yemen's tribes to conquer the capital in 1905; prompting the Ottoman siege and starvation of the population in the months prior to the visit of Aubrey Herbert and Leland Buxton. It was Imam Yahya who rallied the tribesmen to encircle the city in 1911; giving rise to the *Siege in Sanaa* witnessed by Arthur Wavell. It was Imam Yahya who seized control of the country after the collapse of the Ottoman Empire in 1918; swiftly turning his inherited dynastic right to rule into an unassailable autocracy, forming a regular army, placing his sons in key positions of authority, and consolidating personal control of Yemen's infrastructure and administration. And it was Imam Yahya who ordered the construction of the improbable Rock Palace on its sandstone pillar in Wadi Dahr.

Scott and Britton visited Wadi Dahr on one of their many day trips from the capital. There, unmistakably, 'perched on a detached rock' and 'scarcely finished at the time of our visit', they saw 'the amazing new house of the Imam'. But it was February and Yahya would not ascend to his rocky eyrie until summer. So when they met the imam it was at his palace in Sanaa, where 'the Imam was seated on cushions on the floor', surrounded by 'piles of papers of every shape and size', trapped in the micro-management of his own autocratic bureaucracy. The scientists watched as Yahya grabbed at documents and letters, glanced at them, scrawled his signature and any annotations, then tossed the papers to an army of clerks who hammered down the royal stamps and seals. One of these papers included a written request from his son to borrow the car for a day. Another note announced the death of a soldier in hospital, signed, thought Scott, as if 'giving the already deceased warrior permission to die'. The imam showed only marginal interest in the assortment of pinned insects, collecting boxes, nets, and dried plants that the entomologists had carried with them for his inspection. And Yahya's complete indifference to the postcards brought from the Natural History Museum appeared to come as particular disappointment, for 'all the great personages met on our journey saw these cards' and none had failed to be impressed. The Amir of Dhala had apparently been 'particularly amused at the huge skeleton of

Diplodocus'. The imam paused, though, to ask the entomologists whether, in the course of their scientific enquiries, they had encountered a stone that could cure snakebites by its touch. Scott replied diplomatically, claiming that he had heard of such a stone but could not suggest where it might be found. The principal interest of Britton and Scott in meeting the imam, however, was to negotiate their departure from Yemen. They watched as their request to travel out along the old high road via Manakha was written on a slip of paper and passed to the imam, who wrote on it a refusal and handed it back. Scott and Britton would exit Yemen by the new motor route: faster, but far less interesting. They stopped only briefly en route to dig some weevils from under rocks and shake a few ladybirds from a juniper bush.

Scott recalled their 'disappointment' and 'dismay' at Yahya's apparently groundless rejection of their petition. But the imam's reasoning was often incomprehensible to foreigners. He was reputed to be strict and to seem irrational at times. 'Suspicious and xenophobic,' Norman Lewis had suggested, despite having never met him, nor entered his country. 'An all-powerful despot', 'who daily administered the ferocious Koranic justice seated under a tree at the gates of his palace'. Lewis had noted some of the restrictions apparently enforced by Imam Yahya. It was forbidden to sing, to whistle, to walk backwards, to give a horse a human name, to point at the full moon, to wear a watch unless it was left unwound as only an ornament. Smoking was liable to punishment of three months in chains and tennis was soon to be banned because it was a sort of immoral dance. Yahya had outlawed aircraft in Yemen after two German pilots died in an aviation accident near Sanaa, which at least showed a discernible logic.

'Travel documents, medications, wallets, and keys... In clear plastic bags.' Terminal staff shouted out the new restrictions on hand-baggage. Nothing else was to be carried aboard the plane. All other pocket contents, mobile phones, laptops, books and pens were to be placed in the hold. There were armoured vehicles outside Heathrow when I arrived for my return flight back to Sanaa on 12 August 2006. Two days earlier the airport had been the focus of a foiled terrorist plot to detonate liquid explosives on seven transatlantic airliners. If it had succeeded it would have killed more people than 9/11. Heathrow had ground to a chaotic halt. A solid mass of people and luggage became lodged at Terminal Two amid unprecedented emergency security procedures. This was the moment at which the liquids ban on flights began. The only concession was to nursing mothers who were permitted to carry small amounts of bottled milk, so long as they drank some to prove it was innocuous. At the Yemenia check-in desk I watched the airline's staff apologise to an incredulous old man who wished to travel with his Koran. My thwarted alcohol allowance seemed a minor inconvenience.

Besides, when I arrived back home in Sanaa I discovered that Ibrahim had removed the ceramic bathtub from my bathroom, sterilised it, and installed it in the garden for the season's grape trampling. Not long after, we spent an afternoon stomping then squeezing bucket loads of fat, blistering grapes into a dark must that drained slowly through the bathtub's plughole and filled six large plastic jerry cans. The grape juice would remain in the dark coolness of our building's basement for the next six months, before being ready to drink. Wine had once been a passion of imams in Sanaa, but according to Hugh Scott in 1937, those found guilty of drinking alcohol would be flogged 'or in other ways shamed'. The public shaming might involve being tarred or mounted backwards on a donkey. Alternatively, 'a small drum is tied to the culprit's back, and this is beaten while he is led round the town amid the jeers of the people.' In Yahya's Yemen, the punishments seemed as idiosyncratic as the crimes.

In Sanaa, I would not have been the only one among us to have harboured memories of England. And perhaps, after the *qat* chew, when you and I had left the *mafraj* to sit outside in the early evening with Ibrahim and the others, if the *qat* and the company and the drink had succeeded, as they always did, in coaxing a convivial atmosphere, Fuad might have entertained us with his own recollections of an England as idiosyncratic as anything that ever was in Yemen. 'Her husband just sat at the table. Eating his breakfast. Listening to the radio. Reading his newspaper. Not saying anything. He didn't speak a work to her or to me. Until his little dog trotted in and then he'd put down his newspaper and start scratching its belly and rubbing its ears and telling the dog how good it was. And then he'd give the dog a sausage from his plate. And I thought someday the dog might get its own seat at the table. Or take his wife's seat.'

Many years earlier, Fuad had been the childhood victim of some well-meaning cultural programme that placed innocent Yemeni children in typically dysfunctional suburban English homes for mercifully brief periods.

'Every morning the woman made me eat strips of pork and a plateful of watery bean stew. The beans were *bright orange*. And then she'd ask me, "*Fwwwaarrrd. Fwwwaarrrd.* Would you like tea?"' Delighting in his retelling, Fuad would have affected an ever-so proper English accent.

'And I would say, "Yes pleeese!" And she would say, "And how many sugars do you take?" And I'd say, "Four pleeese." And then she'd turn the radio down and say, "Arthur dear, did I hear him say *fawwwr*?!!!"'

By which point the laughter would be belly-aching.

The BBC made its first Arabic Service radio broadcast in January 1938. Assenting to popular request, Imam Yahya lifted his prohibition on the use of wireless sets soon after. In London, the Foreign Office was keen to utilise this newly opened communication channel to conduct an anti-fascist and pro-British media campaign in Yemen. But the BBC refused to broadcast propaganda. And so the Foreign Office recruited the well-known travel writer Freya Stark instead. She was to promote support for the British by showing short propaganda films in Sanaa. So, in February 1940, Stark bluffed her way across the border from Aden into Yemen with a 16mm cine-projector, a portable screen, and three Pathé newsreels, claiming that all these boxes and bits were merely the component parts of a portable commode.

Reaching Sanaa, Stark's opinions of the city were temperamental in the extreme. At first her correspondence crackled with displeasure. 'It is a sordid town,' she wrote; 'the decoration vulgar... the people almost too dingy to be picturesque.' 'If one felt feverish, it would turn into a nightmare.' Yet soon she was cooing about 'this medieval city with its brown minarets against the brown hills and its blossoming trees behind the garden walls. Such luminous high skies!' Stark spent six weeks in Sanaa and later related her experiences in an autobiography, *Dust in the Lion's Paw*, and in her published letters. To her friends she described an 'enchanting holiday'. 'It is all Romance pure and simple,' she wrote to her publisher. Regular messages sent to her mother in Italy revealed only innocent local gossip and goings on, but nonetheless resulted in her mother being briefly arrested by the Italian authorities who were suspicious of Stark's activities. Her most consequential communications from Yemen though, and the reason for her being there at all, were her regular dispatches to Colonel Clayton in Cairo. Stark reported on troop numbers and their condition ('weakened by malaria and the drug kat'). She provided information on Axis propaganda efforts (a German engineer was distributing fascist literature and an Italian woman doctor had been planted in the harems). And she delivered updates on her own propaganda activities ('I have been whispering so hard that *something* ought to come of it').

'All things in Arabia are done by the harem,' Stark had been advised. Night after night she entertained the women in Sanaa's towerhouses with her Pathé newsreels. Flickering scenes in black and white demonstrated the precision flying of the Royal Air Force and the scuttling of the *Graf Spee*, as well as a green and pleasant Britain. '*Ordinary life in Edinburgh* is the present rather surprising favourite: they adore it - just people walking up and down Princes Street!' 'In a chaos of women, children, darkness and general confusion', Stark was able to inform Colonel Clayton that 'the little cinema has penetrated the chief harems'. She even suggested that the imam himself had been watching from behind a curtain at one of her screenings.

It was her role as a spy and clandestine propagandist that intermittently turned Sanaa into the stuff of nightmares for Freya Stark. 'It is *awful* to live in this intriguing atmosphere,' she wrote on 28 February 1940 in a note to Stewart Perowne, the man who later became her husband. She was oppressed by the 'feeling of secret horror and intrigue'. Upon departing Yemen's capital she acknowledged that 'if it were not for the ghastly foreign intrigue one would bring away nothing but kind and friendly feelings.' By then it must have been an open secret in Sanaa that Stark was a British agent. Her letters were apt to be opened by Italian censors after being passed on by a sympathising postman ('an Albanian who wants an Italian passport'). And the authorities in Aden could not be dissuaded from sending messages to her in envelopes stamped 'On Her Majesty's Service'.

Her mission to Sanaa in 1940 was not Freya Stark's first visit to Southern Arabia. She had gained her fame as a travel author for two earlier journeys through the Aden protectorate. Twice she had travelled from Aden in search of the ancient frankincense trade routes, and twice she had fallen ill and called the RAF to rescue her from the desert. The Aden authorities were not amused: the Royal Air Force was not in Arabia to retrieve sun-stroked tourists. Stark herself acknowledged that point. In one of her travelogues she noted matter-of-factly that 'the Se'ar tribe have stolen 42 camels and are probably going to be bombed by the R.A.F.' Britain's colonial administrator Harold Ingrams and his wife Doreen had brokered a truce between conflicting Arabian tribes for whom 'air power would become an instrument of peace'. According to the terms of 'Ingram's Peace', tribes that did not adhere to the Pax Britannica would have their villages bombed. Doreen Ingrams suggested that offenders would welcome the occasional aerial bombardment as an opportunity to submit without losing face. Stark thought this the 'sort of warfare which the medieval courtesy of the Arab can understand'. Norman Lewis, with disappointing disingenuousness, asserted that 'casualties are the consequence of a too complete faith': the tribes, instead of fleeing their villages at the first sign of attack, insisted on reading the Koran 'ceremonially as an anti-aircraft measure.' A 'peace' primarily intended to ease the implementation of British colonial administration, and the use of bombs to enforce it, was accepted with unsettling ease. Behind their travelogues, in their condoning of the use of military force against unarmed villagers, as well as in their apparent complicity with espionage in Yemen, British authors like Norman Lewis, Hugh Scott, and Freya Stark tell a story of close links between travel writing and national interest at a time of impending or actual war.

Hans Helfritz offers a notable counterpoint. 'A horrid stunting German who has already written a *cheap* book about this country,' Freya Stark wrote bitterly of him in 1935. Helfritz had proven more successful than Stark in tracing the incense routes of Southern Arabia and became the first European to enter Yemen's ancient city of Shabwa: something that Stark had hoped to achieve. He made three visits to the region during the 1930s, taking thousands of photographs, writing his own travelogue, and recording Bedouin songs onto dozens of wax cylinders that remarkably managed to survive the heat of the desert and reach the Berlin Ethnological Museum. But Helfritz himself opted never to return to Nazi Germany.

When bombs began dropping in Europe, Yemen had remained distanced from the destruction. 'It was difficult to believe there was a war in Sanaa,' Doreen Ingrams reflected, there being 'no air raids, and nothing to bring war close'. Freya Stark was surprised in 1940 to find the city's two British doctors best of friends with the German residents, even knitting a bonnet for a German new-born. Stark was bemused, 'watching the making of the bonnet in the lamplight, and thinking of all the factories of Europe blazing through the night, turning out bombs.' Doctor Patrick Petrie, whose wife was knitting the bonnet, thought 'Sanaa and the *Qat*-Eaters' had a pervasive mood 'almost of unreality', 'of being outside the world'. 'Few of them have travelled,' he noted. Even Imam Yahya had never seen the sea. If he *had* been hiding behind a curtain at one of Freya Stark's secret cinema screenings, Yahya might have found the scuttling of the *Graf Spee* marvellous, or perhaps no more impressive than Hugh Scott's postcards of dinosaur bones. According to Doctor Petrie, Sanaa's population assumed that Europe's warring nations 'would ultimately call in the Imam': Yahya would act as 'arbiter in the dispute, and that of course would settle everything.' The doctor might have been justified in his scorn for unquestioning faith in leaders, but it was hardly fair to single out the Yemenis for that.

The war was over when I awoke. Sunrise had still been hidden behind the hills of Sanaa when our plane landed, and I yawned through a cab ride from the airport into the city. Snoozing, jet-lagged, through the rest of the day, when I woke the next morning the BBC was reporting a ceasefire. Hundreds of civilians had been killed in the conflict between Lebanon and Israel and many thousands more displaced. In other news, restrictions on aircraft hand baggage had been eased a little, but the carrying of liquids on board flights would remain largely prohibited. Death, destruction, terror; bombs may be instruments for all these, but not for peace, no matter what Norman Lewis, Freya Stark, and the strategists behind Ingram's Peace might have thought in 1937.

Freya Stark returned twice to Sanaa, in March and November of 1976; either side of her visits that year to Paddy Leigh Fermor in Greece, and to the British Royal Family in Caithness, and shortly before she set off on a raft down the Euphrates for another travel adventure. She announced her 1976 Yemen travel plans in a telegram to the Secretary of the British Embassy in Sanaa: 'Arriving Wednesday, Freya.' She was eighty-three. Her memory not yet clouded by dementia, thirty-six years after the event, she vividly recalled an incident from 1940 and her six-day journey between Aden and Sanaa with her film projector and newsreels. Spending a night in the home of the governor of a provincial town, in the early hours, through half-closed eyelids, Stark watched a figure creep into the room and, feigning sleep, she recognised her host. He came close, placed something against her cheek, and then was gone. The object began tinkling tunefully: a musical box. The governor was 'accustomed no doubt to go in and out of his own harem whenever the musical box fancy took him,' she wrote at the time in a letter describing the encounter to her mother. In 1976 she disclosed to the Secretary of the British Embassy: 'I thought I was coming closer to losing my virtue that night than at any time before, and in retrospect since, including the nights I spent with Stewart.' Stewart Perowne, the man to whom she had once written with unusual candour about the horror and intrigue in Sanaa, and the man who ultimately became her husband, had been also a homosexual. Stark found out only after their wedding and struggled to forgive him. 'It was the not knowing, when most others did, that hurt.' After decades without contact following their separation in 1952, it was whilst in Yemen in 1976 that Stark finally wrote to Stewart again, wishing him well from Sanaa. Perhaps recalling her horror of the secrecy and intrigue in the city, she finally acknowledged the secrecy that must have been forced on Stewart in an era when homosexuality was punishable with a prison sentence. Or perhaps it was mere sentimentality. 'I am losing a lot of old friends,' she wrote wistfully during her time in Sanaa, 'not so much old age... but just vicissitude, a word that seems to me to give just the feeling it expresses - a jumble of the unmanageable consonants of life.'

By now the moon would have risen and the bottles would have emptied.

After all the *qat* and the alcohol, the last wisps of cigarette smoke and anecdote would have drifted up into the night sky. And when the murmur of conversation, the burble of the water pipe, and the putter of Ibrahim's old car had ceased, the garden would at last have fallen silent.

- 15 -

Veils

- Louise Février, 1947; Claude Fayein, 1951 -

THERE WAS A STONE FLOOR, there was my body slapped against it, there was heat, and there was pain. And there were three blurred shapes in pristine white underpants sniggering as my toes were clenched, then audibly crunched. I released a muted gasp. Chunks of flesh along my spine had been pinched and tweaked, my arms then fingers had been wrenched and tugged. My calves had been wrung out like wet towels. My head had been twisted like the lid of a stubborn jam jar.

'Ok?'

Face down, an unfamiliar sound seeped out of me in reply, like something that might need mopping up. Then a foot stamped sharply focused into my short-sighted vision. The foot was not mine, but the contortion would hardly have surprised me anymore. Straining with the only muscles that seemed not to hurt, I swivelled my eyeballs to take in the foot's owner as he stood above me. But from the foot, my gaze got only as far as the knee before perspective failed me. Cautiously, rolling my head a fraction further round, from temple to ear against the hot flagstones, I was able to squint myopically up at the hammami. Peering down over his belly, he seemed to be smiling.

'Enough,' he announced.

The hammam had caused an altogether different discomfort for Louise Février. 'We had to keep the windows shut because of our proximity to a public bath,' she explained, for the hammam was 'heated by human or camel dung.' Mostly Février was offended by the smell. But she also intimated distaste at the way in which women trampled the dung 'with their bare feet' and made it into cakes 'with their hands'. It was all very unhygienic.

The Italian doctors encountered by Freya Stark had slipped away from Sanaa, their position becoming increasingly precarious as the Second World War progressed. The English Doctor Petrie and his bonnet-knitting wife departed after a typhus outbreak took the life of their Scottish nurse. When the imam specifically requested a French physician who would be willing to work in Sanaa, Doctor Pierre Février had responded. He arrived in the summer of 1947. Louise Février accompanied her physician husband, along with their three children. The family were given a house in Sanaa, complete with horses and servants. Which caused another dung-related affront for Louise when she found the houseboy cleaning the floor in the traditional manner: 'by scattering horse dung and sweeping up the dust with it.'

The house had no electricity. The entire city was without electric power. Even a generator in the imam's palace could do no more than 'induce a faint glow in a bulb'. The Févriers had brought a wind-up gramophone from France, but they were advised against playing it; just as Norman Lewis had forewarned, 'the Imam had recently made a public bonfire of these potentially irreligious instruments.' Despite their privations, the Février family settled swiftly into Sanaa. They soon befriended an English locust control officer, a Lebanese pharmacist, two Italian mechanics, and a mysterious Frenchman whom they suspected of arms smuggling. Another of their new companions was Yemen's self-appointed Engineer-in-Chief, whose response to newcomers was not always magnanimous (reacting to the arrival of an Egyptian delegation with its own Engineer-in-Chief he promptly promoted himself to the position of 'Engineer-in-Chief of the Engineers-in-Chief'). Following the imam's aviation ban, the Engineer-in-Chief kept the kingdom's only aircraft grounded in his back garden, supposedly for use in event of an emergency. 'He had never flown it but had a book of instructions,' Louise Février noted, amused by her curious new friends. Outside the small expatriate community she was also made welcome. Soon after their arrival, Louise and her seventeen-year-old daughter were invited into a harem where they 'drank mint tea out of Limoges china and watched the elder ladies placidly puffing their narghiles.' The younger women 'tried on our hats, were astonished at our silk stockings and lifted our skirts to admire our underwear.' Hardly the Penetration of Arabia, nor the penetration of harems claimed by Stark, but this was an exploration, and an acknowledgement of being explored. Before long though, Louise's attentions were shifted far from the intimacies of harems, the eccentricities of émigrés, and concerns about domestic cleaning methods or the hygiene of heating hammams.

'In October 1947 my husband died.' Barely four months after arriving in Sanaa, Doctor Février fell victim to some illness that he was unable to treat. Louise Février's published recollection of her husband's death is starkly perfunctory. A sentence gasped, it has the laden brevity of a devastated telegram. The impact can scarcely be conceived. It was a bereavement suffered by a wife and three children in an unfamiliar country where they didn't speak the language and were largely cut off from family and friends. Imam Yahya placed the family under his personal protection. Meanwhile, protracted preparations were made for their departure from Yemen. Then Louise recalled how, unexpectedly, 'on Tuesday, 17 February 1948, at 2 p.m. the Engineer-in-Chief of the Engineers-in-Chief arrived at our house, breathless and trembling.' Imam Yahya was dead.

It hurt to move. It hurt to breathe. My slow inhalations drew in a dense hot vapour, scalding and suffocating. Tentative, testing movements re-established the location and function of body parts. A signal sent to my right arm was answered by a twitch of muscle that felt relatively painless. With a shove and a squirm, I flipped over my tenderised flesh. My palms pressed to the floor, searching for comfort, calm, a neutral position, while the floor slabs seared my buttocks. My eyelids slid down slowly, light filtering through my closing lashes from three tiny alabaster windows in a domed ceiling stained green with mould. Eventually there was only a trio of lurid aura, the receding echo of water, and then stillness.

For all Louise Février's aversion to them, the dung cakes that once heated Sanaa's hammams were part of an impressive self-sustaining system. Donkeys drew water from the city's wells; donkey dung cakes were burnt to heat the hammams' water; ash and wastewater provided fertiliser and irrigation for the city's allotments; and these produced feed for the donkeys. Imam Yahya would have approved. Closed systems epitomised Yahya's Yemen.

The death of the 'King who preferred isolation' was reported in the British press. 'His distrust of foreigners and dislike of Western civilisation' was renowned. Yahya was said to have segregated his country 'from the rest of the world'. No foreign diplomatic representatives had ever been permitted in Sanaa and Yemen's only ambassador was based in Cairo, so it was from there that details dripped slowly over the ensuing days. Yahya had been assassinated. Machine-gunned in his car a few miles outside Sanaa. It was a coup d'état, plotted by disaffected reformers seeking to break Yahya's autocratic sequestration of power. The conspirators took control of the capital and proclaimed a new ruler. But the triumph was short-lived. Yahya's son Ahmad utilised his access to the royal coffers to recruit Yemen's tribes and surround the city. Within a month of his father's death, Ahmad entered Sanaa and had himself proclaimed imam. His father's killers were rounded up, imprisoned, and beheaded. Their heads, gruesomely displayed about the city, were keenly photographed by the Février children. Meanwhile, the tribesmen who had backed Ahmad now ransacked Sanaa. Women had jewellery snatched from their necks, buildings had their doors and window frames lifted, and looters had their own booty looted by other looters who arrived late to the pillage. When the Engineer-in-Chief ventured out in search of his stolen property he had his jacket taken from him, and then his spectacles. 'Finally, saturated with plunder, the tribesmen returned to their mountains' and the impressively resilient Louise Février and her three children were able to return to France. More than three decades later, Lucille Février, middle child and only daughter, returned to the site in Sanaa where her father was buried alongside the two German airmen and the Scottish nurse. And two decades after that, in 2002, by then well into her seventies, Lucille Février published her own account of events, based on the diaries she had written as a seventeen-year-old in Sanaa.

'Tshhh, tshhh, tshhh', three steps. Then a pause, lifting our right legs. Then the left. And three more steps, each accompanied by our hushed intonation, 'tshhh, tshhh, tshhh.' Changing direction, half a dozen half-naked men moved in a circle. 'Allah, Allah, Allah.' Joining hands so as not to lose our pace, 'tshh, tshh, tshh'. Faster and faster, with its rhythmic steps and quiet chanting, the hammam dance continued, round and round, then back again, clockwise then counter-clockwise. A pirouette introduced after the left leg raise set us whirling like spinning tops. Until one by one, from fear of slipping or sheer fatigue, we retired from the hot room dance, excusing ourselves with the assertion that we had worked up sufficient sweat. Strictly speaking, I had been told, this was not a dance but a ritual, a very particular sequence of steps. The distinction would have seemed pedantic, except that dancing had once been frowned upon in Imam Yahya's Yemen.

The hammam was a place of ritual. Of prescribed movements through a labyrinth of hot and cold rooms, a passage between intensities of temperatures and humidities, performing the rites of sweating and rubbing down. Said also to be a place of *djinns* or demons, there were superstitious invocations to be uttered upon entering. Through a nondescript door in an unexceptional alley, down a narrow staircase to a drab curtain that opens with a belch of moist warm air. The underground room beyond is adorned with rugs and rattan, pendentives and squinch arches. There were clothes piled in wall niches, figures dressing and undressing, but there were also a mihrab, an empty *salta* dish, and a water pipe. Not just a changing room, but a place for praying, eating, smoking, chatting, chewing. A social space, open early morning to late evening, on alternate days for men and women. The bathhouse had been embedded in Sanaa for centuries, long before the Turks arrived, even before Islam some said. The public hot baths were born of the cool climate, the necessity of ablutions, the local scarcity of water, and a limited private supply of fuel, which nowadays was as likely to be rubber flip-flops and car tyres as dung cakes. The hammam's hot rooms were said to increase blood circulation and bring countless other health benefits, as well as improving sexual performance. The stimulus for my own visits was the more prosaic removal of my bathtub, not yet replaced following the late summer grape pressing. Having surrendered my spectacles to the care of the hammam owner, I would disrobe discreetly, wrapping a *futah* about my waist before removing my boxer shorts and then entering the baths.

Claude Fayein had been far more brazen. She 'undressed rapidly and completely, in the French manner.' In a hammam on the road to Sanaa, the 'modest Moslem women' had removed their clothes 'with all the skilful technique practised in our Catholic boarding schools, and furtively glanced at me with scandalised eyes.' It was the 'greatest social error of my whole trip,' Doctor Fayein later recalled. An unfortunate faux pas, for genitals were best kept covered in Yemen, even in the hammam. But Fayein was not to know, having been in the country only a few days. In 1951 she roared up from Aden in an old Ford roadster, with a red ostrich plume fitted to the radiator cap. Replacing the deceased Doctor Février as physician in Sanaa, she had been the sole applicant for the job. During the year that Doctor Fayein spent in Sanaa, her four 'judiciously spaced' children remained with her husband in Paris. Arguably Louise Février had shown equal courage in bringing her children to Yemen, but Claude Fayein was undeniably more flamboyantly intrepid than her preceding female compatriot.

Yemen had changed since the death of Yahya and the departure of the Févriers. Sanaa was no longer the capital. The new Imam Ahmad governed from Taiz. He probably didn't trust the northerners after they had murdered his father. They probably didn't trust him after he had allowed their city to be looted. According to Doctor Fayein, Ahmad had bulging eyes, a terrible temper, and was prone to 'periodic mystic seizures'. He was known to the people as 'Ahmed the Djinn'. His bulging eyes were rumoured to have been deliberately induced during childhood by periods of prolonged self-strangulation in an effort to terrorise his peers. He was said to have had several of his own brothers murdered and the beheadings and imprisonments that marked his accession became a pattern of his unforgiving reign. A photograph of Ahmad and his royal entourage 'attending an execution' confirms Fayein's description of his terrifyingly protuberant eyeballs, apparently exaggerated for the occasion by the liberal application of kohl. Unlike his father, Ahmad was not averse to having his photograph taken. Indeed, the strictly regulated adoption of personally gratifying technologies became another motif of his rule. After lifting Yahya's aviation ban, he kept the flight plans of the nation's aircraft under his personal command. Mains electricity was introduced, chiefly, according to Fayein, so that Ahmad could spend hours controlling an electric train set. Despite his resentment of the British, whom he suspected of connivance in Yahya's death and who continued to drop bombs intermittently upon tribes in the south, Ahmad was grateful when the newly-appointed British representative in Taiz began supplying him with film footage of football matches that he was able to view using his newly-obtained cine-projector. He became a Liverpool fan. Restrictions on music were eased so that instead of the bonfire of gramophones reported by Louise Février, Claude Fayein was able to engage an audience by playing *The Sorcerer's Apprentice* with her windows thrown wide open. But there appeared to be little meaningful change for the people of Yemen. Villagers were still impoverished by heavy taxes and mandatory bribes. There were only a handful of schools and the formal health service consisted of just a few foreign doctors like Février and Fayein. Toward the end of his rule, during his visit to Yemen's only x-ray machine in Hodeidah, some disaffected officers emptied their revolvers into Imam Ahmad at point blank range. That he survived this and other attempts upon his life only served to fortify his intimidating reputation.

In Sanaa's hospital, the husband of Louise Février had been frustrated because patients would often take it upon themselves to swap the charts from the ends of their beds when they fancied a change of conversation with their physician. Doctor Claude Fayein was frustrated in her clinical examinations of Sanaa's women because they were 'overwhelmed by modesty, fears, and hesitations'. Even obtaining a simple narrative of symptoms was an arduous task, since her male translator was not allowed to enter the women's rooms, and 'a well-bred wife must hear no male voice other than that of her husband.' The onerous solution was for Fayein to remain alone with the woman, shouting questions in French to her translator who sat outside and spoke quietly to the husband so that he could enter and whisper the enquiry in his wife's ear. Like the Février family, Claude Fayein was given a house and servants, but again, the gender proscriptions caused her problems. She wanted female house staff. But 'this would be impossible'. 'Arab men never allow their wives to serve anybody but themselves,' she remarked begrudgingly. 'If only the Jewish women had still been there!'

But the Jews had all left. They departed en masse not long before Fayein arrived. For centuries the Jews of Sanaa had lived through persecution and public humiliation; from curfews and petty restrictions upon the height of their houses, to having dead cats thrown at them and eating dogs during sieges. Later they also suffered the indignity of having to collect night soil for the hammams. Under the reign of Imam Yahya many Jews felt that they were treated relatively well, and he was regarded by some as their protector. But the murder of the imam in February 1948 triggered volatility in Yemen and a renewed sense of vulnerability among Yemenite Jews. In May that same year the declaration of the State of Israel in Palestine further provoked anti-Jewish sentiments and made life yet more difficult for Jews in Arab lands. But the new state also created a homeland for the Jews to return to. It prompted an exodus from Sanaa as Jews headed south to board planes bound for Israel.

Between June 1949 and September 1950, almost the entire Yemeni Jewish population was relocated to Israel in Operation On Wings of Eagles, known colloquially as Operation Magic Carpet. Hundreds of flights departed from Aden, airlifting close to 50,000 people, many of whom had never even seen a plane before, let alone been on one. Aircraft with a maximal load of fifty passengers carried two or three times that number. The airlift organisers announced that 'the big load is made possible by the fact that the average weight of the Yemenite Jews, who are small in stature, is 85 pounds (about 39 kilos). Seats which normally hold two American passengers hold three and four Yemenites.' In fact, the average weight of the Yemenite Jew was more likely due to their emaciation rather than their small stature. Malnutrition, malaria, and the hardships of the trek south toward Aden had taken their toll. Hundreds died during the long journey from their homes, in temporary camps outside Aden, and on planes to Tel Aviv. According to doctors at Israel's airport, most people arriving from Yemen were so weak that they needed help to get off the plane. Their children made no noise, it was noted, and their infants did not cry. In the birth of the Jewish State, the Yemenite *aliyah* was sombre and silent.

Sound is absorbed by flesh. In the hammam there were no echoes. There were muscular youths, gaunt old men, fathers with paunches, and sons with puppy fat. And there were the three young boys in pristine white underpants lathering soap into one another's hair. The wash room was busier and cooler than the hot room from where I had come. A shoulder flashed brilliantly, in and out of glare, struck by a determined shaft of sunlight that wrestled with writhing steam. Muscles tensed then slackened, powering an arm back and forth, up and down, sponging the spine and shoulders of another man who sat folded forward over his belly. With butchers, barbers, cobblers, and laundry operators, the bath attendants had a lowly status in society. Their work with flesh determined their position, and perhaps it allowed them to vent some small silent fury at the injustice. Grasping my wrist vice-like, the bath attendant twisted my arm and tore a coarse woollen cloth down its length from my shoulder. Shreds of excoriated dirt, sweat, and dead skin fell from me in little dark rolls. Instructed to face the wall while my calves and the backs of my thighs were rubbed raw, wincing, I tried to focus on the moisture that condensed on the whitewashed stone, gathering and running down in lazy dribbles.

Then with gruff discretion I was handed the cloth to clean my crotch.

Sperm might lie dormant in the bathhouses, or so it was said. And since the hammams were often open to men and women on alternate days, and since, through sheer misfortune a chaste woman visiting the hammam might find herself sitting, unwittingly, in a puddle of dormant yet still potent semen where a man had carelessly deposited it on some earlier occasion, it was entirely possible for utterly innocent insemination to occur, or so I had heard. An extra-marital pregnancy might then reasonably be blamed upon a visit to the hammam. Whatever the scientific feasibility, it made some intuitive sense. Hot, damp, and buried underground, the hammam seemed an appropriate setting for the primordial mysteries of fecundity and procreation. Claude Fayein had encountered similar stories. 'In Yemen pregnancy may last four years,' she was told, 'since the foetus has the curious property of "lying dormant" in its mother's womb.' Thus peace might be preserved when a husband who had been away for some time returned home to find his family 'unexpectedly augmented'. The dormant foetus, like the dormant semen, presumably allowed women in Sanaa to express some measure of autonomy over what went on within their wombs. It was rumoured also that pregnancies begun in the hammam might be ended there too. Doctor Fayein 'detected several pregnancies among young girls', but 'never saw one of them come to its term.' As a woman, perhaps more than as a doctor, Fayein was given access to knowledge and secrets not previously revealed to foreigners. 'Sanaa women show great boldness in their intrigues,' she observed, and concluded that 'extra-marital adventures are possible and even frequent.' Which should not have come as a surprise, but it did.

Hana was not from Sanaa. She had been born in Aden and spent several years studying and working in Eastern Europe before returning to Yemen.

'Now I want to learn English very much,' she told me.

I told her how very much I wanted to learn Arabic.

'I study, but it is very hard for me,' she said.

Already we had a lot in common, my own language studies being a bit of a challenge. When Hana and I met at a *qat* chew her presence had been unprecedented. I had become almost inured to the rules that assigned men and women different days at the hammam, that had once intervened to prevent a woman from hearing the voice of a man who was not her husband, that created gender-based seating puzzles on city buses, and that meant outside of work I rarely encountered a woman not wearing a veil that concealed her face and a headscarf that covered her hair. These proscriptions would usually have stopped a Yemeni woman from attending a *qat* chew at which men were present: few women would have been willing to risk their reputation and few households would have wished to host the indiscretion. Exceptions might have been made for divorcees, spinsters, or foreigner women, since their circumstances apparently made their gender ambiguous, but with Hana, the impropriety seemed simply to be ignored. I might have assumed that perhaps this was because she and her family were not Sanaani, but really I neither knew nor cared. I had watched, fascinated, as she entered the *mafraj* and immediately removed her veil.

I was used to my female colleagues arriving at the workplace and unveiling, then putting on their veils again before they left to go home, but though these women might go without veils in the office, they always wore long black *abayas* and headscarfs at work. For a woman to uncover her face was *ayb*: frowned upon by society. But for a woman to uncover her hair was *haram*: forbidden by the Koran. Hoping to better understand these cultural and Koranic rules I once asked why women needed to cover themselves at all. Because, it was explained to me, women were objects of desire. And men were not able to control their desires. So I had been surprised when Hana, having removed her veil, then removed her headscarf and *abaya* too. She sat down next to me and we chatted, ineptly. Aden was ok. I liked Sanaa. She was a year younger than me. We were both unmarried. Switching between my struggling Arabic and her rather more competent English, we partook of the clumsiest flirtations imaginable. And watching her henna-touched fingers delicately plucking *qat* leaves and placing them in her mouth, I was quickly enthralled. She reached toward a bottle of water, and her hair fell forward from her shoulders. She pushed her hair back behind her ear, and her shoulder was exposed and, briefly, the nape of her neck.

Just as her presence at the *qat* chew was unprecedented in my experience, so too was her later presence in my apartment. Once she had cautiously closed all the curtains and locked the door, our faltering conversation finally ceased, breathlessly. And afterwards, and after explaining that she could not, of course, stay overnight, Hana got dressed and called a cab. I made some tea. Then I cleared some space for two mugs among the books and other items on the coffee table.

'Put it down!' There was alarm in her voice. 'It's *haram!*' She pointed to the books that I had lifted. Among them was an English translation of the Koran.

'You should always wash your hands before you pick up the Koran.'

I apologised, dully. Later I would find her sanctimony a little comic and a little hypocritical as I weighed her transgressions of only minutes earlier against my questionable hand hygiene. But Hana was balancing prohibitions far more ably than I could, and moving nimbly among constraints that would eventually impede me. Prompted by a polyphonic ring tone, then the parp of a car horn, she slipped back into her *abaya*, flung on her head covering, and tied the veil across her face. Downstairs, I drew back the bolt and was about to open the huge wooden door when she stopped me, lifted her veil, stood on tiptoes, and kissed me.

'I've seen it all too often,' Richard reflected sternly when I described the encounter over a cup of tea in his kitchen.

'In the Ukraine. Some dim-witted mid-life international employee falls for a stunning twenty-something sex bomb who's quite happy to take his pampering and pull his prick while he gives up a wife and two kids in Surrey thinking that he'll be happy with Natasha living on the edge of a coal mine in Donetsk. Always ends badly. Usually with liver failure.' Though well intentioned, his reflections didn't seem entirely relevant. The problem for me was not one of personal consequences, but of principles or morals. Was it right to continue an incipient relationship with a Yemeni woman knowing that it would offend local mores? Was it right to terminate it on account of religious and social codes that I did not believe in? It felt duplicitous to become subject to those local rules, but disrespectful to knowingly ignore them. My doubts were insoluble and ultimately inhibitory. Hana accepted this, but was disappointed by my timidity.

Claude Fayein faced similar questions more decisively, if inconsistently. 'At one moment in Yemen I believed that God was possible, and I loved a feudal country. Now I continue to be an atheist and a Marxist,' she wrote.

Though open about her own betrayals in retrospect, Fayein was unable to reconcile the compromises that she witnessed in Sanaa at the time. She despaired watching women act virtuously in front of their husbands while knowing of the emboldened sexual adventures that went on clandestinely. And she grew increasingly antagonistic toward the demure women whom she thought had too readily learnt their place in a patriarchal society.

'Surprise, horror, and pity!' Sarcastically, she recalled the day her calloused feet had been remarked upon in a harem. 'The feet of the harem women are as soft as a baby's cheek,' she noted. Fayein reacted forthrightly to the women's horror, challenging the petty concerns of their lives and contrasting them with the freedoms of her own; 'I was *living*.' But to her horror, the women were indifferent. 'My active life as a doctor won me no prestige in the harems.' Shortly before her departure, she argued with 'an assembly of scornful old wise men' over the subject of girls' education. At one of the few schools for girls 'hardly anything was taught but knitting'. The effects were lamentable. Bright enquiring girls became dulled and disengaged women, mere 'objects of pleasure or instruments of procreation'. The men responded, 'That is the way we like our wives.'

The obsession of the harem women with 'fashion magazines' and 'trinkets from France' infuriated Claude Fayein. Perhaps her feminist ideals would still have been offended decades later by the shopping district near Bab-Shuub, at the north end of the Old City. There, high heels and denim hems flashed from beneath *abayas*. Eyelashes and mascara flickered above veils. And the fashion interests of Sanaa's women were exposed among the boutiques. Bin Othman for Silver Objects, Al-Sudae World of The Gold, Al-Murshedi Jewels, and Al-Hamadi House of Perfumes. Al-Khadi Tailor, Al-Oboor Al-Khaled for Sewing, and Albshaer Shose. Heels and handbags cluttered the window display of Mr Albshaer. Elegant evening gowns swayed in the doorway of Mr Al-Khadi, while short skirts and little black dresses dangled on hanging rails. Nearby were *abayas* in polyester, cotton, or satin; loose fitting or figure-hugging; ornamented with sequins, or adorned with embroidered sleeves; all of course available only in black. In the window of a shop selling imported cosmetics was a promotional poster for a new eyelash brush. The text in English promised 'unbeatable volume for maximum impact'. The image showed a woman holding a veil to her face, coquettishly, hiding all but her blue eyes and their 'maximum impact'.

During my brief return visit to Suffolk, friends had asked me about women in Yemen wearing veils and what I thought about it. The enquirer would often proclaim their own feelings about veils being wrong and, perhaps, just a means of subjugating women. I had my own thoughts on the subject, but had never been convinced that they were especially important. Yet subsequently, back in Sanaa, I was surprised when one of my female colleagues asked me about veils. She kept up to date with international news and wanted to better understand the political significance of the issue in the UK. The subject had exploded in Britain that autumn after it was reported that a Labour MP had asked Muslim women not to wear face veils during meetings with him. A public furore had followed, with media calls to ban the veil. The Prime Minister at the time, Tony Blair, had intervened to say that they were 'a mark of separation'.

I replied to my female colleague in Sanaa by suggesting that for a man to ask a woman to remove a veil was probably no better than requiring her to wear one. And that for the majority of a population to define how a minority should dress would do nothing to diminish any sense of their separation.

Hana, covering her face before leaving my house, concealing her indiscretion, and disappearing anonymously into the night, had revealed to me another truth about veils. For while a veil might be a symbol of oppression, it might also (in its dissemblance) be a societal enabler. Perhaps surprisingly then, in simultaneously benefiting and oppressing, the veil may have something in common with high heels, breast enlargements, or other cosmetic embellishments that appear to enhance a woman's attractiveness, whilst endorsing the oppressive myth that her 'maximum impact' might reside in her appearance. Ultimately, focusing on the veil seems merely to exacerbate the prejudices that separate communities and distracts us from the wider realities of domestic violence, gender pay gaps, glass ceilings, and numerous other less visible oppressions that women are routinely subject to, irrespective of which culture or religion they live with.

Claude Fayein's account of her time in Yemen, originally published in Paris, was translated and released in Britain in 1957 as *A French Doctor in the Yemen*. A review was printed in *The Spectator*, a conservative weekly. 'Just what the title says, the doctor being female and endowed with the yelping sort of enthusiasm that is the French equivalent of St. Trinian's.' The anonymous *Spectator* reviewer, being almost certainly male, was unfair in his disparagement. Whatever was implied by the St. Trinian's comparison, it could hardly be applied to a woman who had prepared for her time in Yemen by studying ethnology under Claude Lévi-Strauss at the Musée de l'Homme, as well as completing courses in tropical medicine and Arabic. Moreover, conscious of the value of her learning, Fayein's scathing remarks about the education of girls in Sanaa was a far cry from yelping enthusiasm. By the time I arrived in Yemen, schools were integrated, but the number of girls remained few and they were still required to sit at the back of the class. This, rather than their veils, seemed to me to be the more significant expression of the patriarchy that persisted in Yemen, just as it had existed in Britain's conservative weeklies and persisted in a Labour MP's weekly surgeries.

In the hammam, after the hot room and the wash room, and after the sweating and the scrubbing, I stood in another of the underground spaces beneath a huge shower head that protruded from a tangle of knotted pipework. The air was cooler here and the shower head dribbled a tickle of cold water. Having passed through the fiery insides of the hammam I was slowly returning myself to the temperate outside air. Then suddenly, with a sharp intake of breath, I was momentarily frozen rigid. The hammami chuckled behind me, slapped me on the shoulder, and filled a second plastic jerry can of icy water with which to drench me.

- 16 -

Politics, Violence

- David Holden, 1957 & 1962 -

THE BODY WAS FOUND BY the roadside. It had been laid out neatly. Flat out, face up, arms folded, and feet together. Smartly dressed, but carrying no possessions. No passport, nothing. Nothing to reveal an identity, or nationality. Even the clothing labels had been removed. When the corpse was discovered in a Cairo suburb one morning in December 1977 the authorities were mystified. Foreign embassies in Egypt were contacted and informed that 'an unknown European male' was dead. Who he was and what he was doing here were not immediately clear. All that was known was how he had died. A single 9mm bullet, fired at close range, had entered his back just beneath his left shoulder blade, scorching his jacket and piercing his heart.

I had reached a dead end. It looked, briefly, as though I had run out of writers. Until now I had been guided by Serjeant and Lewcock's book *San'a: An Arabian Islamic City*. The book's bibliography, photocopied for me by the librarian in the Old City, had reliably directed me toward those foreigners who had travelled to Yemen's capital and then written about their experiences afterwards. But the chapter recounting 'Western Accounts of Sanaa' ended in 1962. 'Traditional Sana is the theme of this volume,' Serjeant and Lewcock stated in their opening line. They clarified: 'Sanaa city of the Islamic era up to the officer revolution of September 26th 1962.' That date marked a shift from tradition, through revolution, to tumultuous political and social change. And it marked the end of my bibliographic guide to foreigners writing about Sanaa. If I wanted a witness to that revolution of 1962, and to the events that followed, hereafter I would have to identify my own authors.

David Holden, in his own words, was 'not quite the first professional journalist to enter the Yemen', but he came close. And Holden felt that he was, 'in a little way, a marker as well as a recorder of history'. As Middle East correspondent for *The Times*, he was present in 1957 at Imam Ahmad's first and only press conference. Occurring almost a decade after the machine-gunning of his father Yahya and his own accession topower, Ahmad's press conference was an extraordinary occasion. The imam's words were translated by a functionary of 'feline inscrutability', according to David Holden, while Ahmad's voice 'came in rapid, hoarse gasps, as if he was in pain'. His bulging eyes now 'rolled like white marbles only tenuously anchored to his sallow flesh'. Pained and sallow, Ahmad had by this time developed a morphine addiction. Two years later he was to make his first and only trip to Europe, accompanied by a vast sword-wielding retinue, to have his drug dependency treated in Italy. The imam had also acquired, Holden noted, a particular fondness for Heinz Russian Salad, which prompted the journalist to wonder about the imam's ties to Moscow. But Holden was warned not to read too much into Ahmad's predilection for tinned potato salad: 'He just likes mayonnaise,' an official remarked perfunctorily. And as if to substantiate that claim, Holden reported on good authority that toward the end of his life the imam weighed nearly 300lb and needed to be hoisted in and out of his car on a specially powered seat.

A shrewd political commentator, furnished, he said, with 'bottomless western cynicism', David Holden was also an astute observer of human nature. In his book *Farewell to Arabia*, published in 1966, Holden, then in his early forties, produced an astonishingly vivid portrait of the Imam Ahmad whom he had encountered at his singular press conference. 'Flashes of grim, ingratiating humour, when the full lips were drawn back over broken teeth and the dark brows were lowered over popping eyes, gave an extraordinary humanity to what might otherwise have seemed a mere, broken monster.' It is the monster that reigns in prevailing images of Ahmad; in the photograph of him attending a beheading, in the rumoured murders of his enemies, and in the whispers that he fed his prisoners to lions. 'Both less just and more severe' than his father Yahya, Ahmad 'terrorised his kingdom'. Yet Holden recognised that 'Ahmad the Djinn' was not only fearsome, but full of fear. 'One grasped not only the power, cruelty and suspicion of a total despot, not only the weaknesses of pain, sickness and age,' Holden thought, 'but also the sense of a man fearfully alone... there was probably no-one in the room whom he trusted.' Not the first journalist to enter Yemen perhaps, but the first and last to portray the imam so perceptively.

Imam Ahmad died in his sleep at the age of seventy-one. It was perhaps an undeservedly peaceful end for a ruler whose 'brusque brutality' had become renowned. His son and successor, Imam al-Badr, was reported dead less than one week later. The circumstances were markedly less tranquil. David Holden recalled the *Times* headline: 'Imam of Yemen Killed in Palace Shelling'. On the night of 26 September 1962, tanks rumbled through the city and destroyed the royal palace, burying Imam al-Badr beneath the rubble. A military coup overthrew the imamate and created the Yemen Arab Republic. This was the 'officer revolution' recalled by Serjeant and Lewcock; the event that defined the end of 'traditional Sanaa'.

A bruise marked my jaw, yolky and rotten looking. By the end of Election Day it had already passed quickly from purple to this putrid yellow. Still swollen and tender, it ached when I talked, or when I chewed. So that evening, amid the celebrations after the polls had closed, I pushed my *qat* awkwardly into the other cheek. Violence had seemed inevitable. The only uncertainty was where and upon whom it would fall. In the preceding week, two suicide car bomb attacks had been thwarted and four Al-Qaeda members had been arrested with explosives apparently intended for targets in Sanaa. Less than twenty-four hours before voting began it was announced that another major terrorist operation in the capital had been foiled. The city had an air of tension, as though before a storm. Huge numbers of troops had been mobilised. Journalists had jetted in for the story, diplomats had departed for their safety, and numerous 'democracy development' organisations had established themselves in Sanaa. Intrigued, I volunteered as an international observer of Yemen's elections. President Ali Abdullah Saleh's position was being contested. For the first time in the country's history, the incumbent ruler faced something that looked like a genuine democratic challenge.

At 7:28am on 20 September 2006, I arrived at the temporary polling station housed in the General Investment Authority building. There were thirty-two minutes before the polls were due to open. Already a queue of men extended right around the block. Soldiers guarded the entrance. Inside it was dark and the darkness was accentuated by silence. One of the uniformed officers ushered me into a large gloomy room where figures stood around the walls, silhouetted against the windows like shadows belonging to people I could not see. For reasons that would remain obscure, all the windows had been sealed with black paper and masking tape, blocking out the light. It created a stark contrast to the glare outside, and it seemed at odds with the exhibition of electoral transparency that would shortly commence. Dimly, beneath a couple of low-wattage strip lights, I discerned a number of other foreigners present. Following the news of Al-Qaeda activities, non-Yemenis had been forbidden to leave the capital without an armed escort, and so a visit to the large polling station at the General Investment Authority now featured on the hastily rearranged schedule of several international journalists and election observers. The apparent threat of violence not only hampered election monitoring and reporting, but also looked set to benefit the incumbent president. He had campaigned on a strong platform of national security and stability, putting fear to the service of control.

A grey metal filing cabinet lay on its side in the centre of the carpet. On top of it were three large ballot boxes made of translucent plastic. In a corner of the room a soldier was adjusting the internal tube-frame of a canvas-covered polling booth. The presiding officer of the polling station arrived carrying some papers and a box file. An officious-looking man in freshly steam-pressed pinstripes, he promptly began counting aloud the names of registered voters.

'Wahed, ithnain, delatha, arba, khamza,...' It was a laboured proceeding. '...121, 122, 123, 124, 125, 126...' Hot and stuffy. '...264, 265, 266, 267, 268...' When the presiding officer paused in his enumeration, appearing to have lost count, those present shouted out the last number he had got to, the audience participation adding to a strange theatricality. '...408, 409, 410, 411...' It was a deliberately infallible display of electoral correctitude.

Yemen's last presidential elections in 1999 had been a sham. The country's major opposition party had boycotted them entirely. Three of the thirty-one presidential hopefuls had been disqualified immediately on 'legal' grounds: one for being 'too young' at the age of thirty-eight; another because he had a Russian wife; and the third for having a name too similar to that of President Ali Abdullah Saleh. Of the twenty-eight remaining contenders, only two received the endorsement required to validate their candidacy from the national parliament (which was largely composed of the president's party). Finally, the two presidential candidates were President Ali Abdullah Saleh and one Najeeb Al-Shaabi. Al-Shaabi was a stooge. He was a member of President Saleh's own party, he voted for President Saleh, and he publicly declared that Saleh was the more worthy candidate. Ali Abdullah Saleh ultimately claimed 96.3 per cent of the votes, though it was observed that there were more votes cast than registered voters. The methodical performance that I witnessed seven years later looked like a belated riposte to past accusations of electoral fraud.

While the ballot papers were still being counted, the polling station's opening time came and went. Eventually, a little before nine and a little under an hour behind schedule, its doors were finally opened. I watched the first few votes being cast, but was desperate to leave the airless room where I had stood for two stifling hours. Outside, desperate to enter, were the men who had stood waiting for far longer in the sun. The unexplained delays had created an adversarial mood among the voters that was only exacerbated by the staggered, halting access to the polls as soldiers allowed them to enter just a few at a time. Exasperated men brandishing voter registration cards surged toward the troops who guarded the entrance, and the troops drove the men back with equal force and frustration. Against the tide of men struggling to get in, I tried to squeeze myself out. But as the shouting grew more antagonistic and the shoving became more aggressive I found myself stuck. I was squashed between the front line of soldiers and a squad of reinforcements who had arrived from somewhere inside the building. The soldiers suddenly swept the crowd back forcibly to allow a group of women to enter the building, but in this manoeuvre someone was pushed too far. A *jambiyah* was unsheathed and an AK47 unshouldered. A confrontation unfolded rapidly in front of me. More soldiers collapsed onto the fray, tumbling in to separate the belligerents, but seeming only to escalate the altercation. Then from the scrum a soldier was propelled backwards, cannoning into me. His Kalashnikov cracked hard against my jaw and I fell backwards. The bruise came up quickly, purple, and then yellow before the polling closed.

The cool lines of gun barrels, muzzles, and magazines have long provoked in me a sort of fascinated horror. Partly it is the thought of machines being designed and precision-made for the purpose of puncturing skin, splintering bone, and piercing internal organs. It is also the brutal truths that are expressed in their apparently dispassionate ballistic and ergonomic calculations: truths of biology and politics, of the circular logic of violence and power. It is a logic upheld and not overthrown by a military coup. After Yemen's officer revolution in 1962, the new military rulers promptly executed dozens of their opponents. It was just as might have occurred under the imamate, except that the new regime favoured firing squads over beheadings.

Guns flowed swiftly into Yemen and seeped out across its borders. Following the military coup in Sanaa, David Holden watched the price of a second-hand rifle fall from £100 to £25 in the British Crown Colony of Aden - reflecting the extent of gun running from the new Yemen Arab Republic. The weapons came from Egypt, and from the USSR. Holden had been in Sanaa soon after the overthrow of the imam in 1962 and he personally witnessed the influx of Egyptian troops and Egyptian armoured vehicles. Later, Soviet tanks and Soviet aircraft arrived too. Egypt's President Nasser had backed the military overthrow of Yemen's imamate and sought to bolster the new Republic against 'the threat of counter-revolution'. That threat was realised when Imam al-Badr revealed himself some weeks later. Not dead. Not buried beneath the ruins of his home in Sanaa. Not 'Killed in Palace Shelling', as the world press had reported. When the tanks began shooting up his palace on the night of 26 September, Imam al-Badr rattled off a few salvoes of machine-gun fire in the direction of his attackers, then slipped out of the backdoor. Fleeing north, the ousted imam rallied his supporters and requested firearms and funds from the monarchies of Saudi Arabia and Jordan in order to support his fightback against his foes. King Saud and King Hussain obliged readily, wary of the Nasserite revolutionaries and their republican ideals. Imam al-Badr and his royalist army then established themselves in the caves north of Sanaa and began to wage war against the Egyptian-backed republicans in the capital.

Conflict drew journalists back to Yemen. Filing stories for The *New York Times*, the American Dana Adams Schmidt joined the royalists for a time, risking his neck and then breaking it in a jeep accident, but continuing to write about Yemen from his hospital bed. Richard Beeston broke the story of the Egyptian use of chemical weapons in the *Daily Telegraph*, recounting the horror of blinded Yemeni children coughing up blood while their skin blistered. Meanwhile, David Holden reported from the other side of the war, travelling 'all the way from Sanaa to

Aden' with an ease that he himself remarked upon amidst the Soviet-backed revolutionaries. Among the people of Yemen he found growing resentment of the Egyptian forces, but genuine relief at the overthrow of the imamate. 'Imam fuggoff!' declared an old tea seller in Taiz. Holden later recalled strong emotions in London too as parliament debated whether to recognise the new Yemen Arab Republic and acknowledge that it had replaced the imam's Kingdom of Yemen.

The British government was not keen to be seen supporting the 'blood thirsty' tyranny of the old imamate. But the nationalist revolutionaries and increasing numbers of well-armed Egyptian troops in Yemen's new Republic would make dangerous neighbours to British interests in Aden. Conservative MPs were especially keen to condemn the revolution and to cling on to Aden and the British imperial projects that it enabled. Aden, they asserted, was necessary to access Persian oil, Malayan rubber, and African metals. It should certainly not be allowed to fall into the hands of communist revolutionary types. The right-wing MP Neil 'Billy' McLean was particularly vocal. After King Hussein of Jordan sponsored his visits to the region, McLean denounced Egyptian President Nasser's 'puppet' republican regime in Yemen in a series of articles published in *The Times* and *Telegraph*. McLean also aligned with a group of Conservative politicians who were not only ideologically opposed to Nasser, but eager to avenge their humiliation in the confrontation with him over Suez in 1956. The hawkish Tories of the 'Suez Group' now became the 'Aden Group'. They urged the British parliament not to recognise Yemen's new revolutionary Nasserite Republic.

But that did nothing to stop the second-hand rifles coming across the border and being sold in Aden for £25. And the weapons were accompanied by an increasing revolutionary zeal. Armed and determined to get the British out of Arabia, nationalists in Aden commenced a guerrilla war. The British declared a state of emergency and fought back viciously, equally determined to defend what Holden called 'that curious strip of pink on the old schoolroom maps of Empire known as the Aden Protectorate'. It was an ugly conflict. Cinemas exploded in nationalist grenade attacks and the bodies of dead British troops were mutilated. British soldiers became more brutish with the local population and began abusing prisoners, inflicting callous bruises and cigarette burns.

'No smoking!' Standing next to the blackboard, the headmaster barked his imperative. At the back of the classroom at a desk scratched with graffiti, a uniformed youth moved to stub out his cigarette in an inkwell, but he paused, and instead the soldier pushed the cigarette back between his lips, picked up his Kalashnikov insouciantly, and stepped out of the room with a languid exhalation. Lessons had been cancelled. School buildings had been turned into polling centres. Teachers were charged with invigilating the voting and soldiers had become truculent prefects. Ballot boxes were positioned on the teachers' desks at the front of each classroom, so that the voters dropping off their ballot papers might have been handing in their homework. Except that it was not their name at the top of the presidential election papers, but that of Ali Abdullah Saleh. Perhaps it was merely by chance that the incumbent's name topped the list of the five presidential candidates. And that his only serious opponent, Faisal Bin Shamlan, was listed one up from the bottom.

President Saleh adopted a strongman image, often sporting a military uniform and aviator shades. Meanwhile, seventy-two-year-old Faisal Bin Shamlan's thick spectacles and swept-back white hair gave this presidential candidate an undeniably schoolmasterly appearance. And while Saleh promised security, Shamlan offered change. He was billed as the anti-corruption candidate. Shamlan's campaign slogan was simple but provocative: 'A President at the service of Yemen, not Yemen at the service of a President'. When his bodyguard was arrested three days before polling day on suspicion of being an al-Qaeda operative, some interpreted the trumped-up charges as evidence of Shamlan's threat to the establishment.

As the headmaster gave me a tour of his school that now functioned as a polling centre, our entrance into one of the classrooms was greeted in faultless English.

'On behalf of the People of Yemen we would like to thank you for aiding the progress of democracy in our country and helping to ensure that the elections are free and fair...' It went on, this unexpected eulogy, directed at me by a member of the teaching staff. I felt a little embarrassed. The headmaster gave a sort of irritated snort. Then he hurried me out of the room. 'Huh! The English teacher,' he muttered. 'Words. Words. Words.' He grumbled, closing the door on the upstart behind him. As we crossed the deserted playground, the headmaster remarked upon the large number of women who had turned out to vote at the school. He pointed to the queue that encircled the base of one of the nearby buildings and zigzagged up an external stairwell to the women-only polling booths on the third floor. There were far more women voters than I had seen at the General Investment Authority earlier in the day. One explanation was obvious. With the women voting in an entirely separate building to the men, quite simply, it felt safer.

At the Al-Thowra Hospital later that afternoon there were only women voters present. Expressing my surprise, I was told that 'most men will be chewing *qat* just now.' Outpatient clinics had been postponed and inpatients had been moved upstairs to allow the ground floor and basement to serve the electorate. In a clinic room of white tiles and gleaming steel, ballot boxes sat on an examination couch. On the wall was an x-ray viewing box and a mirror that showed the awkward purple bruise over my jawbone, evidencing my earlier encounter with a Kalashnikov. I saw the same purple smeared in thumbprints on the list of registered voters, next to the names and portrait photographs of those women who had already cast their ballots.

'We check everyone's registration cards when they arrive,' one of the women's polling team explained to me, 'and we take their thumbprint when they leave.' Next to her, reclining in an office chair, her colleague snoozed with her veil drawn up over her eyes. 'And we're supposed to match their faces to the photographs on the registration list. But we don't do that here.' I wondered why. 'Because it's the Old City. Some women don't like to show their faces. Besides, we all know each other.'

A striking poster image had targeted women voters. Alongside the emblazoned invocation 'Your Vote is Your Decision', a woman stood with hand on hip against a sky-blue background, with the national flag billowing about her. As well as clearly endorsing women's suffrage and offering a powerful vision of their role in society, the poster's message was intended to counter the acknowledged fact that women's votes were too often decided by male family members. Still more often though, women did not vote at all. No figures for their turnout at the polls were ever released, but fewer than half of Yemen's women were registered to vote. Two versions of the poster were produced. One in which the woman appeared veiled; another in which her face was visible. It suggested the cautious nudging of a boundary. Similarly, the status quo seemed to be facing questions from the old woman who reportedly declared, 'I couldn't choose my husband, but now I have a chance to choose my president.'

As the 1960s progressed, Aden changed while David Holden watched. From a sleepy colonial outpost of cucumber sandwiches, visiting cards, and pink gins at the Crescent Hotel, it became a crater of burnt-out cars and broken glass, smarting from tear gas borne upon a sea breeze. It marked an especially deplorable end to the years of British occupation. In Sanaa I met a couple of Aden old-timers who recalled quite fondly working alongside the British in earlier times. One of them enquired politely about the health of the queen, and of Cliff Richard. Another, perhaps assuming that all British men of a certain age had passed through Aden, wondered whether he might know my father. But in 1967 this troubled corner of Empire became a battlefront for Lieutenant-Colonel Colin 'Mad Mitch' Mitchell. Quelling the 'Aden insurgency', Mad Mitch captured the attention of the BBC and British press with his brutal enforcement of colonial rule. In one of his many media appearances he described his control of the anachronism that British Aden had become as 'extremely firm and extremely mean'. Under his command the Argyll and Sutherland Highlanders terrorised the people of Aden. 'They know that if they start trouble we'll blow their bloody heads off,' said Mad Mitch with characteristically frank unpleasantness.

In Aden, British troops were fighting nationalists who sought an end to British rule. At the same time, north of Sanaa, British soldiers were fighting republicans who had brought an end to the rule of the imam. But this second British battlefront in Arabia was part of a secret war. While the fighting in Aden was widely reported, British involvement in north Yemen was kept quiet. It was hushed up at the time and remains little known today. Details of the 'war that never was' only came to light long after it was over. In London, Billy McLean and his Conservative colleagues had succeeded in convincing the British parliament not to recognise the revolutionary Yemen Arab Republic. But they quickly realised that they would be unable to gain support for an armed intervention against the troops of Egypt's President Nasser who now controlled much of Yemen.

Instead, McLean and his colleagues agreed that they would secretly assist Imam al-Badr and his royalist forces in their fight against the Egyptian-backed republicans.

McLean had served in Special Operations during the Second World War. Quietly, in the clubs of Mayfair and Chelsea he began to make contact with other ex-Special Ops men. Cloak and dagger ex-military men like David Smiley, Jim Johnson, and David Stirling, founder of the SAS. First they established a private army of English gentlemen soldiers. Then they began acquiring portions of the huge stocks of weapons that remained in Europe after the Second World War. While Britain supplied the men and munitions, King Faisal of Saudi Arabia bankrolled the operation. The British mercenaries started out in reconnaissance, reporting to the Saudis about the positions of Yemen's royalists and advising on armament supplies. Soon they were organising training, advising on tactics, arranging weapons drops, and engaging the 'enemy' Egyptian forces. It was all entirely unofficial and utterly deniable by the British government, and yet the involvement of British mercenaries in Yemen's civil war seemed to have tacit approval. While Mad Mitch was trying to stamp out a guerrilla war in the south of Yemen, Billy McLean was fuelling one in the north.

David Holden suspected something of the sort. Travelling through Arabia he had seen the 'latter-day Lawrences' getting involved. In London he noted the obfuscation of Conservative Prime Minister Alec Douglas-Home in 1964 when he responded to a question in the Commons about 'a clandestine group giving military support to the Imam's forces'. The British Prime Minister denied authorising the group's activities, but did not deny its existence. He denied that British weapons were being supplied to the imam, but did not deny that British actors were purchasing weapons from elsewhere and supplying them to the imam. Meanwhile, Holden had no evidence to connect the British political establishment with the British soldiers of fortune whom he had witnessed in Yemen. And even Holden with his 'bottomless western cynicism' could not have guessed at the Israeli involvement in this covert war. But the Israelis, threatened by Egypt amassing forces in the Sinai, were keen to keep Nasser's troops tied up in Yemen. They made more than a dozen weapons drops to Imam al-Badr's royalist army, delivering guns with their serial numbers brazed out, packed in wood shavings from Cyprus, dropped with Italian parachutes from unmarked Israeli aircraft. In case the drops were intercepted, there was nothing to reveal their source. Their intended recipients on the ground would only have been hinted at by the inclusion of an occasional English newspaper and a bottle of whisky wrapped in toilet roll. The war in North Yemen, nominally between al-Badr's royalists and the revolutionary republicans, had become a battle between the Egyptians and an eclectic collective of Saudi, Jordanian, British, and Israeli interests Holden thought that 'possibly, without foreign intervention, the dispute would have been settled within a few months.' Instead, from 1962 it dragged on until the end of the decade.

Ultimately, the Egyptians pulled out of Yemen in October 1967, bruised after their defeat in the Six-Day War with Israel. British troops left Aden six weeks later, after the Labour government decided to abandon the base. The clandestine British mercenary outfit in north Yemen folded up around the same time, since with Aden lost and Nasser gone they had nothing to fight for and nobody to fight against. Imam al-Badr and his royalist troops kept battling against the republic for a few more years, until the Saudis withdrew their support. Then in 1970, Yemen's conflict ended with compromise: a republican government with some key positions for the royalists. Imam al-Badr retired to Kent.

'He knows all the *djinns*.' As polling came to an end on Election Day I stopped at a teashop and chatted to a man who hinted that President Saleh was on familiar terms with unearthly spirits. I pressed him to elaborate.

'I mean, he knows all the sheikhs. All the tribes,' he said. 'All the people who could cause trouble. Nobody else can control them.' It seemed that the *djinns*, or genies, were merely metaphorical: not supernatural demons, but possessors of earthly political powers. Yet I wondered whether the tea drinker had not divulged something more; a secret truth. After all, there *was* something supernatural about the president.

His portrait was hung on the teashop wall, just as it had hung in the school, the hospital, the General Investment Authority building, and most of the Yemeni homes that I had visited in Sanaa. Public and private life was lived beneath the president's unblinking gaze. And his perpetual presence had somehow become as mundane as doorknobs, windowsills, or wall clocks. Yet in the weeks before the elections President Saleh's image had proliferated. Posters were stuck to walls and taped to car windows, his face appeared on enormous billboards and was plastered in endless repetition across facades, as though the city were gripped by a collective terror of his absence, or as though we were being reminded of his omnipresence.

'He's led this country for twenty-eight years,' the man in the teashop reminded me. Only Muammar Al-Gaddafi of Libya had ruled for longer. Ali Abdullah Saleh had taken power in 1978. Since then he had managed, more or less, to control Yemen's competing military factions, tribes, and local leaders; all the genies.

'He was the only one brave enough to lead the country.' The tea drinker continued his endorsement. In the year before Saleh became president two successive incumbents of the position were murdered by political opponents. He might have been brave to take office, or, it has been suggested, he might have had a hand in the premature departure of his predecessors. Within a month of his succession, Saleh is said to have ordered the execution of more than two-dozen officers who were conspiring against him. Saleh was a survivor. It was safer to align with him. Safer, and more profitable. Many people were rumoured to benefit directly from the president's patronage, and many more benefited indirectly from the complex networks of corruption that threaded through society under his rule. Saleh and his influence were omnipotent.

'So, have you voted today?' I asked the man in the teashop. He replied by holding up his thumb, still purple from the ink of the polling register. The sleeve of his jacket fell back from his wrist, exposing a bracelet made from tiny enamelled portraits of the president. The adornment seemed talismanic. And the repeated images of the president, adhering to bicycle mudguards, motorcycle fuel tanks, *jambiyah* sheaths, and school bags, had begun to seem less like expressions of politics, and more like prayer flags. Thumbs had turned purple throughout the capital, the translucent ballot boxes had taken on the pastel shades of the ballot papers, and by the end of polling I had sensed the common root of votes and votives.

Behind the personality cult, though, there remained an oppressive regime. Two days earlier, at the bus stand on my route to work, there was only a rainbow-coloured slick on the tarmac. No buses, no passengers, and no bow-legged figure calling out destinations. Just the oily stain of a damaged engine seal or gasket. The city's buses and their drivers had all been recruited to shuttle people to one of Saleh's election rallies in the suburbs. I took a cab as far as I could, but soldiers were diverting all vehicles except for the lurching buses loaded with youths who shouted and waved national flags from the windows. I tried to telephone the office, but the signal was down. The taxi driver shook his head, mobile phones were not working today; it happened sometimes at politically opportune moments. On foot I moved slowly amid a press of schoolboys whose khaki uniforms all had a picture of Saleh pinned to their breasts. Open-top lorries crawled by laden with armed troops and jeeps prowled around with soldiers gripping rear-mounted cannons. Overhead there were silhouettes standing on rooftops, cradling weapons, while bristling helicopter gunships beat the air. A vast portrait of the president covering an entire high-rise block was repeated over and over in a crowd of thousands, held aloft on posters and placards, like the thousand reflections of a shattered mirror. The soldiers patrolling the multitude had the same image strapped to their camouflage helmets and taped to the magazines of their automatic weapons. The militarised campaign rally, with its recruitment of schoolchildren and commandeering of the public transport system, belonged to the democracy of a dictator.

Egypt's President Nasser had called Yemen his Vietnam. 'Like the Americans in Vietnam,' David Holden explained, 'the Egyptians had staked their prestige on an overseas war which they showed ever less likelihood of winning.' At the time of Holden's writing in 1966, Yemen was still wracked by conflicts sustained by occupying powers. In Aden, Britain was backing 'reaction against revolution' in trying to put down the nationalists. In the north, Egypt was supporting 'revolution against reaction' in battling Imam al-Badr's royalists (and unbeknown to Holden, the British pro-royalist mercenaries). Both Britain and Egypt were 'well on the way to failure,' thought Holden. 'The result was a nice, historic irony.' Closing his Yemen narrative with a consideration of Egypt's intervention, Holden suggested that 'perhaps the real parallel was less with the Americans in Vietnam than with the British in Aden... In many ways the British and the Egyptians were the mirror image of each other.'

I had to reread these concluding remarks several times. As if the politics and conflicts were not confusing enough already, Holden seemed to be saying two things at once. He perceived a 'parallel' between Britain and Egypt, but they were also 'the mirror image of each other.' For Holden, then, 'parallel' might mean 'equivalent to', but it could also imply 'opposite to' through the wily insertion of a mirror. So, the British and Egyptians were parallel (opposite) when they backed different sides in Yemen, but parallel (equivalent) when they faced the same fate. For a journalist who was so uniquely perceptive and whose prose was usually so lucid, David Holden's final analysis was remarkably obscure. I found it perplexing. But it seemed to hint at how his body came to be found lying neatly at the side of the road in a Cairo suburb, a single bullet having scorched his jacket and pierced his heart. He was identified in the mortuary by a reporter for the BBC who recognised 'an apparent execution'.

'Who assassinated Holden, our chief foreign correspondent, in Cairo in December 1977?' asked *Sunday Times* editor Harold Evans. 'And why?' 'I've brooded on this question for many years,' Evans wrote in his memoir four decades later. 'What I now believe happened has only slowly and painfully been discernible through the shadows.'

Holden was killed just a few hours after he flew into Cairo's airport. His body was discovered at the roadside the next morning, tidily dressed, but stripped of anything that might identify him. His briefcase and portable Olivetti typewriter were later recovered from an abandoned white Fiat. A cartridge case matching the single bullet that had killed him was later found in another abandoned white Fiat. There were bloodstains on the front passenger seat and the headrest had been removed, 'making it easier for the gunman leaning forward from the rear seat to put a bullet through the heart,' Evans suggested. A third white Fiat was also implicated in 'a well-planned abduction'.

At the *Sunday Times* office in London, Evans discovered that telexes sent by Holden in the days preceding his death had been stolen. These telexes detailed his changing travel plans, including his last-minute flight to Cairo. Evans concluded that the newspaper's London offices had been infiltrated and the information obtained from Holden's telexes had been used to arrange his execution in Egypt upon arrival. Evans judged that this could only be the work of an international organisation. He learnt that the both the FBI and CIA held files on Holden, but that these were closed on grounds of 'national security'. Evans knew a thing or two about international intelligence services and how they operated. He had famously exposed Kim Philby as a Soviet spy. Now he suspected that his Middle East correspondent had, in fact, been working for one or more of the CIA, the KGB, MI6, or Mossad.

Holden's CIA connections dated back to the 1950s, when he was in Yemen, attending Imam Ahmad's only press conference and directing his penetrative gaze toward the politics and personality of that lonely ruler with his bulging eyes and broken teeth. Perhaps some other connection had enabled Holden to travel through post-revolutionary Soviet-supported Yemen 'all the way from Sanaa to Aden' with such remarkable ease. And perhaps these different connections were part of the background to Holden's unusual ambiguity about the opposite and equivalent parallels of Cold War military forces in Yemen. Who assassinated David Holden and why? Harold Evans thought that Holden had been caught 'playing a double game'. A game of mirrors. Exactly which agency, or agencies, had employed him, which had uncovered his disloyalty, and which had killed him didn't much matter; his death, thought Evans, had been the 'liquidation of an asset'.

With pinstriped fastidiousness, polling at the General Investment Authority building was declared over on the very stroke of six. The ballot boxes were secured against tampering with great lengths of gaffer tape, and then sealed with ceremonial excess using blood-red paraffin wax before being stamped with an official emblem in the same purple ink that had been discolouring thumbs all day. A soldier began slowly dismantling the grey canvas polling booth. In the centre of the room a grubby circuit had been trampled into the carpet around the upturned filing cabinet where the ballot boxes stood. Opening one of the boxes, the presiding officer in his pinstripe suit began calling out and holding aloft each individual voting paper.

'Ali Abdullah Saleh... Ali Abdullah Saleh... Ali Abdullah Saleh... Ali Abdullah Saleh... Faisal Bin Shamlan... Ali Abdullah Saleh... Ali Abdullah Saleh...'

The process would continue through the night. The final vote count would not be announced for another two days. Despite the displays of democratic diligence, international observation missions ultimately concluded that the results lacked credibility. Women had been comprehensively excluded as candidates and as voters. And there had been numerous instances of unfair use of state resources by incumbents, like the president's commandeering of the capital's public transport network to move people to his campaign rally. Nonetheless, the 2006 elections were said by some to represent a milestone in Yemen's democratic development. Sanguine observers noted that they had strengthened the institutions of democracy and instilled its ideals. Others thought the whole affair little more than a ruse by which the ruling powers could gain some democratic legitimacy.

The election result had never been much in doubt. 'Sweeping Victory for Saleh' ran the *Yemen Times* headline later that week. The death toll, though, had been unforeseen. 'Eight Dead in Election Day Violence'; that figure, too, was swiftly reported. Only eight. Each death was a tragedy, but the election violence was nothing on the scale of what some predicted and many feared. With all 6,025,818 ballots counted, Ali Abdullah Saleh gained 77.3 per cent of the votes and Faisal Bin Shamlan 21.8 per cent. The outcome was declared on 23 September. It was the first day of Ramadan. Some said the elections and the announcement of the results had been deliberately scheduled to ensure that any disaffection and violent reaction among the populace would be assuaged by consideration for the Islamic holy month. By further coincidence or contrivance, Ali Abdullah Saleh's swearing in for a further term as Yemen's president occurred on 26 September - the anniversary of the 1962 revolution, the day that tanks had destroyed the royal palace and the imamate had been toppled in a military coup. 26 September 2006 was a day that celebrated the historical overthrow of the old regime with the interminable power grip of the current one. David Holden might have admired a nice historic irony, or a parallel of the mirror-image sort.

The 'Farewell' in the title of David Holden's 1966 book was intended to express a leave-taking. A 'marker as well as a recorder of history', he was defining an end to the 'promise of escape' and the 'flicker of romance' that Arabia had held out to generations of Englishmen. 'Burton... Lawrence... Wilfred Thesiger... Their names are the record of a love affair, between

mortal men and the immortal image of mystery that Arabia represented,'
he explained in the Introduction. 'This book writes goodbye to all that.'

The British were being booted out of Aden. The dream of Arabia was
over. Or so Holden believed. But even as the televised colonial nightmare
blew up around Mad Mitch and the British troops in Aden, the tarnished
'promise of escape' had been regilded with Arabian gold in north Yemen.
The secret war and the Saudis' rewards lured back a new generation of
English gentlemen adventurers and mercenaries (even Wilfred Thesiger
himself turned up to join the ranks of the ousted Imam al-Badr's royalist
forces for a while in 1966). The litany of Lawrence of Arabia hero figures
would continue to be recited. Some years later, when one of the British
mercenaries divulged a few secrets of their fight against the Egyptian-
backed republicans in Sanaa, the *Daily Telegraph* reported the story
under the headline 'Second "Lawrence" foiled Nasser's army in Yemen'.
When Billy McLean, Tory MP and chief protagonist in Britain's secret
Saudi-funded war in Yemen, died in 1986 his *Telegraph* obituary declared
with admiration that in his character 'there were shades of Buchan and
Lawrence and Thesiger. All seemed to coalesce in the Yemen...' As mortal
men became immortalised, so too were their exploits in Arabia. The 'flicker
of romance' was not extinguished as Holden had supposed; it could be
endlessly rekindled. The allure of Arabia was not over, and neither was
Britain's involvement there.

When Billy McLean and his fighting men returned to London from
Yemen in 1967, they toasted their achievements with champagne at a
Hyde Park hotel. They had much to celebrate. As well as making small
fortunes for each of these mercenaries, the British involvement in Yemen's
civil war created the basis for a lucrative private military industry. Two
members of McLean's team, Jim Johnson and David Stirling, went on to
establish Britain's earliest private military companies. Both Johnson and
Stirling had been pivotal in directing the flow of money and weapons
as Saudi Arabia bankrolled armament supplies to Imam al-Badr's anti-
republican army. When the war in Yemen was over, Stirling was able to
utilise the connections he had established with Saudi King Faisal to broker
the sale of British fighter aircraft to the Royal Saudi Air Force. British arms
manufacturers have benefited from a host of hugely lucrative contracts
with the Saudis ever since.

When the Saudi-led coalition began dropping bombs on Yemen in 2015, they relied heavily upon military hardware and expertise provided by Britain. In January 2016, the British Prime Minister was challenged in the House of Commons about the civilians being killed in Yemen by British-made bombs, dropped from British-built aircraft, flown by British-trained pilots, with the knowledge of British military advisers in Saudi Arabia. The PM denied any responsibility. He cited Britain's 'stringent arms control measures', he asserted that Britain was 'not directly involved' in Yemen's conflict, and he claimed that British military personnel were providing 'training and advice and help' to ensure that the Saudi coalition respected 'the norms of humanitarian law'. But just one week later a confidential report leaked from the United Nations clearly described Saudi-led airstrikes in Yemen targeting civilians and civilian objects, violating international humanitarian law. Which made the Prime Minister's reassurances sound weak at best.

Meanwhile, the British Foreign Secretary was asked repeatedly about Britain's sale of armaments to the Saudi-led coalition. He repeatedly replied that 'we have assessed that there has not been a breach of IHL [international humanitarian law] by the coalition.' But in July 2016 it was admitted that no evidence had informed that judgement and that in fact no assessment had ever been made. The *Telegraph* said it was an 'embarrassing U-turn'. A spokesperson for the Campaign Against Arms Trade observed 'a stunning piece of back-pedalling', pointing out that the Foreign Secretary's original statements 'were either totally wrong or outright distortions'; an abnegation of responsibility, or deliberate deception. The point about international humanitarian law was important. This is the law that governs how conflicts may be conducted. Serious violations of that law, such as the targeting of civilians, amount to war crimes. All nations have a legal obligation to halt the sale of weapons if there is a 'clear risk' that they might be used in serious violations of international humanitarian law. An editorial in the *Guardian* newspaper described Britain's arms exports to Saudi Arabia as indefensible, the need for a suspension undeniable. But the weapons sales continued and so did the bombing of civilian targets in Yemen. Homes, hospitals, farms, schools, and weddings were blown up. Then in October 2016, the Saudi-led coalition dropped two massive laser-guided bombs onto a funeral in Sanaa. More than 150 people were killed and over 500 were wounded. Yemenis called it a massacre. UN monitors said it was a violation of international humanitarian law.

But even after the funeral massacre, Britain's Foreign Secretary urged that British arms sales to Saudi Arabia should continue. Previously he had insisted that the Saudi-led bombing campaign was not 'in clear breach' of international humanitarian law. Those claims were no longer credible. Now he referred to the 'huge economic damage' that would occur if the arms sales stopped. He warned that if Britain stopped selling weapons to Saudi Arabia 'we would be vacating a space that would rapidly be filled by other western countries that would happily supply arms.' The argument was no longer legal; it was economic. By the end of 2016 Britain was estimated to have licensed £3.3 billion worth of arms sales to Saudi Arabia since the conflict in Yemen began. And the flow of arms and money showed no signs of stopping. It was not just Britain: the US was also selling weapons to the Saudis. And it was not just money that was being received in return. Under pressure, successive British Prime Ministers acknowledged a murkier truth. David Cameron, questioned persistently by one veteran interviewer, finally admitted, testily, that 'we have a relationship with Saudi Arabia and if you want to know why I'll tell you why. It is because we receive from them important intelligence and security information that keeps us safe.' The following year, and following Cameron's resignation, Prime Minister Theresa May was called to account for Britain's close ties to Saudi Arabia in the House of Commons. To cries of 'shame' from the opposition, she asserted that the link with Saudi Arabia 'has potentially saved the lives of hundreds of people in this country'.

The potential lives saved in Britain and the protection of business interests in Britain's arms industry have come at a massive cost to the people of Yemen. Clearly, in British government policy and political decisions the lives of those Yemeni people have not been valued especially highly. Just as in the covert war of the 1960s, Britain's actions have fuelled and prolonged a devastating conflict in Yemen. Thousands have been killed, many thousands more have been injured, and millions have been displaced.

Khaled was among the millions. It had been over a year since he left Sanaa.

He had wanted to escape the impact of the war and was determined to avoid active participation in the conflict. When the Houthis took control of Sanaa, Khaled had been under pressure to join their army. Better to die in search of a better life than to be killed in a war that he did not believe in, he wrote on his Facebook page. And so his journey in search of refuge had begun.

The Houthi insurgency, like the British-Saudi arms deals, also had roots in Yemen's civil war of the 1960s. The imams of Yemen belonged to the Zaydi Shia sect of Islam and when the imamate was overthrown in the revolution of 1962, the Zaydis were pushed from power and ultimately pushed back into the northern mountains. They were increasingly neglected in the Yemeni republic. Among the marginalised and disaffected Northern Zaydis was the powerful Houthi tribe. Armed conflict broke out between members of the Houthi movement and the Yemeni Army in 2004. Fighting flared periodically thereafter. With the Arab Spring and the forced resignation of Ali Abdullah Saleh, a power vacuum emerged in Yemen, and the already-militarised Houthis were able to move in. Though they were sometimes accused of seeking to reinstate the imamate, they claimed that their objectives were more progressive. They wanted to end Yemen's corrupt regime. But as they took control of areas where they had no prior claim and imposed their doctrines where they had no support, the Houthis became the new oppressors.

Following his journey across the Red Sea and the Gulf of Aden, through Somalia, Sudan, and the Sahara, Khaled arrived on the Libyan coast and boarded a leaky vessel. He did so knowing that the last boat to depart had capsized, killing everyone on board. The voyage across the Mediterranean was dangerous and unpredictable, but the passengers were desperate and undeterred.

Khaled paid two thousand dollars to join a couple of hundred other people aboard a small wooden boat. He could do the maths: here was half a million dollars' worth of refugee transfer. The black Africans were sent below decks, the lighter skinned Arabs were allowed above. So Khaled sat outside, with a pair of sunglasses, a lifejacket, and a motorcycle innertube across his chest. And unlike most of the people aboard, he knew how to swim. Before they set off, the skipper instructed his passengers not to stand up under any circumstances in order not to overturn the boat. And he reminded them that if they encountered any authorities, they were not to identify him or any of the other smugglers, as the punishments for people smuggling had become severe. In Britain, the Foreign Secretary had recently suggested that Special Forces might be deployed to destroy the people smugglers in Libya. Speaking in a month during which well over a thousand migrants died in the Mediterranean, he asserted that 'you need to chock off the problem at source.' But the source of the problem was not the people smugglers. They were merely meeting the demands of the market; a market created by conflict and political instability. In reasoning that might have been expected to resonate with the Foreign Secretary, their motives were not legal, but economic. If these smugglers refused to accept money from people who were desperate to board boats bound for Europe, they would simply be vacating a space that would rapidly be filled by others. Khaled took a selfie and posted it online. It showed his face, his sunset-orange lifejacket, and the impossible blue of the Mediterranean.

- 17 -

Orientalism

- Jonathan Raban, 1978 -

'YOU COULD LOOK AT THE walls of Sana'a for a year, finding more and more meanings in them,' remarked Jonathan Raban. He 'had never seen a city which was so literally legible.' For Raban, the 'page-like walls' of Sanaa's towerhouses bore 'a dense jumbled alphabet of signs and symbols'. The architecture of the Old City was adorned with 'twin crescent moons... a Star of David, carved water drops, lozenges, triangles, fleurs-de-lys, and some indecipherable calligraphic squiggles'. Islamic, Judaic, and geometric shapes had become a language writ in brick and gypsum. 'The stucco friezes formed a continuous scrawl of handwriting.'

In Sanaa, Raban met a man named Abdurabu, who introduced him to Hussain, who invited him to his home and showed him the view from the rooftop. It was here, high up on the flat roof, looking out across the city shortly before he departed from Sanaa, that Raban stood and contemplated the many meanings written on the page-like walls. He thought that the signs and symbols might 'coalesce into a single simple statement: that the world is infinitely complex, illegible, fraught with paradox'. And he wondered whether 'on *qat*, perhaps', he 'might have been able to read some secrets from the rooftop.'

We too might have tried, you and I, to decipher some of those secrets. After the *qat* chew in the garden *mafraj* was over, with the alkaloids still coursing through our veins, we could have climbed to the top of our building. Minding your footing on the steps, and minding your head against the lintel, we would have clambered onto the flat roof in the dark, high above the street lamps and the toot of traffic horns. Up here, on a clear night, despite the dust and the light pollution, while satellite dishes tilted at the moon, you might have seen the pole star resting above the horizon, and you might have watched the constellations rising and falling. Here, too, were signs and symbols, infinite complexities and eternal mysteries, bright celestial fragments catching the eye and arresting the imagination. And here too, like Jonathan Raban, or like yearning astrologers, we might have searched for meanings in the city walls, or in the stars, stretching toward enigmatic secrets, reaching out to the edge of realities, loosening the ties to all that is solid. It would have been perfectly safe, of course. The rooftops were made for walking upon and the parapet was a sturdy barrier, ideal for being leant upon and looked out from, just as Raban did, on a roof somewhere not far from here, all those years ago.

He touched down in March 1978, a little before midnight, on a night 'particularly black'. There was a bleak taxi ride toward the city, a 'vulpine dog' silenced by a lobbed brick, a hotel receptionist who tried to sleep through his arrival, and then a cell-like room. Raban wanted a glass of whisky. And for a brief moment the hotel receptionist appeared about to soften his landing in Sanaa. 'For the first time since I had woken him, he brightened,' Raban observed. But then, 'a sleepy grin widened his face. "No whisky," he said. "No beer. No alcohol."' This landfall in Yemen was not looking promising.

Raban awoke the next morning in the clothes he had arrived in, as though undecided about whether he intended to stay. The landscape from the hotel window was a 'busy elaboration of stucco, dust and greenery'; there was 'no visible logic, no point for the eye to rest,' he complained. 'No one should catch their first sight of the Yemen before breakfast,' he thought. But breakfast was disagreeable too: just a can of apple juice and an uncooked 'chickenshitty' egg. Later, as he wandered on his first day in Sanaa, Raban was offered 'Yemeni whisky', but he was not much impressed by that either and likened *qat* to 'a mouthful of dry hedge'. Still, he learnt that Yemen was not the teetotalitarian state that the hotel receptionist had implied. He met a man named Hamud, who introduced him to a moustachioed dwarf who was lugging a truckload of bootlegged liquor into Sanaa. 'We have whisky,' said the dwarf, *real* whisky, 'and he patted the hot mudguard tenderly as if it was the rump of a favoured pony.' The logic was instantly apparent to Raban: 'qat keeps one awake; so one needs whisky to get to sleep.'

True, *qat* can be a little stimulating, but as has already been said, it was really only like drinking tea or coffee. I doubt you would have needed whisky to get to sleep, but it might have helped I suppose. And I might even have been able to offer you some, for the bootlegging and the black-market trade in contraband continued. I had been given the telephone number of a man called 'Abud' whose real name I never knew. We met once on the steps of the central post office. It was a conspicuous encounter, between one of the few foreigners in Sanaa and a Yemeni man in a trench coat who shifted in and out of the shadows while glancing about with an expression that said, 'I've got a bottle of whisky under my arm.'

'Abud?' I enquired, as though there could have been any doubt.

He rummaged about in his armpit and withdrew a bottle of whisky from under his arm.

'Four thousand,' he said, which was more than we had agreed on the phone. I didn't bother to argue, but later deleted his number.

On a subsequent occasion I made contact with 'Tariq', who spoke some English, which I had hoped would mean that my pick-up locations were no longer limited to those few municipal buildings and public landmarks that I could name in Arabic. Instead, 'Tariq' suggested that we meet near my home, by the *Sayilah*, opposite the mosque.

'Opposite the mosque?!' But he had already hung up. And that evening, by the *Sayilah*, opposite the mosque, under the glow of a streetlight, a taxi pulled up and the driver stepped out. He opened the rear door wordlessly. I climbed in the back and the door slammed shut. Then 'Tariq' squirmed around in the front passenger seat and slung me a hand like a pile of sausages.

'Don't worry,' he said, wringing my palm. 'We won't kidnap you!'

His driver got back behind the wheel and we trundled slowly up the *Sayilah*.

'Say "hello", Ahmad.'

Beside me on the back seat was a boy, perhaps ten years old.

'Hello,' he said. He had his father's grin.

'Hello Ahmad,' I said.

Tariq dived down between the glove compartment and his paunch, dredged up a polythene bag, then wriggled and twisted to hand me the package with a broad smile. In the bag, wrapped in newspaper, was a bottle of whisky.

'Teacher's,' said Tariq. 'Very good.'

I slipped three thousand riyals into his hand, and Ahmad shyly acceded to his father's insistence that he count from one to three thousand in English for me. The driver pulled a U-turn, we arrived back at the mosque, Tariq handed me the sausages again, and Ahmad waved goodbye from the rear window, having got as far as twenty-three. Teacher's. It was hard to tell.

The torn and faded label barely disclosed the bottle's contents. Instead, it told of a journey from Djibouti, crossing the Red Sea with pirates and sharks, and being bribed or smuggled through numerous checkpoints on its way to Sanaa. Whisky was cheaper outside the city's perimeter: at a shabby building on a hairpin bend on the road to the coast. It was cheaper still at a seaside hotel in Hodeidah: in a backroom littered with empty beer cans, automatic weapons, and drunken sailors. There a bottle of gin could be had for half the Sanaa price, but the rolling bloodshot eyes and the sailors' reeling shadows prompted me to reconsider the trade-off of risk and cost.

'At about ten pounds a bottle,' according to Jonathan Raban, at the time of his visit, Yemeni men were buying 'two or three bottles of black-market whisky a week.' They were spending 'about fifty pounds a week on qat' and 'getting through three or four packets of cigarettes a day.' Raban had arrived to find 'a very poor country which had been on a wild spree.' Oil prices had exploded in the 1970s and oil states had prospered. Yemen had benefited from the new wealth of its oil-producing neighbours by exporting a vast workforce of rig-hands, mechanics, construction workers, and cab drivers throughout Arabia and the Gulf. Since the civil war of the 1960s, Yemen had been broken into two countries. North was the market economy of the Yemen Arab Republic with Sanaa its capital. South was the People's Democratic Republic of Yemen, 'the communist one' to outsiders, with its government in Aden aligning with the Soviet Union, China, and Cuba. But the differences between the capitalist and communist states were not so stark on the ground and both countries relied heavily upon the export of labour. 'Yemen was living on remittances,' Raban noted succinctly. The second-hand wealth sent home to Sanaa was quickly blown on imported consumer goods. 'Rothman's cigarettes, Johnny Walker whisky... Toyota cars, Suzuki motorcycles, Hitachi radios, Sony television sets... What was Yemen's own was the air of glazed fatigue... the dirt... the makeshift, the gimcrack and the tumbledown.' In Sanaa, Raban declared, 'rot was in the air: it smelled of rotten wood, rotten meat, rotten clothes, rotten money.'

Sanaa had been rotting for almost as long as anyone might care to remember. Anyone in Europe at least. In 1839 Charles Cruttenden had viewed the city as 'fast verging to its fall'. Captain Playfair, in his 1859

History of Arabia Felix, also remarked upon the city's dissipation: 'This, the garden of Arabia, has been abandoned to anarchy and confusion,' he said. When Walter Harris visited in 1892, he observed that 'there is, in fact, but little to tell of the former grandeur of Sanaa.' Many years later, the Italian filmmaker Pier Paolo Pasolini appealed to the United Nations to protect Sanaa from the 'contamination' of 'modernity and progress'. 'Save Yemen,' he implored the UN. To support his case, in 1971 Pasolini produced a thirteen-minute documentary film, titled *Le Mura Di Sanaa* (The Walls of Sanaa). Hand-held footage roamed through dusty streets and panned dizzyingly to take in the spectacle of the city's towerhouses. Sanaa had been 'perfectly conserved through centuries,' intoned the film's Italian narration, its beauty had reached 'unreal perfection'. 'So far, the Old City, within the walls, remains completely intact.'

Pasolini visited Sanaa while scouting locations to film his *Arabian Nights*. He wanted to retell his reimagined tales of flying carpets and magic spells in settings that reflected his aesthetic and political ideals. The stories would take place outside the commodification and commercialism of capitalist society, the characters would be liberated from the conventional world and moral conventions. He shot the final scenes in Sanaa. It all went down well at Cannes in 1974, but the copious nudity and at least one semi-erect penis caused offence in Yemen. In part at least, the walls of Sanaa protected an exotic fantasy of Pasolini's own invention. Outside the walls, a 'New City' had arisen after the revolution of 1962. No longer dependent on the aegis of the imamate, the city of Sanaa began to expand in commercial districts and modern suburbs. According to Pasolini, the 'Old City' was now under threat from a rising tide of concrete and tarmac, a rot of plastic shoes, tinned foods, and transistor radios. Pasolini compared Sanaa to Venice; a unique city not of the sea, but of the desert - a Venice of Dust. There were moments, I confess, when the analogy even seemed fitting: in the shadow-filled alleys that terminated unpredictably with a sudden sunlit Campo, or a Turkish-looking dome, or even, just occasionally in Sanaa, a watercourse. But the comparison was not naïve. When the sea-flood of 1966 appeared to threaten the extinction of Venice, the response was an influx of international money and skilled heritage specialists. Five years later, Pasolini was hoping to initiate something similar in Sanaa.

Arabist Robert Serjeant and architect Ronald Lewcock had begun visiting the city around this time, laying the foundations for their comprehensive *San'a: An Arabian Islamic City*. They too described the rot that Raban had sniffed out and the creeping materialism that Pasolini deplored. In the past, Serjeant and Lewcock suggested, 'pride in owning fine buildings' prompted 'decoration and rich finishes'. But they lamented that 'today such expression is diverted to the acquisition of motor cars and relatively impermanent household gadgets.' They witnessed 'the demolition of old Jewish houses', the destruction of ancient buildings to make way for 'ugly ill-constructed edifices', and they watched the bulldozing of bridges across the *Sayilah* 'so that a motor road could run down it'. They saw the walls of Sanaa 'being eaten into by building in many places, or crumbling, not so slowly, into ruin from neglect to maintain them.' Serjeant and Lewcock were concerned with 'traditional Sanaa', 'up to the officer revolution of September 26th 1962'. Since then there had been countless heritage losses. And since the end of hostilities between republicans and royalists, countless interested foreigners had been able to travel to a country that had previously been inaccessible under the imamate, or unsafe due to conflict. This Garden of Arabia, the Venice of Dust, was now open to visitors.

Wilfred Thesiger was in Sanaa only a few months before Jonathan Raban. Years earlier, Thesiger's recounting of sojourns spent with the Bedouin of Arabia and the Marsh Arabs of Iraq during the 1940s and 50s earned him a reputation as one of the great travel writers of the twentieth century. And in 1966 he was in Yemen alongside the British mercenaries and Imam al-Badr's royalist army. He was well into his sixties when he cast his nostalgic eye upon Sanaa for the first time in 1977. He saw 'the disruptive effect' of 'undreamed wealth' in the city. 'In its narrow streets motor-cycles had taken the place of donkeys, and television masts were on every building.' Despite having never seen Sanaa before, Thesiger determined that his snapshot of the city provided evidence of its trajectory. Much like Charles Cruttenden nearly a century and a half earlier who judged Sanaa swiftly verging to its fall, Thesiger concluded that 'everything was changing fast.' And for a traditionalist like Thesiger, who resented the education of 'primitive' people as much as he resented the coming of the motorcar, change was never a good thing.

But change was inevitable. Jonathan Raban described reading Thesiger's *Arabian Sands* on the airplane from Doha to Sanaa's new international airport. His flight path traced the route that Thesiger had taken across the Empty Quarter thirty years earlier. Where Thesiger had been running out of water with his camels in the desert, Raban was smoking cigarettes and munching peanuts at 30,000ft. The moment of contrast neatly distilled a dynamic: Arabia, portrayals of Arabia, travel, and travel writing were all in flux. Raban had distanced himself from an earlier generation of travel writers. Reporting for the *Radio Times* on Freya Stark's televised raft journey down the Euphrates a few months earlier, Raban pointedly remarked that 'Dame Freya and I do not come from the same mould' (in Raban's retelling, eighty-four-year-old Stark is only briefly but ravishingly glimpsed amid the caravan of television crew: 'an enormous cherry-coloured Ascot hat' and a plummy voice remarking upon the genius of the man who invented the omelette). Raban brought a new perspective to Sanaa. Unconvinced by Pasolini's 'unreal perfection' or Thesiger's elegiac refrain, uninterested even in the 'traditional Sanaa' sought by Serjeant and Lewcock, Raban had more in common with David Holden: bidding farewell to the romantic image of Arabia, and being a marker as well as a recorder of history.

Yemen at the time of Raban's visit was a country of imported goods, exported labour, 'spiralling inflation', and political instability. The president had been assassinated six months earlier; a briefcase bomb would kill his successor three months hence. Then Ali Abdullah Saleh would take power. Rot was setting in. Outside Sanaa, Raban stopped in a village. 'It consisted of just eight mouldering towers, bunched around a vestigial market square. There was a well, a pound of smelly donkeys, and half a dozen shops kept by stunted boys who were all ribs and knee-bones.' It was a village 'sunk up to its axles in several centuries of dirt, poverty and inertia'. When Pasolini appealed to the UN to 'save' Yemen from modernity and progress, he had done so 'in the name of the simple people that poverty has kept pure'. Thesiger held very similar beliefs about the purity of primitive people. Raban, however, recognised that 'it is one of the privileges of the rich to idolize poverty from a safe distance.' Sanaa might have begun to rot in its modernity, but mouldering in the poverty and inertia of earlier centuries had little to commend it. Unsentimental, disconsolate even, Raban's apparently despairing view ultimately gave some room for optimism. Shunning the inherent dishonesty of nostalgia and its betrayal of hope, he rejected the falsehood that our past was better than it is possible to make our future. Raban did not set out to witness a world before it changed, or to prevent it from changing. He was interested in change itself.

For the thirty-five-year-old who had escaped from his father's staid Norfolk vicarage and his boarding school upbringing to become an adventurous writer, the journey to Sanaa began on the Earls Court Road. It was spurred by a 'calligraphic revolution'. 'Stylish, looping letters' had appeared on the municipal litter bins of west London. 'A script of ripples and flourishes' adorned the doors of dentists and kebab houses. 'A *halal* butchers opened up, its window a pretty conundrum of red squiggles and dots.' Raban wandered through 1970s Kensington, contemplating his new neighbours who had lately arrived from Middle Eastern oil states. Lost in 'an impenetrable labyrinth of consonants', he stared at the signs in Arabic, 'taking pleasure in their meaningless elegance'. And he planned the trip that would take him from London through Bahrain, Abu Dhabi, Dubai, Doha, and on to Sanaa. Changes at home motivated Raban's exploration of a changing Arabia. That journey of exploration was described in *Arabia Through the Looking Glass*, one of his earliest books. The title might have been an allusion to the Arabic writing on the Earls Court Road, for 'like mirror-writing, it worked back to front.' But a journey 'through the looking glass' inevitably also hinted at a Lewis Carroll world, 'back to front' spatially, perhaps also logically and morally.

Yet even as Raban's book went to press in 1979, the metaphor of the Arab world as a mirror image had been shattered by the publication of Edward Said's *Orientalism* the year before. Said exposed the European invention of the Orient. He argued that Europe's representations of Arabs were rooted in a self-serving opposition of West and East, Occident and Orient, Us and Them. In this opposition, West was invariably best. The East was everything the West was not; opposite, but far from equal. West was logic and good sense; East was irrationality. West was honour and decency; East was immorality. East too was racial inferiority, religious fanaticism, and fundamental weakness; it could be subject to 'penetration' and domination by the West. In this distorted mirror, Said argued,

'The Orient' had become not only a repository for European fantasies, but a justification for imperial ambitions. It was not a perfect theory, but it would have a powerful impact. And perhaps it is of note that in a subsequent edition, Raban's book would lose the Looking Glass moniker; its title abbreviated simply to *Arabia*.

'Latent orientalism' was the phrase used by Edward Said to describe the way in which our ideas and assumptions of the 'Orient' are bred into us and perpetuated, almost unconsciously and often unquestioningly, in words and images. Having been exposed in the course of a lifetime to so many invented words and images about the Orient, as well as invented versions of Arabia and Islam, it is hard to escape their influence. Latent orientalism, regrettably but nonetheless undoubtedly, imbues my own experiences and depictions of Sanaa; it is, after all, by Said's definition 'almost unconscious' and to recognise and challenge it takes a determined effort.

'No fucking sand dunes,' decided Raban, making just such a determined effort. He was intent on avoiding the repetition of hackneyed tropes. Eschewing the desert, the belly-dancers, and the Bedouin hospitality favoured by earlier travellers, he instead encountered cityscapes, novelty car horns, and the economics of oil. Raban's was a realist Arabia, urban, modern, and mechanised. Perhaps because he anticipated some of Edward Said's contentions, because he determinedly avoided clichés, or simply because he sought out actual conversation with real people on his journey, Raban rarely succumbed to orientalist banalities. He met a Yemeni man named Ahmad who more or less expressed Said's thesis. 'It is very difficult,' said Ahmad, 'for someone from the West to understand. Either he sees a hopeless chaos, or he thinks it is all very pretty and quaint. I would like you to see that it is something else.'

'The Yemen had been known to older travellers as *Arabia Felix* - the happy corner of fertility in a desert continent,' Raban noted, remembering his boarding school Latin. But he thought the place had gone feral, creating 'an Arabia which was not so much Felix as Demens.' There had been no Latin at my comprehensive, so I had to look it up. *Demens* - 'demented, mad, wild, raving' or 'reckless, foolish'. Raban's initial impression of Yemen, in short and in spite of Ahmad's advising, was of a hopeless chaos. He was not the first to say so. 'The *normal* state of al-Yemen through history has been chaos,' declared the British colonial administrator Harold Ingrams in 1963. Ingrams was torn by the dichotomy of chaos and quaintness. He recalled having 'found life in Sanaa much as did my first English predecessor, John Jourdain of Lyme Regis, in 1609.' Quaint, in a gothic sort of way. Ingrams' wife Doreen saw the city as 'a living picture of medieval towns in Europe'. It was already a familiar trope. Freya Stark called Sanaa a 'medieval city'. The entomologist Hugh Scott brooded over 'to what century the life of Sanaa, so largely medieval, chiefly belonged.' Claude Fayein considered it 'still in the Middle Ages'. Arthur Wavell made the medievalism manifest by travelling to Yemen with a suit of chain mail. Jonathan Raban reported a remark made by a foreigner in Sanaa: 'They're dragging this country by the scruff of its neck into the middle of the fifteenth century.' 'It was the kind of remark which custom required one to make about the Yemen,' Raban observed with disdain; 'a standard cliché', and he detested clichés.

By such clichés Sanaa had been denied entrance to the twentieth century. For European observers, the paradigm of a twentieth-century city was a European one. Yet in the face of the acknowledged social, economic, and technological change occurring in Sanaa, charges of medievalism were hardly tenable. In fact, they were grossly hypocritical. But it was in accord with the dichotomy of quaintness or chaos, and consistent with a lingering orientalist superiority, that Sanaa was condemned to be either not modern, or modern only in an ugly, rotten sort of way. Europe, it seemed, provided the only proper model for modernity. Even Raban, while not objecting to change, disapproved of the nature of change he saw in Sanaa.

Yet beyond superficial appearances, Yemen's capital seems to have had much in common with Britain's. In 1937 Hugh Scott recognised in Sanaa a medieval background with some nineteenth-century buildings, but then 'quite modern inventions such as bicycles, motor-cars, wireless and aeroplanes'; which made it sound rather like parts of pre-war London. And the Western goods imported into Sanaa in the 1970s seemed in some ways only the equal of the Arabic script that Jonathan Raban witnessed being imported onto Earls Court Road.

I had been confounded by the Latin epithet *Demens* that Raban applied to

Yemen. But I was also puzzled by the definite article that he attached to it too. Why did Raban refer to 'The Yemen', rather than just plain 'Yemen'? None of Doctor Finlay, Charles Cruttenden, Charles Millingen, General Haig, Joseph Wolff, or Reverend Stern had written about *The* Yemen when they visited Sanaa in the middle years of the 1800s. But from the end of the nineteenth century, and through to the last quarter of the twentieth, almost all English visitors added a definite article to their destination. Walter Harris, Aubrey Herbert and Leland Buxton, Arthur Wavell, Freya Stark, Norman Lewis, Harold Ingrams, and now Jonathan Raban had all passed through *The* Yemen. The label apparently had its own history.

'The Yemen,' I vaguely thought, might have been an abbreviation of The Kingdom of Yemen, or The Yemen Arab Republic, but 'The' was already being applied in the Ottoman era - well before either of those states came into existence. In fact, the moment at which travellers began to apply 'The' to Yemen seems to coincide with the second Ottoman occupation of the country and the British establishment of the Aden Protectorate. Still, I wondered, *why* had 'Yemen' become 'The Yemen', and why *then*? In Arabic, a definite article commonly precedes place names, so perhaps 'The Yemen' was simply 'Al-Yemen' translated too literally into English, as though this territory beyond the edge of British influence in Arabia had been labelled, but the label had not been finished with care. A definite article usually implies some familiarity with its subject, but here it sounded like the opposite, or indifference. As well, 'The' is more often applied to regions than to nation states; as in The Levant, The Hejaz, or The Maghreb. The haziness of Yemen's borders meant 'any exact description of the country is impossible,' claimed Walter Burton Harris (who nonetheless considered the border clear enough to necessitate him dressing up as a Greek shopkeeper in order to cross it in 1893). So 'The Yemen' expressed some uncertainty over the country's perimeter. And if 'The Yemen' denoted geographic ambiguity, it also called into doubt the country's validity as a political unit. Just like the paradigm of a 'modern' city, the model of a sovereign nation was a European one. And that European model was not matched by Yemen's vaguely bordered domain of tribal affiliations that were intermittently and incompletely occupied by the Turks.

'The Yemen' was a colonial title, dating back to the carve-up of

Southern Arabia between the Ottomans and British. 'The British rescued Aden in 1839,' suggested the Colonial Administrator Harold Ingrams rather provocatively in 1963, just as the nationalist rebellion against British troops in Aden was firing up. In the nineteenth century, while the British asserted power over Aden and the Aden Protectorate, the Ottomans claimed control of the rest of the region. It was these offcuts of British territory, badly managed by the Turks according to British visitors, that the Brits themselves named 'The Yemen'. According to Ingrams, 'The Yemen' was merely a territory 'in effect created by the British', in what he thought was a province of historical and geographical chaos. When Ingrams attached 'The' to 'Yemen' it was knowing, deliberate, and disparaging. When Jonathan Raban described his time in 'The Yemen' it is hard to imagine that he could have been aware of the colonialist heritage of that definite article. Latent orientalism at times seems like an inescapable inheritance.

Perhaps that inheritance put writers off. After the publication of Said's *Orientalism* in 1978 there was a gap in Western travel writing. I could not find a single European travel book about Yemen from the 1980s. And I struggled to find any about the Middle East too. Maybe would-be travel writers had been prompted to pause and reconsider their representations of the 'Orient', as Edward Said would have wished. Or perhaps 'The Orient' ended with the oil boom and the increasing impossibility of applying the old clichés, as Jonathan Raban suggested. Or perhaps travel writers were put off by the regional instability and the tensions of the Cold War. In any event, after the British abandoned Aden, after the 'oil crisis', and after *Orientalism*, the landscape for travel writing in Arabia had altered, politically, economically, and intellectually.

Raban, having observed change in Sanaa, seemed to experience some personal change there too, or at least a change in his perception. After his unpromising arrival and his chickenshitty breakfast, he had found the Old City overwhelming; 'maddening'. 'Its walls were oppressively high, its corridors narrow.' Whichever way he turned, he said, 'there were new riddles and contradictions.' The streets became a labyrinth. Raban became 'a scared rat in a psychologist's maze'. It was not an experience I ever shared. I never felt myself oppressed by Sanaa's walls, was never remotely unsettled when I lost myself in its knotted alleys. But I was reminded of the giddy sweep of Pasolini's hand-held cinematography with its vertiginous panning vistas. And I recall a sensation from my explorations not just in Sanaa, but also from my roaming through Edinburgh, Paris, or Amsterdam. It is a malady of travel, a sort of motion sickness, brought on by walking with an eager gaze through a city of towering terraces. Raban complained that there was 'no point for the eye to rest', and therein lies the beginnings of this ailment. As you walk, an urban panorama scrolls out from foreshortened buildings; as you glance up, the structures taper loftily; and as you continue past narrow side streets, the sky cleaves open beside you in elongating triangles and stretching parallelograms, like a slowly warping puzzle.

Only up here, on a rooftop, shortly before his departure, did Raban begin to feel better. It was here, at this altitude, looking out over the city, that the motion abated, the chaos ended, and he began to see something different. Alighting first on far-off rooftops, then upon the facades near-to, at last his eye came to rest. On the towerhouse walls he recognised the 'scrawl of handwriting'. In the stucco friezes he saw a 'dense jumbled alphabet'. Here were the 'signs and symbols' that had inspired his journey. On Earls Court Road, Jonathan Raban had seen only the 'meaningless elegance' of Arabic script. In Yemen, he saw that 'you could look at the walls of Sana'a for a year, finding more and more meanings in them.' Each towerhouse might bear a verse; each view from a rooftop might be a poem; and the Old City that Raban considered 'so literally legible' might then become an urban anthology of sorts. Far from being meaningless, there were multiplicities of meanings, if you only looked.

At night, looking out from up here on the rooftop, after the kids had been called home and my neighbour the camel had taken his rest, we would have watched the vehicles streak along the *Sayilah*, the figures chatting at Abdul's Sobermarket, the movement in and out of the *ful* shop, and the pools of light radiating from the mosque. We might have recognised that what we saw was neither simply quant or chaotic, and we might have found any number of meanings if we had searched for them. Once, I stood here looking for a very particular meaning. High above the streets, above the signs and the symbols on the city walls, above the horizon, high up, on a clear night, when it looked as though the old moon had been smashed and blown in powder across the sky, I was searching for the new one. I was looking for the *Hilal* Moon, a slender silver crescent arcing into the firmament, like the ibex horns that curved out from the rooftop's corners. The *Hilal* Moon would be the sign that marked the start of Ramadan...

- 18 -

Questing

- Eric Hansen, 1978 & 1989 -

AT 2AM ON THE MORNING of 2 February 1978, a storm was rising on the Red Sea. Eric Hansen was aboard a yacht, manning the bilge pump as it churned out a foul soup of diesel fuel, sump oil, warm brine, and vomit. A decade later, Hansen would go in search of this moment. Or if not this moment exactly, then moments close to this, and moments far from this. Moments at Tahitian waterfronts and Tibetan monasteries; moments that included secret Mekong River journeys and smuggling trips into Rangoon; days in Afghan villages near the Russian border and nights with village girls in the Indian Ocean. All these were moments from Hansen's youth, preserved in years of travel journals, and he was determined to revisit them. The trouble was that all his journals lay buried on a tiny island off the coast of Yemen.

Hansen wanted 'to remember what it was like to let go completely, to abandon all caution and feel the freedom of floating in the world.' With this floating freedom, in the ebbing days of 1977, he and four others set sail from the Maldives on their forty-two-foot yacht, bound for Athens via the Red Sea. But once through the Bab al-Mandab the sky darkened, the wind blew up, the waves swelled, and a powerful roller slapped open the skylight, emptying seawater into the yacht's cabin. As the tempest grew, Hansen knelt in the darkness next to the engine, manning the bilge pump, cursing and struggling not to pass out amid the heat and diesel fumes. Through the night he was at the helm, pitching and rolling into rain and salt spray, getting pounded by twenty-foot breakers that thundered beneath the keel and washed over the deck until dawn. Finally, the yacht beached on Uqban Island, just a few miles off Yemen's coast. For two weeks in February 1978 Hansen and his comrades were shipwrecked on this desolate sandbar. And somewhere on this deserted island Hansen buried his travel journals. A decade later, exhuming the journals and the moments they contained would prove to be no easy undertaking, but the challenge animated an enthralling travelogue. 'Part of my desire to return was purely sentimental,' Eric Hansen explained in his book *Motoring with Mohammed*, 'but I also felt that the journals held significant moments to be relived - scenes from a past life. I wanted to find out who I was as a young man.'

There had been an explosion of shattered glass. Shards scattered over the cobbles and spots of sugary tea spattered my trouser legs. Glancing up, already a throng had surrounded the two men whose angry disagreement had sent a tea glass flying toward me across the *suq*. Their argument escalated quickly. Gesticulations became shoves, shoves became punches, and then, above the heads of the assembled audience, there was the flash of a *jambiyah*. There were screams and the crowd surged forward to separate the two combatants. No deathblow fell; no mortal wound was inflicted. But three or four more times a blade was raised aloft, as though to deliver the opponent a fatal stab. And three or four more times the impending impalement was followed by the shrieking and then surging of spectators. This climactic sequence was repeated as if in a choreographed melodrama - a flashing blade, a collective scream, the crowd sways, and the moment is defused - until at last the foes were disarmed and toppled to the ground. It was minutes before *iftar*. We had fasted all day and I had been sitting at a tea stall, quietly contemplating a handful of sticky dates that glistened, succulent in the fading light. Having no inclination to watch a fistfight, when the brawl showed no signs of abating and the bundle of furious limbs came rolling toward me, I grabbed my dates and hurried away as the entangled pair continued thrashing on the floor in their violent embrace.

On Friday evening I had been reliably assured that the holy month would definitely not begin on the following day.

'No, no. Not tomorrow. After tomorrow,' Mansoor the fruiterer told me.

'Sunday. It will begin on Sunday,' Mohammed confirmed at the Sobermarket.

But if I had watched television later that night, listened to the radio, paid attention to the mosque announcements, or climbed up to the rooftop just a few hours earlier to glimpse the moon before it set, I would have known that the *Hilal* moon had been sighted. That first clipped edge of silver visible after the new moon signalled the start of the ninth month of the Islamic lunar calendar. The Holy Month of Ramadan would begin the next day: Saturday. I woke late that morning and had not been woken. Instead of the usual chug and honk of traffic on the *Sayilah* that routinely dragged me from sleep, I rose to light and birdsong. The first day of Ramadan had taken me by surprise. Neither Mansoor nor Mohammed was available for redress. Not a single shop front opened and none of the stalls on Bab as-Sabah stirred from their tarpaulin-draped slumber that morning. My footsteps on the street made the silence stark.

I hadn't been alone in failing to recognise Ramadan's arrival. Richard drove on deserted roads to a near-deserted office. 'It was just me and the teaboy,' he told me afterwards. 'And the teaboy lives in the basement, so he's always there. Anyway, I had four cups of English Breakfast and got some work done until everyone else turned up around noon.' Overnight, body clocks were adjusted and the city adopted new routines. Government ministeries pushed back their working times by three hours. Banking occurred between ten a.m. and two, then from eight p.m. until eleven at night. Shops stayed open until two or three in the morning. Manual workers avoided daylight entirely and more than once I was awoken by the screech of a circular saw in the early hours as a new storey was constructed on a nearby house under cover of darkness. Even my neighbour the camel shifted his working pattern, circling the sesame mill from seven to eleven in the evening. Sanaa had become nocturnal. The hardship of fasting and abstinence during daylight hours was ameliorated somewhat as people spent more of those hours asleep, and more of the night awake. *Qat* served to sustain, or necessitate, the schedule. Once meals had been shared and mosques attended after sunset, *qat* chews commenced only around eight in the evening. They continued until midnight. And the stimulant's effect made it difficult to sleep much before dawn.

'We pray at least five times every day. Even if you don't usually pray, you must pray during the holy month.' A religious colleague reminded me of Ramadan's proscriptions in the preceding week. 'And no food, and nothing to drink,' he told me. 'No smoking and no sex from sunrise till sunset.'

With nothing to pray to and nobody to reliably have sex with, these edicts seemed hardly to apply to me. I could fast though, and I proposed this, anticipating that the suggestion would be suitably regarded as a magnanimous gesture of solidarity, yet certain that it would be roundly discouraged as unnecessary since I was not a Muslim.

'But of course you'll fast. It's Ramadan.' It was not the response I had expected and I reconciled myself to a challenging month.

On the first day of Ramadan, as I hurried away from the *suq* in the moments before *iftar*, an opening door splashed the sounds and smells of cooking into the emptying street. The clattering of crockery, a shout to take the bread from the oven, and the mingling scents of sweet buttery baking and piquant simmering stews were almost overwhelming and my legs slowed of their own accord as I passed by, drinking in the air. Reaching Bab al-Yaman, I pushed my way through the crowd surrounding three giant teapots with gas flames roaring underneath, then thrust some coins into the hand of the tea stall owner and snatched a glass of milky tea. Belatedly I acknowledged that I had jumped the queue. It didn't matter. My heart was pounding and a cool sweat pricked my spine. I sat down on the pavement.

'Are you fasting?' An affable old man sat next to me and attempted conversation.

I was.

'Are you Muslim?'

I was not. And I was in no state to discuss it. Brusquely I steered the conversation toward the single subject occupying my mind. 'How much time left?' I asked.

'One minute... Maybe two...'

One consequence of my fasting was a modest understanding of what would otherwise have been an incomprehensible month. I shared the sleep deprivation and the deranged blood sugar levels, and all the physiological and emotional turmoil that followed. And I recognised how a fight could break out in the *suq* in the minutes before sunset on the first day of Ramadan. But I also felt the inestimable preciousness of the moments around *iftar* and the sanctity of fast-breaking.

Soon, somewhere west beyond the mountains, well beyond the walls of the Old City and out of sight, the sun's burning rim would drop at last below the horizon. At that moment, as we were plunged into the earth's shadow, we would finally break our fast. But for now, dusk lay waiting, biding its time in the trembling shadow of my tea glass. With my thoughts focused elsewhere, I didn't notice the girl until she was standing before me. She could have been no more than six or seven years old and as I sat on the cobbles our eyes were almost level. We looked at one another. She seemed a little uncertain; I must have seemed surprised. Then, wordlessly, she held out her hand toward me and in her palm was a deep-fried samosa.

I hesitated, she stepped forward, and I accepted the proffered gift. Still without speaking, she turned and picked her way carefully between the men sitting around untouched dishes of rice and stew, re-joining her father who squatted on the other side of the square. I was left speechless too. And then the sound of the prayer call from the al-Rudwan mosque declared the sun's disappearance. Immediately the news was answered with bismillahs and fast-breaking. Again I hesitated, breathing my own thanks for the gifted triangle of deep-fried lentil-filled pastry and the unspoken act of kindness.

'Fourteen days on this waterless island?' The Eritrean goat smugglers were aghast. Though their own food and water supplies were almost depleted, the Eritreans' first act upon finding Eric Hansen and his four companions shipwrecked on Uqban Island was to gift them two handfuls of dates. Hansen buried his travel journals and other possessions on the island, intending to return and collect them later. Taking with them only the provisions essential for their journey, he and the others boarded the goat smugglers' boat. The Eritreans took them to Kamaran Island, from where they reached Hodeidah, and from there they took 'a spectacularly uncomfortable and scenic five-hour drive' to Sanaa. With only a few dollars in traveller's cheques, Hansen entered the US Embassy to ask for assistance. He was met by marine guards, bulletproof glass, and a decidedly unhelpful consular official. Next he approached the airline offices, hoping to find a discounted flight out of Yemen. He carried with him the conviction that gift-giving is a mutually gratifying exchange; that the experiences of both generosity and gratitude offered fulfilment. But even Hansen was stunned by the sagacious response of the Yemenia airline manager who unhesitatingly handed him a free flight. 'The next time you see someone in need, I want you to pass on this favour,' the manager told him. 'It was given to me, and now it is yours.'

In 1978, still salt-crusted from his Red Sea shipwreck, the young Eric Hansen had arrived in Sanaa and found a sugar-coated city. It was 'a gingerbread fantasy', adorned with 'squiggles of white cake icing'. His analogy felt unusually fitting during Ramadan as I wandered hungry in the late afternoons, beset by intrusive thoughts, beneath candied glass *qamariah*, past stucco frosting on the Old City's buildings, along cinnamon-dusted alleyways. In 1989, Hansen returned to recover his buried journals. He, too, wandered distractedly, washed out by a transatlantic flight, on his first day back in Sanaa for over a decade, and he was retiring to his hotel room for a jet-lagged mid-morning nap when he encountered the locust seller.

'We consider the locust to be a delicacy,' the locust seller told him. Hansen pinched the wings off one of the insects, popped the legs and body in his mouth, and thought it tasted 'like crunchy, smoked milk powder'. He wondered if it might have been improved by a little salt.

'But a ram's head is preferred to a sackful of locusts,' said the locust seller cryptically before Hansen returned to bed. Surprisingly, even the locust seller's enigmatic dictum and Hansen's motives in this unexpected encounter would come to make sense during Ramadan.

Hurtling out of the sun, swerving on the oily smear of its heat-hazed shadow, the bus veered across the road towards me. Skidding, it stopped, and I stepped aboard warily. It was the eighth day of Ramadan, half an hour before *iftar*, and the city's roads were a dangerous place to be. Everyone had somewhere they wanted to get to for fast-breaking. Throttling the engine, the driver launched the vehicle violently forward. He stamped the accelerator, punched the horn, and yanked the wheel aggressively. I clutched the seat in front of me, bracing myself for impact as the driver repeatedly chose to swerve rather than to slow, to honk and not to brake. It was maniacal behaviour. Careering back toward the kerb he targeted an old lady. She was frantically flagging down the bus from the roadside, all shopping bags and flapping black fabric. With more horn and a miraculously avoided collision, we swept in front of a speeding Landcruiser that had been overtaking on our inside lane and came to a short-lived standstill alongside the old woman. Clambering aboard, she cried out briefly about being late to join her daughter for *iftar*, before an especially pitiless acceleration threw her into the lap of a young soldier. Thus was the seating conundrum overcome in a busload of men in the minutes before *iftar*; any impropriety overlooked in the urgency of the situation.

Valuing self-preservation over speed of passage I hopped off the bus at the next red light. Walking on past Zubeiry Street's closed banks and shuttered shopfronts, only the baklava stores continued trading, crowded with men carrying Kalashnikovs, all jostling to buy confectionaries. Toward the Old City I passed two men with ragged clothes and dirty beards sitting on the ground beneath the city walls. Spread between them in torn-open polythene bags was a meal of rice, beans, and bread. Already they were eating.

'Could your appetites not wait until after *iftar*?' asked another passer-by. He turned to me, shook his head and tapped his temple. 'They're crazy!' he declared, as we walked past, leaving the pair unperturbed and cheerfully pushing food into their faces: eating because they were hungry and because they had food; crazy because they were not following the rules. With its strict schedule, its shared denying and satisfying of appetites, and its observance seeming to override all other concerns, Ramadan was a powerfully cohesive experience. Even the collective moments of madness before *iftar* seemed sanctioned, so long as they adhered to some generally acknowledged formula.

My plan was to reach Bab al-Yaman, as I had come to enjoy the sociability of the square around sunset. But my path was blocked by a sea of blue tarpaulin that overflowed across the pavement, between parked cars, and out into the road. Upon the tarpaulin sheets, crossed-legged around *iftar* fare, dozens of men chatted and shouted in the excitement before fast-breaking. Traversing this ocean of dishes and diners seemed an improbable undertaking. Even the nimble-footed serving boys bearing laden platters from nearby restaurants were struggling to navigate the busy impromptu outdoor picnic area. A uniformed policeman stood up suddenly and signalled to me. I thought at first that he was offering directions, but his hand gesture was an invitation to join him and his colleagues. Gladly I accepted and was welcomed to a patch on the blue tarpaulin. We exchanged greetings and introductions.

'Andrew.'

'Mohammed.'

'Ibrahim.'

'Yasser.'

'Goat,' said Mohammed, noting my gaze. The animal's boiled head stared back at me from a puddle of broth on a tin plate. Its skin had been stripped away, both eyeballs had hardened into unfathomable black globes, and the skull wore a ghoulish turmeric-coloured glow.

'You eat it?'

'Not yet.'

'No. Of course. But, after *iftar*?'

'Yes.'

'Is it good?'

'Excellent! You should have one.'

Grabbing the attention of a passing waiter, I ordered a cup of tea and a boiled goat head.

'Just one?' asked the waiter.

Zubeiry Street's engine roar had faded, replaced by the noise of discussion and demands for tea and goat heads. Then conversations began to quieten amid an air of mounting expectation. Mohammed glanced at his watch and smiled at me. My goat head arrived, smiling at me too. A dirty whiff of tobacco pricked my nostrils and I turned to see a jet of cigarette smoke exhaled into the purpling sky. Nobody had heard the muezzin's voice and we looked about in vain for some other confirmatory sign. A few hesitant hands reached out toward plates and a few dates were tentatively nibbled by mutual consent as collusion spread cautiously across the tarpaulin. Then shouts and fingers pointed toward a figure coming from the direction of the mosque inside Bab al-Yaman. Chomping upon a bread roll, he was the unwitting herald of our fast-breaking. Dates and samosas swiftly disappeared. Then the smile vanished, replaced by a fleeting expression of astonishment, as the jaw dropped, dislocated, and came away from the skull in Mohammed's hands. Already he had ably dismantled his own goat head and now was helping me with mine. He peeled a sliver of flesh from the jawbone and passed me this morsel between finger and thumb. It was a little sinuous, but quite palatable. I watched him extract the tongue from his skull and did my best to copy what he had done, removing bits and pieces from the cheeks and temple. When I had finished tearing meat off the bone Mohammed reached over again and lifted the remnants. Grasping the skull in one hand, he rammed one end of the disconnected jaw into its base, and wrenched with his improvised skull-splitter. There was a splintering sound as the cranium was levered open.

Mohammed held out the shattered skull to me, as though the exposed grey matter were a rare treat, which it was of course. A ram's head is preferred to even a sackful of locusts, after all. But it looked decidedly unappetising. And yet like Hansen with his locust eating perhaps, I was overcome by eagerness to please, anxiety not to offend, bravado, and maybe some notion that someday this episode might be retold. And I sank two fingers into the bony cavity and scooped out a pallid gob of warm soft cerebrum. The boiled brain quivered on my fingertips, then fell apart against my palate like tofu or a flavourless jelly. It might have been improved by a little salt.

It was here, or very close to here, that Eric Hansen took a detour. He had returned to Yemen in 1989 intent upon unearthing the travel journals that he left behind a decade earlier. But after two unsuccessful attempts to reach the spot where they were buried on Uqban Island he came back to Sanaa. The first attempt saw him turned back by soldiers on the highway north of Hodeidah because he lacked written authorisation to visit the coast. At the second try, he reached the harbour town from where Uqban lay just offshore, but was stopped as he boarded a boat: the island lay within a strictly prohibited military zone, the local police chief informed him. Exasperated, Hansen managed to find a group of local fishermen who were able to recall the white people who had appeared upon the island ten years before and the boat that they had left behind with its many bounteous treasures. Encouraged, the fishermen were happy to dig up their own stories of the shipwreck. The ropes, radio, batteries, gas bottles, flare guns, sails, compass, and engine had all been stripped from the vessel. Only the skeleton remained, picked clean.

'She has been in the sea for so long, and now she is very tired,' a local boy explained sweetly.

'The boat is finished,' one of the fishermen confirmed. 'Everything has been taken.'

But Hansen's journals remained buried.

Back in Sanaa, just outside the gate of Bab al-Yaman, near where I had sat upon the ocean of tarpaulin and sucked the dribbling remnants of goat brain from my fingers, Hansen met Martin and Kevin. Both were English teachers in Sanaa. It was the start of the school holidays and Hansen needed a break from his journal hunt, so they set off together to spend a few days in the mountains. In retrospect their trio was a remarkable literary constellation. All three - Hansen, Martin, and Kevin - would subsequently write books about their experiences in Yemen. Kevin Rushby, inspired by the journeys of Richard Burton and intrigued by the prospect of following the path by which 'both coffee and qat entered arabia', later embarked upon a *qat*-fuelled journey from Addis Ababa, across the Red Sea, through Mocha, then Aden, to Sanaa. At the time of Hansen's visits in 1978 and 1989 such a journey would have been impossible. Aden had been separated from Sanaa since 1967 by the border that separated the Yemen Arab Republic in the north and the People's Democratic Republic of Yemen in the south. Travelling between the two cities, and the two countries, meant flying via Djibouti. But 1990 saw the unification of North and South Yemen. And subsequently, Kevin Rushby was able to move across the united Yemen with relative ease. His Red Sea passage was much smoother than Hansen's too, but his travels were not without risk. Piracy was a burgeoning enterprise in the waters off Yemen's coast and kidnappings were rife at the time of Rushby's visit.

The problem of foreigners being kidnapped persisted while I was in Yemen. Shortly after I had arrived in November 2005, two Swiss tourists were seized. An Austrian couple were taken the following month. And two weeks later a former German Deputy Foreign Minister, his wife, and their three children were abducted. When the German family were released after three days in captivity on 31 December, the celebrations were short-lived. A group of four Italian tourists were kidnapped the very next day. Each of these kidnappings had been carried out by different tribes in different regions, but they followed a consistent, customary pattern. Typically, the foreigners would be captured while they visited some far-flung corner of the country, then they would be held for a few days while their captors aired their grievances, and eventually they would be released unharmed. Demands of the kidnapping tribesmen varied but might include the release of kinsmen from government jails, or provision of government jobs for fellow tribesmen, or the delivery of government services like schools, clinics, or paved roads for their communities. The common theme was the tribes' perception of being over-legislated and under-served by the state. When tribes felt wronged by one another they might kidnap other tribesmen; when they felt wronged by the government they kidnapped foreigners.

Usually, the captives seemed to be released before the complaints of the tribes were resolved, which made the tribal kidnappings look less like hostage situations than publicity stunts, and the kidnapped foreigners look less like bargaining chips than poster children for the tribesmen's cause. Anecdotes abounded of the hospitality shown to foreigners by their kidnappers. A group of French retirees were entertained with folk dances and gifted *jambiyahs* and jewellery upon their release. One young French couple were happy to carry on with their honeymoon after being kidnapped for two days. 'Too bad it's not possible to organise holidays like this!' an Italian remarked when he was freed from five days of captivity. And then there was the apocryphal tale of a Japanese tour group being kidnapped, held, and released without any of the tourists realising that their unscheduled detainment was not part of the tour.

Sometimes there was violence and kidnappings occasionally ended disastrously when security forces bungled a 'rescue'. The disincentive to foreign visitors and investors prompted President Saleh to announce a crackdown on kidnappings. At least two convicted kidnappers were executed as a deterrent. And the kidnappings stopped, for a while. Until the same tribe that had kidnapped the German diplomat nine months earlier, harbouring the same complaint about relatives wrongly imprisoned in a Sanaa jail, abducted four French tourists.

'Yes, yes, it's really terrible. Really, really, very terrible.' By chance I had met the Yemeni tour operator for the four Frenchmen during the period of their captivity. He was wretchedly despondent.

'It's been ten days now. Ten days. Really, really, a very terrible disaster.' The outcome for the tourists remained uncertain, but the tour operator believed his own fate sealed.

'Already I have paid all their hotels, all their airfares, and all their guides. All of them. And the French would pay only at the end of their tour. So now I have nothing. All lost. And other tourists are cancelling their visits.' I never heard what became of the tour operator, but the Frenchmen were released unharmed in the first week of Ramadan.

So the scheduling of a television comedy based on the kidnapping of two tourists in Yemen seemed oddly prescient. It was broadcast one evening during Ramadan.

'TV or television?' asked Kaid.

'Either is fine. Or in England we say "telly".' Kaid had invited me to share *iftar* at his home. Waiting for sunset, we watched *Yemen TV*.

'I thought "telly" was for telephone?'

'No, "telly" is for television.'

'OK then, telly is always better during Ramadan.'

The television tourists were being placated by their comedy kidnapper with the assurance that they were merely being invited for lunch. The joke was Yemen's inescapable hospitality.

Kaid worked mornings at one of the government ministries and had spent his afternoons teaching at one of the city's Arabic language institutes until a dispute with the language school's director ended the arrangement. We had met one afternoon, and several times subsequently, at one of the city's teashops. I enjoyed the company and the insights that our conversations provided, while Kaid practised his English and collected my idioms. The black box in the corner of his *mafraj* crackled and blinked.

'We don't have a satellite dish, so we only get *Yemen TV*.'

Kaid stood up and adjusted the television set.

'Usually it's just full of the president. President Saleh got up, President Saleh had a cup of tea, President Saleh had a bath, President Saleh had lunch...'

I perceived the contempt for authority that might have riled the director of the language school. The television image settled and Kaid sat back down.

'But everyone is at home for *iftar*, so the telly people try and make the shows as good as possible.'

The comedy kidnapper of prime time *Yemen TV* shot a lamb and demanded that the foreigners prepare it for dinner. But he was deeply disappointed by their cooking skills. When the police arrived and asked what the kidnapper was demanding for the release of the tourists, he shouted back: 'Bread and *salta*!'

Bread and *salta* appeared immediately upon the television announcement of *iftar*. Kaid and I ate with his fourteen-year-old son. When I asked about his children, Kaid reminded me proudly between mouthfuls that he had five. 'My son here. And my four daughters, the oldest is fifteen and the youngest is three weeks.' Two of the girls were playing boisterously when I arrived and the happy wrestling between father and daughters gave the impression of a loving home. I wondered, though, how difficult it was for young children during Ramadan.

'They have a great time,' Kaid assured me. 'Shorter school hours and there's Eid at the end of it, with celebrations and new toys.'

And what of his wife who looked after them while they were off school?

'I think she enjoys it too. She's able to go out shopping and meet her friends after dark. And she only has to cook once a day.' Our bread and *salta* had, of course, not simply appeared by itself.

'But you know, I had a friend who said that Ramadan in England was brilliant and fantastic. He spent six months in your country, many years ago.'

I had imagined it would be difficult to fast in a context where most other people were not Muslim.

'Not at all,' said Kaid. 'Best Ramadan he ever had. He made lots of friends at the mosque. And it was winter so your English days were short and he only had to fast for about eight hours. Actually, he said that Christians fasted too. But only certain foods, and for longer.'

It took me a while to comprehend what Kaid was talking about. When I did figure it out, the forty days of Lent and their optional abstinence from indulgence seemed considerably less testing than Ramadan.

Forsaking *qat*, we drank mint tea and talked about the future. Kaid was looking for another language school job. He enjoyed learning and teaching English and he was bored by his work at the Education Ministry. Meanwhile, I was approaching the end of my contract in Yemen. I had to choose between taking a contract extension in Sanaa or accepting the offer of a clinical job at a London hospital. I was hesitating before the decision. And my indecision itself was unsettling. In a few days I would turn thirty, and I had no idea what or where I wanted to be. Before I left, Kaid toured me through his home, pointing out the small patch of cultivated dirt where he grew his mint leaves, and the unfinished staircase that would someday lead to a second storey once his son had married and started his own family. Then he peeped around a curtain and drew it back to introduce me briefly to his unveiled wife and mother-in-law.

'I'm sorry that you will be leaving Sanaa,' Kaid told me, anticipating my decision. 'But of course you must go,' he said as I struggled to find my shoes among the assorted footwear piled next to his front door. 'You must start your own family.' His six-year-old daughter appeared and presented me with my shoes. 'A big family!' he advised me. 'Yes, you must go home.'

But home? Where was that? No longer in Suffolk, nor yet in London. Was I not at home in Sanaa? It had felt so, however briefly. Years before, Najiba had arrived in Yemen from France and made a home in Sanaa too. Eric Hansen met her in the Old City and devoted a chapter to describing his encounter with the elderly Frenchwoman and recounting the events of her life. It was a poignant meeting.

Crumpled by time and smelling of dust and dog hair, Najiba reminisced about arriving in Aden by steamship in 1949 and watching the English women waltzing on a hotel rooftop. A three-day truck ride took her north to Taiz and to the Yemeni husband she had met in Paris. Yemen under Imam Ahmad, she recalled, had been a country suspended in 'terrible isolation. Beautiful and complete isolation.' The absence of paved roads and the occasional public executions were startling, but worse was to come in her new domestic role. Her husband beat her to the floor with his fists for not putting enough sugar in his coffee. In Sanaa's hospital she was cared for by the French doctor Claude Fayein. Najiba divorced, remarried, took a job as a translator at the hospital, and chose to remain in Sanaa, looking after her dogs, tending to her invalided second husband, and growing old behind her dusty windowpanes. 'Memories...' she remarked wistfully, 'they are our souvenirs from a lifetime of forgetfulness.'

Hansen did not record a response to the Frenchwoman's lament. Perhaps he might have wished to contend that memories are not the whole story; that his buried journal would contain some more reliable keepsakes from his past than the blurred outlines that history impressed upon his brain. Or perhaps he no longer perceived a contradiction. He may already have realised that the search for his journals was no longer a search for his past. He might by now have recognised that what had started as a pursuit of 'significant moments to be relived' had become a journey of living moments. Hansen's personal journey was a paradigmatic traveller's tale: a quest. But his progress appeared paradoxical, for the closer he came to his objective, the less important it became. 'They represented a lost segment of my life,' he wrote of his lost notebooks, 'and for that reason I found it disconcerting that the longer I stayed in Yemen, the less I worried about finding them.' Gradually, the yearning for his journals gave way to the fulfilment of the journey.

Something similar occurred in my experience of Ramadan. Though at first I spent my days longing for the moment of *iftar*, I came ultimately to find satisfaction in the hours of fasting. Partly it was the quietude of mornings, when it seemed that I had the whole city to myself. But mostly it was the light. Later I would swear that it had altered. As after a thunderstorm, or as if still strewn with the glittering fragments of broken glass and sugary tea, Sanaa sparkled during Ramadan. Each day, soon after the onset of fasting, when the sun tipped over the eastern mountains, a honey-coloured light poured into the Old City. Towerhouses became drenched in a rich liquid radiance. The colours and contours of their walls became enlivened. Every trowel mark on their plaster cut an intricate shadow. Every handprint, brush stroke, or surface imperfection on the stucco became an impeccable marker of the earth's diurnal rotation and our turning about the sun.

I was spellbound. During Hansen's visit, Najiba recalled how entering Sanaa for the first time in 1949 had felt like 'walking into a church'. My own dreary recollections of churchgoing had never before been much called to mind. But this new luminescence was transformative. And like Hansen's gingerbread description of Sanaa, the church analogy felt suddenly apposite during Ramadan. I recalled the rare transcendent beams that had once fallen between Norman arches, through the dust of a gloomy sermon, turning the unbelieving religious observances of childhood into something transiently magical.

I did not want my Ramadan days to end. Perhaps Eric Hansen came to feel something similar about his own journey. But then, incredibly, abruptly, and almost unbelievably, he eventually was able to return to Uqban Island. Locating the spot in the sand where he had buried his journals in a length of sailcloth years before, he was finally able to uncover the lost pages. And almost unbelievably, too, I recalled that he had already disclosed their eventual discovery in his book's opening chapter. Yet this apparent plot-spoiler did not, in fact, spoil the story at all. Instead it allowed me to share Hansen's sense that his apparent objective had become almost irrelevant. His book was not about the stories buried in his old journals, it was about his Yemen journey. Beginning with a shipwreck and ending with the discovery of buried treasure, his tale has the shape of a classic seafarer's yarn, and it is an affectionate portrayal of Yemen and the people who lived there.

Sanaa's aura during Ramadan might have been just autumn's slanting rays. Or some physiological effect of sugar deprivation. Or even a sort of pre-emptive nostalgia brought on by my impending departure. For the city's amber glow was of the sort in which past fragments become preserved; as fossil resins, or as memories, to be buried and then unearthed. Everything seemed enlivened, but then everything passes. And at night, the blazing electricity demands of the sleepless city brought ever more frequent power outages. As the moon tide surged, we were submerged in its phosphorescence, but as the nights rolled by the moonlight waned. And as I walked in darkened streets, the headlamps of the cars that rumbled past sent my shadow spinning around me, as though in a burlesque acceleration of time, gently mocking me, my enthralment with the earth's turning, and my coming departure from this city that had become too briefly my home.

- 19 -

An English
Sheikh

- Tim Mackintosh-Smith, 1982 to date -

'ARRRGGGH.'

Startled, I turned on my heel.

'Whoooaaa.'

Glancing up and down the alleyway I could see no sign of where the noise had come from.

'Arrrrrghh, whoaaa!'

Again the sound, but on the narrow lane behind Sanaa's donkey market nothing stirred. The woman selling herbs sat motionless, watching. It was she who had directed me toward the 'House of Dim'. Once more I rapped the metal knocker against the door. Once more came the guttural moan of camels mating. It seemed to emanate from somewhere deep within the looming towerhouse. Looking up, I saw a pair of eyes peering down.

'Arrghh!' Tim was peeping from an overhang in the wall several storeys above. It was from him that the groaning arose; it was a throaty way of catching attention: a sort of Yemeni 'Oi!'

'Just give the door a good shove!' he cried. 'It tends to stick on the hinges.'

That was the first time that I had visited Tim at his home, but I might have recognised the sounds. On the first page of his book *Yemen: Travels in Dictionary Land* Tim Mackintosh-Smith described the 'strange, strangulated syllables' muttered and mumbled amid a gruff fug of 'peat smoke and roll-ups' as he grappled with his early Arabic studies in the isolation of a crofter's cottage on the Isle of Harris. An Arabic dictionary opened up a strange and alluring lexical landscape. 'Somebody once said that every Arabic word means itself, its opposite, or a camel,' Tim noted. *Qamus*, the Arabic word for dictionary, also means the ocean and ignoring the advice of his undergraduate tutor in Oxford, Tim left the university's ivory towers behind and dived into his dictionary land in Yemen. He had lived there ever since.

'Parp! Parp!'

I looked up, but no face gazed down. I shoved the door, but it didn't budge.

'Parp! Parp!'

The same woman watched me from among her mint and basil sprigs as I hammered the doorknocker one afternoon during Ramadan on this, my second visit to what she called the House of Dim, or Tim.

'Parp! Parp!'

The tooting echoed my knocking.

Knock knock, parp parp; like a flatulent punchline. This, too, I might have recognised, since Tim was by no means averse to toilet humour. I turned and saw him at the far end of the lane, smiling and waving astride a fat black motorcycle.

'Just let me park this thing,' he yelled, then fired the engine and growled around the corner. Again I might have recognised it. Tim's *Dictionary Land* contains a memorable allusion to his 'fiery bicycle' being impounded by Yemen's customs authority. The anecdote neatly satirised a particular strain of pen-pushing bureaucratic obfuscation. It ended with a fart joke.

'Now, um, I've been running about a bit today,' Tim said, pocketing the motorcycle keys. 'And I haven't managed to get any *qat* yet.' He swept off his chequered headscarf and we shook hands. 'So perhaps that's, er, something that we, might...'

Our first stop was Tim's *qat* seller.

Tim had lived in Sanaa for twenty-five years. Arabist, author, traveller, he had been called 'The English Sheikh' and 'The Sage of Sanaa'. He was also an inveterate *qat* chewer. Some months earlier I was waiting for a share taxi to fill up near Bab al-Yaman, quietly reading my paperback edition of *Dictionary Land*, when a fellow traveller jabbed a finger at the portrait picture of Tim on the book's back cover. 'He's chewing,' he said. It was true. The author photograph that I had glancingly thought captured merely a rather blank expression in fact contained the subtle bulge and drawn lips of a young man harbouring a cheekful of *qat*. I wondered if his publishers had twigged. Tim's hair had receded a bit since then and his gaze had become bespectacled, but he retained a youthful ebullience in his manner.

'I don't really consider myself to have an addiction,' he replied chattily when I asked whether he ever managed a day without *qat*. 'And I don't really think of *qat* as a drug or substance,' he continued as we muddled our way through the throng. 'Or at least, not in the way that people think of substances, you know? Salaam Abdullah, keyf ant?' We paused as Tim exchanged greetings with one of his Yemeni neighbours, shifting smoothly from soft-spoken Oxford English to the gentle susurration of Sanaani dialect. 'Alhamdulallah... I mean, it's no more a substance than, well, a cup of Earl Grey or something.' Again the tea analogy, but with discriminating nuance.

Tim's *qat* man reclined in the cubbyhole of his shop front. Shaking hands then kissing their knuckles, they each expressed an enduring bond. Invited to inspect what was on offer, Tim lifted half a dozen small plastic bags in turn and sniffed their content like a discerning sommelier. I recalled his book's description of an especially delectable *qat* stalk.

> It was as thick as asparagus, its leaves edged with a delicate russet, and it tasted nutty, with the patrician bitter-sweetness of an almond. There was a tactile pleasure too, like that of eating pomegranates - a slight resistance between the teeth followed by a burst of juice.

This was not addiction. It was an enthusiast's fervent appreciation. Even before I arrived in Yemen Tim's writing taught me that there were *qat* connoisseurs, *qat* snobs, and *qatal* - the cheaper leaves of the lower branches. 'Everything has pubic hair,' Tim was told once by a *qat* snob. 'Qatal is the pubic hair of *qat*. Besides, dogs cock their legs over it.'

Flexing a stem, then massaging a leaf between forefinger and thumb, Tim appraised our *qat* while I looked on. Assuming that I was unable to speak Arabic, or simply mute perhaps, the *qat* seller nodded in my direction and enquired of Tim, 'Does he chew?' Tim laughed and looked at me to answer.

'Today I'm chewing,' I said. 'But usually I only chew on Thursdays.' Thursday, after all, was the equivalent of a Saturday night in a country where the Islamic weekend finished on Friday. The *qat* vendor's rapid-fire response had me glancing back at Tim for a translation.

'He says he knows about men who only chew on Thursdays. He says that they only chew so that they can go up the fig tree.'

Still I was uncomprehending of the meaning and Tim explained the idiom with a smirk. It was not the first time I had heard of the supposed association between chewing and enhanced sexual performance, but the euphemism was beguiling. *Going up the fig tree?!* I had never heard it called *that* before. And had I not been busy attempting to convey the innocence of my intentions to the *qat* vendor I might have pressed Tim to explain the metaphor. It would have been just his sort of erudite and ribald gossip. In *Dictionary Land*, Tim was charming and scurrilous, chatty as well as scholarly. His account of Yemen's imamate, for instance, began with reference to Imam al-Mansur Ali (found invariably intoxicated by Charles Cruttenden and Joseph Wolff) who apparently relished an aphrodisiac 'prepared from the engorged pizzles of thoroughbred donkeys'. A chapter on Aden commenced with a literary quote from Kipling before promptly introducing a nightclub dancer whose 'stupendous breasts could be seen shuddering beneath her abayah, like a couple of hippos trapped in a marquee.' Within the space of a few pages his references ranged from the pre-Socratic philosophers to Lee Van Cleef, from Giacometti to Bavarian Bierfests. His footnotes were a repository of the fascinatingly arcane, like the medieval debate about whether eating mermaids would be *halal*. It was as though the most irreverent moments from the most illuminating or intriguing *qat* chews had been quietly bottled and preserved. 'I have merely quoted from the books of learned men,' Tim wrote, citing the disclaimer used by Yaqut al-Hamawi, the thirteenth-century Arab chronicler.

Having purchased our *qat*, we returned to the house behind the donkey market, and in his kitchen Tim began emptying the courier bag that had journeyed with him on his motorcycle excursion about town. Half a kilo of vacuum-packed coffee, three cartons of long-life milk, and two jars of marmalade.

'Very difficult to find marmalade in Yemen,' he observed, kneeling and opening the doors of his low kitchen cupboard. 'Honey is abundant, of course, but marmalade uncommon.' He peered into the cupboard. An unopened jar of marmalade stared back at him from the shelf. 'Hmmm.' Tim withdrew the jar and glared at it for a moment, then reached inside the cupboard to retrieve two more identical unopened jars. 'Though having said that, I seem to have found quite a bit in here.'

Tim had already been living in Sanaa for six years when Eric Hansen wrote to him in 1989, asking for assistance in the search for his buried journals. In Hansen's account Tim Mackintosh-Smith is concealed behind the pseudonym Martin Plimsole. After an exchange of letters, but before they actually met, Hansen described his imagined correspondent:

a kindly middle-aged man who favoured grey herringbone blazers and wool gabardine slacks cut generously at the waist - perhaps the sort of out-doorsman who might take along a tin box containing a set of hairbrushes, binoculars, and a silver butter knife for spreading gentleman's relish on dry biscuits imported from England. If there was a shop in San'a selling Wilkin and Sons apricot preserves, Martin Plimsole would know the place.

The humour lay in the discrepancy between the invention and the reality; Tim was then in his twenties. The young man pictured on the back cover of my copy of *Dictionary Land* was not wearing a herringbone blazer, but a denim jacket. And in Tim's description of exploring Yemen's hinterland, he was not equipped with a silver butter knife, but a penknife that once belonged to Imam Ahmad's chauffeur. He did not carry a set of hairbrushes in a tin box, just a biography of Vita Sackville-West in a mildewed rucksack. He ate bread rolls and cheese triangles, not imported biscuits spread with Gentleman's Relish. But years later, as I stood in Tim's kitchen, Hansen's vision of a somewhat obsessional procurer of English preserves appeared remarkably foresighted.

When Hansen described his meeting with Kevin and 'Martin' in front of Bab al-Yaman, he noted that their rendezvous occurred an hour later than scheduled because 'Martin had overslept'. In Hansen's story, Tim or 'Martin' came close to becoming a stereotype of the English eccentric: learned, but always late; distracted, if not a little dotty. And he came close to leading Hansen and Kevin over a cliff edge during a deluged hike in the Haraz Mountains: Tim was blithely ornithologising African sunbirds, hammerkops, rock buntings, and 'I say, wasn't that Tristram's grackle?' until he wiped his rain-spattered spectacles on a shirttail and perceived the precariousness of their footing.

Tim also appeared in Kevin Rushby's account of his *qat*-tour from Addis to Sanaa. Here, Tim's absent-minded idiosyncrasies were rather less indulged. 'Shut up and let him drive!' cried Kevin, irritated to the point of despair by Tim's immersion in a discussion of thirteenth-century Yemeni poetry with a pick-up driver who was motoring them around a steep, boulder-strewn mountainside. The driver could not talk without gesticulating and his enthusiastic distraction by Tim's conversation sent the wheels of their pick-up spinning perilously over precipices. Tim arrived an entire day late for their meeting ('not altogether a surprise,' Rushby noted drily) and he had barely appeared in Rushby's narrative before he was accidentally setting fire to a tablecloth in a crowded restaurant.

His own account, Tim admitted, was 'perhaps unfashionably digressive', but at least not dangerously so. I found his book a pleasantly rambling companion on my travels in Yemen. Describing one of his own share-taxi rides out of Sanaa, for instance, a discursive detour took Tim to a far corner of dictionary land, towards a contemporary Yemeni bestiary. There he found 'the *fukhakh*, the hisser - the Yemeni name for the chameleon. Its blood taken externally is a cure for baldness, but its breath makes your teeth fall out. The gecko... eats the remains of food from round your mouth as you sleep, pisses and gives you spots...' Unfashionable? It was timeless. Herodotean.

I have often found that characters in novels tend to appear to me like the featureless faces found in dreams: real and definite, yet somehow indistinct and indefinable, as though seen in peripheral vision, or passing, like Herbert and Buxton's Arabs, as mere shadows. Until, that is, some minor detail in the text clangs discordantly, at which point I realise that I had in fact formulated the person distinctly in my mind all along, just as Eric Hansen had once imagined Tim. It doesn't take much: perhaps a passing reference to someone being thin when I had imagined them to be fat, or short when I had thought them tall. The phenomenon is less apparent in reading travelogues. Perhaps, simply, fewer of those elemental details that might be rendered by a novelist are revealed to clash with my conceptions. Authors tend not to spend time describing their own height or body habitus after all. The discordant clang can still occur though. So, for example, the Aubrey Herbert of my imagination strides confidently into Sanaa and taps deftly on the typewriter that he carried with him, until I remind myself that he was half blind and must have stumbled and squinted. More usually though, it is a jarring action or opinion that forces me to acknowledge that the writer is not who I thought they were, or perhaps, who I wanted them to be. But there was nothing discordant about Tim. In the flesh and in his writing I found him consistently entertaining and eminently likable. But then, of course, he never came close to leading me over a cliff edge, or setting fire to my tablecloth.

While I watched, Tim placed the five unopened jars of marmalade back in the kitchen cupboard, along with the milk cartons and the coffee, which, I noticed, also contributed to small collections of identical items.

'These cupboards are simply so deep you tend to lose stuff in them... And so you go shopping and then you come back to discover the stuff that you thought you'd lost...' He offered up a tenuous rationalisation of his accidental stockpiling before returning to the task of emptying his courier bag.

'Now... I didn't get around to paying this, so that goes all the way down... And I didn't drop that off, so that goes down again too...' The commentary seemed to be entirely for his own benefit as he pulled out an electricity bill and an undelivered letter and left them on a step just outside the kitchen.

'This goes *half*-way up.' A bundle of papers was removed from the bag.

'And this goes *all* the way up.' He held aloft a British passport.

'And so does this!' Our two bags of *qat* were placed on the kitchen sideboard with the papers and the passport. 'One problem with this house is that unless you're sort of strategic about where you put things, you spend your entire time going up and down stairs to get the things from the bottom that you need at the top.'

Tim's house in fact seemed scarcely plausible. Barely broader than its own front door, it wound tightly around a central spiral staircase from which rooms flew off occasionally as the construction spun upward. There might have been five floors, or more, or fewer if one or two of them were considered mezzanines. It was impossible to say. The staircase had a dizzying effect which, combined with the concentration required to avoid bashing my forehead on a succession of low beams, prevented me from tallying the levels passed in our ascent. Suffice, perhaps, to acknowledge that every room seemed to be at a different altitude. Tim's tiny bedroom and bathroom were on the first horizontal plane after the ground, further up was his library, the kitchen was at greater elevation, then (and I might have lost a room or two) his study, before a climb to the narrow room at the front of the house that Tim called 'The Bus'.

'Because there's lots of horns tooting from the street outside?' I ventured gamely. Tim laughed. 'Er, no. A friend of mine who once visited England says that sitting here reminds him of riding through London on the front seat of a double decker.' The room spanned the width of the house, but was barely three feet deep, so that sitting with your back against the wall, your nose was almost pressed against the window, thrusting one into the bustle of streets far below. The bus analogy made sense. And there the building ended. Until Tim added its highest point. Desiring a spot for chewing that felt more salubrious than the front seat of a bus, and aspiring to a view uninterrupted by neighbouring rooftops, Tim had done as the locals did and added another storey. Crowning his home there was now a cosy *mafraj*, permitting perhaps half a dozen chewers and providing them with enviable panoramas across the city in all directions.

According to Tim, Sanaa's Ghumdan Palace, built sometime in the second century and reduced to rubble long ago, was the model upon which all the city's towerhouses were based. Much like Tim's own house, the palace was of uncertain height, but its shadow was said to stretch all the way to the edge of Wadi Dahr, some dozen miles distant. Another of the palace's noted and exaggerated features was the alabaster ceiling of its topmost room. It was claimed to have been so translucent that looking skyward through it you could still tell kites from crows. 'Every upper room is a memory of that alabaster belvedere,' Tim wrote. And in his own lofty *mafraj*, like many others in Sanaa, thin pieces of alabaster the size and shape of dinner plates were set above the broad windowpanes. The alabaster circles were hand-sawn from gypsum blocks in a method that dated back centuries. At night, when lamps were lit, they emitted a buttery glow and, seen from the street, hovering over the city, their luminous discs elucidated the alabaster's Arabic name: moonstone. Above these translucent portholes, encircling Tim's *mafraj*, was a stucco frieze in calligraphic Arabic. The verse praised Sanaa, esteeming it above all the cities of Europe and America; an apt touch for an Englishman who had made the city his home.

'Now, I thought we could break our fast here with a sort of appetiser before we go on to have dinner proper at Ali's. I have some frozen pea and ham soup that I was given by the ambassador's wife.'

'Very kind of her,' I said, wondering how that particular ambassadorial bestowal had come about, and whether the ambassador's wife would expect the return of her Tupperware. As the block of frozen soup fell with a thump into a black and battered saucepan the irony of our unorthodox *iftar* dish was not lost on Tim.

'Quite a Ramadan-buster,' he remarked. 'Could do with a glass of English ale to wash it down.'

Idly I watched the twist of a gas knob on the stove, the flick of a lighter, and a valiant effort to break up the frosty olive-green lump with a wooden spoon, until Tim's mobile telephone emitted an electronic tone and I was obliged to take over. While I knocked the soup about in the saucepan, Tim held a long and nattering conversation about visa stamps, ancient tombs, and a temple where someone was said to have once deflowered virgin maidens. At the end of the telephone call Tim apologised and explained. He was half-way through filming a BBC television series documenting a journey from Morocco to China in the footsteps of Ibn Battuta, the fourteenth-century Moroccan scholar and explorer, and there were still some arrangements to be finalised before Tim departed in four days' time for his next filming location: India and the Maldives. Apology accepted. For Tim, Ibn Battuta, or 'IB', was one of the most remarkable travellers to have ever lived. From his home in Tangier, IB journeyed more than 75,000 miles, encountering dervishes, fire-eaters, magicians, hermits, holy men, and countless concubines; surviving shipwrecks, pirates, Black Death, imprisonment, the mercurial volatility of the Sultan of Delhi, and ten marriages. Upon his eventual return to Morocco in 1354 he dictated an account of his travels. Yet not until some four centuries later was his travelogue 'discovered' by Europeans. That his achievements remain largely unknown in the West, and his name far less familiar than that of his contemporary Marco Polo, owes much to the historical accident of Battuta having been born in Tangier and not Venice, and to his account having been written in Arabic. Tim had edited an English translation of Battuta's travelogue and IB was the subject of two of Tim's published books, with a third in progress. There was nobody better qualified to bring Ibn Battuta's travels to life for an English-speaking television audience.

Still, I found it difficult to picture Tim in the Maldives. To picture him anywhere other than Sanaa in fact. Yet his British passport, collected this afternoon with a freshly stamped visa from the Indian Embassy in Sanaa, lay on the kitchen worktop.

'Do you still think of yourself as British, Tim?'

'I sort of think of myself as having dual nationality... Having said that, I do actively miss Yemen when I'm not here. And there's always something of a sinking feeling when I arrive back at Heathrow, so... Um, I think that might be ready.'

The brick of pea and ham had long since thawed and was now beginning to boil.

'And I think the timing might be perfect.' As the sound of sunset reached us from a nearby mosque, I took the saucepan from the stove and filled two small bowls with the steaming dark green liquid.

'Bismillah,' Tim declared.

Begrudgingly, I acknowledged that the soup from the ambassador's wife tasted pretty good. Perhaps at last this was some slight recompense for my having been left off the guest list for the Queen's Birthday party.

Before moving on to our main course at Ali's restaurant, Tim was obliged to deliver the motorcycle to the friend with whom he shared ownership of the machine. I sat comfortably behind as he motored us through the Old City streets, tooting children out of our path and halting for oncoming Toyotas. The other part-owner of the fiery bicycle turned out to be the stonecutter who had rendered the alabaster for Tim's *mafraj*. As we arrived at his home just outside the Old City walls, the stone-cutter's young son and daughters leapt upon Tim, eager to play with their adopted uncle. One of the children then inexplicably placed his head inside an upturned plastic wastebasket. Tim removed it, plopped the wastebasket on his own head, and began bumping about with his arms outstretched exclaiming 'Exterminate! Exterminate!' The performance was sufficiently absurd to entertain the children, even if the Dr Who reference was lost on them.

Rereading *Dictionary Land* I was occasionally reminded of this scene. It not only epitomised Tim's playfulness, but the way in which, as he travelled through Yemen he would embellish an Arabic scene with a British analogy. On the coast, guests at the local flophouse were wrapped in blankets 'like Henry Moore's sleepers in the underground'. In Aden, dog turds were sun-bleached 'to the colour of Cheshire cheese'. Heading east from Hadramawt, where the place names recall a Semitic language that predates Arabic, seemed to Tim like driving through the Welsh borders 'and suddenly seeing a sign for Llanwyddelan'. Definitely British. Unequivocally English.

Tim was still very much in touch with the country of his birth, and still capable of being touched by it, even in Sanaa. One of the most memorable passages in *Dictionary Land* occurs when he spots a Yemeni boy wearing an ankle-length shirt and *jambiyah*, and 'a piece of clothing as familiar to me as my own body…'

> There it was, grey flannel with navy piping and a fleur-de-lis on the breast pocket: my prep-school blazer. I looked inside. "Steer & Geary Gentlemen's outfitters". There was the ghost of an inkstain on the pocket, where my birthday Parker had sprung a leak in 1972.

As the boy scuffed away there was a wave of nostalgia, then 'a strange, deep stillness of spirit. It was the calm of completeness.' Even if the blazer in Sanaa hadn't *really* been Tim's hand-me-down, the motif fitted neatly. His interest in Yemen had been piqued as a schoolboy while visiting the 'Nomad and the City' exhibition at London's Museum of Mankind. For the World of Islam Festival in 1976, the museum 'recreated a corner of the market of Sanaa,' Tim recalled. 'Yards from Piccadilly was a secret, labyrinthine microcosm of the *suq*.' The display was largely based on the fieldwork of the authors Serjeant and Lewcock. It included reconstructions of half a dozen stalls from Sanaa's *suq* selling daggers, pottery, grain, coffee, spices, and perfume. 'Even its sounds and smells were reproduced,' Tim remembered. Years after this recreation of Sanaa enthralled the schoolboy in London, the boy in the reused blazer enthralled the man in Sanaa. 'The wheel,' as Tim put it, had turned 'full circle'.

Barely half an hour had passed since *iftar* by the time we arrived at Ali's restaurant, but already the place had emptied out. There remained only a debris of dirty dishes and an atmosphere of deflation. When we were told that all the meat had been eaten I shared none of Tim's evident disappointment. I would have preferred a sackful of locusts to another goat's head, and even his carnivorous enthusing about boiled lamb that 'falls from the bone' could instil in me no sense of loss. But I eagerly anticipated the *shafoot*, *salta*, and *fatah bi asal* that we ordered.

'I hope you don't mind,' Tim offered as we waited to wash our hands before eating. 'This place is a bit *gabili*.' The term meant 'tribal' and was employed in the way that 'bumpkin' might be used in England, or 'redneck' in America. In front of us at the washbasins, two satiated Yemenis shouldering AK47s over dirty camouflage jackets were rinsing the grease from their hands with laundry washing powder. But the tribesman was also a man of honour. I had been paying attention when, in his book, Tim described how, 'if you give a taxi driver a hundred-*riyal* note for a short ride, by saying "Give me *qabyalah*" - what a tribesman would give - you are honour-bound to accept whatever he hands back, he not to overcharge you.' I tried it once. The taxi driver laughed in my face and kept the change.

We took our seats and the requisite sheet of newspaper was laid upon the table. Our food arrived almost instantaneously. Leaving our *salta* to cool, we tucked into the *shafoot*. The appearance of this traditional dish of sorghum pancakes soaked in herb-infused buttermilk was one of the unexpected pleasures of Ramadan. The *shafoot* served at Ali's was especially good.

'Mmm... Yes, one of the best restaurants around in my opinion. And you're right,' Tim concurred between shovelling spoonfuls of the stuff inside himself. 'The *shafoot* is outstanding.'

No amount of effort to accelerate my eating would have allowed me to keep up with him. And no attempt at conversation could distract him from his task. Tim had adopted the Yemeni velocity of food consumption. He gained a substantial head start upon the *salta*, tearing up bread rolls and dunking chunks into the stew as it ceased erupting and began merely to bubble more benignly. And when he finished, as local custom dictated, he got up from the table without excusing himself and wandered back to the washbasins to wash his hands.

When we returned to Tim's house he ducked into the kitchen to put the kettle on and rinse our *qat* while I, stooping and squeezing, climbed the narrow staircase to his *mafraj*. Among the cushions lay a few scattered Arabic tomes, while beyond were superlative views across the blinking Ramadan night and the city's alabaster moons. As a reading room or study, I thought, the *mafraj* might by turns be distracting or inspiring. Tim entered carefully bearing a tray laden with *qat* and fresh-brewed tea. Some mutual friends would be joining us shortly, but we agreed that there was no sense in waiting and so settled ourselves into the business of chewing and chatting. We talked about Tim's upcoming travels, his feelings toward filming compared with writing, and the experience of missing *qat* while he was away. He admitted that there was a substantial part of him that would be content to stay put. Which prompted me to wonder how he had come to be a travel writer.

'Well, I'm not sure I am a *travel* writer really. I wasn't even always a writer. I was an organ scholar at Oxford. And an English teacher when I came to Sanaa. Writing only came much later.' With a little prompting he related how his writing career had started.

'There was a girl teaching at the British Council at the time. And we went off to the Haraz Mountains together, along towards Hodeidah. Well, during that trip she told me: Look Tim, you're a fool, you've lived here for years, you speak the language, you read all the books, you should write about this stuff, otherwise you'll just be an English teacher forever. And, well, I didn't look back. But that was only after I'd been here a decade or so.'

He poured us each another cup of tea.

'20 November 1982,' Tim shot back in response to my asking when he had arrived in Yemen. His unhesitating precision might have been a consequence of the innumerable administrative forms that routinely demanded 'Date of first entry to Yemen'. But it might also have reflected a critically affecting moment. In the closing pages of *Dictionary Land* Tim alluded to another impactful time and date.

At 8.10p.m. on Wednesday, 4 May 1994, while I was in the room on the roof, the lights went out and stayed out. The night was abnormally quiet.

The blackout in Sanaa on 4 May 1994 had marked the beginning of a civil war.

Political differences had persisted between North and South ever since the unification of the Yemen Arab Republic and the People's Democratic Republic of Yemen in 1990. Tensions were exacerbated after the Iraqi invasion of Kuwait and President Saleh's refusal to support military intervention by non-Arab states; a position that caused outrage among American war hawks and their allies in Saudi Arabia. Meting out punishment, the US cancelled aid programmes and the Saudis expelled close to a million Yemeni workers, creating dire economic and social strains in Yemen as the influx of remittance money witnessed by Jonathan Raban suddenly stopped and the exported labour force of rig-hands, mechanics, construction workers, and cab drivers returned home. When conflict erupted in Yemen, the south of the country bore the brunt of it and the northerners would ultimately claim victory. But still, in the two months of fighting, Sanaa was hammered by air raids and by the SCUD missiles that had gained notoriety during the Iraq war. Tim recalled the SCUD as 'a weapon of terror, a monstrous airborne carbomb'. One of them landed close to Kevin Rushby's house in Sanaa. When Tim visited soon after the explosion he found a home reduced to wreckage. Fallen plaster and broken glass had been blown throughout the building. Children's drawings on the kitchen table were covered with the dust that described loss.

Rushby and his family had already returned to the safety of England. Tim never made plans to leave Yemen, but I wondered how he had felt watching others depart, how it had felt to be standing in the ruins of his friend's empty house, and how he had felt at 8.10p.m. on Wednesday, 4 May, 1994, when the lights went out and stayed out. I had wanted to ask Tim about loneliness, and even fear, but a knocking on the door echoed up the stairwell and the questions went unasked. As Tim dashed out of the *mafraj* to welcome his visitors I had to suppose an answer. Despite the ugliness of conflict, and by a choice that was broad-minded and bold, Sanaa was Tim's home. And having embraced Sanaa he had been embraced, with all his baggage of Earl Grey tea and English ale, double-decker buses and Daleks. It was here that he had found the calm of completeness. I heard him yelling from the overhang.

'Arrrgh! Whoaaa! Just give the door a good shove.'

- 20 -

Those Remaining

STREETLAMPS WOULD HAVE THROWN DOWN their orange light to rest on the pavement. Cloud cover, drawn low over the rooftops, would have reflected the city's nocturnal glow. Night would have resided in the tops of towerhouses, black against the discoloured sky. And as the last bulbs and flames were extinguished, the last alabaster moons would have been eclipsed. The day long gone, it would have been quiet now, and cool. If, after the *qat* chew, we had climbed up here to the rooftop, as Jonathan Raban once had, to look out across Sanaa, to contemplate its many mysteries and wonder at its secret dreams, we would have found by now that the air had a definite chill. Hardly cold enough to bring on the hoary frost described by John Jourdain in 1609. Nor the finger-thick ice recorded by Sir Henry Middleton the following year. But sufficiently brisk to prompt us to return indoors, descending carefully on the unlit stairs.

Scraping a match in the kitchen to light a candle, then another to fire the gas stove, I would have made us some mint tea. Soon we would have settled ourselves back in the *mafraj*, that cushioned space between earth and sky. On the low mattress seating we would have adopted the now-familiar semi-recumbent sideways slouch. When the city rests like this, when the faintest sounds come as crashing disruptions to the silence, and when electric lights might come too abruptly in the darkness, it might have been hard to imagine. But at this hour during Ramadan, and almost until dawn, I could have looked out of the window and watched the traffic streaking up and down the *Sayilah*, seen the shops still busy and bright lit on Bab as-Sabah, and observed an additional storey being noisily constructed under arc lamps on the house opposite. The Ramadan nights seemed to last forever, until they ceased just as suddenly as they began.

With the end of the holy month, the morning traffic returned, grumbling and honking, and the waking city seemed to have reverted to its usual routine. But the atmosphere remained subdued. The Ramadan pavement stalls had disappeared, but still the markets were deserted and the shops were shuttered. Mansour's grocery, Nabil's boutique, and Abdul's Sobermarket were all closed. Another new moon brought another new mood: this was the three-day holiday of *Eid al-Fitr*, marking the end of fasting. Soon after leaving my house that morning I was approached in broad daylight by a boy levelling a pistol at me. With one eye squinting to take aim and a finger squeezing on the trigger, he demanded my money. Smiling, I wished him *Eid Mubarak* and the seven-year-old lowered his plastic weapon, grinned cheekily, then returned the greeting before scarpering off. Two young princesses tottered by, identically dressed from their glittering tiaras to their sparkling shoes. The twins summoned me to take their photograph and posed proudly in fur-collared sequinned dresses before processing away, holding henna-patterned hands. Sanaa's residents had departed in droves to spend the holiday with extended families in the countryside. The few children remaining in the city reclaimed the streets, scuffing footballs along deserted alleys, squirting waterpistols at their shadows, and wearing outfits bought in the Ramadan *suqs*. Slowly learning that there was no substitute for friendships, they sought to entertain themselves with new toys and new clothes until their playmates returned from vacations.

Once, they might have found an American kindred spirit. Many years before, a lonely Californian boy named Bruce had written to Yemen's Imam Ahmad. In his letter the boy asked the imam for a penfriend and someone with whom he could swap stamps. It was an improbable request. But a reply had come from the imam's son: 'His Majesty has commanded me to be your friend.' Decades later, David Holden was surprised to be introduced to an American in the imam's retinue, 'blessed, so he informed me, with the unlikely name of Bruce Alfonso de Bourbon Condé.' Orphaned at an early age, the stamp-obsessed Bruce at some point adopted the family name of Bourbon Condé. Later, Bruce Condé converted to Islam, renamed himself Abdhurrahman, renounced his US citizenship, and relocated to Yemen. There, under the auspices of his childhood penfriend, he was put in charge of the Post Office. After Imam al-Badr was ousted in 1962, Condé joined him in the guerrilla war against the republicans. The British mercenaries fighting with the royalists didn't trust him and thought he was a spy. Wilfred Thesiger felt Bruce Condé was 'a strange character... with an extraordinary craving for self-aggrandisement'. Holden had the measure of him: 'an odd and slightly pathetic figure, somewhat out of both his time and his depth... he seemed to belong nowhere and to be yearning romantically for the impossible.' Throughout the 1950s and

60s, Condé issued frequent updates of philatelic interest from Yemen that were published in *Linn's Weekly Stamp News*. After the war and the end of the imamate, he settled in Spain, then Morocco, dying in a drab suburb of Tangier, stateless, alone with his fabulated honorifics and family titles: Major-General Prince Bourbon H.S.H. Abdurrahman B.A. de Bourbon, Prince of Condé, Postmaster of Yemen.

Only the *qat* sellers were open for business, and one or two shops selling sweets and plastic ware to children who still had holiday money to spend. Walking around on that first morning after Ramadan I found nowhere to have a cup of tea and struggled even to find somewhere that could sell me a bottle of water. Eventually, in a corner store amid a gaggle of four young girls who yelped excitedly among the fizzy drinks and confectioneries, I managed to purchase a few provisions, while the plastic bustles of four ostentatious frocks rioted against my calves during a scramble for the contents of a jar of boiled sweets that had been knocked to the floor. The shop owner threw his hands up in despair. I decided to head to the mountains.

At the share-taxi station near Bab al-Yaman few passengers were arriving and few were leaving. It was late in the morning by the time I had stuffed a few things into a bag and joined the wait for a Peugeot headed west. It was well into the afternoon when we set off. And it was almost sundown when we reached Manakha. From the mountain town near where Joseph Wolff had once encountered the Rechabites, where George Wyman Bury had once spotted serins and finches, and where I had once arrived sprinkled with goat piss, I walked along a familiar twilight track toward al-Hajarah.

The white shapes of half a dozen Landcruisers were parked outside the hotel. In the candle-lit lobby staff greeted me with *Bonjour* and *Guten Tag* before Mohammed, the owner and manager, welcomed me in Arabic. 'Yes, we have a room,' Mohammed announced after opening a large ledger and scrutinising a gridlined page that looked surprisingly busy with biro scrawls. 'And we have dinner almost ready,' he said. 'But we have no electricity.'

An LED headtorch illuminated the annoyance of two foreigners who sat next to one another in the *mafraj*, struggling to read a guidebook by the light of their battery-powered headgear. The pair muttered in French, ignoring me as I settled myself comfortably in the dark.

'*¡Hola!*' A Spanish couple entered carrying candles. They were followed by a foursome from the Netherlands. Then a group of ten ageing French tourists arrived, along with the electricity that blinked and buzzed in dangling strip lights. The illumination revealed walls hung with antique *jambiyahs*, flintlock rifles, faded photographs of the mountains, and a picture of the president; and it exposed our awkward bottom-shuffling along the mattress-seating to make room for all the newcomers. I had never seen so many guests at the Hotel Al-Hajarah. The evening meal was soon brought in on huge metal platters, held shoulder-high by hotel staff who carefully unloaded dishes of okra, omelettes, beans, grilled chicken, flat rounds of handmade bread, and also spaghetti and French fries.

Such concessions to Western palates were a relatively novel phenomenon in Yemen. So too, according to past visitors, was the provision of comfortable accommodation. In Sanaa, as Major-General Haig reported in 1886, earlier Europeans often preferred to forsake local guesthouses and lodge 'beneath the hospitable roof of the Messrs. Caprotti, two Italian gentlemen'. The Caprotti brothers, Luigi and Giuseppe, were businessmen who had relocated to Sanaa from Lombardy in 1883. Under the Turks they obtained a monopoly on tobacco sales within the city. Hugh Scott later suggested that they were part of an early Italian effort to infiltrate Yemen. Luigi Caprotti died in 1889. His brother Giuseppe outlived him by thirty years and stayed on in Sanaa. When Aubrey Herbert and Leland Buxton visited in 1905, Giuseppe Caprotti was 'the only foreigner in the town'. In 1912, Signor Caprotti was still 'the only European in Sanaa', according to Arthur Wavell, and it was Caprotti who kept Wavell supplied with old French periodicals during the siege that year. Alone in Sanaa, collecting out of date European newspapers and accommodating any passing European visitors, the surviving Caprotti brother sounded just a little forlorn.

At the Hotel Al-Hajarah, while the Europeans equipped themselves with cutlery and chatted in their respective languages, I tore into our meal hungrily with both hands and fell into conversation with their tour guide. He was not eating and I assumed that his appetite was already sated by *salta* and *qat*. But no, he told me, his home was nearby and he would return there shortly to his wife's cooking. 'I haven't chewed at all,' he said, looking aghast, then nodded toward the tour group. 'I had to show them the mountains... I've been with them since they came from Sanaa,' he explained. 'But tomorrow they will leave and I will chew until my tooth aches.' From here the group would head to the coast, stopping at Hodeidah and continuing to Aden on their three-week tour of Yemen.

What brought these European holiday-makers to Yemen in 2006? The Yemen Tourism Promotion Board had lately begun publicising the country's many UNESCO-listed heritage sites: the Old City of Sanaa; Shibam, the 'Manhattan of the Desert'; and Zabid, Yemen's ancient capital. Then there was the remarkable stone bridge of Shaharah to the north, the towns of the ancient incense routes out east, and south, off the coast, was the island of Socotra with its unique biodiversity and Dragon's Blood trees. Yet soon the unsuspecting Yemen Tourism Board would be inundated with ill-informed enquiries about Salmon Fishing. Meanwhile, the Lonely Planet guidebook described a 'beguiling land of mud-brick sky-scrapers and labyrinthine medinas', 'a medieval time capsule', 'probably better known by its historical epithets... Arabia Felix, the Land of the Queen of Sheba'. Despite the best efforts of the Tourism Board, and perhaps despite the visits of these few intrepid travellers and others like them, Yemen, to the outside world, remained beguiling, medieval, and unknown.

After appetites had been satisfied and dishes only half-emptied had been collected and carried away, Mohammed the hotelier returned to sit down with the hotel staff. One of them held a drum beneath his arm, another positioned a metal tablah between his knees, and at the centre of the small ensemble a man with an oud began plucking swiftly at the instrument's strings. The notes trembled and twanged while fingers and thumbs beat on the tablah, calling forth a rhythm of brisk tapping and deep resonating thumps. Doum, tek-tek, doum, tek-tek, doum. Then the oud-player began to sing, accompanied by hand claps and vocals from the men sitting around him; tremulous verses, words I couldn't catch, but a sentiment I yearned to grasp. I asked the *qat*-deprived tour guide if he knew the song. 'Of course,' he replied. 'It's a very famous song. It's about love.' He turned to me. 'It's always about love.'

In 1937, Norman Lewis, voyaging by dhow, had improbably encountered love's timeless symbol: a single cherished rose. He was still hoping to reach Sanaa when the vessel he was aboard stopped at Kamaran Island, five miles off Yemen's coast. Here, amid the incessant sandflies and the furious heat, Lewis came upon the solitary rosebush, sheltered in a tent. Since 1915 the island had been under dubious British control; occupied, but never formally claimed. As Lewis explained, 'Kamaran had been part of the Kingdom of Yemen until a few years before our arrival, when quite suddenly, and without explanation or published excuse, it had been taken under the control of a British administrator.' There was, though, Lewis observed, 'in reality nothing to administrate'. Eleven miles long, the island had no roads and was swept with quicksand, and yet somehow the British administrator, one Captain Thompson, convinced the authorities in Aden to provide him with a Model T Ford. Thompson would spend seventeen years on the island. He polished his automobile. His wife pruned the rosebush. Lewis thought 'the captain and his charming young wife were possibly the two loneliest people I had ever seen.'

Untouched by the tune's wistful strain, some of the tour group began to look bored. But then the oud-player picked up the pace. A quick tempo melody spurred the tablah to a galloping rhythm. Doum, tek-tek, tek-tek-tek, doum, tek-tek, tek-tek-tek, doum. Mohammed the hotelier jumped to his feet, pulled a partner from among the Yemeni men and with precise, practised steps they began to dance, circling one another, crouching, rising, leaping, landing. The pair drew *jambiyahs*, the tourists drew cameras; flashing blades duelling electronic flashes. Mohammed and his agile companion danced the length of the *mafraj*, forwards, then backwards, pirouetting and kicking their heels high until, breathless and their brows beaded with sweat, the pair retired. Two more Yemenis took to the floor and each took the hand of one of the tourists to teach them a few steps. Before long the entire audience was on its feet, dancing in a spontaneous fusion of hesitant jive, highland dance, and enthused disco. It was the sort of experience that guests could enjoy in Yemen, at a time when tourists could still visit. Quietly I crept away, departing self-consciously, having not quite found my place among the local men or the foreigners passing through, and feeling not quite in the right frame of mind to dance. Instead, anticipating the weather and the forthcoming day of hiking, I climbed to the roof of the hotel, to watch the sky and the clouds as they shifted over the mountains. There was a new moon and an old familiar mood, reflective and a little melancholic. I was booked on a flight back to London that would leave in less than three weeks. I had barely as much time remaining in the country as the tourists downstairs. Departures had always been difficult. My diary entries had become sentimental and disconsolate. I sought to reassure myself that this was an inevitable change, a necessary next step. My departure from Sanaa was scheduled a year to the day after my arrival, but even the sense of a wheel turning full circle could not smooth this hard edge.

Next morning the tour group decamped in a convoy of Landcruisers, with sunglasses set on foreheads and backpacks strapped to roof racks. I watched while breakfasting on an oily omelette that Mohammed prepared for me, along with a bowl of *ful* and a thermos full of sugary tea. Then I set off on my own journey, on foot toward the nearby village of Kahil. I no longer needed the biro sketch map that Mohammed had once given me; I had walked the path alone often enough. But on this occasion the day of hiking would never materialise, and I would never reach my intended destination. Barely had I set off from the hotel and begun to ascend the mountain path when my footsteps were slowed then stopped by the sound of thunder. The low pounding rumble persisted, growing louder, but seeming to come from behind me, and below. I turned to look back the way I had come, but saw nothing. Until a small boy in a white shirt and a pair of ragged shorts appeared on the track from Manakha. As he walked, the boy was beating out a rhythm on a wooden drum. Behind him came two more drummers, marching around the mountainside, hammering on two huge booming drums that hung over their chests. A procession of men followed, smartly dressed in jackets and *jambiyahs*. They halted below my vantage point, then drew their blades and began dancing to the drumbeats that thumped at the mountains. They moved in circles, a ring that turned while each man spun. Off to one side a short figure stood watching. He wore a green and golden turban with a matching tabard, and in his hand was a silver-sheathed sword. He didn't dance but remained apart, as though not quite in the mood. His dress and demeanour embodied the dignity and distraction befitting a bridegroom on his wedding day.

When the drummers had ceased their rhythm and the dancers had sheathed their *jambiyahs* the company marched on. But one of them remained and called out to me.

'Helloooou!'

I squinted.

'Hellooooo!'

He was waving and beckoning. So I scrambled back down the mountain, hurrying and stumbling. Reaching the bottom, it took me a moment to recognise the man in his elegant white *thobe* with his gelled hair and his embroidered scarf folded neatly over his shoulders, but it was Arif. The last time I saw him he was wearing a black leather waistcoat and a pair of winkle pickers. We had met just once before, a month or two ago, on a wet afternoon in Manakha. Both of us had intended walking on to al-Hajarah, Arif to his home, and I to the hotel, but both of us decided to wait until the rain eased. Drinking tea together, we chatted in English while the downpour continued outside. Arif was a student at Sanaa University, but his family lived in al-Hajarah and he made the journey back to visit them on occasional weekends. Despite being aged twenty-five he was not married, he told me, and he was determined to complete his studies before contemplating marriage. 'Besides,' he disclosed, 'university is the best way to meet girls.' Meeting Arif again unexpectedly at the foot of the mountain, we had barely shaken hands when he set off running after the wedding party. 'Come on, we'll miss the celebration,' he shouted. And I jogged after him. The men had halted again when we caught them up and they were circling once more, *jambiyahs* twirling, drums pounding. Arif introduced me to the groom and we talked for a while and watched the dancing. I felt uncomfortable though, in my old worn chinos, grubby t-shirt, and hiking boots, still carrying my rucksack and still intent on following the trail round to Kahil, then looping back down to Manakha and maybe catching an evening ride back to Sanaa. My place was not among the local men, I was really just passing through.

'Arif, I probably should get moving,' I said, explaining my plans.

'You can't leave now,' he replied. 'It's already late. Besides, it will probably rain.'

It was not yet eleven o'clock. The sky was overcast but hardly threatening a deluge, and the dirt road had none of the rutted muddy puddles that I recalled from previous visits. Nearby, the dancing men were kicking up dust.

'Has it rained much here recently?' I asked.

'Not a drop,' Arif admitted.

A young man with an ancient camera positioned me next to the bridegroom and took a couple of photographs, fixing me scruffily among the finely attired Yemenis and the remarkable setting of al-Hajarah's cloudswept mountains. When a flock of marauding sheep brought the photo shoot to an abrupt end I apologised for not being better dressed and for not wearing a jacket or carrying a *jambiyah*.

'Here, have mine!' someone cried, thrusting a blade into my hand and seeming to have taken my remark too seriously. But then I was pushed into the circle of men dancing with their *jambiyahs* held aloft and I realised that my remark had not been taken seriously at all. There was cheering and some laughter as I tried to match the steps of the group, just as the tourists had done the night before. I had seen countless wedding dances during my time in Yemen, but this was the first in which I had participated and my awkwardness was apparent. I was ungainly and unsynchronised. Until at some point I realised that the movements were roughly those of the hammam dance in Sanaa, with three steps, pause, then three steps, pause, and I managed, more or less, to keep the pace. And at some point as we circled I was no longer following the movement of the man next to me, but with my arm holding high a *jambiyah* and my feet marking time, I was circling, turning, following the pounding of the drum. It was a beat that resonated in all of us; a steady, animating, unifying pulse. If the rhythm were to speed we would speed, and if it were to slow we would slow, and if it had stopped then we would not have gone on. Doum, doum, doum. There must have been two or three dozen of us, moving together like this, circling, circling, a wheel turning, turning. Until eventually I lost the pace and retired to the sidelines, returning the dagger to its rightful and amused owner. Two tiny boys took my place among the dancers and an old man with spectacle lenses like bottle ends was cajoled into a few good-humoured and stumbling steps.

Wedding guests continued to turn up, having walked from neighbouring villages, or driven from Sanaa or Taiz. Arif introduced me to more of his friends and family members. The groom's father approached, tall and proud, wearing an elaborately embroidered shawl, a new jacket, and a newly polished assault rifle over his shoulder. Shaking me by the hand he told me I would stay for lunch, and my day was decided. There would be no departing: I would remain. Then the sky exploded with firecrackers and the men shouted chants, wielded blades, and held their Kalashnikovs high as the wedding drums thumped and the sky shattered under another barrage of fireworks. The air still smelt of sulphur as a gaunt figure made his way through the celebrants and the drifting gunpowder smoke to kneel before the bridegroom. His skin was marked by vitiligo and with a mottled hand and a mumbled incantation he smashed a hen's egg on the ground at the groom's feet.

'What's the egg for?' I asked the man beside me, struggling to make myself heard above the continued noise of firecrackers.

'To protect him from *djinns*,' the man yelled in my ear.

The blotchy hand cast rings of brown powder around the groom's shiny shoes.

'And what's that?' I shouted.

'Henna,' the man next to me shouted back.

'What for?'

'The same.'

'*Djinns*?'

'Yes.'

Later I found an opportunity to ask Arif if he could offer any further explanation of the egg and the henna powder, but his reply remained vague: it was just what was done in the village. The man with the spells and the skin condition was 'just a sort of holy man'.

John Jourdain had encountered a similar character. Returning from Sanaa in 1609, he 'passed the tyme with an old blind Portugall renegade witch'. Presumably a Portuguese sailor who had washed up on Yemen's shores, the old man 'could doe a fewe of the Divells myracles,' wrote Jourdain, 'and was taken here to bee a saint.' He had made a deal with the devil, 'but the Divell will have his due,' Jourdain noted, and the old witch had paid dearly. The devil had killed his sons and daughter, he said. And it had been the devil that appeared to him one night in the shape of a fawn, 'dancinge round aboute', burning with such an extreme heat that the eyes of the old man had been scorched blind in their sockets, so he claimed. The witch's stories, Jourdain wrote, 'weere too tedious to sett downe, although pleasannt to heare', and he was content to listen to the forsaken sailor's account of witchcraft and devilish pacts. 'Thus with many other tales which he tould me of the Divell, and of his cominge into the countrye and of his marriadge and other histories, wee passed the time.'

When the spells and the ceremony were over, the men cheered louder, until the firecrackers were all used and the drumming ended. *Jambiyahs* were then sheathed once more, the shouting ceased, and the crowd walked slowly through the village, away from the henna circles and the yolk-spattered dirt towards the mosque, with the familiar wedding-day conflation of tradition, superstition, and religion.

The prayer call reverberated from a pure white minaret that rippled gently in its reflection as the first hands broke the surface of the outdoor ablution pool. Steps led down to the water where wedding guests crouched, washing their hands and feet before entering the mosque. Prayers were kept brief and the men re-emerged promptly while I waited outside. We walked on to a house that had been newly decorated with whitewash daubed around the windows. Inside, at each turn of the staircase, smiling, smartly attired boys ushered us up to the second floor where the father of the bride welcomed us to his *mafraj* and a lavish wedding banquet. A fat man with varicosities that wriggled up his hairy calf sat beside me and I asked if he was a friend of the bride's family, or of the groom's. He looked at me suspiciously. 'It's all the same family,' he said. The groom, it turned out, would be marrying his cousin. After eating, as we departed, the same shiny little boys stood by the door, wiping our hands and squirting perfume onto our wrists. From here we were all led to a relative's house for coffee and then to the house of a local sheikh who was displaying his largesse by hosting the afternoon *qat* chew.

I positioned myself next to Arif as we pushed *qat* leaves into our cheeks and discussed weddings with Waleed, a local schoolteacher, and Adel, who worked at the Italian Embassy in Sanaa.

'My family let me finish my studies before I got married,' Adel said. 'I don't think I'd have got my job at the embassy otherwise.'

Arif reiterated his determination to complete his own education before marriage.

His decision was endorsed by Waleed. 'You need to have a job before you have a wife. My teacher's salary is only 30,000 riyal per month and a wedding like this could cost ten times that amount. Finish your studies, get a job with good money, and *then* get married.' It seemed an appealingly simple plan. My own marital status had already been established, along with the fact that I would be soon be leaving Yemen, but now Arif asked about the monthly income that I would receive for working in a UK hospital; apparently seeking to gauge whether it would be enough to fund an extravagant wedding. I avoided answering, partly because I genuinely didn't know, but also because my best guess would seem obscene next to the £100 per month earned by the village teacher. Adel spotted my evasion and laughed out loud.

'Ha! So it's true what they say about the English: you really don't like to talk about money! The Italians don't mind. And Yemenis don't either.'

It was surmised that I was returning home to make my fortune. I said that was unlikely. To find a wife then. I said that wasn't exactly my intention either. I was sorry to be leaving Yemen, I told them. So then, Adel asked, if not for love or money, why was I leaving? And if I was so sorry about it, why didn't I stay?

Perhaps it seems absurd that I should have seriously considered the question. Or perhaps not absurd at all. Absurd, though, that I could not provide any answers. I didn't know. My departure defied explanation. It had seemed a necessary next step. But other foreigners before me had chosen to remain in Yemen. Many of the past travellers who journeyed to Sanaa had encountered non-native residents. Bruce Condé, the orphaned American stamp collector; Signor Caprotti, the Italian newspaper hoarder; Captain Thompson, the British island administrator and his wife with their useless car and their lonely rosebush; the blind Portuguese witch; and Najiba, the Frenchwoman whom Eric Hansen had described clinging on to her memories in 1989. Those who remained in Yemen appeared to share a common trait: they had been lost, lonely souls. Tim Mackintosh-Smith might have been the exception, but I didn't know him well enough to say, and I had missed the opportunity to ask.

Why was I leaving, if not for love or money? Perhaps for fear of losing myself. Or perhaps for fear of finding myself. After all, part of me wanted what I had glimpsed in Yemen; what I thought the young men at the wedding had, or what they would have once they had completed their studies. Companionship, stability, a steady unifying pulse, a simple plan. It felt intensely appealing, but it also felt a world away from anything I knew. While completing my own studies I had never really settled, positioning myself on the edge of friendship groups, leaving the country whenever I could afford, always travelling alone. And in the years since then I had moved around a lot; too much to allow myself to feel that there was a viable alternative. I had always found departures difficult, but *not* departing appeared even more challenging. The anxieties and insecurities that made it uncomfortable for me to stay anywhere for very long were, in fact, the very same ones that made it difficult for me to leave. What if people were bothered by my departure? What if they were not? Better then to slink away, hoping for some Norman Lewis-like invisibility. The quiet departure also served somehow to avoid confronting the decision to leave, as if I could avoid having to face up to an ending. Yet here I was in Yemen, among newfound friends, having my departure acknowledged and questioned, and being prompted to question it myself. In my unpractised response I might have muddled sadness with self-doubt, and mistaken the pain of leaving for a reason to stay, but I was at last contemplating the alternatives and the possibility of remaining.

'Alemani? Franci? Ameriki?' While I might have been wondering where I was going, the man at the teashop on the edge of al-Hajarah asked where I was from.

'English,' I had replied, 'Engliterra.'

I had left the wedding party and the *qat* chew just before sunset, not slipping away this time, but apologising, explaining that I wanted to secure a room at the hotel, and assuring the company that I would return to join them later, for there were further celebrations planned for the evening. Besides, I had chewed rather more *qat* than I was used to and as the *mafraj* filled with smoke and the windows clouded with condensation, I began to feel a little nauseous. I was happy to be back out in the open air, carrying the backpack that I had dragged around the village all afternoon as we moved from venue to venue. Returning to the Al-Hajarah Hotel, Mohammed the manager seemed unsurprised by my reappearance *Of course* they had a room for me. There would *always* be room for me. Later I realised that an absence of tour groups meant that I was in fact the only guest at the hotel that evening. The electricity was out again and I did not stay much beyond dropping off my bag. At the teashop at the edge of the darkening village, a group of old men sat, their faces ghoulish around a single gas lamp, their hands tapping dominoes like bony fingertips upon a tabletop. When the victor held out his palms, empty for all to see, they glowed with a supernatural luminescence in the lamplight, before the dominoes were swept away and a new game began with murmurings and the clacking of tiles. I had just ordered a glass of milky tea when the man asked where I was from, and I had just replied that I was from England when a second man approached and called me a liar.

'Engliterra? Ha! You're from the Old City!' he declared, laughing.

I could not recall having met him before.

'I saw you at the wedding,' he said. 'And I've seen you in Sanaa.' He introduced himself as Ghaleb. He had come from Sanaa to attend the celebrations. We drank our tea together and I acknowledged that I had come from England, but that I did indeed live in the Old City.

'So you come from Sanaa too,' he told me, smiling and clapping a hand on my shoulder. It seemed a friendly remark, whether embracing me as a fellow Sanaani, or just playing on the fact of my arrival from Sanaa the day before, but I gave it no more consideration. We talked, and soon we walked back to the open ground where the dancing had occurred earlier in the day. Dozens of men had gathered and formed a circle once again, but now they stood still, under the village streetlamp, holding hands, and singing in the night. At the centre of the ring was the bridegroom, with his gold sash and turban and his ceremonial sword, and his appearance of being slightly shy and a little overawed. We joined the circle and though I didn't know any of the songs, I sang along anyway, as the sound and the resonance seemed more important than the words. And in the singing, as in the dancing, there was a ready connection. It might have been the same sort of quick essential understanding that the tour group had intuited the night before. Except that none of this was being put on for my benefit. It was not for me. But for a moment I might have allowed myself to imagine that it could have been. We were observing a rite of passage. We were honouring change; a next step. And we stood for over an hour, holding hands in a circle, among the clouds that blew up from the valleys and ravines, singing beneath the streetlamp, into the darkness beyond.

Abruptly the bridegroom was thrust upwards on the shoulders of two of his companions. The circle then imploded as the others crowded in around him, voices rising and falling. Amid the crests of *jambiyahs* held high once more, the figure dressed in gold bobbed away on a sea of chanting men. That night, from the rooftop of the hotel, I watched a slow caravan of tooting off-road vehicles set off from the home of the bride where I had lunched in the afternoon. In the dark, the building was still recognisable by the incandescence of its whitewashed window frames, as if light were bursting from the household. At the front of the bridal procession, fireworks began blasting from the tailgate of a pick-up truck, releasing crackling showers of explosions and swirls of smoke that twisted and flared in the glare of headlights. Arif had explained how the bride would be escorted to the house of the groom, and how the bride and bridegroom would then be united. If not the first time that they had met, it would be the first time that they were alone together. Crudely I had wondered whether they would be expected to consummate the marriage, but Arif was appalled at the suggestion: they would barely know one another. Hearing the rapid crumping patter of an automatic weapon, I watched the flecks of celebratory tracer fire being spat into the night sky, like ricocheting meteors sparking back toward the stars.

To connect and to intuit, to know, however roughly, the steps in a dance, and to learn the tune of a song: this might seem unremarkable. But if there was one recurring contention in the accounts of past travellers to Sanaa, one claim that was repeated almost as often as the myth of Yemen's medievalism, repeated so often in fact that it had begun to take on the appearance of truth, it was that Yemen was impenetrable and mysterious; unknowable and unknown. It was an 'unknown country' to Reverend Stern in 1856; 'unknown' to Leland Buxton in 1905; a 'terra incognita' to Norman Lewis in 1937. Mistakenly, in fact, Lewis supposed that Yemen had only been 'previously visited by two or possibly three Englishmen'. But even those visitors who were better acquainted with the country and with the narratives of earlier travellers could still remain none the wiser. Hugh Scott spent months in Yemen, collecting insects and information that would later serve the Admiralty. He read Robert Playfair's 1859 history of Arabia Felix, and he cited the earlier visits of Jourdain, Niebuhr, Harris, Wavell, Wyman Bury, and Freya Stark, but in 1942 he still thought that Yemen remained a 'mysterious country', 'strange and little-known'.

The apparently unshakable belief, in Britain at least, that Yemen was mysterious and unknown might appear to explain why so many of these authors had gone there in the first place. Yemen had been a destination for British spies ever since 1823 when Doctor Robert Finlay was instructed 'to avoid all political discussions and also the appearance of being on a political mission, but to collect every information relative to the country and its politics.' In the wake of Finlay came Norman Lewis with his 'spy camera', then Freya Stark with her cine-projector disguised as a portable commode. There is a fair chance, too, that Hugh Scott with his later position in the Admiralty and David Holden with his 'bottomless western cynicism' were also engaged in espionage while in Yemen. Less politically motivated knowledge and less covert methods had been on the agendas of other visitors to Yemen: from Ludovico di Varthema's intended witnessing of 'new manners and customs', through John Jourdain's trade prospecting, and Carsten Niehbuhr's scientific learning, right up to Serjeant and Lewcock's comprehensive studying of Sanaa. Yet despite all the spying and the knowledge seeking, Yemen remained startlingly obscure. Despite all the visits of past travellers, despite all that they witnessed and experienced, and despite all their published opinions and assertions, Yemen, they said, was still unknown. Yemen had become *known* for being unknown. Visitors readily perpetuated that reputation, seeding the perceptions of those who came after them. At the end of the twentieth century, in the 1999 edition of the Lonely Planet guide, Yemen was still 'beguiling', 'medieval', and unknown. It irked Tim Mackintosh-Smith. When the

American edition of his *Yemen: Travels in Dictionary Land* was given the title 'Yemen: The Unknown Arabia', he appeared uncomfortable with the marketing decision. 'Yemen might have been "unknown" in the past; but I was putting that right, wasn't I?' he wrote in the afterword to a later edition. But he also acknowledged that, regrettably, in recent years Yemen had become known only 'as a lair for those lurking terrorists'. If only it could have become known for its singing or its dancing instead.

There was a spare seat in Ghaleb's Toyota the next day and I was grateful for a ride back to the capital. An easy camaraderie filled the journey, a holiday feel spilling over, and the *qat* stalks, carelessly tossed, collected in the collar of my hiking boots. The sun burnt off the last of the morning's autumn mist as we wound back along the mountain roads and it was almost noon when we curved around the last bend, over the last rise, and gained our first glimpse of the city spread beneath us. A few cars sat parked at the roadside; couples and unconventional *qat* chewers enjoying the view. Coming this way a century and a half earlier, Reverend Henry Stern had remarked on the vista of 'tapering minarets' and 'glittering cupolas'. They were still there, those minarets and cupolas, but amid the sprawling expanse of breezeblock suburbs and glittering plate glass they were more difficult to spot. Marvelling at the city laid out before him, crowning his progress and the triumph of his pilgrimage, Stern told his readers that Sanaa was 'one of the most ancient and famous cities'. But if Sanaa was famous, it was, like Yemen or The Yemen, famous only for being unknown. Aubrey Herbert, justifying the decision to try and reach Sanaa that he and Leland Buxton agreed upon in the lobby of the House of Commons in 1905, explained simply and sufficiently to his readers that Sanaa was a place of 'mystery'.

And like Yemen or The Yemen, in the religious ecstasies of Rev Stern, or the sexual fantasies of Walter Harris, the heroic dreams of Arthur Wavell, or the furtive nightmares of Freya Stark, the city of Sanaa had been endlessly imagined and reimagined by Western visitors. And like Yemen or The Yemen with its 'historical epithets' Arabia Felix or Land of the Queen of Sheba, Sanaa had been given a good assortment of labels by foreigners over the years. For the egotistical preacher Joseph Wolff, Sanaa was 'Uzal', so-called 'in Genesis, chapter x. verse 27'. For Captain Playfair, in his history, it was The Garden of Arabia. For Pier Paolo Pasolini, it was the Venice of Dust. And for academics Serjeant and Lewcock, Sanaa was the scholarly Arabic Islamic City. Meanwhile the city's Arabic name was variously rendered. In 1609, Westcountryman John Jourdain referred to it as Senan - just like the Cornish coastal village near Penzance. In 1823, Doctor Finlay called it Senna - just like the laxative. Then for a while Yemen's capital became Sanaa in English, until the twentieth century when apostrophes began to be variously inserted and vowels were added or removed. For Freya Stark and Hugh Scott it was San'a; the same for Tim Mackintosh-Smith, Kevin Rushby and Eric Hansen. For Norman Lewis and Jonathan Raban it was Sana'a. Then Serjeant and Lewcock did something unusual like San'a', but with a dot added beneath the S and a line above the a: Ṣan'a'. For David Holden, though, it remained plain old Sanaa.

'One problem that besets all writers on Arabia,' Holden observed, 'is how best to reproduce in their own language the manifest signs and sounds of Arabic.' In an appendix to his book he added 'a last word on words' and asked, 'Mohammed or Muhammed, Mahomet or Mehemet?' Or equally, we might wonder, qat or gat, kat or khat? 'Personal preference,' Holden admitted, determined his response to the lack of spelling convention. And as for the 'ain', the apostrophe sounded like a glottal stop, 'I have cast it out without mercy,' Holden announced. 'No doubt Sanaa should properly be Sana'a... But not here. Except for quotations from other writers whose idiosyncrasies I have left intact'... By now it will of course be clear that I have followed his approach, though not without reflection. For punctuation continues to come and go in this corner of Arabia: Al Jazeera currently favours Sanaa; the BBC Sana'a. The spelling might be immaterial, the position of the apostrophe inconsequential. But somehow the inconsistency seems relevant. Sanaa or Sana'a, Sana or San'a? It might seem to remain beguiling and unknown.

Yet as so many travellers to Sanaa have demonstrated, to know a city or a country is by no means an inevitable consequence of visiting. Like getting to know another person, or ourselves, getting to know a place requires effort and openness: an acceptance of difference and things disliked, a willingness to make mistakes and to learn from them, and an acknowledgement that there are things that we will never wholly comprehend. There may be only fleeting moments of insight or intuiting, brief feelings of connection or disconnect, or of something shared or withheld. And from these transitory perceptions, mere glimpses when the clouds roll back, our knowledge remains inherently personal. We think we know a place, but we know too that someone else will know it quite differently. Much like the 'truths' set down by Ludovico di Varthema all those years ago, what we know is the product of our own unique experiences, perceptions, and memories.

In Sanaa I came to know a city founded where a bird had once dropped a stone. A city once ruled by a man who refused to be photographed, then ruled by a man whose image adorned amulets and covered entire buildings. A city with a river that flowed through its centre for just a few weeks each year, and I came to know which way the water flowed. I was taught the steps of the hammam dance and how to snap open a goat's head. I learnt not to grab at cactus fruit, not to clean my teeth with *miswak*, and not to attempt cycling on Sanaa's roads. Sorely, I learnt the difference between the museum and the airport. I became familiar with the different quarters of the Old City and I could find my way through the labyrinthine medina along its unnamed streets. In the *suq* I knew where to obtain the finest coffee from Al-Kabous, and I eventually knew my way to the library, though I could never comprehend the opening hours. I understood how to appraise a *jambiyah* and how to tell a man's occupation from his dagger sheath, but I never figured out the secrets of the Mokeets, Beloweets, and four different types of headscarf on my laundry list. I knew the fire of the *salta* shop and the quiddity of the *qat* chew. I knew amber days under alabaster moons and I knew rising dust and falling rain. I knew a steady unifying pulse and the blue of the prayer call before dawn. It was all my own reimagining and it was all true.

Many visitors before me were affected by their time in Yemen and many returned, or tried to. Lucille Février returned and wrote about her experiences as a seventeen-year-old in Sanaa some fifty years afterwards. Eric Hansen returned after a decade to hunt for his lost journals and lost youth. Ann Wyman Bury attempted to return on the anniversary of her wedding to George, the ill-fated ornithologist. Norman Lewis returned again and again to the memory of his thwarted attempt to reach Sanaa. Tim Mackintosh-Smith chose to remain. And he warned me before I left that Yemen had a habit of bringing people back. In a sense, that is what happened as I returned to my diaries and the travelogues of others. But in an important sense, reading and writing about these past visitors and my own past experiences has been no match for returning. It is not just the distinction, noted once by Ludovico di Varthema, between seeing with one's own eyes and hearing the report of an eyewitness. It is the difference of seeing one's friends and experiencing the feel of homely places.

Ghaleb stopped at Tahreer Square and I climbed from the back of his Toyota, thanking him for the ride back from Manakha and flicking the *qat* stalks from my shoes. A few public buses were emptying out and filling up nearby and there were people busying about the post office. A television screen had been installed on a plinth at one corner of the Square and it was showing a looped movie trailer of *The Incredible Hulk*; the green superhero bursting repeatedly out of his shirt. Sanaa had rallied from its quiescence. The city's inhabitants had recovered from the Ramadan inversion of their collective body clocks and returned from their vacations. On Bab as-Sabah, Mansour waved from behind his fruit stall and Nabil, the seller of embroidered scarves, insisted that I join him for tea. Crossing the footbridge over the *Sayilah*, my neighbour the camel was enjoying an extended holiday, standing outside the sesame mill, chewing on a mouthful of alfalfa. Yusuf, the youth once painted purple, was booting a football about the cobbles with some of the other neighbourhood kids. In the garden behind our house Ibrahim was blinking in and out of the trellis shade, preparing food for a few guests who would be arriving soon and, of course, I was invited. I realised then that Ghaleb was right: I came from here too. And ever since, I always have; for so many journeys seem to have begun in Sanaa, including this one.

And at the end of every journey is the point where we discover why we made it. It may not be the place that we set out for, but it is nonetheless our destination. John Jourdain would have known that, for in its archaic meaning, destination was not merely a location, but the fact of being destined; it was the act of God's destining or appointing; it was our fate. Tim Mackintosh-Smith might have quoted the poet TS Eliot, who wrote that the end of all our exploring will be to arrive back where we started and know the place for the first time. Our destination is a state of knowing.

It is our fate. It is where we start from, and where we return. It is a circle of friends, and of family, it is a home. Ibrahim once remarked that my departures were only apparent when I returned having remembered what I had left behind. But that changed. My departure became apparent because Ibrahim organised a leaving party for me in the garden. And I knew what I was leaving behind because I wrote it all down in my notebook in the blue before dawn. That was where I started and it was where we might have ended; seated in the *mafraj* on the mattress, the faintest scent of incense on the air and a low round table scattered with notepads and stationery, a few books and a layer of dust that bore the memory of absent things. With the last stars swept away and the first silhouettes of towerhouses inked against the sky, we would have heard the call to pray. And long before the sun climbed over the eastern hills to pour light into the city, we would have faced our destination and our departure.

Epilogue

IN THE SQUARE OF THE Sailors, I stood at the entrance to the Bahnhof, just as we had agreed. Nearby, a clutch of seagulls flapped and pecked among the parked cars while clouds pushed past a retiring sun. Slowly the Square shifted back and forth between light and the cooling shade of late spring. Occasional passengers hurried toward afternoon trains, dragging wheelie luggage, rumbling and clacking, across the paving slabs. Waiting, glancing around expectantly, I felt self-conscious, a little apprehensive, as I looked at my mobile phone, at my watch, or at the station clock, and then went back to contemplating the gulls.

So far, the day had been marked by a sort of distracted anticipation. My flight had coincided with a royal wedding and in the departure lounge at Heathrow the rolling television footage from Windsor Castle provided a welcome hypnotic. For years air travel had never really troubled me. I had taken countless flights and covered innumerable air miles, crossing continents and oceans, troubled by no greater mental strain than deliberating over which of the in-flight movies to watch, or whether to have chicken or fish. But my last time on a plane had been an unsettling experience. Returning from Greece and another summer of work in a refugee camp, mid-flight, some slight change in the engine tone, or some small adjustment of the aircraft's trim was enough to momentarily unbalance my mind. Immediately, and with absolute certainty, I knew that our plane was about to fall from the sky. It was an unusual sort of conviction, unexpected and incongruous. My heart pounded wildly in my chest, my thoughts ran out of control, and I guessed madly at how long it would take for everyone to recognise the imminent disaster. Meanwhile the cabin crew continued to tootle calmly up the aisle with their duty-free trolley. Gripping the arm rests either side of me I ached for some reassuring sign, or for an announcement from the captain to say that all was well, but there was only the continued beating of my heart, which gradually began to slow, and with that my terror gradually subsided, as strangely and seemingly inexplicably as it had arisen. Departures had never been easy, but this was different. Later I supposed that my episode of acute anxiety was some sort of delayed reaction to the stories that I had heard in the Greek refugee camp; stories of real danger and actual loss in conflict zones and on migration routes; stories that continued to be enacted and retold by their often-traumatised survivors long after they faded from the media coverage.

Perhaps the televised pageant of guests arriving serenely for the marriage of Harry and Meghan helped to numb my thoughts this morning. The flight went smoothly. My journey, in fact, could not have been easier: an early start, a bicycle ride to the bus stop, a bus to the airport, followed by an airplane to Hamburg, and then another bus here to Kiel, and the Square of the Sailors.

Khaled's journey to this German harbour town could not have been more different, or more difficult: from Yemen, across the Red Sea and the Gulf of Aden, through Somalia and Sudan, across the Libyan Desert in a cramped truck and then across the Mediterranean Sea in a flimsy boat. He had been rescued off the Italian coast eighteen months earlier, during the region's deadliest season of migration on record. In a succession of shipwrecks, drownings, and bodies being washed ashore, almost 5,000 people are known to have lost their lives that year while trying to reach Europe from Africa. Many more are likely to have tried and died without acknowledgement, sinking without trace, and many continue to attempt the journey. The selfie image that showed Khaled haloed by his sunset orange lifejacket against the blue of the Mediterranean might have prefigured a tragic obituary. But soon after, another photograph, of Khaled standing in front of a Baroque Italianate fountain, announced his safe passage. I experienced a wave of relief and sent him my congratulations, uncertain though whether that was exactly the sentiment I wanted to express. Later, after a year spent in Naples and then Rome, the Italian authorities informed Khaled that he was going to be relocated. He was to be given a home in one of the European Union's member states as part of the refugee resettlement scheme. That beleaguered European scheme was the continent's response to those hundreds of thousands of people fleeing conflict and persecution who had lately arrived in Italy and Greece. For months, then years, I watched the scheme failing. Huge numbers of refugees remained in squalid and overcrowded 'temporary' shelters, like the makeshift camps in old factories and derelict warehouses where I worked in Greece. Those inhuman conditions, in which angry young men and families with young children were detained together, offered few resources to help people deal with their traumas, and left many vulnerable to mental health problems, exploitation, or abuse. Meanwhile, the absence of any schooling or employment opportunities in the camps was slowly undermining the future prospects of a generation, and eroding their aspirations.

Khaled did not have much faith in the scheme either. He had heard it rumoured that Romania and Hungary were possible resettlement destinations, and neither of those locations held much appeal. The few Syrian refugees who arrived in Italy from Greece had nothing good to report from their friends who had taken the alternative overland route through Eastern Europe. So Khaled contacted a Yemeni he knew in Germany, where the situation was said to be more favourable for refugees. Khaled was relocated to Germany in December 2017, shortly before Christmas, and was promptly greeted by the first snow that he had ever seen. He had never encountered ice before either and would later recall slipping and sliding perilously about the streets of his new home. But the dangers were otherwise behind him and he quickly found his feet.

Now it was springtime and I had arranged to visit Khaled for the weekend. The arrangements, truth be told, were pretty cursory. Unable to write Arabic, I had sent Khaled a few Facebook messages in English to explain my travel plans, and he had responded with a few cryptically misspelt replies. I realised only after booking my flights that I had thoughtlessly timed my visit for the first weekend of Ramadan. And I realised too that observing Ramadan in Northern Europe during May would mean fasting from 3am to 9pm, and I wondered how Khaled would cope, and how I would cope while I was with him. Telephoning him on his German mobile number, we managed a halting conversation as each of us struggled to recall fragments of one another's language. During that phone call I attempted to confirm my arrival date. But there was no reply to the text message I sent from the departure lounge at Heathrow that morning. And though my flight was not disturbed by another episode of anxiety, there remained some niggling uncertainty about what would unfold when I arrived. Khaled had said that I might be able to stay at his place, so I hadn't booked a hotel and instead just packed a sleeping bag. But later, as I waited outside the Bahnhof in Kiel, watching the seagulls squabble, knowing that the station clock had already declared the passing of our appointed meeting time, I began to have doubts about whether I had been clear in communicating my plans, and whether Khaled had understood. And if he had, and if we met, I was unsure whether our communication would remain so stumbling and uncertain. And if we met and were able to converse, I began to ask myself whether we would still get on. It had, after all, been a dozen years since we had last seen one another and, until our shakily-made arrangements to meet, the directions in which life had taken each of us had been utterly divergent. For the past four years Khaled had been putting distance between himself and Sanaa. I meanwhile had spent that time circling the city in my notebooks and in the narratives of travel writers; from Ludovico di Varthema's unbelievable truths and John Jourdain's adventures in the spice trade, through the shifting rememberings of Norman Lewis and the questing of Eric Hansen, up to and including the revisiting of my decade-old diary of a year spent in Sanaa. Both of us had been driven by memories of what we had left behind in Yemen at different times, but there was otherwise little equivalence between my bookish journey and Khaled's dangerous escape from a deadly conflict. Waiting in the maritime breeze, I thought of Khaled's sea voyages, of his dream, early in Yemen's conflict, of reaching Aruba, a tranquil island in the Caribbean, then his crossing of the Red Sea, the Mediterranean, and his eventual arrival here on the edge of the Baltic. Having left his home, his friends and his family, risking his life at each step, I half expected his resentment, and Khaled's landfall on European shores remained an uncertain occasion for congratulations.

Not so long ago, we had stood on opposite sides of the Mediterranean, Khaled in Libya while I was in Greece, and I had questioned how the war in Yemen could be 'forgotten'. How could something as drawn out and destructive slip from our collective consciousness? By now I had worked out some answers. I knew only too well that stories of human suffering could evoke unpleasant feelings; if not acute anxiety, then confusion or unease. And I understood the urge to suppress those feelings, or avoid them entirely by distancing ourselves from their source. I had become accustomed to the political and economic concerns at stake; the arms sales, oil supplies, and antiterrorism intelligence. And I understood that those national interests were being invariably prioritised, while their devastating consequences in faraway countries like Yemen were inevitably marginalised. Finally, I had come to question the role of travel writing. I had become familiar with the role of travel writers and their writing in wartime. I had read about Freya Stark in Sanaa during 1940; observed Arthur Wavell's *jambiyah* description in the 1917 *Handbook of Yemen*; and acknowledged the active roles of George Wyman Bury and Hugh Scott in drafting military handbooks during the World Wars. But had the narratives of these travellers somehow facilitated our forgetting? From the sales trips of the East India Company, through the proselytising of missionaries, and the adventurism of the English upper classes, could these travellers and their writings reveal anything further about our apparent failure to remember the current conflict?

Packing for his journey to Sanaa in 1912, Arthur Wavell had filled a tin box with scientific instruments and a chain mail shirt. He also carried with him a weighty baggage of colonial-era stereotypes. Later he wrote of Yemen that 'Western Europe knows little and cares less about what goes on there.' For a moment it sounded like a reproach to his readers. But then Wavell appeased his audience's lack of knowledge and absence of concern with his refrains about Yemen being 'unknown' and 'impenetrable', as well as the Arab inhabitants of Sanaa being the 'laziest' people he had 'ever come across'.

Over the years, the ways in which Yemen and the people of Yemen have been presented or misrepresented, even by authors less partial than Wavell, have often done little to aid our knowledge and concern. There is a connection here, I sense, between the travel writers' 'unknown' Yemen and Yemen's 'forgotten war'. Travel writing has not always encouraged our understanding and empathy. More usually it has sustained an uncomprehending and indifferent vision of Yemen through the repeated myths of medievalism and mystery. Those myths perpetuate an unwarranted and unhelpful perception of difference. Unintentionally perhaps, but inescapably, keeping Yemen unknown and mysterious stifles empathy and compassion. The unknowing permits 'forgetting'.

There is another connection, again doubtless unintended and unconscious, but still oppressive, like the latent orientalism once described by Edward Said. Attaching the term 'forgotten' to Yemen's war reveals the same muddling of reproach and collusion shown by Arthur Wavell. It appears to be an attempt at redress, a rebuke to our forgetting. But at the same time it upholds underlying misconceptions. Those misconceptions include the spurious notion that Yemen's war might have been merely 'forgotten', rather than deliberately overlooked on account of the national interests at stake. There is also the painful fact that the war in Yemen will never be 'forgotten' by those who have lived through it and whose lives have been disrupted by it, just as Yemen was never 'unknown' to the people who lived there. The suggestion that Yemen's war might have been 'forgotten' in any meaningful sense only validates a naive and insular vision.

'Androo!'

In the Square of the Sailors, the seagulls arched their wings and suddenly took flight. I turned around to find my friend from twelve years ago and three thousand miles away. He looked older, his hair much longer, and he was smiling, and he might have observed the same things about me. As the gulls soared away and my doubts about our meeting arrangements instantly dissipated, Khaled and I shook hands and embraced. It was an extraordinary and yet somehow prosaic reuniting. Extraordinary were the dozen years and the distances covered, but mostly the unimaginable circumstances of our encounter. I had thought I might return to Sanaa. When that became impossible I had not thought that Khaled would arrive in Europe. And neither of us could have guessed at our meeting here, on the Baltic coast, in a German town that only a few months ago neither of us had even heard of. It was not the destination that I had anticipated. And yet, at the same time, the overlapping of lives and the reuniting of friends seemed, if not prosaic exactly, then natural at least, and normal. Or had I taken the ease of travel too much for granted? It was anyway the sense of the extraordinary that stayed with me; the feeling that our meeting here was not quite impossible, but at least unlikely. It was a feeling not immediately dispelled by the handshake and the hug. But my concerns about Ramadan disappeared promptly when Khaled bought us some beers. Clearly he was adapting to the local culture. The sky had cleared and we sat down by the harbour, cracked open a couple of cans of Heineken and remembered how, in Sanaa, we would have sat in Tahreer Square and drunk sugary tea from re-used tins of Al-Momtaz evaporated milk. The water sparkled, we felt the warmth of the sun, and my uncertainties about communication and whether Khaled and I would have much in common vanished as words and memories came to light afresh.

Watching the sailboats, Khaled recounted his voyage from Libya, reliving the moment when the Italian coastguard sighted their vessel, and recalling how people leapt to their feet, how some surged to leap overboard, and how the boat tipped dangerously toward the waves.

'The Nakhoda cried out for everyone to sit down and stay calm.'

I knew the Arabic word from one or other of Norman Lewis' rememberings. The Nakhoda, or skipper, in Lewis' *A Voyage by Dhow* called the passengers to prayer when the sun fell to the horizon. And according to Lewis, the Nakhoda regaled them with stories when the wind dropped. As Khaled continued his tale I began to think that his story was surely as compelling as anything that Lewis or even his Nakhoda could have offered. As a travel narrative, it was gripping, packed with obstacles and dangers met with courage and determination. As a human drama, it was powerfully emotive, with its themes of separation, survival and resilience. Yet Lewis, that most moral if inconsistent of storytellers, had never ventured to recount the Nakhoda's stories second-hand. And likewise, I don't feel it is my place to relate the events that Khaled described. Besides, as we sat at the harbour side, I could scarcely keep pace with the catalogue of frightening and extraordinary experiences; each episode calling out for explanation of how it came about, or of what happened next. Perhaps, once his story has come closer to a conclusion, Khaled will have the opportunity to narrate it himself, and to have his story heard. Meanwhile, he was still searching for a satisfactory ending, and the readiness with which his Mediterranean boat journey resurfaced and the urgency of the retelling gave me the impression that Khaled's account had not yet been much retold. Or not much listened to. Like the stories of so many refugees, whether Khaled's odyssey would ultimately be a tale of triumphant overcoming, or of tragedy, and whether his story would ever be heard at all, remained out of his hands.

Once upon a time, his story might have been met with compassion. Around the time that Khaled left Yemen in the autumn of 2015, a surge of concern for the fate of migrants was prompted by the death of Alan Kurdi. The three-year-old Syrian boy drowned while trying to reach Greece by boat from Turkey. Images of Kurdi lying dead, face down, washed up on a Turkish beach, dramatically symbolised the tragic fate of many refugees and the moral crisis facing Europe. For a fleeting moment across the continent there was a shared horror at our having allowed this to happen. Four days after Kurdi's death the tragedy looked briefly set to be turned into something else as the television news in Britain showed refugees arriving at Munich's rail station being greeted by clapping and cheering crowds.

- EPILOGUE -

But the welcome extended to refugees in Europe had cooled considerably since then. In Germany, the challenges of cultural integration, perceptions of strains on social services, and a small proportion of immigrants committing criminal acts, had caused compassion fatigue toward refugees among some locals and exacerbated xenophobic attitudes among others. The situation in Germany was made more difficult by the fact that many other European countries were seen to be refusing to admit anything close to their fair share of refugees. On a per capita basis, the number of refugees being permitted entry to Britain was one of the meanest on the continent.

Khaled had been granted a one-year German visa. Five months had passed already, and it was not clear what would happen when his visa expired. For the present, though, his home lay out beyond the airport, six miles north of central Kiel, in an old military base. The barracks that had once accommodated servicemen now housed refugees. We spent the evening there with friends of Khaled's; a young husband and wife from Eritrea. Like Khaled, they had survived the journey across Libya and the Mediterranean before their arrival in Germany and the birth of their beautiful two-year-old daughter. We talked and the room became colourful with languages; Arabic, English, Tigrinya from Eritrea, then the German that Khaled was struggling to learn, and something none of us understood that the daughter had picked up from the Kurdish boy down the corridor. We talked, about the totalitarian regime in Eritrea, the destructive war in Yemen, and the perilous journey to Europe, while in the corner of the family's single room a television with the sound turned down showed highlights from the day's Royal Wedding. My thoughts flicked back and forth, skipping from the silent television images to an airport lounge, my in-flight anxieties, and the vessels that continued to go down in the Mediterranean with all the fatality and human tragedy of a plane crash, but none of the publicity. I tried to imagine my companions of this evening on the Libyan coast, boarding boats. I tried to think how they would have weighed up the risks and chosen to undertake the sea crossing. Or how they would have found the mental and emotional strength to continue at every stage of their journey. But the dangers and the decisions were impossible to grasp. Of course, I had taken the ease and safety of travel too much for granted. They might never have survived their voyages. The babbling two-year-old might never have been born.

- 323 -

'We could not have gone back even if we wanted to,' my new Eritrean friend told me. 'We had no choice.'

'There was nothing else,' said Khaled. 'Only the sea.'

That night, after insisting that there was no reason for Khaled to give up his bed, and after rolling out my sleeping bag on the floor of his small room, I lay down and my thoughts unravelled back through my own journeys. From a locked refuge and a single night under the stars in the Greek mountains, to an episode of anxiety in the safety of a flight home. It was not only the relative ease and safety of my travel that I had taken for granted, but the fact too that my journeys had never been forced. And before falling asleep I reflected on being made welcome, here, as in Sanaa, by the very people who themselves now needed to be made welcome after their unwanted but necessary journeys. Then I drifted off to the sounds of Ramadan cooking, of children running up and down corridors, and Khaled's snoring. Sometimes, he told me the next morning, he still woke back in Yemen. At some point I asked him about Aruba.

'*Aruba*?!' replied Khaled.

That had been my response more than three years earlier, but I was surprised by Khaled's bemusement.

'Yes, you sent me a message on Facebook when you were in Yemen. You said you wanted to leave and go to Aruba.' I had not forgotten, and besides, the internet keeps a record of these things.

'*Aruba*?' He seemed never to have heard of the Caribbean island.

'Yes, Aruba. I think it's part of the Netherlands,' I said, trying to jog his memory.

'Aruba? No, *Europa*! *Europa*!'

That made more sense. We shared the humour of Khaled's unconventional spelling and my own credulous misunderstanding. And our meeting, specifically the fact that our meeting arrangements had been successful, seemed all the more extraordinary.

The next day we borrowed bicycles and took a bike ride, and Khaled reminded me of my abortive attempt to pedal to work in Sanaa; my near miss with a motorcycle and my mangled rear wheel. He hadn't witnessed the incident, but we must have joked about it afterwards over a cup of tea. Now, once more, we couldn't help laughing. The memory was comically absurd, but there was something else, something unexpected. It was, I realised, the comfort of knowing that the memory was shared, that it existed outside ourselves, and that each of us had carried a little bit of the other with us during the intervening years. I thought I glimpsed something similar when, on along the coast road, we spotted seals. In Arabic, Khaled told me, they were *Kalb al-bahr*, dog of the sea, and in German they were *Seehunde*: sea dogs too. The words seemed to hint at something else shared, far back. And when the rear wheel threatened to fall off my borrowed bicycle and I used my rusty German to cadge a wrench from an old man, we learnt that in German the word *Schlüssel* is used both for spanner and for key, and with the memory of my cumbersome door key in Sanaa I recalled that the Arabic word *Miftah* sometimes has the same dual meaning too. Again, the commonalities of language seemed to point reassuringly toward some common perspectives, if only from long ago.

We pedalled on and I remembered my efforts to learn Arabic in Yemen, recalling the many conversational taxi drivers who aided me in my struggle. Khaled was now facing a similar challenge with German. I listened to him wrestling with the *Sch* sound in *Schlüssel* that does not really exist in Arabic, which was unfortunate because the street where Khaled lived and the bus stop where he had to get off when his own bike broke down was called *Schusterkrug*. Khaled had a free bus pass, but little money for talkative taxi rides. Moreover, the uncertainty about how long he would be allowed to remain in Germany did little to encourage his language studies. And we both observed how, when he approached someone to ask if he could borrow a bike tool, their face would tend to cloud over. Despite our shared memories, and despite my clutching at sea dogs, Schlüssels, and whatever other sparse linguistic clues existed to what might once have been common experiences and perspectives, there was no disguising the frustrating separateness that Khaled confronted. I had imagined something cyclical, a wheel turning, the Englishman once in Yemen now accompanying the Yemeni in Europe, but the disparity was painfully clear. In Sanaa I had a job that had given me purpose and enough money to pay for my choice of apartment, my dining out with friends, and my travel around the country on weekends and on holidays. And I always had a choice about my departure. In Kiel, Khaled had acquired a few possessions, some cooking utensils and clothes, but his state income was minimal, he was not permitted to work, he had no option over his accommodation and no control over whether he would be allowed to remain in Germany. And then there were the ugly suspicions that he encountered on the street; the confused fears about refugees bringing religious extremism and terrorism, or contradictory concerns about them taking jobs and social benefits. Ultimately, there were stark differences in our origins and, consequently, in the privileges granted to us. We had been opposites and we had lived in opposite worlds. There seemed to be little in common between my past experience in Yemen and Khaled's present life in Europe.

Sitting once more on the quayside before my bus back to Hamburg and my flight back to Heathrow, our last conversation was about books and authors. Khaled had discovered the public library in Kiel, and discovered that it held a small Arabic language collection. Our feet dangled above the waves that slapped the harbour wall as Khaled scribbled down the names of two authors in Arabic. Mohamed Choukri and Tayeb Salih. Both were unknown to me, but Khaled urged me to look them up. Once back home I found that their work had not only reached Europe, but arrived in translation. Intrigued, I read *For Bread Alone*, Choukri's tough memoir of poverty, migration, and coming of age in Morocco. In the book's final chapter, on the outskirts of Tangier, Choukri gets into a fistfight over a few pesetas on the shore in front of Villa Harris. The setting caused me to draw breath. Villa Harris was the sumptuous home of Walter Burton Harris, who in 1892 had gloated about crossing the border into Yemen dressed as a penurious Greek shopkeeper. Choukri's reference to Harris was fleeting, but it delivered a striking counterpoint to Harris' own romanticised travel narratives.

Later I became immersed in the other book that Khaled recommended, *Season of Migration to the North*; Tayeb Salih's turbulent novel of lives lived adrift in the wake of colonialism and the dangerous eddies of orientalism. Again I was jolted - this time by Salih's narration of a truck ride across the Sudanese desert. 'There is no shelter from the sun,' he wrote, 'no shelter apart from the hot shade inside the lorry - shade that is not really shade.' The description brought vividly to mind Khaled's account of his own journey through that same scorched landscape. He had endured that same insufferable heat. He had resorted to sucking moisture from grimy puddles. He had told me of the trucks that overturned or broke down or got lost in the silent desert, the passengers who were abused, extorted, or left for dead beneath the pitiless sun. He had made a journey that nobody would choose to make, a risky and agonising route from conflict to an unwelcoming continent.

For a moment all the travel narratives that I had read seemed superfluous. All the words that I had written seemed redundant. Everything to be said about the encounter between East and West had already been said by Salih. Everything about journeys and endurance had been said by Choukri. And yet the conflict continued in Yemen, refugees continued to be scorned in Europe, and Khaled's situation still looked uncertain. No story is definitive. Stories of travel are not just stories about where we got to, but how we got there, where we came from, and, perhaps, where we can go from here. If, in the past, European travel writing about Yemen, and other places too no doubt, has tended toward complicity in our forgetting, there surely remains the potential for that writing to move on, to undertake a journey of its own, to go further in aiding our understanding, our engagement with other voices and other stories, and our empathy for others. To do so requires not only contending with the disparities of our experiences, but acknowledging the possibilities of connection, and strengthening what is shared.

Later, thinking back to the quayside in Kiel, I thought of Choukri's figure on the shore in front of Villa Harris; of the jarring conflict between the view from the window of a privileged English expatriate and the world seen from behind the migrant's bloodied fist. I thought of our very different experiences of being foreigners: mine in Sanaa; Khaled's in Kiel. I thought of our very different journeys: mine through the pages of old travel writing; and Khaled's from Yemen, across the Sahara and the Mediterranean, on through Europe's increasingly hostile environment for immigrants. And yet despite the contrasts, and no matter how little we might have in common, the sharing of memories and of stories had reconnected us. At the harbour, near the Bahnhof; gripping cans of sweet milky tea in Tahreer Square. On the cycle path, along the Baltic coast; abandoning a hapless bicycle ride down Zubeiry Street. And then, if only briefly and imaginatively, I had felt Khaled's burning truck ride in the desert, just as I had felt the perilous boat journeys on my flight home from Greece. There would be other memories and other stories, beginning elsewhere, from other times and other places. In Kiel, when Khaled and I shook hands again, back at the Square of the Sailors, our journeys were not over. We parted with stories yet to be shared.

Acknowledgements

I AM GREATLY INDEBTED TO Khaled al-Shanoon, for allowing me to share part of his story. In Sanaa, Abdurahman Almoassib was a singular host, Peter Boswell was a valued companion, and Abdulghani Al-Iryani was a generous source of knowledge. Others who helped to make my time in Yemen possible and so enjoyable are too numerous to mention, but their number includes: Ramesh Shrestha, Heidi Larson, Dan Siskind, Najla al-Shami, Alice Wilson, Walid Rabeh, and Adnan Jumman. Tim Mackintosh-Smith was kind enough to chew qat and to chat, and to read through the manuscript and suggest amendments. In Britain, in the writing and realisation of this project, I am grateful to Ian Huish who was there at the inception, Jonathan Gregory who saw the potential and provided valuable advice, and James Ferguson without whom it would never have been published, and published so stylishly. I must thank my parents, for encouraging my travels in Yemen and elsewhere, and for tolerating one or two anxious moments. Especially my Old Man for visiting me in my towerhouse. For all the time that I have spent working on this book, for supporting me in doing so, and for putting up with the moments when, like the librarian in Sana, I might have appeared only partially present, I am thankful to my wonderful partner Eike. And now also to Artus.

Glossary

Abaya	Women's robe worn over clothes, covering all but the head, hands, and feet; in Yemen the colour is invariably black
Aga	Title used in the Ottoman Empire
Ayb	That which is proscribed by societal norms, also used in remonstration, like 'shame'
Bab	Gate or door
Beit / bayt	House, home, or family, as in 'Beit Zaid' (Zaid's House), but also used in village names, like Beit el-Fakih
Beni / bani	'Children of', used in village names and in the names of some tribes
Dar	Palace
Djinn	Genies, supernatural spirits or demons
Ful	Stew of cooked fava beans, seasoned and served with oil
Funduk	Hotel
Futah	Sarong-like garment worn by men
Halal	Permitted by Islamic law
Hammam	Bath house
Haram	Proscribed by Islamic law
Hijab	Women's clothing item for covering hair and neck
Hilal	Crescent, denoting the crescent moon seen after a new moon and marking the start of a new month in the Islamic calendar
Iftar	Fast-breaking evening meal enjoyed after sunset during Ramadan
Imam	Yemen's ruler, used elsewhere for the leader of a mosque or community
Inshallah	If God wills it, used when speaking of future events
Jambiyah	Traditional dagger worn sheathed and tucked in an ornate belt
Jumhuri	Republic
Mafraj	A room traditionally furnished with mattress seating, used for social gatherings (especially qat chews), often located on the top floor of a building, but may also be situated in a garden

- THE CAMEL'S NEIGHBOUR -

Miswak	*Twig of the arak tree used for cleaning teeth*
Muezzin	*Person who calls out the times of prayer at a mosque*
Muwalad	*Pejorative label applied to a Yemeni with non-Arab parentage*
Nazarene	*A Christian (from Jesus of Nazareth)*
Niqab	*Face veil concealing all but the eyes*
Pasha	*Honorific used in the Ottoman Empire, reserved for high officials*
Qamariah	*Stained glass windows, the coloured glass held in place by plaster*
Qat	*Stimulant leaf chewed socially during afternoons*
Qishr	*Hot drink made from coffee bean husks, flavoured with ginger and served sugary*
Ramadan	*Holy month of fasting, ninth month of the Islamic calendar*
Rashoosh	*Flatbread made with ghee, cooked in a tanoor oven*
Salta	*Meat stew topped with fenugreek froth (hilbeh), served at lunch*
Sayilah	*Dry riverbed in Old Sanaa, carrying water after heavy rain*
Suq	*Market*
Tahreer	*Freedom, as in 'Tahreer Square'*
Thobe	*Men's ankle-length robe*

Notes on Sources

THIS HAS BEEN A BOOK about books, almost as much as it has been about people and place. In the course of writing, I have benefited enormously from access to the Bodleian Library in Oxford. I have also made use of the remarkable resource that is the Internet Archive (archive.org): a freely-accessible digital library of public-domain books. In the outline of my sources below I have identified those that are presently available online - a quick internet search should locate them. Beneath each chapter heading primary sources are listed first and, where they are multiple, they are listed in order of their appearance or use in the chapter.

Introduction

- Patrick Leigh Fermor. *Mani: Travels in the Southern Peloponnese.* London: John Murray. 1958. Chapter 1 describes Paddy's journey into the Taygetos.

- Freya Stark. *Letters, volume 8: Traveller's Epilogue, 1960-80.* Edited by Lucy Moorehead and Caroline Moorehead. Salisbury: Michael Russell. 1974. Page 269.

Throughout the conflict in Yemen, media reports have referred to a 'Forgotten War':

- Gabriel Gatehouse. 'Inside Yemen's forgotten war'. BBC News. 11 September 2015.

- Editorial. 'The Guardian view on Yemen: remember the forgotten war'. *The Guardian*. 13 September 2015.

- Editorial. 'Yemen's Forgotten War'. *The Times*. 22 September 2016.

- Con Coughlin. 'We must find a way to end the bloodshed in Yemen, the forgotten war in the Middle East'. *Daily Telegraph*. 11 October 2016.

- Joe Sommerlad. 'Yemen civil war: The facts about the world's "forgotten war"'. *The Independent*. 15 October 2018.

---

1. Truth

The *Itinerario* of Ludovico di Varthema (c. 1470-1517) has been translated twice into English; by Richard Eden in 1576 and John Winter Jones in 1863. Both translations are accessible online, though the Jones version is easier to read and has been reprinted many times, meaning that it is also available in hard copy. The 1532 world map referred to is the *Typus Cosmographicus Universalis* commonly attributed to Sebastian Münster.

- Lewes Vertomannus. The Navigation and vyages of Lewes Vertomannus, Gentleman of the citie of Rome, to the Regions of Arabia, Egypte, Persia, Syria, Ethiopia, and East India, both within and without the river of Ganges. In the year of our Lorde 1503. Conteynyng many notable and stranuge thinges, both hystorical and natural. Translated by Richard Eden. 1576. Contained in: *The history of trauayle in the West and East Indies, and other countreys lying eyther way towardes the fruitfull and ryche Moluccaes. As Moscouia, Persia, Arabia, Syria, Aegypte, Ethipoia, Guinea, China in Cathayo, and Giapan: With a discourse of the Northwest passage. Gathered in parte, and done into Englyshe by Richarde Eden. Newly set in order, augmented, and finished by Richarde Willes.* Volumes 4 & 5. Pages 371 to 77 describe events in Arabia Felix.
- Ludovico di Varthema. *The Travels of Ludovico Di Varthema in Egypt, Syria, Arabia Deserta and Arabia Felix, in Persia, India, and Ethiopia, AD 1503 to 1508.* Translated by John Winter Jones. London: Hakluyt Society. 1863. Pages 59 to 80 describe Varthema's arrival in Arabia Felix and his journey to Sanaa.
- Tim Youngs. *The Cambridge Introduction to Travel Writing.* Cambridge University Press. 2013. The introductory chapter discusses the nature of travel writing and considers the question of 'truth'.

2. Myths of Strangeness

Pedro Páez (1564-1622) wrote his account of captivity in Sanaa some two or three decades after the events that he described. The story remained in manuscript form for another three centuries. Eventually, in 1905, the original Portuguese text of Páez's *History of Ethiopia* (which included his Sanaa narrative) was printed in Rome under the auspices of the Catholic Church. The first complete English translation was published in 2011.

- *Pedro Páez's history of Ethiopia, 1622.* Edited by Isabel Boavida, Hervé Pennec, Manuel João Ramos. Translated by Christopher J Tribe. London: Published by Ashgate for the Hakluyt Society. 2011. Yemen and Sanaa are described in Book III, chapters 17-21, pages 112-133.

- Beckingham CF, Serjeant RB. *A Journey by Two Jesuits from Dhufār to San'ā in 1590. The Geographical Journal.* 1950. Vol 115, pages 194-207.

- Robert Silverberg. *The Realm of Prester John.* London: Phoenix. 2001. Better known for his science fiction, Silverberg's readable history of Prester John also describes the role of Pedro Páez and the Portuguese.

- Matteo Salvadore. The Jesuit Mission to Ethiopia (1555-1634) and the Death of Prester John. In: Allison B. Kavey (ed.), *World-Building and the Early Modern Imagination.* New York: Palgrave Macmillan. 2010. Pages 141-172.

3. Journal Writing

John Jourdain (1572-1619) delivered his journal to the London office of the East India Company in 1617.

- *The Journal of John Jourdain, 1608-1617, describing his experiences in Arabia, India, and the Malay Archipelago.* Edited by William Foster. Cambridge: Hakluyt Society. 1905. (Accessible online).

- John Keay. *The honourable company: a history of the East India Company.* London: Harper Collins. 1991.

- Nick Robins. *The corporation that changed the world: how the East India Company shaped the modern multinational.* 2nd ed. London: Pluto Press. 2012.

4. Global Health & Global Wealth

The narrative of Henry Middleton (d. 1613) was included among the travel stories collated and published by Samuel Purchas in four volumes in 1625. Purchas' collection was reprinted in 20 volumes in 1905.

- The sixth voyage, set forth by the East Indian Companie in three ships... written by Sir H. Middleton. In: *Hakluytus Posthumus* or *Purchas his Pilgrimes, contayning a History of the World in Sea Voyages and Lande Travells, by Englishmen and others, 1625.* Glasgow: University Press. 1905. Volume III, Chapter XI, pages 115-193. (Accessible online).

- Eric Macro. *Yemen and the Western World since 1571.* London: Hurst. 1968.

- Andrew Moscrop. 'Yemen embarks on its seventh round of polio immunisations'. *British Medical Journal.* Volume 331, issue 7529, page 1358. 10 December 2005.

5. On the Origins of Coffee

Englishman Joseph Salbank's 1618 journey to Sanaa is related in the journal of one of the crewmembers of the East India Company ship *Ann Royal*. Dutchman Pieter van den Broecke (1585-1640) wrote an account of his travels in Asia, but it has never been translated into English. His portrait though hangs in Kenwood House in London. It was painted by Frans Hals, famed for his Laughing Cavalier, and shows van den Broecke looking rather amused too.

- Voyage of the *Ann Royal* from Surat to Mocha, in 1618. In: *A general history and collection of voyages and travels, arranged in systematic order: forming a complete history of the origin and progress of navigation, discovery, and commerce, by sea and land, from the earliest ages to the present time.* Volume IX. By Robert Kerr. Edinburgh: William Blackwood. 1829. Section XI. Pages 490-506. (Accessible online).

- CG Brouwer. *Under the Watchful Eye of Mimī Bin cAbd Allāh: The Voyage of the Dutch Merchant Pieter Van den Broecke to the*

Court of Djacfar Bāshā in Sana'a, 1616. Itinerario: International Journal on the History of European Expansion and Global Interaction. 1985. Vol 9, No 2, pages 42-72.

- Brian Cowan. *The Social Life of Coffee: the Emergence of the British Coffeehouse.* New Haven: Yale University Press. 2005.

6. Freedom of Expression

Carsten Niebuhr (1733-1815) wrote three volumes of travel accounts. The 1792 English translation by Robert Heron is notorious for being inaccurate and incomplete. Heron worked from a French version of the text that had already been translated from Niebuhr's original German and he was inclined to omit the parts that he found dull. In fairness to Heron, he was in prison for non-payment of debts at the time and he was honest about his shortcomings, remarking frankly in his Introduction that 'as to the translation; I cannot indeed say much for it.' Other sources for this chapter included the brief hagiographic biography of Niebuhr written by his son. Also the Danish novelist Thorkild Hansen's adventure-filled retelling of the Arabia Felix expedition. Surprisingly, Niebuhr's companion Peter Forsskål has his own website (www.peterforsskal.com) which includes the text of his 1759 pamphlet.

- Carsten Niebuhr. *Travels through Arabia and Other Countries of the East.* Translated by Robert Heron. Edinburgh: R. Morison and Son. 1792. (Accessible online).
- Early scientific expeditions and local encounters: new perspectives on Carsten Niebuhr and 'The Arabian Journey'. In: *Proceedings of a Symposium on the Occasion of the 250th anniversary of the Royal Danish Expedition to Arabia Felix.* Edited by Ib Friis, Michael Harbsmeier and Jorgan Bæk Simonsen. Copenhagen. 2013.
- Thorkild Hansen. *Arabia Felix: the Danish expedition of 1761-1767.* London: Collins. 1964.
- Barthold Georg Niebuhr. Life of Carsten Niebuhr. In: *The Students' Cabinet Library of Useful Tracts, Vol. III: Biographical Series, Vol. I.* Edinburgh: Thomas Clark. 1836. Pages 1 to 77. (Accessible online).

7. Intolerance

- Frankl PJL. *Robert Finlay's description of San'a' in 1238-1239/1823*. Bulletin (British Society for Middle Eastern Studies). 1990. Vol 17, pages 16-32.

- William Milburn. *Oriental Commerce*. London: Black, Parry & Co. 1813. (Accessible online).

- *The British and Foreign Anti-Slavery Reporter*, published in London by the anti-slavery society. 21 February 1844. Page 27 describes British slave trading in Mocha.

- CJ Cruttenden. *Journal of an excursion to Sanaa, the capital of Yemen*. Journal of Bombay geographical society. Sept to Nov 1838. Pages 39-55. (Accessible online).

- *South Arabia: the 'Palinurus' journals of Jessop Hulton*. Edited by W.A. Hulton. Cambridge: Oleander Press. 2003.

- Captain R L Playfair. *History of Arabia Felix or Yemen, from the commencement of the Christian Era to The Present Time; including an account of the British Settlement of Aden*. Bombay Government Records. 1859. (Accessible online).

- FM Hunter. *An account of the British settlement of Aden in Arabia*. London: Trübner. 1877. (Accessible online).

- Caesar E. Farah. *The Sultan's Yemen: 19th Century Challenges to Ottoman Rule*. London: *Tauris*. 2002. Describes Anglo-Ottoman confrontations in Mocha.

- Millingen, Charles. *Notes of a Journey in Yemen*. Proceedings of the Royal Geographical Society of London. 1873. Vol 18, pages 194-202.

- FT Haig. *A Journey Through Yemen*. Proceedings of the Royal Geographical Society. 1887. Vol 9, No 8, pages 479-490.

- Christian Ann Haig. *Memories of the life of general F.T. Haig, by his wife*. London: Marshall Bros. 1902. Describes the letters sent to his daughter and includes an obituary.

8. The Gift of Reading

As well as dictating his own *Travels and Adventures*, Joseph Wolff (1795-1862) is referred to in numerous sources and has been the subject of several articles and two full-length biographies. He would have been pleased. Henry Stern (1820-1885) wrote several travelogues, including the account of his journey in Yemen and *The Captive Missionary*, which describes his later role in prompting the British expedition to Abyssinia.

- RB Serjeant and R Lewcock. *Ṣanʿāʾ: An Arabian Islamic city*. London: World of Islam Festival Trust. 1983. (Reprinted in 2013).

- Ronald Lewcock. *The old walled city of Ṣanʿa*. Ghent: UNESCO. 1986.

- Joseph Wolff. *Travels and Adventures*. 2nd edition. London: Saunders, Otley, and Co. 1860-1. Pages 500 to 511. (Accessible online).

- Fanny Parkes. *Wanderings of a Pilgrim in search of the Picturesque*. Vol I. London: Pelham Richardson. 1850. Pages 268-272. (Accessible online).

- 'The Travels and Adventures of the Reverend Joseph Wolff'. *The Spectator*. 4 August 1860. Pages 741-742.

- Joseph Leech. *The Church-goer. Rural rides; or, Calls at country churches*. Bristol: John Ridler. 1847. Pages 232 to 241 describe Wolff's sermon at St Peter's Church in Bristol. (Accessible online).

- Joseph Wolff. *Dr Wolff's New Mission* (Eight-page pamphlet). London. 1860. (Accessible online).

- Hurly Pring Palmer. *Joseph Wolff: his romantic life and travels*. London: Heath Cranton. 1935.

- Hugh Evan Hopkins. *Sublime Vagabond: the life of Joseph Wolff, missionary extraordinary*. Worthing: Churchman. 1984.

- HA Stern. *Journal of a missionary journey into Arabia Felix, undertaken in 1856*. London: Wertheim, Macintosh, and Hunt. 1858.

- Albert Augustus Isaacs. *Biography of the Rev. Henry Aaron Stern*. London: James Nisbet. 1886. (Accessible online).
- Alan Moorehead. *The Blue Nile*. London: Hamish Hamilton. 1962. Pages 203 to 274 describe the British military expedition to Abyssinia. (Accessible online).

9. Pictures Taken

The published account of Ḥayyim Ḥabshush (c. 1833-1899) represents a unique local perspective on a European traveller in Yemen. For those able to read French, Joseph Halévy (1827-1917) gives his own version of events in the 1872 *Rapport sur une mission archéologique dans le Yémen*. Halévy's work is accessible online. So too is the travelogue of Renzo Manzoni (1852-1918).

- Ḥayyim Ḥabshush. *Travels in Yemen: an account of Joseph Halévy's journey to Najran in the year 1870*. Translated by Shlomo Dov Goitein. Jerusalem: Hebrew University Press. 1941.
- Renzo Manzoni. *El Yèmen: Tre anni nell'Arabia Felice. Escursioni fatte dal settembre 1877 al marzo 1880*. Rome. 1884. (Accessible online).

Sources relating to the Saudi airstrike on the Old City are as follows.

- *At Least 6 killed in the Old City of Sana'a on Friday*. Yemen Times. 12 June 2015. (No longer accessible online).
- Lizzie Porter. Y*emen: the Unesco heritage slowly being destroyed*. *Daily Telegraph*. 16 June 2015. Includes the quote from the UNESCO head. (Accessible online).
- Amnesty International. *Yemen: Airstrike and weapon analysis shows Saudi Arabia-led forces killed scores of civilians*. 2 July 2015. (Accessible online at amnesty.org).
- Jamila Hanan. *Saudi led coalition airstrikes hit a UNESCO protected heritage site, Old Sana in Yemen, killing 6*. Yemen War Crimes blog. 12 June 2015. Includes the interview with Mohamed al-Mansour. (Accessible online at: http://yemenwarcrimes.blogspot.co.uk/2015/06/12-june-2015-saudi-

led-coalition.html)
- UNESCO. *Yemen's Old City of Sana'a and Old Walled City of Shibam added to List of World Heritage in Danger.* 2 July 2015. (Accessible online at: http://whc.unesco.org/en/news/1310/)
- Amnesty International. *UN resolution on Yemen fails to launch international investigation into war crimes.* 2 October 2015. (Accessible online at amnesty.org).

10. Passports and Their Uses

Walter B Harris' (1866-1933) Yemen story was originally published piecemeal in the *Illustrated London News* and *Blackwood's Magazine,* then printed in book form in 1893, and has lately appeared in an ebook edition. Biographic sources include Harris' *Times* obituary, John Fisher's essay, and a brief but informative sketch by Patrick Thursfield.

- Walter B Harris. *A journey through the Yemen: and some general remarks upon that country.* London: William Blackwood and Sons. 1893. (Accessible online).
- Obituary - Mr. Walter Harris. *The Times.* 5 April 1933. Page 16.
- Walter B Harris. *Morocco That Was.* London: Eland. 1983 reprint. With an introduction by Patrick Thursfield.
- John Fisher. 'An Eagle Whose Wings Are Not Always Easy To Clip': Walter Burton Harris. In: John Fisher And Anthony Best. *On the Fringes of Diplomacy: Influences on British Foreign Policy, 1800-1945.* Ashgate Publishing. 2011. Pages 155-177.
- Mark B Salter. *Rights of passage: the passport in international relations.* London: Lynne Rienner. 2003. Pages 1-9 describe the role of passports, including their *request* for protection in the absence of capacity to intervene. Pages 25-33 describe the historic upper class privilege of British passports.

11. Costume & Class

Aubrey Herbert (1880-1923), composing his memoirs shortly before his death, was clearly indebted to Leland Buxton for the details and impressions of their journey together through Yemen in 1905. Yet it was

Buxton (1884-1967), four years younger, who felt beholden: he named his son Aubrey and requested Herbert to write the introduction to his 1920 book about the Balkans. Herbert acceded, fondly citing his memories of travelling with Buxton fifteen years earlier through 'the fabled valleys of Arabia Felix, where the wind is scented and there is a glory of sunshine'. Soon it was Buxton's turn, in a eulogy written for *The Times*, to recall their journey 'into the wilds of Arabia', and to commemorate Herbert and 'the extraordinary affection which he inspired'. The journey to Sanaa, having featured prominently in both men's lives, was remembered at their deaths. Herbert's 1923 *Times* obituary noted of Sanaa that 'in those days hardly an Englishman had visited'. Over forty years later, when Buxton died at the age of 83, *The Times* still recalled his youthful journey with Herbert, suggesting that so few outsiders had visited Sanaa that the pair 'may have been the first or second Europeans'.

- 'Undergraduates' Hoax'. *Whitby Gazette*. 10 March 1905. Page 6. See also: 'A Mayor Hoaxed'. *Taunton Courier, and Western Advertiser*. 8 March 1905. Page 3.

- Leland Buxton. 'A Journey to Sanaa'. *Blackwood's Magazine*. May 1906. Pages 597- 617.

- Aubrey Herbert. *Ben Kendim: a record of eastern travel*. London: Hutchinson. 1924. Pages 51-78. (Accessible online).

- Margaret FitzHerbert. *The Man Who Was Greenmantle: a Biography of Aubrey Herbert*. London: John Murray. 1983.

- Patrick Leigh Fermor. Book review: 'The Heroic Aubrey Herbert'. *The Spectator*. 24 September 1983. Pages 20-21.

- Eric Macro. *Leland Buxton in the Yemen, 1905. Journal of The Royal Central Asian Society*. 1961. Vol 48, pages 168-172.

- 'Death of Col. Aubrey Herbert'. *The Times*. 27 September 1923. Page 13.

- Leland Buxton. 'Colonel Aubrey Herbert'. *The Times*. 29 September 1923. Page 12.

- 'Obituary - Mr. Leland Buxton'. *The Times*. 15 March 1967. Page 14.

The prospect of famine in Yemen was made clear to the UN in 2016:

- Stephen O'Brien, Under-Secretary-General for Humanitarian Affairs and Emergency Relief Coordinator. *Statement to the Security Council on Yemen*. United Nations. 31 October 2016. Includes the quotes about 'desperation, fear, and resignation' and Yemen being 'one step away from famine'. (Accessible online).

12. Heroism

Two years after the death of Arthur Wavell (1882-1916), the account of his pilgrimage to Mecca, without the Yemen journey, was republished in a 'new cheaper impression'. This economical edition included an introduction by Major Leonard Darwin, son of the naturalist, who in 1908 had been President of the Royal Geographical Society when Wavell requested the loan of the Society's equipment to take in his tin box to Yemen. Leonard Darwin went on to become Chairman of the British Eugenics Society and he mourned Wavell's death, he said, 'for he was of the race of Empire-builders'. A new and cheap posthumous impression of Wavell's journey to Sanaa was planned but never published.

- Arthur Wavell. *A modern pilgrim in Mecca: And a siege in Sanaa*. London: Constable. 1912. (Accessible online).
- David George Hogarth. *The Penetration of Arabia: a record of development of western knowledge concerning the Arabian Peninsula*. London: Lawrence and Bullen. 1904. (Accessible online).
- David George Hogarth, Kinahan Cornwallis. *Handbook of Yemen*. Cairo: Government Press. 1917. Page 16 includes the description of the *Jambiyah*, copied from page 247 of Arthur Wavell's book.
- Richard F. Burton. *First Footsteps in East Africa*. London: Tylston and Edwards. 1856. Published in two volumes in 1894. (Accessible online). The quoted passage comparing *qat* to green tea comes from a footnote on pages 54-56 of Volume I. On page 31 of Volume II Burton states his preference for Ethiopian *qat*.
- PJL Frankl. *Wavell, Arthur John Byng (1882-1916), army officer*

and explorer. Oxford Dictionary of National Biography. Oxford University Press. 2014.

13. Impermanence

George Wyman Bury (1874-1920) put his Arabian thoughts and travels into three books. For the first of these, *The Land of Uz*, published in 1911, Bury used the identity with which he travelled; so the title page names the author as 'Abdullah Mansur', and the frontispiece photograph of Bury shows 'the author in native dress', wearing a turban and holding a spear. For subsequent works he dropped the pseudonym and costume. Bury was not credited in DG Hogarth's 1917 Arab Bureau Handbook to Yemen, though parts of his *Arabia Infelix* are clearly reproduced in the Handbook and Hogarth ended up writing Bury's obituary three years later. Two biographical articles written about Wyman Bury by Eric Macro have an intriguing provenance: Macro describes working under Hugh Scott (see chapter 14) in the Naval Intelligence Division during World War Two and being asked by Scott to interview the long-widowed Ann Wyman Bury. Hugh Scott later produced another military handbook on Yemen that appears in the next chapter. As for the bird skins sent from Yemen to the Natural History Museum in London; Bury received full acknowledgment when they were described in *Ibis*, the journal of avian science. The specimens themselves were sold to the private collection of Lord Rothschild, a man once notorious for riding in a zebra-drawn carriage. Later the Wyman Bury birds were sold on again, to satisfy the blackmail demands of Rothschild's former mistress.

- George Wyman Bury. *Arabia Infelix, or, The Turks in Yamen*. London: Macmillan. 1915. (Accessible online).
- George Wyman Bury. *Pan-Islam*. London: Macmillan. 1919. Pages 75-76 relate the murdered German gunboat crew and the bloody copy of Bury's book. (Accessible online).
- WL Sclater. *The Birds of Yemen, south-western Arabia, with an account of his journey thither by the collector, Mr. G. Wyman Bury. Ibis.* 1917. Vol 59, pages 129-186.
- David George Hogarth, Kinahan Cornwallis. *Handbook of*

Yemen. Cairo: Government Press. 1917. Numerous passages are clearly drawn from Bury's *Arabia Infelix*, including the racial profiles of Yemen's population, parts of the country's history, and the Handbook's description of *qat* on page 34 echoes that of *Arabia Infelix* on page 113.

- DG Hogarth. *Obituary: Lieut. G Wyman Bury RNVR*. The *Geographical Journal*. 1920. Vol 56, no 5, pages 423-424.

- Eric Macro. *George Wyman Bury, South Arabian Pioneer*. Proceedings of the 16th Seminar for Arabian Studies held at Oxford, 20th-22nd July 1982. Seminar for Arabian Studies. 1983. Vol 13, pages 93-100.

- Eric Macro. *The Red Sea and Wyman Bury - The Last Seven Years, 1913- 1920. New Arabian Studies*. 1997. Vol 4, pages 168-180. A footnote in this paper refers to Ann Wyman Bury's return voyage to Hodeidah and her wedding photo with its handwritten note.

14. Returning

Norman Lewis (1908-2003) was lauded in his own lifetime as one of the greatest writers of the century. Most of his books remain in print, though not the large-format *Sand and Sea in Arabia* with its abundant photographs. Lewis' 1985 retelling of the Yemen voyage originally appeared in his autobiography, *Jackdaw Cake*, and was later included in an expanded edition, published in 1994 as *I Came, I Saw*. The most polished (and plausible) version is contained in *A Voyage by Dhow*.

- Norman Lewis. *Sand and Sea in Arabia*. London: Routledge. 1938.
- Norman Lewis. *Jackdaw Cake*. London: Hamish Hamilton. 1985.
- Norman Lewis. *A Voyage by Dhow*. London: Jonathan Cape. 2001.
- Julian Evans. *Semi-invisible man: the life of Norman Lewis*. London: Jonathan Cape. 2008. Lewis' remark about entering and leaving a room without being noticed is quoted on page 602.
- Julian Evans. 'Obituary: Norman Lewis'. *The Guardian*. 23 July 2003.

The entomologist Hugh Scott (1885-1960) was elected a Fellow of the Royal Society in recognition of his scientific achievements. His book on Yemen appears to sit strangely amid the extensive catalogue of his academic articles with their esoteric subject matter and obscure titles ('*Some malformations of aedeagus and cases of probable parasitic castration in Coleoptera of the family Anobiidae*', for example). Still, when Scott died, his obituary in the science journal *Nature* was written by Everard Britton, his travelling companion on the road to Sanaa.

- Hugh Scott. *In the High Yemen*. London: John Murray. 1942.
- Hugh Scott, Kenneth Mason, and Mary Marshall. *Western Arabia and the Red Sea, Geographical Handbook series*. London: British Admiralty, Naval Intelligence Division. 1946. Page 336 lists the punishments used under the Imam's rule.

Much has been written about Freya Stark (1893-1993), much of it by herself. There are her own four volumes of autobiography, eight volumes of published letters, the travelogues of her journeys through Arabia, Persia, Afghanistan, and Turkey, as well as at least four biographies. Shortly before she died, when Molly Izzard produced an ungenerous portrayal aimed at debunking the myth of the centennial and then senile Stark, other travel writers came to her defence, or to debunk the debunking. 'She has got on in the world not just by writing successful books, but by advertising herself, exploiting her frailties (and her femininity), courting the rich and powerful and never neglecting the main chance. These sound unimportant crimes to me', wrote Jan Morris. 'There is nothing new here', thought Dervla Murphy, who suggested that Stark's own writings already revealed how 'she has always been vain, ruthless, manipulative, hypochondriacal, emotionally unstable, intolerant of criticism and hopelessly addicted to aristocrats.' The subject of real interest, suggested Murphy, was not Freya Stark's many flaws, but the question of 'how, thus flawed, did she inspire so much affection among so many for so long?' Most of her books remain in print.

- Freya Stark. *Dust in the Lion's Paw: Autobiography, 1939-1946*. London: John Murray. 1961.
- Freya Stark. *Letters*, edited by Lucy Moorehead and Caroline

Moorehead. Salisbury: Michael Russell. 1974-1982. Volume 4, *Bridge of the Levant, 1940-43*, pages 7 to 43, includes Stark's forty-six letters from Yemen. Volume 8, *Traveller's epilogue, 1960-80*, contains the letters that Stark wrote from Yemen in March and November of 1976 on pages 259 and 273-275.

- Freya Stark. *A Winter in Arabia*. London: John Murray. 1940. The RAF bombing of the Se'ar tribe is referred to on page 124.
- Hans Helfritz. *The Yemen: a Secret Journey*. Translated by M Heron. London: Allen & Unwin. 1958.
- Doreen Ingrams. *A Time in Arabia*. London: John Murray. 1970.
- William Robertson. 'San'a and the Qat-eaters'. *Scottish Geographical Magazine*. 1942. Vol 58, No 2, pages 49-53. William Robertson was the pseudonym of Dr Patrick WR Petrie.
- Hugh Leach. *Seen in the Yemen: Travelling with Freya Stark & others*. London: Arabian. 2011.
- Malise Ruthven. *Freya Stark in Southern Arabia*. Reading: Garnet. 1995.
- Caroline Moorehead. *Freya Stark*. London: Allison & Busby. 2014.
- Molly Izzard. *Freya Stark: A biography*. London: Hodder & Stoughton. 1993. (Reviews were published in *The Independent* newspaper by Jan Morris on 30 January 1993 and by Dervla Murphy the following day).

15. Veils

An editorial note at the beginning of Louise Février's brief account of her time in Sanaa states that it was written partly as a memorial to her husband and partly as a memento for her children. It is partially accessible to the public online. Readers of French may be interested to get hold of her daughter's account, published in France in 2002 as *Yemen: Evénements vécus: médecine cooperative française sur fond de révolution;* Lucille Février. Claude Fayein's narrative was first published in 1955 as *Une Française médecin au Yémen*. It was later translated into English, German, Polish, and Arabic. The *Spectator* review appeared on 17 May 1957, page 23.

- 'A French Family in the Yemen'. Louise Février. *Arabian Studies* III. London: C Hurst & Co. 1976. Pages 127-134.

- *A French Doctor in the Yemen*. Claude Fayein, translated by Douglas McKee. London: Robert Hale. 1957.

- Tudor Parfitt. *The Road to Redemption: the Jews of the Yemen 1900-1950*. Leiden: EJ Brill. 1996. Describes the background to the movement of Jews from Yemen to Israel.

- Esther Meir-Glitzenstein. *Operation Magic Carpet: Constructing the Myth of the Magical Immigration of Yemenite Jews to Israel*. Israel Studies. 2011. Vol 16, No 3, pages 149-173. Describes the harsh realities of the mass exodus and includes the quote about the small stature of Yemeni Jews.

- BBC news. 'Remove full veils' urges Straw. 6 October 2006 (Accessible online at: http://news.bbc.co.uk/1/hi/uk/5411954.stm)

- BBC news. Blair's concerns over face veils. 17 October 2006 (Accessible online at: http://news.bbc.co.uk/1/hi/uk_politics/6058672.stm)

16. Politics, Violence

The complex intrigues and conflicting interests alluded to in this chapter cannot easily be condensed. For more on the civil war in north Yemen and the British departure from Aden, of course refer to the book by David Holden (1924-1977). For the circumstances and investigation of Holden's assassination, see Harold Evans' biography. For details of the British role in Yemen's civil war, see Duff Hart-Davis' history. For the role of Israel in that conflict, see the article by Clive Jones. For anecdotes of the more prominent British figures involved, see their obituaries. For a critical analysis of these events and their connection to the arms trade and Britain's post-imperial role in Arabia, I recommend the work of Adam Curtis; both the blog article cited below and episode one, 'Who Pays Wins', of his 1999 BBC documentary *The Mayfair Set*, which is accessible online.

- David Holden. *Farewell to Arabia*. London: Faber and Faber. 1966.

- David Holden. 'At cross-purposes in the Sands of Yemen'. *The Reporter*. 14 February 1963. Pages 37-41.
- Harold Evans. *My Paper Chase: True Stories of Vanished Times*. London: Little Brown. 2009. Pages 365 to 391.
- David Smiley. *Arabian Assignment*. London: Leo Cooper. 1975.
- Duff Hart-Davis. *The War that Never Was*. London: Random House. 2011.
- Clive Jones. 'Where the state feared to tread: Britain and the Yemen Civil War'. *Intelligence and National Security*. 2006. Vol 21, No 5, pages 717-737.
- 'Obituary - Lieutenant Colonel Neil 'Billy' McLean'. *Daily Telegraph*. 20 November 1986.
- 'Obituary - Colonel Jim Johnson'. *Daily Telegraph*. 13 August 2008.
- 'Obituary - Colonel David Smiley'. *Daily Telegraph*. 9 January 2009.
- Adam Curtis. *Yemen - the return of the Old Ghosts*. BBC Blogs. 8 January 2010. Accessible online at: http://www.bbc.co.uk/blogs/adamcurtis/entries/684a90bc-6149-399d-b9ab-9ff1e02b0564

Sources relating to Britain's complicity in the later war in Yemen are as follows.

- The House of Commons exchange in January 2016 during which UK Prime Minister David Cameron referred to Britain's 'stringent arms control measures' and training the Saudi coalition on 'the norms' of international humanitarian law can be found in Hansard:
  House of Commons Debate. Volume 604. Column 1411. 20 January 2016.

- The UN document describing Saudi violations of international humanitarian law that was leaked one week after Prime Minister David Cameron's statement is reported here:
  Ewen MacAskill. 'UN report into Saudi-led strikes in Yemen raises questions over UK role'. *The Guardian*. 27 January 2016.

- The EU Common Position on Arms Export Controls which requires arms sales to be halted if there is a 'clear risk' of their use

in violations of international humanitarian law can be found
here:
European Union. Common Council Position. 2008/944/CFSP.
8 December 2008.

- The six answers to parliamentary questions on the subject of
international humanitarian law violations in Yemen that were
later acknowledged to be false and subsequently 'corrected' can
be found here:
*Corrections to Parliamentary Questions and Westminster Hall
Debates: Written statement.* HLWS120. 21 July 2016.

- The UK Foreign Secretary's assertion that the Saudi-led bombing
campaign in Yemen was not 'in clear breach' of international
humanitarian law is reported here:
Patrick Wintour. 'Boris Johnson defends UK arms sales to Saudi
Arabia'. *The Guardian.* 5 September 2016.

- The UK Foreign Secretary's rejection of the need for an
independent inquiry into war crimes in Yemen is reported here:
Jamie Doward. 'UK accused of blocking UN inquiry into claim
of war crimes in Yemen'. *Observer.* 25 September 2016.

- The 'Great Hall' funeral massacre that occurred in Sanaa on 8
October 2016 is described here: Shuaib Al-Mosawa and Ben
Hubbard. 'Saudi-Led Airstrikes Blamed for Massacre at Funeral
in Yemen'. *New York Times.* 8 October 2016.

- The eventual Saudi admission of guilt for the funeral massacre
is reported here: 'Saudi-led coalition admits to bombing Yemen
funeral'. *The Guardian.* 15 October 2016.

- And the verdict of the UN that the funeral massacre violated
International Humanitarian Law was reported here:
Michelle Nichols. *Saudi coalition violated law with Yemen
funeral strike: U.N. monitors.* Reuters. 20 October 2016.

- The subsequent parliamentary debate in which UK Foreign
Secretary Boris Johnson referred to the funeral massacre but
refused to stop the sale of arms to Saudi Arabia, citing the 'huge
economic damage' that would result, is detailed in Hansard:

House of Commons Debate. Volume 616. Column 348. 26 October 2016.

- And it is reported here:
Patrick Wintour. 'Labour call for UK to withdraw support for Saudi-led coalition in Yemen fails'. *The Guardian*. 26 October 2016.

- The UK Foreign Secretary's continued support for the arms trade is further described here:
Alice Ross. 'Boris Johnson urged UK to continue Saudi arms sales after funeral bombing'. *The Guardian*. 10 February 2017.

- Prime Minister David Cameron's testy justification of Britain's relationship with Saudi Arabia appears here:
Rose Troup Buchanan. 'Jon Snow challenges David Cameron over deal with Saudi Arabia: Read the transcript of the interview in full'. *The Independent*. 7 October 2015.

- Prime Minister Theresa May's claim of potential lives saved is in Hansard:
House of Commons Debate. Volume 637. Column 298. 7 March 2018.

- Foreign Secretary Boris Johnson's earlier remarks about sending the SAS to sort out Libya's people smugglers are included in this article:
Rowena Mason. 'Cameron and Clegg admit axing search and rescue in Mediterranean has failed'. *The Guardian*. 22 April 2015.

17. Orientalism

The journey narratives of Jonathan Raban (b. 1942) have recently been republished. Among the new editions are his Arabian travelogue and the essay collection that includes his encounter with Freya Stark on the Euphrates. Disingenuously, Raban recounts in that piece his inclination never to travel further east than Norwich. Much later, his feelings about sand dunes were made known in an interview with James Canton. Edward Said's *Orientalism* has been inexhaustibly critiqued over the years. It remains undeniably ground-breaking, surprisingly readable, and, essentially, true.

- Jonathan Raban. *Arabia through the Looking Glass*. London: Collins. 1979. Pages 198-257.
- Jonathan Raban. Freya Stark on the Euphrates. In: *For love & money: Writing, reading, travelling, 1967-1987*. London: Collins Harvill. 1987. Pages 233-238.
- Wilfred Thesiger. *Desert, Marsh and Mountain: the World of a Nomad*. London: Collins. 1979. Pages 269-299. Includes photographs taken by Thesiger in Yemen during and after the civil war of the 1960s.
- Harold Ingrams. *The Yemen: Imams, Rulers, and Revolutions*. London: John Murray. 1963. A Prefatory Note defines Ingrams' terminology.
- Edward W Said. *Orientalism*. London: Routledge. 1978.
- James Canton. *From Cairo to Baghdad: British Travellers in Arabia*. London: IB Tauris. 2011. Pages 245-253.
- Sam Rohdie. *The Passion of Pier Paolo Pasolini*. London: BFI. 1995. Pages 183-6.
  Note also, Pasolini's 1971 documentary *The Walls of Sana'a* is accessible online, so too is his 1974 film version of the Arabian Nights, *Il Fiore delle Mille e Unna Notte*.

18. Questing

In *Motoring with Mohammed* Eric Hansen (b. 1947) delivers a first rate adventure story. Stories salvaged from the journals buried in Yemen feature in his later book, *The Bird Man and the Lap Dancer* (2005). Here, Hansen recalls the time he was employed as the resident carpenter and post-brawl repairman at the Grand Hotel on Thursday Island, and the time he spent trying to smuggle Maldive fish to Sri Lanka, and the time he worked at Mother Teresa's Home for the Dying Destitute in Calcutta, and so on. His stories are all the more remarkable for being true.

Kevin Rushby writes a regular travel column for the *Guardian* newspaper.

- Eric Hansen. *Motoring with Mohammed: Journeys to Yemen and the Red Sea*. London: Hamilton. 1991.
- Kevin Rushby. *Eating the Flowers of Paradise: a Journey through the Drug Fields of Ethiopia and Yemen*. London: Constable. 1998.

19. An English Sheikh

Tim Mackintosh-Smith (b. 1961) has edited the principal English text of Ibn Battutah's Travels and published three volumes of his own journeys in the footsteps of IB: *Travels with A Tangerine* (2001), *The Hall of a Thousand Columns* (2005) and *Landfalls* (2010). The three-part television series that he was working on when we met is accessible online, under the title *The Man who Walked Across the World*. His much-lauded *Arabs: A 3,000 Year History of Peoples, Tribes and Empires* was pubished in 2019.

- Tim Mackintosh-Smith. *Yemen: Travels in Dictionary Land*. London: John Murray. 1997.

20. Those Remaining
- Alan Rush. 'Obituary - Bruce Condé'. *The Independent*. 4 August 1992.
- David Holden. *Farewell to Arabia*. Pages 73 & 83 describe Bruce Condé.
- Arthur Wavell. *A Siege in Sanaa*. Giuseppe Caprotti is mentioned often, especially Wavell's dependence on him for money (p 263) and periodicals (p 269).
- 'There's no salmon fishing in Yemen, tourist board warns'. *Daily Telegraph*. 2 May 2012.
- Norman Lewis. *A Voyage by Dhow*. Pages 42-46 describe the British administrator on Kamaran Island.
- John Jourdain. Describes the Portuguese witch on pages 96-97.
- Tim Mackintosh-Smith. His thoughts on the 'Unknown Arabia' title are included in an afterword to the 2014 American edition of his book on Yemen.

Epilogue

Mohamed Choukri (1935-2003) was born in Morocco's Rif Mountains. Poverty forced his family's move to Tangier, then his father's violence forced Choukri to leave home. Destitute at the age of eleven, he entered a world of prostitution and petty crime. It was not until the age of twenty that he learnt to read and write. *For Bread Alone* is essentially autobiographical, but it seems to express a universal experience of being downtrodden and desperate. Paul Bowles, the American writer and resident of Tangier, translated Choukri's work from Arabic into English. Later it was translated into French by the Moroccan writer Tahar Ben Jelloun. And in 1982 *For Bread Alone* was published in Arabic, though it remained censured in Morocco for years.

Tayeb Salih (1929-2009) grew up in Sudan and studied in Khartoum and London. *Seasons of Migration* draws on his own experiences. Frequently cited as a classic of postcolonial literature, it deals with the encounter of Occident and Orient, the movement of people between those spaces, and the ideas that they hold about one another. Written in Arabic but widely translated, it was banned in Sudan for years.

- Nick Squires, Peter Foster. 'Image of dead Syrian boy captures human tragedy of Europe's migrant crisis'. *Daily Telegraph*. 2 September 2015
- Melanie Hall, Nick Squires, Matthew Holehouse. 'Migrant crisis: Refugees welcomed in Germany like war heroes as Berlin expects 10,000 in one day'. *Daily Telegraph*. 6 September 2015.
- Mohamed Choukri. *For Bread Alone*. London: Peter Owen. 1973.
- Tayeb Salih. *Season of Migration to the North*. London: Heinemann. 1969.